Match Game 101

Match Game 101
A Backstage History of Match Game
by A. Ashley Hoff

An icon of an era, *Match Game* had everything: Stars! Prizes! Orange shag carpeting!

The premise was simple: as the host read off a racy fill-in-the-blank statement, two contestants competed to match answers with a panel of six celebrities. But the score was secondary to the banter between the panelists and host. The modern-day equivalent to lunch at the Algonquin Round Table, *Match Game* has run on American television in six separate incarnations (thus far) beginning on NBC in 1962 and was successfully remade abroad (in Australia and the U.K. the format proved as popular as in the U.S.).

But it was the second U.S. version that proved most popular with American audiences. In this best-known version of *Match Game* (which ran nine years beginning in 1973) host Gene Rayburn played ringmaster to a circus full of celebrity panelists who tried to match contestants' answers to naughty questions written by a team of comedy writers. While other game shows focused on intellectual stimulation and physical challenges, watching *Match Game* in the seventies was like being invited to the hottest cocktail party in town. The set was shag-adelic, the humor was cutting-edge, and the celebrity guest panel smoked, bickered and bantered like they were at a party in a friend's living room, rather than in a TV studio.

But it wasn't called the 'Match' Game for nothing, so the panel had to judge contestants' likeliest answers for themselves—knowing when to answer with wit, and when to answer like a nitwit.

Hugely popular in the U.S., it proved just as durable abroad, spawning hit spin-offs in both the U.K. and Australia. When reruns of *Match Game* began airing daily on GSN (the Game Show Network) they inspired a growing cult among couch potatoes of all ages.

Match Game 101
A Backstage History of Match Game
by A. Ashley Hoff

It goes behind the scenes and gives game show fans the scoop on what went on behind the scenes of their favorite TV game show. Colorful and fun, it's chock full of rare publicity photos and fun stories told by the people who were there.

Within the pages of *Match Game 101* readers can find out the answers to these mystifying questions:

* What did Brett Somers and Charles Nelson Reilly really *do* besides *Match Game*? Anything?

* And where did Fannie Flagg get her trademark wacky t-shirts—and where are they now?

* Did the cast members really have a bar backstage, and just what was in those styrofoam cups from which they drank?

* What was Richard Dawson like on the set, and was he really as difficult as *E! True Hollywood Stories* would have you believe?

Author A. Ashley Hoff has had exclusive, one-on-one conversations with many of the celebrity panelists and surviving hosts who made each viewing of the show—in each of its incarnations—an eagerly-awaited event. And to make this a thorough and even educational tome, he tracked down the writers, directors, and producers of the show to get the complete behind-the-scenes scoop on the people and the product, letting readers in on the secrets of creating a classic game show!

Match Game

101

A Backstage History of

Match Game

By

A. Ashley Hoff

CASTLE TNT PRESS

2019

Published by Castle TNT Press, a subsidiary of WHW Press

Match Game 101: A Backstage History of *Match Game*

Cover art and dust-jacket design by Alan White at PixelMotel.com

Unless otherwise noted, all photographs are from the collection of the author.

ISBN Number 978-0-9908800-2-8

First Edition

This book is dedicated to the staff and crew members, celebrities, and contestants who made *Match Game*, in each of its incarnations, so entertaining.

And

To my mother and to Gloria Grote Baird, both of whom introduced me to the world of daytime television at an early age.*

*=P.S.—*Thank you, Jacqueline Susann!*

CONTENTS

Eavesdropping At The Algonquin

"Why *Match Game*?"

That was the question everybody asked, and it was a good one at that. My friend John and I were sitting around and talking about all the books and films that had come out of late about or based on popular TV shows from the nineteen-sixties and seventies. From *Scooby-Doo* to *Charlie's Angels*, nothing, it seemed, had not been done. Or re-done.

"Has anybody ever written a book about *Match Game*?" one or the other of us asked. We couldn't think of anything, but coincidentally, he happened to know Kay Henley, who worked as celebrity coordinator on the program.

"She should write a book about her years on the show," I said. "*I'd* buy it." He mentioned it to her, and she replied with a simple no. "But," she added, "If *you* want to write a book about it, I'll gladly talk to you about the show."

That offhand comment blossomed into this colorful little investment you are currently perusing.

Why *Match Game*? Like so many of my generation, I was over-televisionized as a child, and one of my favorite shows was *Match Game*. And since nobody else bothered to ask Brett and Charles, "So, during the 'Super Match,' when Gene said, 'Slide it, Earl!' just who *was* Earl?"....well, my destiny seemed clear.

I began combing through new and used bookstores. Lots of books were written about the game show genre and particular game shows, but surprisingly none had been written on *Match Game*. I wondered what I was getting myself into by writing this book. I felt it would be

George Kennedy, Barbara Rhoades, and Bill Daily join Brett Somers, Charles Nelson Reilly and Betty White on the *Match Game* celebrity panel.

marketable—the success of the old *Match Game* reruns on GSN (The Game Show Network) and later Buzzr was proof there was a built-in audience for it. But what kind of research would this require? Who could I talk to? And how would I track them down? Like everyone else, I never thought much about the behind-the-scenes workings of the show—except possibly for Earl. Besides, it was a game show! Yeah, it took a lot of work, but how hard could it have been?

I soon found out.

The more research I did the more respect I had for a genre that I (like so many others) took completely for granted. This gave me another reason to write the book: for years, people like Charles Nelson Reilly have been dismissed as mere "game show personalities" (which partly explains Charles's love-hate relationship with his game show past) no matter how many Tony or Emmy awards grace their mantles. Giving them some long-deserved credit was another reason for writing this.

On TV shows and in film, you memorize a script, rehearse and know your blocking; on a TV game show, it's all improvised. When asked a question, it's the celebrity or host (or contestant) you are listening to, not a writer or editor or director. It's really like eavesdropping at the Algonquin—with Brett Somers and Charles Nelson Reilly filling in for Dorothy Parker and Robert Benchley. To come up with a clever remark and witty repartee takes a certain amount of intelligence and work. Even Peter Marshall conceded in his memoir that the grand majority of clever "zingers" delivered by celebs on *The Hollywood Squares* in its heyday was pre-scripted (which, by the way, does not diminish Paul Lynde or Rose Marie in the least).

But *Match Game* is more than just Brett and Charles and Richard and Fannie and Gene—even though we love them a lot. A lot of people made these shows work—and oh, yes, there was more than one show we're talking about here. Six versions of *Match Game* have been done for American television (and counting!) and there have been some nifty foreign versions of the show done, too. Wanna meet Australia's answer to Brett Somers? You'll meet her inside!

Is that more than you expected in a book about an old game show? It's fascinating stuff and that's why I'm going to share all these stories with you. But if all you care about is Brett dishing the goods on her co-stars, by all means, skip ahead to chapter nine, because it's in there. And if you also want to know how you get to be a game show host, well, that's in here too. And if you're interested in learning about what it was like to be a woman producer working in a man's world—the man's world of *very* early television—well, *that's* in here too. There's something for everybody in this book.

Another thing I'd like to point out—lots of people keep asking, "Whatever happened to so-and-so?" (Translation: "Isn't that person a washed-up, old has-been?") as if they were sitting on a shelf collecting dust. Granted, a few are retired, but you'd be surprised how little dust they are collecting. Our *Match Game* alumni of celebrity panelists, contestants, and even the staff, crew and writers have moved on in some very surprising directions—you'll meet people who are writing books and screenplays, taking cooking classes, directing Broadway shows and award-winning films, winning the Super Bowl, going off to war-torn countries to report what's *really* going on in the world, and even creating...more game shows!

How do you end up talking with the stars you grew up watching? Mostly luck. Living in L.A. helps—and working in an L.A. talent agency *really* helps. I began researching this book just prior to the rise in social media; Facebook and Twitter would have helped immeasurably, but they were only just coming into vogue when I started this book. So I had to play sleuth—checking local theatre notices to see who was onstage and therefore accessible; checking websites to see what people were currently working on (and which cities they were currently in); calling up SAG / AFTRA, and rifling through *The Academy Players Directory* to track down the representatives of the remaining actors and actresses.

So I would like to extend a very special thank you to all the very helpful managers, publicists, agents, assistants, friends-of-friends, and others, who helped me in my quest for The Holy Grail and the long skinny microphone. Everyone is thanked individually in the chapter titled *And Now a Word from Our Sponsors....* I would also like to give a special thank you to all the staff, crew, host, and panel members who never had me arrested for stalking them. My gratitude is sincere.

A. Ashley Hoff
Los Angeles

Part I

In The Beginning

1940's-1969

"The excitement comes from it being undecided.
Anything can happen at any moment. There is also
the element of people-watching in game shows. It
has hundreds of analogies. Why do people go to
cocktail parties, for instance? Not to drink,
certainly. You can do that at home. You go to
people-watch, to be watched, to dress-up."

—Mark Goodson

Producers Mark Goodson, left, and Bill Todman, center, make a final check on the format for *It's News to Me*, shown here with the show's director Jerry Schnur in the early fifties.

1

"This Has Been A Mark Goodson-Bill Todman Production"

"Experimental television had been in the works as early as 1928, and by 1939, at the New York World's Fair, NBC presented the first television demonstration to the American public. After a few years of finding its footing, by 1947 programs were being telecast regularly from Chicago and from New York. It was soon obvious that the new kid on the block was here to stay..."

—Betty White in *Here We Go Again*

So begins Betty White's memoir *Here We Go Again*, and so begins our own story. (Don't worry, folks—Betty will be showing up later in the book!)

Once TV became a fixture in American life, the early networks started scrambling, looking for entertaining (and easy to produce) programming. Quiz shows were already a mainstay on the radio, and now there was a picture to go with them! Of course, not all of the radio shows translated well to the new medium, so new games had to be created that would both involve and entertain the viewing audience.

The "Gold Dust Twins":Bill Todman (left) and Mark Goodson (right) after winning one of their many Emmy awards.

Game shows were hugely popular both with networks and audiences. The networks loved them because they were cheap to produce: a single standing set with a host and announcer, and contestants instead of actors requiring pay; prizes and prize money were provided by sponsors, rather than by the networks' own pockets, in return for advertising. Profits for some game shows have been estimated up to 600 percent! Audience appeal is easy to figure out: real life drama featuring ordinary mortals (just like you and me!) competing for big-bucks, or small bucks, or thirty-five bucks and a carton of smokes. The prizes were secondary to the sense of competition and the novelty of watching your own mini-movie screen right in your very own living room. And once celebrities began to be thrown into the mix, you had a ratings hit!

Maxene Fabe explained the audience appeal of the celebrity-panel game shows, especially in those earlier days of Television before *People Magazine* flooded the market with unflattering photos of stars going to supermarkets: "Viewers could watch a celebrity agonizing and exulting, triumphant or thwarted, competing and suffering every bit as intensely as the contestant. You no longer had to wonder, 'What's he like?' You knew."

The technical marvels of TV entranced even world leaders. President Dwight and Mamie Eisenhower were such fans of the classic game show *What's My Line?* during their White House years that, at their request, tapes of the show were flown to Augusta, Georgia, several times when they missed the show on the air. The creators of this very show that so impressed the Leader of the Free World, and the mavericks who pioneered the celebrity-studded panel TV game shows, were Mark Goodson and Bill Todman.

Mark Goodson was born in Sacramento, California on January 24, 1915. An introverted kid from a poor family, he headed to New York after finishing law school at the University of California at Berkeley. While working several radio announcing and writing jobs, he met William S. Todman (born July 31, 1916 in New York City), a radio director and advertising copywriter from a wealthy New York family. They joined forces and began creating radio quiz shows; when TV arrived, they had found their medium, creating such staples of the 1950s as *Beat the Clock*, *I've Got a Secret*, and the long-running hit, *What's My Line?*.

These master showmen figured out how to effectively use famous people on game shows and get good ratings: the secret lay, not in the quantity of the fame, but the quality of the game, and (as they later found out with *Match Game '73*) if the game is good enough, you can even create your own celebrities! Along the way, a lot of people got their start with Goodson-Todman Productions, among them Merv Griffin and James Dean. In fact, the Goodson-Todman production company would go into *The Guinness Book of World Records* for having the most television shows ever produced—over 39,000 episodes.

Mark Goodson was once asked whether he would become a game show producer if he could start his career again. "It wouldn't be TV at all," he replied. "It would be theatre or movies. I myself don't watch a lot of TV. When I do, it's usually PBS." Ah, there were many possibilities in young Mark's life, but lucky for us, Fate decreed he would become a TV game show producer.

> "Creativity lies essentially in attention to detail."
> —Mark Goodson

Scandal!

Then came 1958, and the quiz show scandals.

For those who missed Robert Redford's movie *Quiz Show*, here's the low-down on the scandals: It was revealed that answers were being given to the contestants on the wildly successful prime-time show, *Twenty-One* (How successful was it you ask? It out-rated *I Love Lucy*—*that's* how successful it was!). Charles Van Doren (February 12, 1926-April 9, 2019) became a national celebrity as he remained champion week after week; decades before 'reality television shows' became a phenomenon, audiences watched Van Doren breathlessly agonizing over each question, sweating, mopping his brow, and, at the last moment, producing the correct answer. He amassed over $120,000 and triumphed over Herbert Stempel, who, filled with resentment either because Van Doren replaced him in the spotlight or because Van Doren won so much more money than he, blew the whistle.

Even those in the game show field seemed astonished by this revelation, though Ira Skutch, who worked for G-T for some thirty years, quotes Mark Goodson as saying, "I knew all along that the contestants weren't behaving naturally; they had to have been coached. If you know the answer to a question, you say it. Only occasionally do you have to hesitate, and you certainly don't struggle and sweat and then suddenly come up with the answer."

A Grand Jury investigation began, and the packagers, fearing the public would stop watching fixed shows and bring cancellation, denied everything. When perjury was committed to the Grand Jury, a congressional investigation followed—and decimated the ranks of the major game show producers.

Talk about *drama*! The revelations shocked the nation; Even President Eisenhower was compelled to comment, "What a terrible thing to do to the American public." In the end, the testimony before the house committee investigating the game show scandals filled two volumes totaling 1,156 pages. Skutch continued, "I've often wondered whether the legal uproar would have subsided had the producers forthrightly admitted they were merely producing entertainment shows in what they felt was the most dramatic and diverting manner. Programs were canceled right and left. When the dust settled, Goodson-Todman was the only major game show company still in business."

"The big-money quiz-show business had done itself in," Betty White relayed in her memoir *Here We Go Again*, "and from then on, some stringent rules were put into effect and enforced in all game shows to preclude a repetition. The Goodson-Todman shows made it through the storm with a clean record, and for one simple reason: there was no big payoff involved. Questions were worth perhaps fifty dollars, and totals might not make it to four figures."

Moreover, as R. Patrick Neary, a writer for *Match Game '73*, observed, "When the game show scandals of the fifties came around, none of Goodson's shows were affected because for the most part they weren't hard knowledge games. For example, in *Match Game*, there are no right answers to be known ahead of time. Everything happened in front of the cameras."

The Gold Dust Twins

These little differences were what would make or break Goodson-Todman Productions—and as it turned out, those differences *made* them. By 1964, Goodson-Todman Productions was producing twenty hours of network programming each week, "an unprecedented output," said Ira Skutch, "even more than MCA in its glory days." He estimated profits generated by the company "were certainly in the neighborhood of $100,000 a week. It's not surprising that Mark and Bill were known in the trade as 'The Gold Dust Twins.' At its height, the firm occupied not only the entire thirtieth floor of the Seagram Building, but also substantial space on three other floors." Bill Todman's business skills eventually expanded the Goodson-Todman empire to form Capitol City Publishing, which included the Ingersoll newspaper group and other publishing holdings (including Bernard Geis Associates, the book publisher of such classics as Helen Gurley Brown's *Sex and the Single Girl* and Jacqueline Susann's bestselling potboiler *Valley of the Dolls*).

While their focus remained on game shows, Goodson-Todman also produced early primetime live dramas like the anthology series *The Web* (CBS 1950-1954) and primetime Westerns including *The Rebel* (ABC 1959-1961), starring Nick Adams, and *Branded* (NBC 1965-1966), starring Chuck Connors.

Mark Bowerman, who worked for the company in California beginning in the mid-1970's, says "Mark Goodson possessed the ability to assemble a group of creative people and use the strengths of each member of his team to mold one major hit show after another."

Mark and Bill were not without their critics, however. Comedy writer Allan Sherman recounted his experiences with Mark and Bill in his bittersweet memoir *A Gift of Laughter*. He had co-created *I've Got a Secret*, and sold the show to Goodson-Todman for a pittance (he and his partner each got $100 for all world-wide rights; a revised version ran for fifteen years on network TV). Sherman was hired as executive producer of the show, and later was made a full producer with the company—minus a raise in salary—before being replaced in 1955. The book, according to Maxene Fabe, described Mark and Bill as "petty despots in a barony now equipped with a grey flannel men's room with gold fixtures, monogrammed towels, and seven kinds of cologne. He would depict Goodson seated behind a desk that had once belonged to Napoleon, dictating blizzards of memos...Todman spoke an advertising man's double-talk Sherman labeled 'Todmanese'...Sherman would be in Todman's office the day he ordered a custom-made Lincoln directly from Henry Ford himself." Sherman had better luck later on when he came out with the hit record, *My Son, the Folksinger* and wrote the classic summer-camp song *Hello Muddah, Hello Fadduh*.

Mark Bowerman described his impression of Mark Goodson: "Old school style of running a company. He surrounded himself with people that were great at what they did and then, running his company in a committee style, had the ability to take in all the ideas and criticism regarding a given show and then cull the important elements from all the input and make a decision. His track record speaks for itself. He was always interested in everybody's opinion whether you were the highest paid producer or the guy from the mailroom. Mark Goodson liked good music and enjoyed keeping up with the latest groups. He collected art and created one of the most impressive personal collections of contemporary art in the United States."

"He was, I think, a perfectionist, and it paid off," observed Diane Janaver. "He was very fair. He was very bright. And he was very perceptive. You'd bring in a show idea, and of course you would think it's all worked out. 'Oh, it's terrific, wouldn't that be good? Wouldn't that be good?' and Mark Goodson would point out all the holes in it. And he was right! He was terrific that way. I have nothing bad to say about him.

"Bill was the salesman," she added. "He was mostly selling the shows to the network. It got to the point where he didn't even have to really sell. Their reputation was so good. He could say, 'We're thinking of a new show that we might call—.' He'd come up with the title, whatever it was, and the networks would be willing to buy it based on Goodson-Todman. When you think of all the stuff they did, all the panel shows—God, *Price is Right* is *still* on the air. Isn't that amazing? Not bad, huh? The other ones keep coming back, versions of *I've Got a Secret*, *What's My Line?*, and *Match Game*."

In his memoir, Ira Skutch recalled, "As I settled in as a producer, I began to learn more about Mark and Bill and their relationship. Bill had been a radio writer and director, Mark a radio announcer and producer. Becoming partners some twelve or thirteen years before I joined the company, they produced a number of game shows for radio and entered television in 1948 with *Winner Take All*. Those who had been with the company longer than I told me that primarily Bill had been in charge of sales, Mark of the creative end.

> "They were the class act of the western world."
> —Betty White

"It became obvious that Mark was a dynamo. He monitored almost every episode, wrote critiques of many of them, spent untold hours struggling with new concepts, involved himself in the smallest details, and supervised the operation of the office.

"In the classic manner, each partner blamed the other when an unpleasant decision had to be made. Mark hated personal confrontations, so Bill was assigned the unpleasant task of firing people and informing them of pay cuts."

"Mark and me are very interesting chemistry," admitted Bill Todman. "We argue constantly. If we both agree, one of us is not doing anything."

"On the surface, it seemed a harmonious and complementary alliance," observed Ira Skutch, but "below lurked fathomless tension."

"Bill Todman was totally emasculated," admitted Gene Rayburn. "*Mark Goodson* was the company. He was never allowed really to make any important decisions. He handled the routine stuff but the creative brains were in Mark Goodson's head."

Yet Bill Todman was fondly remembered by Bob Barker. "He was a delightful man. He personified a man you might aspire to be: a gentleman, personable, successful, handsome and very intelligent. He had the attributes to sell you anything, and the intelligence to sell it beautifully. On one of my first days there, we chatted alone. His kindness and flattering remarks, that he'd admired my work [as host of *Truth or Consequences*] made me feel very comfortable, very much at home. "

A Record Holder!

By the time he died, Mark Goodson had entered the Guinness Book of World Records for having produced the most television shows—over 39,000 episodes! The list of Goodson-Todman shows included some of the most successful and long-running programs in Television history:
Winner Takes All, Beat the Clock, What's My Line?, It's News To Me, The Name's The Same, I've Got a Secret, Two For the Money, Judge For Yourself, Feather Your Nest, The Price Is Right, To Tell The Truth, Play Your Hunch, Split Personalities, Number Please, Password, Say When, The Match Game, Missing Links, Get The Message, Call My Bluff, It's Your Move, Snap Judgment, He Said, She Said, Concentration, Now You See It, Family Feud, Tattletales, Showoffs, The Better Sex, Card Sharks, Mindreaders, Blockbusters, Child's Play, Match Game/Hollywood Squares Hour, Body Language, Trivia Trap.

Review Questions

How well did you pay attention to the chapter? Here's where we test your *Match Game* knowledge!

1. Goodson-Todman Productions was founded by <u>BLANK</u>.

a. Merv Griffin and James Dean
b. President Dwight and Mamie Eisenhower
c. Mark Goodson and Bill Todman

2. Goodson-Todman Productions went into the *Guinness Book of World Records* for <u>BLANK</u>.

a. Most produced television shows
b. Ordering the most Lincolns from Henry Ford himself
c. Writing the best-selling novel of all time

3. The Quiz Show scandals prompted President Eisenhower to say <u>BLANK</u>.

a. "Big bucks, no whammies!"
b. "You're in *trouuuuuuuble*!"
c. "What a terrible thing to do to the American public."

Answers: 1. c, 2. a, 3. c

2

How To Create A Game Show

Thomas Edison once famously said that invention was 1% inspiration and 99% perspiration, but there's a lot to be said for just getting a group of people in a room together and bouncing ideas off one another.

Mark Goodson was once quoted as saying, "Creating a game isn't like conceiving a drama when you say, 'Let's do something about a transit cop' or 'Let's do something about a woman private eye who does karate.' In drama you can reach out and pick up a start-off notion. In games you begin with a blank page. It's almost like trying to create a new sport. Think of a new sport. Think of how many new sports come along."

What exactly makes a great game show work? Goodson-Todman staff members were taught the principles of game show construction. The key ingredient, according to Ira Skutch, is simplicity. "The greatest chance for success lies with the show having the fewest rules, the greatest clarity, and the most apparent goals. Fairness is important, as is availability of material, whether it be questions, pictures, words or stunts. The drama of the game must develop naturally, and the scoring ensure that the game ends with a climax, not a foregone conclusion. Generally, the least important element is the prize structure. Except for merchandise shows like *The Price Is Right*, you can plug in whatever the budget will bear."

SUNDAY NEWS TV week

May 9 to May 15 1965

host Gene Rayburn

The MATCH Game.

Mark Goodson oversaw weekly evening meetings in the Executive Conference Room, remembered Ira Skutch, attended by "eight to ten people he considered to be the creative heart of the company. We gathered to work on the new program ideas, essential to the continued health and growth of the company..."—and it was during one of these meetings that *Match Game* was created.

Now comes the $64,000 question: Just *who* created *Match Game*?

According to Ira Skutch, "*Match Game* began the day that Frank Wayne said to several of us, 'Try this. Write down something about an elephant—and try to write the same thing that the others do.' One wrote, 'It's large.' Another, 'It's gray.' Two matched with, 'It has a trunk.' There were no right or wrong answers, only matching answers counted. It was a totally new idea, a breakthrough game which could be used in many different formats. *Match Game*, itself, had long runs in two different forms: in the Sixties as a game played by two teams of three people, where the object was to match one's teammates; in the Seventies as a game played by two individuals who tried to match the answers given by a panel of six celebrities. Furthermore, the idea of matching answers was the progenitor of many games that followed, such as *The Newlywed Game*, *Tattletales*, and *Family Feud*."

Robert Sherman pointed out that "few of Mark Goodson's shows are created in such a way that you really can point to one person and say, 'That's who created it.' Most of them were a much more circuitous path. *Family Feud* is really a good example of that. Mark Goodson was definitely the impetus for that. He had shortly after *Match Game* went on [in its second run in the 1970's] said, 'Gee, it's a shame we're not using half of these thousands of questions [from the original 1960's run of *Match Game*]. And they were good questions, but they don't seem to fit with *Match Game* anymore. Maybe we should come up with some kind of show that uses them.' And later shortly after that suggested something akin to the poll in the *Match Game* 'Audience Match' with more than the three answers we had. And after that point there were a good half dozen major contributors and probably a dozen more minor contributors to the various aspects of what ultimately became *Family Feud*. It's really hard to point to creators."

Of course, no matter who individually thought up the initial premise, the overall show was shaped and developed collectively by the good staff at Goodson-Todman Productions. Period.

"It's the greatest challenge in the world to invent a new game," Mark Goodson once said. "For every one you see, every concept that ultimately is refined and developed, a dozen are worked on and not worked on or almost worked on or dropped because they don't read any more. We test and hammer and test and hammer. When you finally get it down so that it looks very simple, that one has had the most complicated amount of work."

The Rules

The initial run of the show was a pretty staid affair, with a simple premise: "At that time, the game was played by two teams," explained Ira Skutch, "with a celebrity and two contestants on each side. Each person was trying to match his teammates. The game was much straighter than it is now. They'd ask questions like, 'Name a kind of muffin,' and the players would try to write down the most common answer. If two people matched, the team would get 25 points. If all three matched, the team would get 50 points. The first team to get 100 points would win the game.

"The next step was to play the audience match for money. The audience match, in those days, would go something like this...'We asked 100 people in the audience to name their favorite movie star.' Then the three people on the winning team would each guess, giving the same or different answes. When the answer was revealed, the contestants would get $50 fo each guess that had matched the answer."

The Pilot

The pilot episode was taped on December 5, 1962 and was hosted by Gene Rayburn. It featured Peggy Cass and Peter Lind Hayes as the celebrity players, and still exists today in the collection of the Library of

The opening of the original *Match Game* pilot, taped on December 5, 1962

Congress as well as in the trading circuit. The show featured a theme song by Bert Kaempfert, a nifty little ditty called *A Swingin' Safari* that sounded vaguely 'Calypso' and, as one website put it, "was a staple of supermarket music and provided background music for countless home movies of summer vacations." The show was taped at NBC in Studio 8H at 30 Rockefeller Center in New York City (today, *Saturday Night Live* is taped on that very soundstage) and ran successfully on NBC from December 31, 1962 to September 29, 1969 in the 4 p.m. time slot.

"I really don't have very much memory of the pilot," says *Match Game* producer Diane Janaver, "because I was working on *I've Got a Secret* at the time it was being made. I was just doing a little of this and a little of that, and so I really can't tell you much about the pilot. But usually there are bugs that have to be worked out. The staff, when we were doing *Match Game* in New York, was a terrific staff, and we were called on to do many pilots while we were doing the show. And pilots are murder to do! They're like twenty-two-hour days, several in a row, to get all the stuff worked out on them."

The wood-paneled set (which on-camera vaguely resembled a mid-century Hi-Fi stereo) was designed by Otis Riggs, Jr. According to Mark Bowerman, who worked for Goodson-Todman beginning in the late seventies, "I never met Otis and he was not an exclusive to Goodson. He was a freelance designer in New York who was contracted to design the old show."

Match Game was an immediate hit with audiences. "I have no specific memory of reviews of any of the game shows," says Ira Skutch today. "They were of no intrinsic value, so reading them was purely for ego reasons: pumping up or bringing down. The show was a rating success immediately, as I recall, and was part of NBC's successful afternoon bloc of shows."

We'll just have to take Ira's word for it. If you're interested in judging the show for yourself, you're going to have to do some hunting around. Finding the master tapes of episodes of NBC's original *Match Game* is about as easy as tracking down lost Fabergé eggs. NBC routinely erased tapes in order to save space and money—so the story goes—and as a result, many early classic game shows, like so many early silent films, are lost to posterity. Of the approximately 1,760 episodes taped between 1962 and 1969, only eleven are known to exist. Nine episodes of *Match Game* (including the original 1962 pilot episode) are located in the Television Collection of The Library of Congress. One episode currently exists in the collection of The Museum of Television and Radio in New York City. At least two episodes can be found in the trading circuit, including the pilot (which was included on the *Match Game* DVD set). In fact, it's interesting to note that (legal ramifications aside) collectors and fans provide as much or more preservation service for old TV shows and recordings than any official agencies or, often, the rights-holders themselves.

Will additional tapes ever be found? Only time will tell, but here's a little story to give you some hope: *Hollywood Squares* host Peter Marshall related in his memoir *Backstage With The Original Hollywood Square* that NBC also recycled the original tapes of that show (supposedly), along with most of their other game shows. When he made the attempt to track down and buy up the master tapes, he was told the tapes had all already been destroyed. A quarter century later the tapes were found in a media storage warehouse in Burbank, and after skillful negotiations with the rights-holders, began airing on The Game Show Network.

A Kids Version of Match Game

Hollywood and Broadway stars weren't the only ones invited to play *Match Game*. "I even used my kids—my second kid's class," remembereed Jean Kopelman. "We decided we would try and do a kids version of *The Match Game*. And so we figured the third graders were about the right age. They were eight, were smart enough and cute enough. And I tried it out with the kids in his class and I let them do the answers, the polling we did for the Audience Match. We polled that class, and it really was adorable. My kids weren't on the show, of course, but we did use their class as the experiment, and then we went out and got kids. And it was just adorable and they were cute as can be, a lot of fun."

Videotaping the Show

While some sources claim *Match Game* ran live, at least in the beginning, associate producer Jean Kopelman said it was always taped, and taped in color from the very beginning. "It was, absolutely. It was the first one on tape and the first one in color at NBC, which is why they put it in 8H." Studio 8H had color cameras, and Jean remembered, "They were very big and very cumbersome."

"I have no idea when the show went to color," admitted Ira Skutch. "*Play Your Hunch* was colorized in 1962, and the network was pressing to convert all the shows at that time because RCA was selling color sets." Ira did however have a funny story about the show's color cameras.

"*The Match Game* and *Snap Judgment* were produced in Studio 8H," Ira remembered in his memoir. "That beautiful radio facility had been gutted, converted for television, and equipped with huge color cameras which had been built by NBC engineers. After a while, this ungainly gear was replaced by RCA's TRK-40 color cameras, which were so unreliable that the engineers nicknamed them 'turkeys.' One morning I noticed that a small set had been erected and lit in a storage room off the entry to the studio; and engineers were running tests on other makes of cameras. After examining a number, they settled on Norelco equipment, and, in due course, these new cameras were installed.

"When General Sarnoff presided at the annual RCA stockholders meeting in 8H, he was obviously embarrassed when a stockholder asked why NBC was not using RCA gear. The next day, the engineers covered the Norelco name with overlays of the RCA logo."

Videotaping TV game shows revolutionized the industry, and Jean Kopelman explained why: "They didn't really tape because they wanted to make it look better or anything, they taped because it was the cheapest way for them to handle their real estate. That's what tape was all about. It was not about doing things so you could have it for posterity...The reason for the taping was instead of tying up a theatre for five days, you could do—in two days you could five shows, and in three days you could do ten, which made the whole real estate portion of television a lot cheaper. The same studio could be used for three shows as opposed to one."

Videotaping the show, instead of doing it live, of course made it easier to edit any mistakes that might occur during the taping. "We had a couple of mistakes and they were usually corrected," admitted Jean Kopelman, "but nothing really bad or unpleasant ever happened. It was always pleasant—except when the lights went out in the Seagrams Building during the blackout. That was kind of bad, but that was the Seagrams Building's fault, because they didn't have lights in the stairways."

Above, a shot of the *Match Game* set taken during a rehearsal in December, 1968 for an episode airing on NBC on February 2, 1969 and featuring Gordon MacRae and Meredith MacRae as the celebrity captains, with Dick DeBartolo sranding in for Gene at his podium. "That way, Gene could rest between shows," recalled Dick. During rehearsals, the production staff sat in for the celebrities. "I don't know who it is sitting in for Meredith," Audrey Davis informed me, "but it is Jerry Layne for Gordon. And, of course, Dick DeBartolo, filling in for Gene Rayburn."

Above is another shot of the set, taken from a different angle. According to Dick DeBartolo, "We did the whole week in one day. Two shows, Monday and Tuesday, in the morning. Lunch break, then the Wednesday, Thursday and Friday shows. We had stand-ins for the celebrities too. The idea was to run through the game for the benefit of the contestants. How to enter, where to place your cards after you wrote your answer, how to dispose of the used cards, etc. We used old *Match Game* questions for the rehearsals." (Both photographs taken by Bob Batche, December, 1968.)

"

These rare behind-the-scenes shots were taken by NBC cameraman Bob Batche during a *Match Game* rehearsal. As Ira Skutch related, Studio 8H was equipped with color cameras. These are the RCA TK10 models nicknamed "the turkeys" by the crew.

After he was drafted, Batche, who worked on the show as a sound mixer and cameraman took these photos on a visit while on leave from the services. "When I was so much younger, I was offered several jobs by *National Geographic* as a Field Photographer and NBC Engineering. Since I didn't really want to work in jungles, swamps or hot or cold climates, I selected an indoor job at NBC near where I grew up..

"I started to work on *The Match Game* in June of 1967 as the audio mixer for the studio audience. A long-time cameraman became ill and needed to be replaced, so I was chosen. I was Camera #1 on Gene. In late November 1967, I received a Letter from President Johnson. The first sentence was, 'Greetings. You are hereby ordered to report for Military Service...' But I wanted to work indoors, not in the Army! Therefore, I only worked on *Match Game* and other live or taped shows for five months. Some of the photos were taken on a visit during Army Leave Time by myself."

The Machine

"During each taping," recalled Dick De Bartolo, "I wore a headset, and Jean Kopelman, one of the producers, would be sitting in the control room talking to me. For the most part, I would just grab a question, and I'd hand it to a stagehand, and he would clip it to this small wooden board that had a paperclip on the end, and force the board through a tunnel, and the question card would pop out through a slot on the machine that we had on the side of Gene's podium. And as I recall, the sound effect man would cue the sound of an old crank-style cash register to make it seem like it was really, you know, a machine. But it was just the stagehand forcing the card through the tunnel.

"The reason we did it that was so I could change up the material based on how well the contestants were playing that day. If it was going poorly and nobody was matching, Jean would say, 'Give 'em an easy one,' and I'd look at my wall of questions and grab one that had some really obvious answer that everybody would be inclined to write, and that way a lot of points would be scored. And by the same token, if the contestants were doing so well that it seemed that the show was moving too quickly, I'd grab a card that had a broader range of answers and there wouldn't be any matches made in the next round, and that would slow things down. So that's why I was always in the studio."

The Telephone Match

In 1967, they added *Telephone Match*, a feature on the show in which Gene called and chatted with a home viewer, who was given the opportunity to win a cash prize by matching answers with one of the celebrity panelists.

"It was all very odd at the time," admitted producer Jean Kopelman, "because this show came on after the big quiz show scandals, and NBC had Standards and Practices, and they decided that they would follow me around, and whatever I did was going to be what they were going to make everybody do. And one of the things was how you pick these telephone contestants. And as I recall, we basically picked the cities we would call that actually took the *Match Game* on the network. And so we had all these phone books that we would—I guess someone from NBC overseeing us, would pick a different town for each show, and then somebody would just open up a phonebook and just point a pen at a telephone number and call, and then we just kept going until we got an answer. And then we asked people to hold onto the line, and they held onto it until it was time for this feature on the program, and then off we went. And we talked to them and they could be heard on the air giving their answer. What they had to do was match someone in the audience who, before the show, had written down an answer to a question, and the person at home had to figure out what the person wrote down as an answer. And if they matched, everyone got prizes—or money, I guess. I really don't remember too well."

Jean Kopelman admitted that Gene Rayburn was able to keep cool under pressure. "Even in his crankiest mood he was fun—he was never cranky, but occasionally things would go wrong." One of those things concerned the telephone segment of the show...and the time the stage phone went dead during a taping of the show.

"One day the phone lines went down, and I guess they decided we'd better do it anyway. On we went, and so there was Rayburn [in] the area backstage hanging onto the payphone, and I don't even remember if the person won or not. I don't remember too well except that I remember poor Gene Rayburn ended up on the wall of Studio 8H with a pay phone calling someone, and I don't know how we ever—I don't think we ever got it hooked up so you could hear the other person talk."

"Oh, yes," exclaimed Diane when I asked about the incident. "God, there was always something, *always* something like that would happen. When you think you've got everything covered, you know, then suddenly—phone company! It was so crazy. I was not directly involved with that part of it, I was probably down in the wait room with the celebrities when that happened." Of course, on-set mistakes were par for

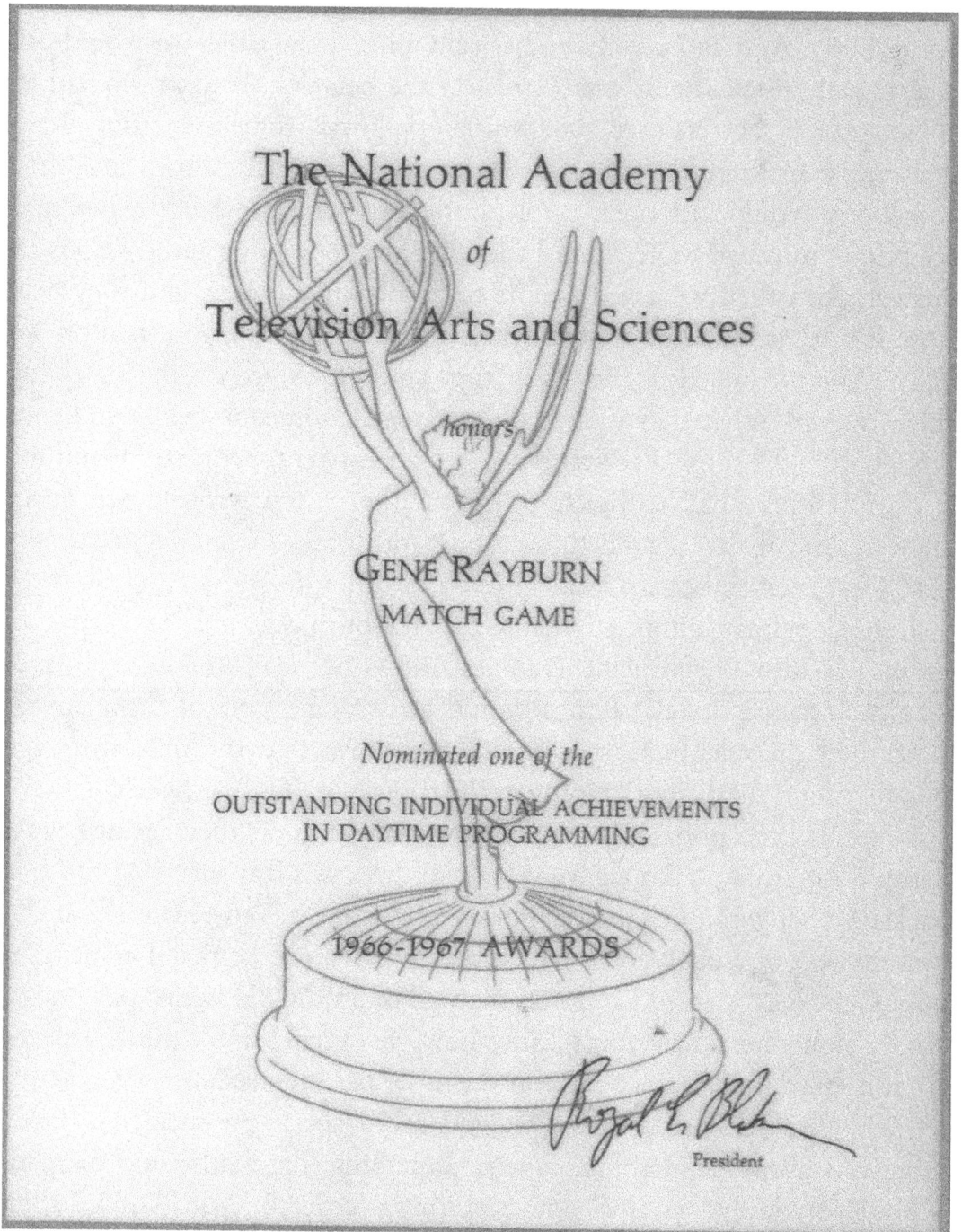

The National Academy

of

Television Arts and Sciences

honors

GENE RAYBURN
MATCH GAME

Nominated one of the

OUTSTANDING INDIVIDUAL ACHIEVEMENTS
IN DAYTIME PROGRAMMING

1966-1967 AWARDS

President

One of the five Emmy nomination certificates received by Gene Rayburn, mounted and glazed, that hung in Gene's office.

the course during the seventies run of *Match Game* (for instance, when the turntable bringing contestants out onstage wouldn't turn), and Diane admitted, "That was the good part, yes. And the nature of the game lent itself to that kind of thing. Everybody loved anything—anything *funny*!"

They Worked On Game Shows, Too...

Some notable talent got their start working on Goodson-Todman game shows. I couldn't help but ask *Match Game* producer Jean Kopelman about some of the young talent she worked with on *Beat the Clock* during the fifties, before she started on *Match Game*.

Playwright Neil 'Doc' Simon began a writer on the show, and I asked Jean what he was like. "Young," she replied. "He and his brother did it. It was Doc and Danny Simon, and he was basically at the time—the guys we got to write *Beat the Clock* were basically comedy writers. He was a young guy. He wrote some stunts for us. I remember sitting in Goodson's office, and he was there with his brother. All I remember doing was laughing, everybody was funny."

Some famous character actors also got their start on *Beat the Clock* before making names for themselves, among them Warren Oates. "Yeah, he was a stand-in, as was Jimmy Dean. Or *James* Dean. Absolutely *intense*. If he couldn't do a stunt...

"What they did was, we would try out stunts before they actually went out on the air with actual contestants, and we would do it with three different stand-ins, to see basically how much time we should give to a stunt, and see if things didn't work out quite right how we could change it, and so on and so forth. And he—I remember just basically, we would have three different groups of stand-ins. He would come in and he was given a stunt, and if he couldn't do it, he would go off in a corner and keep doing it."

So James Dean was one very determined youth, eh?

"Oh, very, and very intense about it. Warren Oates was just a sweet guy. These were all kids. We were paying them ten bucks an hour to do this kind of work; they were clearly starving actors. Some of them didn't care, and when they didn't care, we didn't use them again. They had to really try to do the stunts for us. It was important they do that because that was the only way we could make any kind of judgment as to whether or not the stunt was going to work on the air. Would it be amusing, would it be funny, would they be able to do it?"

Not A Fan of *Match Game?*

Before we move on to the next chapter, I'd like to close with one last ironic little vignette: Brett Somers was an actress living in New York City at the time the original *Match Game* aired. When I asked if she ever watched the show, she replied "The original version of *Match Game* was a very straight, unfunny and—it's very interesting enough—I hated it. I finally happened to have my set on, looking for the news or something. I would *leap* across the room to turn it off. I *hated* it!"

Review Questions

1. According to Ira Skutch, the key ingredient to making a game show work is <u>BLANK</u>.

a. Simplicity
b. Bribing the network honchos
c. Cigarettes and whiskey and wild, wild women

2. The creator of *Match Game* was most likely <u>BLANK</u>.

a. Drunk
b. Gertrude Ederle
c. Frank Wayne

3. The original *Match Game* theme song was <u>BLANK</u>.

a. Henry Mancini's *Baby Elephant Walk*
b. Bert Kaempfert's *A Swingin' Safari*
c. Allan Sherman's *Hello Muddah, Hello Faddah*

Answers: 1 a, 2 c, 3 b

3

The Host With The Most

Unbeknownst to most fans of *Match Game*, during the time Gene Rayburn was making America laugh while hosting the show, he was secretly working for the CIA as a paid undercover assassin...

Oh wait, wrong game show host! But hey, that long skinny mike he used during the seventies version of the show sure looked like a deadly weapon, didn't it?

In any case, James Bond wannabe or not, Eugen Peter Jeljenić was born on December 22, 1917 in Christopher, Illinois. His father died when he was still an infant, and the family moved to Chicago. His mother remarried a man named Milan Rubesah, and young Gene took his stepfather's name (slightly altered to "Rubessa"). The two were very close. Gene acted in plays at the Lindblom High School in Chicago, and won a scholarship to Knox College in Galesburg, Illinois.

A year later, he moved to New York, determined to become an actor. He worked at NBC as a page and usher by day and at night attended the network's announcing school. He was in the same page-training class as future *Today Show* host Dave Garroway, and also became friends with another future game show host, Peter Marshall.

"I knew his brother first, Jim Rubessa," recalled Peter, who would later host the original *Hollywood Squares*. "When I was fifteen, I was a pageboy at NBC in New York. Jim was a pageboy, then I met his brother Gene who

Young Gene in his first school play, dressed as Abraham Lincoln.

had been a pageboy...Through Jim, I met Gene and we became good acquaintances."

It was while working at NBC that he met Helen Tricknor, and the two married in 1940 and had their only child, a daughter named Lynne, in 1942. According to one early bio, "Between guide tours, he attended the network's announcing school, where out-of-town station managers hired young men aspiring to careers in radio. He landed his first announcing job with a Newburgh, New York station. Later he landed a job in Baltimore, where he stayed until enlisting in the Air Force, becoming a bombardier-navigator in B17s."

After time in the Air Force, he worked on WNEW in New York. Radio's first morning team was introduced in 1946: Jack Lescoulie and Gene Rayburn. Six months later, Lescoulie left and was replaced by Dee Finch, forming the highly successful team of *Rayburn and Finch*; their show proved a hit comedy program. In 1952 Gene moved over to WNBC Radio to do *The Gene Rayburn Show*, where doing live radio broadcasts trained him for working as a television host.

The Music Man

Looking for a bit of trivia on Gene that you never knew before? Here's one: while shopping around on *eBay*, I discovered a piece of sheet music for sale. For four dollars, I purchased *Hop Scotch Polka (Scotch Hot)*, published by Cromwell Music in 1949 with words and music by William (Billy) Whitlock, Carl Sigman, and *Gene Rayburn*. The cover featured a picture of Gene with his radio partner Dee Finch.

"When Rayburn and Finch set out to demonstrate their ability to create a hit song on the air," according to Nightingale Gordon, "they asked a music publisher for the worst song he could find. Playing the recordings five times a day, they generated tremendous popular demand. Rayburn and Finch commissioned a full orchestral arrangement and produced a new version featuring a young singer just out of high school. *Music! Music! Music!* sold over a million copies and made a star out of Theresa

Together, Gene Rayburn and Dee Finch practically invented the morning talk radio format that is so familiar today.

Brewer. To prove it wasn't a fluke, Rayburn and Finch did the same thing with *Hopscotch Polka*, which also sold millions."

Tonight's The Night!

By 1954, Gene made television history as the first announcer for *The Tonight Show* with Steve Allen. While he found announcing to be a bit confining, he asked for and got a chance to exercise his comedic skills in a news and weather segment he delivered from a soundproof studio NBC carpenters had constructed in the basement of the theatre where the show was taped. In his book *The Tonight Show*, Robert Metz wrote that "Gene began doing the weather in a humorous fashion—he had had a hundred hours of Air Force meteorology. But then Gene was staggered by hepatitis and couldn't leave his home in Westchester County. Broke and about to go off the payroll—he was on an appearance-by-appearance basis—he appealed to producer Mort Werner for help. Werner, never one to desert a talent in trouble, promptly ran a broadcast-quality telephone line from the Hudson to Gene's house. Thereafter, a leggy model in an abbreviated nurse's uniform would stand before the weather map and Gene's mellifluous voice would say, 'There's rain over Appalachia—put some measle marks over the mountains, nursey. No, no, not over Canada, over Pennsylvania, that's it—just a little to the left now. And there's snow in Ironwood, Michigan'—a running gag; there was always snow in Ironwood."

A versatile performer, Gene had appeared in a number of TV dramatic roles, and cited his most satisfying to be a starring role in a *Robert Montgomery Presents* program called *The Man Who Vanished*.

Along the way, there was Theatre, and Gene performed in comedies like *The Seven Year Itch*, *The Love of Four Colonels*, *Will Success Spoil Rock Hunter?*, *Who Was That Lady I Saw You With?*, and *Come Blow Your Horn*. Then in 1960, Gene starred in the huge Broadway hit *Bye, Bye, Birdie* and met an actor by the name of Charles Nelson Reilly, who replaced Dick Van Dyke as Gene's understudy. In fact, it's interesting to

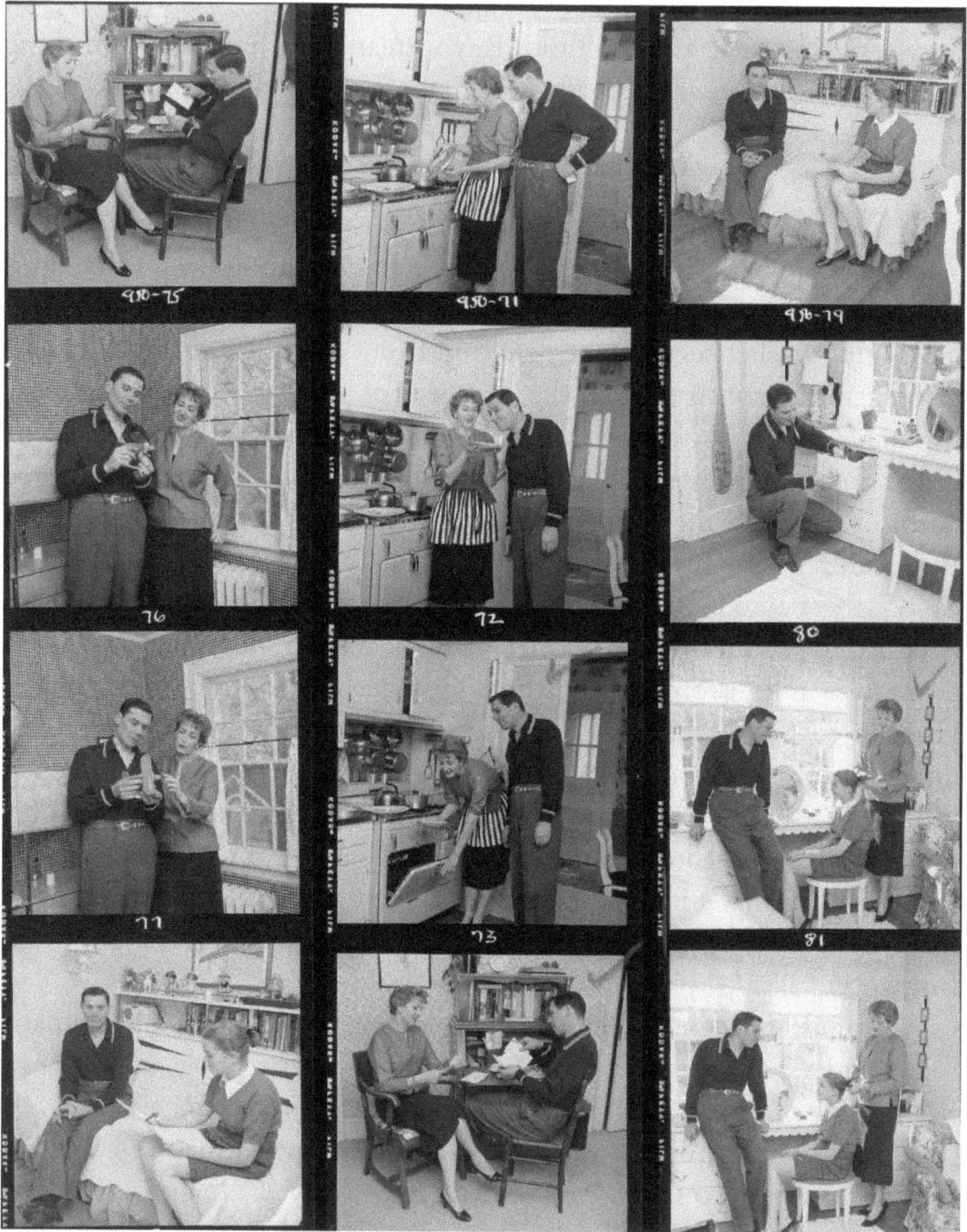

A proof sheet of photos taken by Barry Blum, showing Gene, Helen, and daughter Lynne at home in Massachussetts.

note just how many actors who later worked on *Match Game* had already known or worked with Gene.

His theatre bios contained such tidbits as, "Until he sold his Piper Pacer in the summer of 1953, his favorite hobby was flying. Skiing then became number one for a five year period until he broke his leg. At the moment it's tennis in the summer and squash in the winter." An NBC press release for *Match Game* dated fall 1969 states: "Gene Rayburn is a health food and exercise enthusiast. When he's not sharing a recipe for low-calorie pasta or riding a bike in Central Park, he's displaying his multi-faceted talents as host of NBC Television Network's *Match Game*...Gene is a regular performer at the Bucks Country Playhouse, where he appeared in *The Impossible Years* with his wife, Helen, and their daughter Lynn."

Yes, even while hosting *Match Game*, Gene continued to perform in live theatre, even co-starring with his wife Helen and his daughter Lynn in *The Impossible Years* at the Bucks County Playhouse in the mid-1960s. "It was like the old days in the theatre," quipped Gene. "People waiting at the stage door, mostly to meet Helen and Lynn. A lot of them watch *The Match Game* and said they were wondering who in the world would actually marry me."

The Game Show World

"I didn't start out to be a game show host," Gene admitted, years later. "I happened to be pretty good at it and had a long run with it. But I would say to anybody starting out, don't stick to one thing. Try and vary your interests as a performer. Do different things. It'll make you a better 'whole' entertainer."

By the time he began hosting *Match Game*, Gene was no stranger to game shows. At NBC he appeared in many of its panel shows, including *The Name's the Same*. He first hosted the Goodson-Todman celebrity panel show *Make the Connection* in 1955, and the following year worked on *Choose Up Sides*, a children's game show. In 1956 he acted as substitute host for Jack Barry on *Tic-Tac-Dough*, and in 1958 began a three year stint hosting NBC's *Dough-Re-Me*.

This Rayburn family portrait of Helen, Gene, and Lynne was among the many personal photos Gene kept over the years.

In 1962, Gene Rayburn was hired to replace Merv Griffin as host of *Play Your Hunch*. Ira Skutch remembered, "I knew him by reputation as a shining example of an ex-page who had achieved fame and prosperity, but this was our first meeting; the beginning of a twenty year career connection, and an ongoing personal one. Gene's a thorough professional with little of the ego problem that afflicts so many performers. He told me he'd managed to overcome those tendencies through personal soul-searching and psychoanalysis; a good example of the value of that much-maligned discipline. Gene was easy to work with, and in all our time together we had few problems between us.

"However, when Merv Griffin left *Play Your Hunch* and the ratings began to drop, the network panicked, and after five weeks, Gene was replaced as host."

Ira continued, "In the curious way that fate takes and gives, this turned out to be a bonanza for Gene. Preparing to launch *The Match Game*, Goodson-Todman was searching for an emcee. I persuaded the management to give Gene a chance, and not penalize him for NBC's precipitous decision. It proved ideal. For sixteen years, in its two separate runs, *Match Game* provided Gene with an advantageous and lucrative vehicle."

Match Game was popular because, Gene told a reporter, "For the first time, the audience can participate in the quiz game to the same extent as the contestants on-camera. The panelists represent the viewers." In a 1965 interview, Gene was quoted as saying, "This show is filled with fun, too—the format seems to inspire humor in our contestants." He cited the following example: "Once I asked the teams to name a canal. Most contestants replied 'Panama' or 'Suez'—but one gentleman answered 'Guadel-Canal.' The audience burst into laughter."

"I wanted to do my own thing," Gene admitted years later. "I wanted to do it in my own style. And my style is to do it with humor. Humor was part of my nature. And I'll never forget, in the beginning Mark Goodman used to write these long memos to the producers. 'What is Rayburn doing? He's getting laughs. He's getting *laughs*!' He thought that was terrible because he thought the most important thing was the game. Well, if you're talking about something like *Password*, he's right. But if you talk about a weak format like *The Match Game*, you've got to do something to jazz it up or make it fun or light or whatever. So that's what I did."

Match Game producer Jean Kopelman had worked with Gene Rayburn prior to his hosting *Match Game*. "He did one show for me. I did a show very early on, *Choose Up Sides*, which was a kids show. This was live. We did it on Saturday mornings and it was a kids' stunt show. We put two teams competing against each other, kids doing stunts, blah, blah, blah. We did that at noon on Saturday, and then we rushed from whatever studio that was in and went over to *Beat The Clock* in the afternoon, and it was on in the evening...I remember there was about twenty-six weeks of Saturdays where I started at six in the morning and finished at around eight at night doing live television shows.

"And Rayburn was the emcee on that. And everybody knew who he was and everybody liked him, and he was absolutely wonderful. I think we auditioned a bunch of guys, but I think he got the job kind of hands down. I don't really remember too well. There was no question in any of our minds that he was wonderful, and he was.

"Rayburn was a talented guy. I don't know whether the radio helped at all or not. I mean, he was doing something quite different than quiz shows. Running a quiz show is not the same thing as having a disc jockey show with Finch, because the problems are entirely different. But he was very, very good at it, and he was very likeable, and he played it with just the right light touch."

Ira Skutch had nothing but praise for the man. "Oh, he was terrific... We had a lot of good times together...I was one of his biggest fans."

Review Questions

1. In Gene Rayburn's dramatic debut he played President <u>BLANK</u>.

a. George Washington
b. George Jefferson
c. Abraham Lincoln

2. To prove they could create a hit song on their show, Rayburn and Finch asked a music publisher for <u>BLANK</u>.

a. The worst song he could find.
b. Britney Spears' phone number.
c. A harmonica and a washtub.

3. Gene Rayburn's microphone was <u>BLANK</u>.

a. Long and skinny
b. A Sony ECM-51 Telescopic Microphone.
c. All of the above.

Answers: 1. c., 2. a, 3. c.

4

The Voice of Daytime Television

Johnny Leonard Olson (May 22, 1910-October 12, 1985) was a skinny kid, the youngest of six boys and five girls and grew up on his Norwegian family's eighty-five acre dairy farm on the outskirts of Windom, Minnesota.

According to Randy West's tribute website dedicated to Johnny, "John Olson's broadcasting career began when Windom electrician Oscar Estenson wired a crude radio transmitter in his electrical repair shop. Fourteen-year-old Johnny sang *No, No, Nora* into the microphone during a break from his part time job in a local jewelry store. Encouraged by his brother Curt who worked at the electrical shop, Johnny took to the air for three more afternoon pirate broadcasts. The thrill of the experience lasted even after a man from the Federal Radio Commission, precursor of the FCC, paid a visit to suggest they add frequency control to their crude apparatus to avoid blotting out all the stations up and down the dial for a 50 mile radius."

Johnny Olson, photographed in 1956 for an ABC publicity shot.

Ah, how a child's interests can grow into his future.

Johnny credited his distinctive speaking voice to his mother's hearing problems coupled with her difficulties with the English language. As he recalled, "She just demanded I 'speak up' when I began to talk and read. She wanted to hear me, and I 'spoke up' when I acted in high school plays and began to sing and talk before audiences before I was fourteen years old. Because of her interests and demands, I amplified an average baritone voice into one that is loud and clear."

In an unpublished memoir, he wrote, "It takes a good voice to grab [an audience's] lethargic, wandering attention and hold it long enough to tell them what you and your sponsor want them to hear. A good voice involves more than a high decibel level...A voice without undue inflection may charm, soothe, calm or arouse. A voice can also repel, infuriate or actually make a listener ill."

After graduating high school, he began working at a radio station ("The Friendly Farmer Station") in Poynette, Wisconsin, before moving on to another station in Madison, Wisconsin. At eighteen, he became the youngest station manager in the country, making $25 a week at KGDA—writing, singing, and acting in radio skits, news, and children's programs. Over time he juggled radio work with odd-jobs, working variously as a soda jerk, court reporter, short-order cook, and a singer and manager for music groups traveling the big-band circuit.

In 1938, he was in Iola, Wisconsin performing with *The Rhythm Rascals*—a five-piece jazz band he organized for Milwaukee's WTMJ radio station—that he met Penelope Powers, a young school teacher who sang and danced in community productions and local radio. Not only would Penny eventually become Johnny's wife, but also over the years she would perform as his on-air co-host, vocalist and occasionally associate producer on a number of radio programs, as well as some of Television's earliest talk, variety, and game shows.

Work with the jazz band took him across the country, and into radio, where he announced and hosted a mind-boggling array of radio programs.

By 1949 he was presiding over twenty half-hour shows a week—quiz shows, talk shows, you name it.

Then came Television.

His success in hosting a radio program called *Ladies Be Seated* led to the show debuting on TV. He recounted his first experiences in the new medium:

"We did what rehearsing we could...We studied the lighting arrangements and visited the control room where engineers had the choice of images from three live cameras and from three reels of film. I was very impressed with it all." He continued, "I hopped out of a Valentine-like cardboard entrance in a minstral costume and we had our usual opening....Our audience was lively and responsive...There was only one incident. Lights became so hot they melted mascara on women's faces in early television. GE tried to lick the problem with a type cooled by water. In the course of our program, one of these exploded and sprinkled part of the studio audience with warm water. 'My God, my time has come,' shouted a pregnant woman caught in the downpour. When she found it hadn't, she laughed. Penny and some others wiped up the water. We finished the program with everybody convinced that television had great possibilities."

> "If you would like to appear in person in the television audience of *Match Game '75*, forget it! —I mean, don't forget to write to this address."
> —Johnny Olson

Later, Johnny hosted the first daytime network TV show to originate from New York, *Johnny Olson's Rumpus Room*, which aired daily on the pioneering DuMont Television Network from 1949 to 1952. The list of TV and radio shows and specials he worked on is far too numerous to

Johnny Olson at work on the later version of *Match Game* in 1975. Photo by Gary Kleinman.

mention here, but two are worth noting: in 1955 Johnny was teamed with Jackie Gleason for work on *The Honeymooners* for DuMont, and he hosted a radio pilot entitled *Time's A-Wastin'* for ABC from a new producing team—Mark Goodson and Bill Todman.

Needless to say, they seemed to like Johnny's work—at least well enough to let him announce for game shows like *What's My Line?*, *I've Got A Secret*, *To Tell The Truth*, and a brand new show set to debut in December 1962 called *The Match Game*; in time, he would also work on the classic 1970's version of *Match Game*.

"Johnny Olson was the announcer the entire run of both shows," remembered Ira Skutch. "I worked with him on many series and pilots. He was not only the best at what he did, he was the most even-tempered person I have ever known; always pleasant, cooperative, and helpful."

"I Loved Johnny O.," said *Match Game* production assistant Audrey Davis. "Best announcer in the business. Friendly with everyone. He was the announcer on several shows I worked on."

"Evidently Jackie Gleason would not tape his show unless Johnny Olson warmed up the audience, because he was so good at it," remembered Dick De Bartolo. "And so, sometimes we would start taping an hour earlier so Johnny could jump on an airplane because, you know, Gleason did his show in Miami."

When *Match Game* moved to the west coast, Johnny kept up his jet-setting ways, dividing his time between Los Angeles and the home he maintained in West Virginia. By this time he was already making over $100,000 a year, and had become one of the most in-demand and respected men in radio and television. Over the years he interviewed three sitting U.S. Presidents, and shared stages with a wide variety of great and talented performers including Bob Hope, Frank Sinatra, Kate Smith, Johnny Carson, Bing Crosby, Jack Benny, Jackie Gleason—and yes, Gene Rayburn.

Johnny was remembered affectionately by his co-workers. Elliot Feldman, who worked as a writer on the seventies version of Match Game, remembered, "Back then I shared the front of the stage with the late great Johnny Olson. I helped him cue the audience to shut up or laugh at bad jokes. Sometimes we cued them to groan. He was a supreme mensch."

The other writers shared Elliot's respect for Johnny and paid tribute to him, 'the *Match Game* way.' While working as the announcer and opening each show with his familiar catch-phrase, "Get ready to match the stars!" before listing off the celebrity panelists appearing in each episode, he was also the announcer on Godson-Todman's *The Price Is Right*, hosted by Bob Barker. When the contestants' name was read on that program, Johnny offered up the invitation to "Come on down!" to the foot of the stage for a chance to play on the show. That phrase became Johnny's signature line, even after fellow *Price* announcers Rod Roddy, Rich Fields, and George Gray succeeded him, each putting their own spin on it. But the phrase "Come on down!" is forever identified with Johnny Olson. Inspired by this, *Match Game* writers immortalized him in one of their questions.

Gene read off the fill-in-the-blank statement: "Johnny Olson's beautiful wife Penny said, 'Last night it was very hard to sleep because all night long Johnny kept shouting BLANK.'" While Scoey Mitchlll and Brett missed the boat, Gary Burghoff and Richard Dawson came up with the definitive answer, Johnny's by-now-familiar "Come on down!"

We'll give the final tribute to Gene Rayburn, who once admitted, "I did a show without Johnny once, and I never realized how good he was until I tried to do a show without him."

Review Questions

1. Johnny Olson's broadcasting career began when he <u>BLANK</u>.

a. Shouted "Come on down!" to a guy on the 3rd floor
b. Sang *No, No, Nora* into a crude radio transmitter
c. Tattled on his sister on *The Maury Povitch Show*

2. Johnny credited his distinctive speaking voice to <u>BLANK</u>.

a. His getting the good genes and his brother getting the beat-up old Levi's
b. His mother being a hard-of-hearing foreigner
c. Steroids

3. According to Johnny, it takes a good voice to grab <u>BLANK</u>.

a. Jackie Gleason
b. An audience's attention
c. A pregnant woman sitting in a studio audience

Answers: 1 b, 2 b, 3 b.

5

The Staff Who Made It All Work

"There was never anything hard about this show," admitted *Match Game* producer Jean Kopelman, "except the ten shows in three days. By the time we got finished, I didn't know if my name was Kopelman or Rayburn or whatever, and I don't think *any* of us did. That was hard. But nothing else about it was hard. Everybody had a good time.

"We had this Roselle Bernhard who got the contestants for us, and she was terrific. She was an 'older woman,' if you will. If I was in my thirties, she was in her fifties. And I think she just worked the *$64,000 Question* or something, and she and [Robert] Noah actually had come out of places that had been involved in the Quiz Show scandals. And Goodson nicely hired them and nicely paid them and everything else, and they all worked out very well. But they had a very tough time for a couple of years before that whole thing kind of disappeared. And Roselle was marvelous. She got these marvelous contestants.

"It was really a very happy crew. I mean, I'm sounding boring saying how wonderful everybody was, but they were."

Match Game 101

Diane Janaver agrees with that statement. "As a matter of fact," she told me, "the staff of that show—it was incredible!—we got along so well we made a movie. The first movie we made was *How the West Was Won, Barely*. We got Freedomland to open for us one morning, you know, when nobody else would be there, and they let us shoot all the scenes of *How the West Was Won*. We had a premiere of it in New York where everybody came, celebrities, everybody came, it was covered by Dorothy Kilgallen. It was this little eight millimeter thing that we did. It was great, it was fun, and it was Dick De Bartolo that was behind that."

"*How The West Was Won, Barely* was all Dick De's doing, I'm pretty sure," remembered *Match Game* production assistant Audrey Davis. "I don't remember who secured Freedomland, but probably [it was] Dick De. As I remember it, the crew [was made up of] the staff with help from some others like a friend of Ken's. I don't really remember the plot, but I played a blonde Indian. I wore a shirt and jeans and had a feather in my hair. And I think I held a tomahawk. I think Diane played a damsel in distress. I remember Rae in a huge hoop skirt who had trouble walking down the aisle of the train because of the big hoop.

"It was very funny. And there was a great fight scene on top of the train, I think between Dick and Ken. Don't know how they didn't kill themselves doing it. If I remember correctly, the film took more than one day to shoot. But don't trust my memory."

"Later on we did another second feature called *242nd Street*, " remembered Diane. "And that was a big deal. Remember the old *42nd Street* movie? And when we'd go to the studio at NBC, take the camera, and we would get our celebrity guests to do little cameo appearances. So there would be a row of ladies turning their umbrellas and you'd see our cute little chorus girls, and suddenly the next face up would be some famous person. It was cute. It was great, and we had another big premiere of that. Those were all on the side. It was the *Match Game* staff, but it was not on the air.

The 2nd *Match Game* Movie: *242ND Street*

From Dorothy Kilgallen's nationally syndicated column, June 24, 1964:

"Members of the 400, the jet set, and stars of show business are still talking—and probably will talk for a long time to come—about the glittering premiere of the new cinema extravaganza "242nd Street" at Delmonico's Ballroom. After the laughter and the cheering died, it was generally agreed that Sam Spiegel, Joe Levine, Jack Warner, and all the other giants of Hollywood had better move over just slightly to make room for writer-producer-director Dick DeBartolo, who was responsible for this delightful confection starring two discoveries, Imie Lane and Diane Janaver, and a host of more familiar talents, including Joan Fontaine, Don Ameche, Arlene Francis, Audrey Meadows, Phyllis Diller, Jane Withers, and Van Johnson.

"The story, a classic in the movies, delineates the tribulations of a small town beauty as she tries to make the grade in the theater, but under Mr. DeBartolo's masterful direction, the old tale takes on new dimensions and seems as fresh as any turgid drama ever dreamed up on Swedish celluloid.

"The production numbers, skillfully choreographed by Ken Abernathy, are lavish, and the special effects should win an Academy Award. There are scenes of New York, its skylines and its tall buildings, that could not have been more realistic if they had been filmed in front of the Seagram Building."

While the film was directed by Dick DeBartolo, he conceded the camera work was a team effort. "Anybody who wasn't in the scene shot the film," he admitted. Imie Lane, who worked at Goodson-Todman, starred as "Ruby Feeler," and accoding to Dick, "She worked for *Price Is Right*, so she got great props for us, all the furs that the women wear." Dick even made a cameo as a "starmaker" producer. The screen grabs on the opposite page illustrate the star power captured by the lens: Arlene Francis and Van Johnson posing with umbrellas; Gene Rayburn with Peggy Cass, Henry Morgan, Robert Q. Lewis and Betty White in the MAD Magazine offices.

WITH A FLASHING
GLANCE OF

GENE RAYBURN
BETTY WHITE
BENNETT CERF
HENRY MORGAN
JOAN FONTAINE

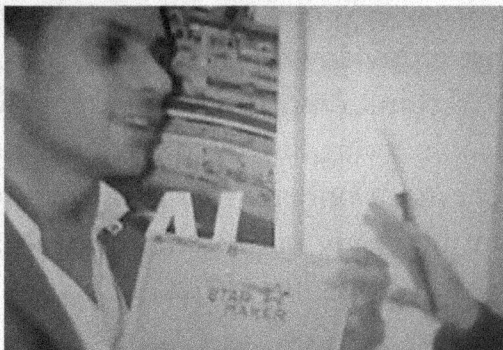

"I think they were probably close to an hour, fifty minutes. Dick De Bartolo I'm sure still has them. I *know* he does. We had posters made up, premiere, and again, all the celebrities, coverage in the press, the whole thing. It was great fun, a really good time."

"*242nd. Street.* was a hoot," Audrey Davis recalled. "I played a French maid to the 'star,' Imie Lane. I wore a short, black, ruffley maid's costume with a white apron, very high heels and black stockings with a diamond pattern, I think. Those scenes were shot in my parents' bedroom in Brooklyn. I was helping Imie try on fur coats and jackets. And there was a scene with 'reporters' rushing in to talk to her at the entrance to our living room. My father played a reporter. So did Lenore Goldstein-Hatch. Maybe Rae also, don't remember.

"We also shot several scenes in the Seagram Building. There was a Busby Berkley scene on the steps leading to the Four Seasons restaurant with lots of ladies dressed in costumes. My sister was one of them and wore a two-piece bathing suit. They all wore these crazy head pieces *à la* Berkley. I'm pretty sure that one of Mark Goodson's secretaries was one of the girls. I'm blocking out other scenes we shot.

"We had so much fun. It was the craziest thing I'd ever done and I had a ball. Gene Rayburn narrated both films."

The Directors

A director's job isn't as easy as it looks, even in the world of game shows. "Nobody was moving, but a lot of stuff was going on," observed *Match Game* producer Jean Kopelman. "My having done *Beat the Clock*, where everybody was all over the place, it was a pleasure to have people just sitting down.

"I think *Beat the Clock* was much harder to direct. You had stuff going, people going, in all directions; balloons, what have you. You could rehearse it only up to a point because the contestants never did anything until they got on the air. So that was more like shooting a baseball game [than] things like *What's My Line?* and *To Tell the Truth* and *Password* and *Match Game*, where everybody sat very quietly, nobody slightly out of frame."

Ira Skutch directed the New York version of *Match Game* (and later produced the West Coast version in the 1970's). "I worked very closely with Jean Kopelman," Ira told me. "I didn't do any of the booking or anything. We worked very closely together, and we all used to have lunch together during the break between shows. She and I used to take the stars out to lunch. I said, 'I never thought when I went into this business I'd wind up directing lunches.'"

Three men besides Ira have been credited with directing *Match Game* between 1962 and 1969: Jim Elson, Mike Gargiulo, and Rodger Wolf. The first was James Elson. "Poor Jimmy died of a brain tumor," said Jean Kopelman. "He was very young, as I recall. Jimmy was super. That's right, I forgot he was the first director. Ira came in after Jimmy died. Jimmy was a lot of fun. He was a pal of the guys that did all the *That Was the Week That Was*, and Doug Hemming, they did all these kind of wonderful specials, musical comedy kind of things. They were all of his pals. It was amusing to hang around with them."

Next came Rodger Wolf. "I always used to rub his fuzzy balding head for luck," remembered *Match Game* production assistant Audrey Davis. "Rodger was the associate director, and he worked for NBC," said Jean. "I worked with Rodger. He was a very, very nice guy. They were all nice. Everybody was very pleasant.

"Mike Gargiulo did it for awhile. I can't remember. Ira was both a producer and a director. I know Ira ended up doing it until we went off the air."

"Mike and I were really good friends for quite a while," said Ira. "We first worked on *Play Your Hunch* together. I was producer and he was director. We did that for four years, and then we did a show called *Missing Links* together for a year. And then after that, that's when I went on *Match Game*, when that went off. And he stayed with Goodson-Todman until the company began to shrink, which, as you probably know, [was] during the latter part of the sixties. We went from one week where we had fifty half-hours of programming on in one week to where there was nothing left on the networks at all in 1969."

The Writer

The questions used on the show were written by Dick DeBartolo. While he parlayed his lifelong passion for gadgets into a role as 'the Giz-Wiz' and these days often appears on talk shows as a pundit for technical wizardry, Dick DeBartolo is probably best known by pop-culturati as being for over fifty years one of 'the usual gang of idiots' writing for *MAD* Magazine.

Dick began his game show career by climbing from office boy to writer for Barry-Enright Productions, and as he recalled, "Bob Noah, one of the producers at Barry-Enright, left to join Goodson-Todman Productions, where he was involved in developing a new show called *The Match Game*. Bob had liked my writing on *Winky-Dink*, which by then was history, so he asked me to submit sample questions for *The Match Game*. I did, and he liked those, too, so I got the job writing the questions for the show. Hard-hitting questions like: Name a red flower. Name a kind of sandwich. Name a president whose picture is on currency.

"Well, the show was canceled after a year and a half and when that happened, I got an idea. I went to Mark Goodson and said, 'Mark, I write silly stuff for *MAD*, how about doing silly questions on *The Match Game*? I had written a couple of samples: John liked to put gravy on his (blank). Mary had a flower growing out of her (blank). Goodson said, 'Dick, we have six more weeks of the show to tape. Do what you want. Since *The Match Game* is already canceled, they can't cancel it again!'

"The new questions brought lots of laughs, as Gene Rayburn, the original host of the show, read the word 'blank' for the missing part of the question. Of course (at least in their minds), people couldn't help but fill in the blanks with all sorts of weird things, and a whole new life was given to the show. *The Match Game* got renewed, and it ran for about a total of twelve years, with a break somewhere in between. When the show moved out to California, Mark asked if I wanted to relocate to the West Coast. I told him I really loved New York, and that *MAD* was in New York, and I'd rather stay. He told me he'd never forget what I'd done for *The Match Game*, and I'd always have a job at Goodson-Todman, no matter where I lived..."

"He was amusing and fun," Jean Kopelman said of Dick, "and we had a grand time doing it. It was great fun writing those questions, working with him as he wrote the questions, and what he did. When I did the show he would sit on the floor and feed out the questions, and we would pick them out as we were going. We set up the first three questions before we went on the air, and then just—there were like forty questions on the board that we could use, and depending on how I wanted the show to go. I'd pick a question I either thought was amazing or tough or whatever. He was down there with me, and we were both on the headsets all the way through the show...it was all five cents, everything was easy."

"Being involved in TV has given me some unique opportunities," admitted Dick, "like getting to meet celebrities who are interested in buying comedy material, not just taking the *MAD* tour. I've written jokes for Phyllis Diller, and I've done a lot of work with Soupy Sales. I got to write two one-hour TV specials Soupy starred in. One was a Saturday morning kids' show, and the other was a basketball special featuring Soupy and the Harlem Globetrotters. Soupy and I also went to Canada to work on a version of *Helzapoppin'*. Talk about *off*-Broadway!"

It's nice to know that the behind the scenes people occasionally get a nod of recognition for their contributions to their shows. Dick told me, "Very early on there were nominations for game show writing, and I was nominated for two years." That category was later dropped from Emmy consideration before he had the chance to actually win one. "Well," reasons Dick, "They were trying to streamline."

The Production Assistants

Producing a TV show requires more than just actors and sets. Most audiences are probably familiar with the duties of producers and directors.

Gene Rayburn on the *Match Game* set, surrounded by production assistants (back row, left to right) Ken Abernathy, who organized the scripts for Gene's live commercials; Lenore Goldstein, who operated the show's scoreboard; Jerry Layne, who conducted warm-up games with the contestants prior to taping the program; (Front row, left to right) Audrey Davis, office receptionist; Gene Rayburn; Rae Pichon, who acted as the show's judge and helped book some of the celebrity guests. (Collection of Adam Nedeff)

But most people outside the business are not familiar with the function of the production assistant, a position in which many producers started their careers. The sixties version of *Match Game* used five P.A.'s, as production assistants are called.

Rae Pichon was the first P.A. hired for *The Match Game*. Previously she worked on Westinghouse's syndicated show, *PM East* (co-hosted by Mike Wallace and Joyce Davidson). Rae was Jean Kopelman's secretary, and she decided whether or not a match has been scored, except in doubtful cases, when Jean herself made the decisions. A newspaper article from 1965 also said of Rae, "She also reads all mail from viewers, and swears that the audiences' letters are the kookiest whenever the moon is full!"

Jerry Layne started out in show business as a ventriloquist and did nightclub work in New York and Miami before joining Goodson-Todman in December of 1960. During the show, Jerry was responsible for making sure the audience applauded at the right time, and assisted announcer Johnny Olsen with the audience match that was conducted before each show. Other times, Jerry worked with the contestants, booking them for participation and teaching them how to play the game.

Ken Abernathy started as a page at NBC, and was hired as a production assistant on both the daytime and night versions of the original run of *The Price Is Right*. Ken was the commercial coordinator on *The Match Game*, responsible for making sure the commercials were in the right positions in the show. He also made sure Gene had the copy for the introductions or "lead-in" that he would read before every commercial.

Even while working for Goodson Todman, Ken was moonlighting as a producer in his own right. In 1964, he and a friend formed University Concerts, a company that produced various kinds of shows for colleges throughout the New York area. Ken handled all talent booking promotion and production for colleges, and was proud that the Serendipity Singers made their first public appearance for the company in a concert at West Point.

Lenore Goldstein came to Goodson-Todman in 1961 as a production assistant on *Play Your Hunch* with Merv Griffin. After *Hunch* went off the air, she joined the *Match Game* staff when the show was still in the planning stage. Lenore was in charge of the scoreboard during the show and was also responsible for keeping records of answers and contestant's winnings, as well as making sure Gene Rayburn had the questions.

Audrey Davis joined Goodson-Todman in 1961 as a receptionist, after working for a magazine for six months. When the *Match Game* staff was being organized, Audrey told producer Jean Kopelman that she wanted to get into production. Jean told her to submit a list of questions that could be used on the show, liked them, and soon after, Audrey was made a production assistant.

Audrey Davis Remembers...

"I was nineteen when I started working for Goodson-Todman," remembered Audrey Davis. "I was the receptionist/relief switchboard operator at Goodson-Todman and when *The Match Game* was sold, I asked Jean Kopelman how I could join the staff. She asked me to submit *Match Game*-type questions, which I did. Apparently she liked them and I was hired as a production assistant."

Audrey remembered Mark Goodson as rather "intimidating and a fabulous dresser," and Bill Todman she described as being "somewhat quiet and very much a business-type. I didn't know either well at all.

"I was very impressed to work for them. I loved television and they were the kings of game shows. The Seagram Building was the most elegant building in New York City. And, of course, I always thought of the iconic scene from *Breakfast at Tiffany's* [between Audrey Hepburn and George Peppard, shot by the fountain in front of the Seagram Building]. I adored Audrey Hepburn. Thought I was extremely grown up when I went into Al Schacht's [restaurant across the street] which wasn't often. Everyone looked so sophisticated to me.

"I did general P.A. work: typing, filing, and if I remember correctly, I sat with a stagehand at the scoring machine in the studio when we taped and at one time, I sat with the stagehand that pushed the questions out of the chute so Gene could read them. Since we were not union, we couldn't touch anything that would take work away from a stagehand, but I wore a headset and got instructions from Jean in the control room as to which questions they wanted read. I also tallied the answers that the studio audience filled out which were later used for The End Game.

"The best thing was that I was earning my own money, had more independence and I was in 'Show Biz.' The worst was that I had to travel back home to Brooklyn on the subway and had little in common with my friends that were still in college or teaching.

"And I had such fun, especially when we made the Dick DeBartolo movies. I did not love going to school but I loved working. And I've been addicted to television since I was very young.

"Game shows were available to anyone that had a television and they could play along. Also, you didn't necessarily have to be super smart and Goodson-Todman's games were fun to play."

The crew occasionally played little practical jokes on one another; not enough to disrupt things, simply to have a little bit of fun. "I also remember telling you a story about Dick DeBartolo putting everyone up to wearing a turtleneck sweater one day to a taping. Cameramen, staff, electricians, guest stars, etc. This was when turtlenecks were quite in fashion and Gene Rayburn wore them sometimes on the show, but Dick never told Gene what he was up to. So Gene was introduced and came on stage and it took him a little while to notice that everyone was in turtlenecks. Everyone had a good laugh about it.

"Rae and I are still good friends, even thought at one point there was a twenty-year gap in our friendship until we reconnected. She was fun to be around. I don't remember Brian Hennessey working on *The Match Game*. I did work with him on another game show later on, but it was not a G-T show. I thought Roselle was very sophisticated—I thought everyone was when I was twenty—and she was always nice to me. So were Jerry, Lenore and Ken. I remember us all getting along well. I don't remember any fights or big disagreement. Of course I could be blocking that out, but I really don't. Sometimes they treated me and joked about me being a kid ... but I was! My sense of humor is much better now.

"To this day, I still prefer the New York Gene Rayburn version of the show. It was something different from other game shows which were on the air. Since there were only two celebrities and four contestants, the fun was more evenly divided. Also, it was new. And the first game show I worked on, so I guess I'm partial. We had so much fun and the staff was pretty close. I think that was helped so much because of Dick DeBartolo and the 8 mm movies. "

A Swingin' Safari

Just who wrote that catchy theme song to the original 1962-1969 version of *Match Game*? It was songwriter Bert Kaempfert.

Born in Hamburg, Germany, in 1923, Kaempfert studied music and began performing professionally at the age of sixteen. He was drafted into the German Navy during World War II and played with a military band; while a prisoner in Denmark near the end of the war, he formed his own big band, and after his release toured Allied officer's clubs in Germany. After the war he returned to Hamburg (then the center of the German music industry) and over the next decade became one of the top music producers in Germany and honed his songwriting skills.

While he provided some tunes for Elvis Presley's film *G.I. Blues*, he is best known by the pop-culturati for giving the Beatles their first commercial release: In 1961 British singer Tony Sheridan, backed by the Beatles, recorded the songs *My Bonny Lies Over The Ocean* and *When The Saints Go Marching In*; the Beatles recorded *Ain't She Sweet* and George's *Cry For A Shadow*. Kaempfert was so unimpressed he released the single under the name 'The Beat Brothers'.

Kaempfert began focusing on his orchestra and recording, rarely touring or appearing live. Between 1959 and 1973, he released over thirty albums for Decca records. His success as a composer was assured with hits like *Spanish Eyes*, *Danke Schoen*, and *Strangers in the Night*, as well as *A Swingin' Safari*, a popular song of the era used as the theme for the original version of *Match Game*. In the early 1970's he bought a large estate in Majorca, Spain, and began touring with a live band. He died unexpectedly in Majorca on June 21, 1980.

I asked *Match Game* producer Jean Kopelman whose idea it was to use *A Swingin' Safari* as the show's theme. Without hesitation she replied, "Goodson's. He wanted to use it. He loved it. He'd heard it—it was very hip, and he had heard it, and it was marvelous. Of course, they took it off at the end because they discovered they could make more money if they made up their own song and reap the ASCAP royalties for it. So they took it off, but it was a marvelous idea."

The Associate Producer: Diane Janaver

"I worked on the one in New York, and then I worked on the new version out here [in Los Angeles]. Then I worked on the *Match Game-Hollywood Squares* one. And I worked on the nighttime syndicated one which began at the same time as the first California version.

"I worked originally at ABC. I went to work as a secretary and I heard about an opening, that Mark Goodson needed a secretary, and I was very good as being a secretary. I had shorthand awards and all of that stuff, but Mark did everything very fast. And I went in for an interview and he hired me as a secretary, and then from there I moved on to other things in that company. I think *Match Game* was my second show. The first show I did was *I've Got a Secret*. I was a P.A., production assistant."

Diane's primary duty as an associate producer on *Match Game* was booking the celebrities. "Yeah, that was the main thing of it, because that was a big thing. Well, it's a matter of getting together with these people and teaching them how to play the game, make sure they understand what they're doing, and how to watch contestants, and how it works. And then arranging for them to get to the studio and talking with them about what clothes to bring, and then being with them at the studio, going out to lunch, taking them to lunch, all that. Now, people think nothing five, six shows a day, but in those days in New York in the early version we did two in the morning, one in the afternoon, and back the next day, two in the morning, and a leisurely day. My day was taken up with celebrities each time.

"We wanted names that people would recognize, and we wanted people that could relax and enjoy themselves and do a show like this without a script, which isn't everybody's cup of tea. But most people who were willing to do it all liked that... Other people I found interesting because, as you say, of their reputation. There were people you knew of forever. And yeah, they really were real people. Like Ethel Merman, a Broadway legend forever, and there she was—the *real* Ethel Merman! And then there were people around the show that were just good on the show and so funny, and we really laughed, like Henry Morgan, who was great and became a personal friend."

The Stars!

The sixties version of *Match Game* featured a wide variety of celebrity captains, remembered with fondness by the staff half a century later.

"The celebrity booker for *The Match Game* in New York was a woman named Rae Pichon," remembered Dick DeBartolo, "and very early in the series we said, 'Let's just try to book every famous person that we've ever wanted to meet.' And so many of them said yes! But that was all there was to the booking process. Rae just tried to book celebrities that we would be excited about meeting backstage."

And of course, those were the same celebrities the television-viewing audience also wanted to see on the show. But even the network executives had no idea which guest stars would garner the highest ratings with their appearance on the show.

As Ira Skutch recalled, "My favorite story about that was—we were doing a show called *Snap Judgment* in the late sixties. Ed McMahon was the emcee, and he managed to get us two bookings. One was Johnny Carson and the other was Bob Hope. And the two weeks that those fellows were on the show were the poorest ratings we had, I think. I always was very skeptical about the power of names to bring people to game shows because that was what the network wanted. They said, 'Oh, you've got to get better names.' And that generally degenerated into saying, 'Well, book people from soap operas,' and 'Book people from sitcoms, because they're big television stars.' That was their idea of great *promotable* stuff. I never thought that worked either."

Still, a lot of big stars played *Match Game*; among them was Lauren Bacall. "She was very nice, too," said Ira. "I'll tell you who else did the show a few times: Shirley Jones and Jack Cassidy. They were a nice couple. Particularly Shirley. I was very fond of her. Joan Rivers did the show a lot because Gene liked her a lot, and she did it a number of times. Soupy Sales used to do the show quite often, too. Oh, he's a really nice fellow. He's been very ill lately, but he's a lot of fun."

"They were all, almost all of them, wonderful," reports Jean Kopelman. "Florence Henderson was an absolute doll, Peggy Cass was a doll, Kitty Carlisle was fun. The only one that wasn't fun was Gladys—no, not Gladys. What the hell was her name?—Gloria Swanson—who came in and said, 'I wish to talk to the producer.' And I said, 'I am the producer.' She said, 'Don't be ridiculous. I wish to speak to the *producer*.' That didn't go too well.

"But other than that—Lauren Bacall was a little bit of a tough cookie. The rest of them were all marvelous. Orson Bean was a doll, Tom Poston—even Henry Morgan turned out to be an absolute sweetheart. They were all great fun. They enjoyed doing the show, they were very nice about it.

"We had Dusty Hoffman on before *The Graduate* became big, and we had Liza Minnelli on before whatever she did became big. When they came on, they were just terrific. Ed McMahon used to do the show a lot, he was lots of fun. Aside from Miss Swanson, I can't really remember anyone who was anything but pleasant and fun and enjoying themself."

"We had Raymond Massey, of all people, on the show as a celebrity," said Diane. "We had one week where we had Liza Minelli playing against Dustin Hoffman. And these are all just gone! It's incredible. Ethel Merman was on it too. A lot of people like that. It's too bad. NBC, in all their wisdom, I guess, erased them. Mickey Mantle. They were really good shows."

When I ventured that it was possible there might be tapes lost in storage somewhere, waiting to be discovered, as happened with a cache of master tapes from the old *Hollywood Squares*, Diane replied, "But I have the feeling New York has much less storage space than California, and I have the feeling they recycled them all. Too bad."

Snippets of Stardom

Some celebrities left a deep impression on production assistant Audrey

A special "all-stars" celebrity-themed week of episodes in 1964 featured Bennett Cerf, Henry Morgan, and Robert Q. Lewis playing against Joan Fontaine, Betty White, and Peggy Cass.

Davis, while others rated hardly a blip. As she pointed out, "In fact, I have very little memory of most of the celebs who appeared on the show. It was over fifty years ago and I was just a PA who got them coffee," she laughed. "I don't even know some of the people you listed. Also, some of my memories may be mixed up when I worked with these celebs on other shows. I'm trying very hard to give you only facts, so please forgive my poor memory."

About Ray Bolger, best known as The Scarecrow in *The Wizard of Oz*, she recalled, "Nice man. Loved when he danced a shuffle for us. I think he did the shuffle as he was introduced and came out on stage from backstage. Most likely it was Diane who booked him.

"As far as Douglas Fairbanks, Jr. goes, I remember Jean Kopelman calling him or referring to him as 'Captain.' Maybe it was because he wore a double-breasted navy jacket with gold buttons."

The Godfather of Soul, James Brown, appeared as a celebrity captain on *Match Game* in 1968, competing against Meredith MacRae's team; the following year he competed against Rita Moreno's team. When I asked Audrey about his appearances on the show she admitted, "Believe it or not, no memories!"

Selma Diamond was "LOUD." Jack E. Leonard was "brash (could have been his act)." Broadway playwright and director Abe Burrows—Really liked him. Smart, funny. I remember he autographed something for me —maybe a playbill." About one actor who appeared in Western movies and at the time had a successful television career, Audrey described him as "handsome, great body without being over-muscled. Maybe not the sharpest knife in the drawer." James Farentino also inspired one word: "swoon." John Forsythe: "double swoon. Later, I worked slightly with him when [I was] one of the publicists on *Dynasty*. Still super nice." She remembered Joe Garagiola as a "very nice man. Also worked with him later when he hosted a non Goodson-Todman quiz show I worked on." George Hamilton was "TAN!" When I asked about Dorothy Loudon, Audrey replied, "I didn't see it at all, but I remember someone saying that I looked like her." On Rod Serling: "I had such a crush on him at that time, I could hardly speak. I just thought he was so brilliant." Florence Henderson was "lively and fun. Amazed that she was one of ten children." When Van Johnson appeared on *Match Game*, Audrey reported, "I looked to see if he was wearing red socks and now I don't remember if he was!"

Alan Alda and Robert Alda
(Robert Alda: February 26, 1914-May 3, 1986)

"Oh, I'll tell you who did the show a number of times," Ira Skutch told me, "Bob and Alan Alda, the father and son. Alan was just starting out in the business, so Bob was the one we booked actually; we booked Alan as his son, you know, make a pair out of them. And of course Alan was wonderful—we had them back several times."

Judy Carne, the "Sock it to me!" star of *Rowan and Martin's Laugh-In*, showed up to play *Match Game* in 1968 (along with an unpictured John Forsythe).

Diane Janaver remembered Robert and Alan Alda's "lovely father and son relationship. They had this card game they played in the pick-up room that they had played since he was a little kid, with a lot of yelling and screaming and slapping of cards, and they just had such a good time. It was very cute. Nice people."

"One of my pets, of course, was Alan Alda," recalled Jean Kopelman, "who I had discovered in some kind of a crappy play down in Florida, and I said 'Something big is going to happen to this kid.' The first thing we did, we put him on with his father, and that was absolutely *amazing*. They were just terrific together, and they loved each other, and they—it was the first time I ever saw a man and his son hug each other in public. Just to see each other.

"And I have a cute Alan Alda kind of follow-up story. He did the show a lot, and because of my pushing for him and so forth, he ended up doing *Password* and other shows. And he had made *The Paper Lion*, and it was before *MASH*, and it helped him along when he was trying to make a name for himself. Many years later he became a client of my son's, and my son did his grounds out in Bridgehampton.

"He has a wife and three daughters, and they're all just terrific people. And they decided to start a children's museum for the East End of Long Island, that is—and they did a big charity bash at The Russian Tea Room, and of course Alan was there with his wife. And I went up to him and I said, 'I'm sure you don't remember me, but I produced *The Match Game*.' And he said, 'Oh, my God!' and he turned to his wife and kids and said, 'This is the woman who kept me alive for years.' I said, 'But that is not really why I am talking to you.' I said, 'You're going to be even more thrilled for me to tell you my son is your landscape architect.' Well, I thought they were going to fall over, they were so tickled.

"He is just one of the most wonderful men I've ever met in my life, Alan Alda. Just a first class peach. I guess I would call him my favorite, only because I did see him, as I said, in this terrible play and I said something good would happen, and everything I could do I did for him. It

In 1963, as TV Westerns ruled the airwaves, Dennis Weather of *Gunsmoke* and *Bonanza*'s Michael Landon showed up as competing team captains.

wasn't very much, but it made *me* happy, and it kept him going for a few years."

Lauren Bacall

(September 16, 1924-August 12, 2014)

"I will always do *The Match Game* because I love Rayburn," Lauren Bacall once told a reporter.

"Lauren Bacall was a favorite," remembered Diane Janaver. "I love Lauren Bacall. She did the show first because she was in *Cactus Flower* on Broadway, and Abe Burrows, who wrote *Cactus Flower*, used to do our show whenever we wanted him. So I sent him [a note] asking if Lauren would do our show. That kind of networking worked too, in getting people. So I asked Abe and he asked Lauren Bacall, and sure, she came! She had a wonderful time, and, of course, we sent a limo to pick her up and she got all the star treatment, and she said she'd come back anytime. She had a really good time, and I'd call her from time to time, and she'd come back! I liked her a lot."

Dick DeBartolo remembered, "She was on *Match Game* so many times, backstage we got to call her 'Betty,' a name she preferred. And I remember one day after Gene Rayburn introduced her [she came out onstage]. I sat three feet from Gene, just slightly off camera, and we picked the questions that we sent down. If it looked like the show was sort of a little bit quiet, then I would try to pick a very silly question [to liven up the audience]. Gene Rayburn noticed that Lauren was staring off-camera, seemingly just staring into space, and asked her, 'Lauren, what are you looking at?' 'Oh, I'm looking at Dick DeBartolo. I'm *in love* with Dick DeBartolo.'

"And they cut to a shot of me, which I saw on the monitor, and I pretended to be shocked, and I jumped up and I actually knocked the table over. I'll never forget that." In fact, somewhere in his collection, Dick has a rare 16 millimeter print of that very show. The real topper for that little moment, says Dick, is that "she did it without prompting!"

Shelley Berman
(February 3, 1925-September 1, 2017)

"In the days you speak of," said Shelley Berman, who made quite a few *Match Game* appearances over the years, "there were many, many shows for actors and performers to appear on—many variety shows and game shows and even talk shows. These shows did, of course, offer essential exposure though that was never the main reason for doing them. There was fun in doing them and being paid for having fun was certainly a bonus. Naturally, for a performer, exposure is a needed ingredient in keeping the audience aware of one's presence. But thinking a performer would do a game show purely for the purpose of exposure is not exactly flattering. There was never the opportunity to do improvisation on a game

Game show pro Peggy Cass (best remembered today as the stalwart secretary Agnes Gooch taught to "live, live, live!" by *Auntie Mame*) appeared opposite John Lind Hayes in the pilot for *Match Game*, taped December 5, 1962.

show. Ad-libbing maybe, but improv, no. Fast thinking is the comedian's would of course, but trying to win at a game show is not always the way to win. I loved the fun of trying, just as did the others. Doing so without making a fool of oneself was the idea."

Peggy Cass
(May 21, 1924-Mach 8, 1999)

The raspy-voiced actress and comedienne Peggy Cass is best remembered for her Tony Award-winning role as Agnes Gooch in the Broadway stage and film versions of *Auntie Mame,* but she made frequent appearances on game shows and talk shows throughout the fifties and sixties.

"Peggy was just always there whenever you needed her," remembered Diane Janaver. "Always funny. You could depend on her to give you a good show. She was terrific. Peggy we knew because she did *To Tell the Truth*. She was one of the top people. We could go through her agent or call her direct. It didn't matter, she would come. She was terrific and she had a good time with everything.

"Gene Rayburn introduced her," continued Diane. "It was one of those things where he just got his tongue twisted, introduced her as 'Ziggy Ass.' Ziggy Ass! Everybody got hysterical and I think it came out of the tape. Never played. He realized it after it was out of his mouth, he just didn't realize it at the time to stop it, but he just came out crooked. We all recovered. It was funny."

Bill Cosby

Stand-up comedian Bill Cosby was already a nightclub sensation when he appeared in a number of episodes of *Match Game*, playing opposite Florence Henderson in January, 1965 and then Gisele MacKenzie a few weeks later. Soon after, he was cast as the lead in the hit TV series *I Spy*.

"I remember Bill Cosby as being so nice and fun to be with," remembered Audrey Davis. "He invited the staff to come and see his stand-up act at some nightclub in New York City. We had such a good time and we met [his wife] Camille. And I think we had very good seats! I don't remember too many details but only pleasant memories of him being on the show."

Bill Cullen

(February 18, 1920 – July 7, 1990)

Audrey Davis fondly remembered "Dean of Game Show Hosts" Bill Cullen as a "quick wit, always was so nice and funny."

Dick DeBartolo told me about "a very funny thing when Bill Cullen showed. The celebrities, everybody milled backstage, waiting for the show to start, and Bill said to everybody backstage, "No matter what the question is, everybody's very first question, let's all write the answer 'pickle.' And so I don't even know the question, but certainly pickle was not a viable answer...Gene said, 'Pickle? Okay, I don't know what you're thinking, but okay." And the next contestant matched 'pickle.' And Gene said, 'I don't understand it.' Well, Gene gets.....and then he starts yelling. Gene said, 'Listen, if you have pickle, I'm leaving the set and I'm going to let Johnny Olson'—you remember Johnny Olson?—'emcee.' And the next person of course said pickle and Rayburn as a joke left the set and Johnny Olson came and said, 'Alright, here's the question,' and said, 'If you say pickle, *I'm* leaving, and of course the next person said pickle. And Johnny left, and then so I got up 'cause I was the only one left on the stage and asked the final question and someone said 'pickle' and then Rayburn came back...So, I got to emcee *The Match Game* for about two minutes!"

Dustin Hoffman and Liza Minelli

Diane Janaver remembers when a young Liza Minnelli appeared on the show with a young Dustin Hoffman. "She was still appearing in *Flora, the Red Menace*, which was an off-Broadway play," remembered Diane, "but you knew her because she was Judy Garland's daughter and got a lot of publicity. And I told you I booked her at the same time with Dustin Hoffman. Dustin Hoffman had just finished his first big movie, you know, the one with Mrs. Robinson, *The Graduate*. It was playing in all the theatres and getting him great reviews, and he was collecting unemployment because he was not working! So, again, his agent—I said, 'You think if he's not doing anything right now, would he want to do the show?' 'Well, yeah, let me ask him.' Sure enough, he came and did the show, and he was funny. He and Liza hit it off just fine."

They may have hit it off, but Ira Skutch had a different memory of that week. "Dustin Hoffman did the show one week, but he hated it. In fact, I don't think he ever did game shows again." I asked if it was because he didn't like the improvisation involved with doing a game show, as opposed to studying a script.

"I don't know," replied Ira. "I had no idea. I just think he was very—disappointed. Had the same experience with Michael Landon. He did the first week of [the seventies version of] *Match Game*, and he hated it so much he would never do it again. He said it was very unfair, and he thought it was awful. He wouldn't do it anymore."

Sandy Koufax

"Sandy Koufax had an interesting motive for appearing on the program," Adam Nedeff revealed in his engaging biography *The Matchless Gene Rayburn*. "An arthritic elbow had prematurely ended his career and he was beginning a new career as a sportscaster for NBC. He appeared on *The Match Game* because he admitted in his first year that broadcasting wasn't coming naturally to him, and he needed some practice.

"Gene, to loosen him up, walked into the make-up room while Koufax was getting his face powdered and instructed the make-up woman to put some make-up on Koufax's elbow to make it feel better."

June Lockhart

Dick DeBartolo wrote in his memoir *Good Days and MAD*, "When June Lockhart was a *Match Game* guest, she was still filming *Lost in Space,* and I got to give her a copy of the latest *MAD*, which featured my spoof of her show. (What timing!) In *Loused Up in Space*, the Robinson family's space capsule lands on a planet where everything is of enormous size—in one panel they come across a giant watermelon which turns out to be a REALLY giant pea! After she read the piece, June said, 'You're not only funny, you have ESP! We're shooting a show now where we crash land on a planet where everything is giant-sized!'"

Jayne Mansfield
(April 19, 1933-June 29, 1967)

"We had Jayne Mansfield on a couple of times," remembered Diane Janaver. "She was very sweet. She really was very nice. She always came with her little Chihuahua pup dog which she would always kind of hold against her bosom...She was very cooperative, very sweet, funny. Cute little girlish voice, you know, and she was fine. No problem at all."

Well, Jayne Mansfield wasn't a problem in the *conventional* sense. Production assistant Audrey Davis remembered, "Jayne appeared on the show twice, I think. She usually brought some of her children along. At that time, two boys and a girl, all of whom I kept an eye on while Jayne was taping the shows.

"She also brought one or two chihuahuas which took quite a nip at me, but not serious. Since we taped five shows in a day, the celebrities were told to bring changes of clothes. One time, Jayne was short an outfit. She saw me in a short-sleeved black cotton t-shirt and asked to borrow it. Who was I to say no to Jayne Mansfield? I think I wore a make-up smock while she had my t-shirt on. When I got the shirt back from Jayne, needless to say, it was quite a bit stretched out!

"I remember her being very nice and sensing she was a lot smarter than people believed her to be.

"As life will have it, many, many years later I was doing television publicity and one of our clients was Dick Wolf, of *Law & Order* fame, and I wound up being one of the people who represented his show *Law & Order: Special Victims Unit*, starring none other than Jayne's daughter, Mariska Hargitay! She didn't remember me (not surprised) but I remember her!"

Ethel Merman
(January 16, 1908- February 15, 1984)

Asked if there were any stars he was surprised who did the show, Dick DeBartolo said, "Well, we had a couple of people that were on the show— Ethel Merman, and she was backstage, she said to me 'This is absolutely crazy! What am I doing here? I'll never—"

"I said, 'You know, it's just a silly [TV show].' I said, 'There's nothing you can say that will make you look wrong. It's just fun. You can't be right or wrong because there are no answers.'" Once she relaxed, and got on the set, she was perfectly fine and ended up having fun with the show, even working on the later seventies version of *Match Game*.

Rita Moreno

"Oh, and then I have a very funny story about Rita Moreno," said Dick DeBartolo. "We were going down in the elevator and she didn't know who I was. She just knew she saw me in the studio, and she said, 'Is that a stupid show or what?' I said, 'Well, I think it's kind of fun.' 'Oh, what do you do there?' I said, 'Well, I write the questions.' 'I'm so sorry! Oh, well, when I said stupid, I meant silly.'" "Well, that's what it's meant to be.'"

Audrey Davis remembered Rita Moreno as being "quite the whirlwind—in a good way! Everybody that I know of loved her."

Burt Reynolds
(February 11, 1936-September 6, 2018)

Gene Rayburn recalled, "Don Meredith was on the show and he said to me, 'Hey, listen, why don't you use my old buddy on the show? We went to college together.' I said, 'Who is he?' Don says, 'He's the guy who plays the Indian on television. He's Burt Reynolds.' I said, *'Who's he?'"*

George Segal

In *Good Days and MAD*, Dick DeBartolo remembered, "I've gotten to meet many of the people we've satirized in *MAD*. For example, a l-o-n-g time ago...when *The Match Game* was taped in New York City, George Segal was a guest on the show and I got to tell him that he was featured in the new issue of *MAD*, in our version of *The Owl and the Pussycat*—'The Foul and the Prissy Cats.' George was so excited he told me to meet him at the beginning of the lunch break, so I could take him to the nearest newsstand. He bought ten copies of the magazine."

"Rae [Pichon] and I had a quarter bet," Audrey Davis recalled of the first time George Segal appeared on the show. "Because we were both fans, the first person to touch him would win. I waited by the elevator and when he got off, I took him by the elbow to escort him to the dressing room, so I won!"

Nancy Sinatra

"What I remembered most about Nancy Sinatra was that I was the hugest fan of her father," admitted Audrey Davis, "and just assumed she would have all these exciting plans for her evening in NY after she finished taping with us. I was quite taken aback when she told me she was just going to go home and wash her hair."

Since we were discussing Frank Sinatra's daughter, it made sense to ask about other members of the Rat Pack who appeared on the show, and Audrey continued, "I was thrilled he was one of the 'Rat Pack.' I was a huge Sinatra fan. My memory of Peter Lawford may not be associated with his appearance on *The Match Game*...but I do remember him sitting in the audience with his current lady friend (don't know who she was) during rehearsal and looking absolutely thin and very haggard. I thought it must be from drugs but I really didn't know and thought what a waste if it were true.

"As far as the Rat Pack goes, I just thought how much fun they must have. Also, Joey Bishop was on the show. Wasn't he a minor member of the Rat Pack?"

Jacqueline Susann

(August 20, 1918 – September 21, 1974)

Since I myself was writing a book I hoped would hit the bestseller lists, I asked about another bestselling author, who just happened to do *Match Game* back in 1966. "Oh, Jacqueline Susann, yeah," Ira Skutch replied of the author of *Valley of the Dolls*. "Yeah, I remember her. She was married to Irving Mansfield. And of course she wrote all those books. Well, she was a personality in New York. She'd been an actress for years, and of course everybody knew her husband. My recollection is that Jean knew her, that she and Jean Kopelman were sort of social friends or knew each other. But when the book came out and they offered her to us, it seemed like a good booking, and as it turned out it was. She was good."

Since Irving had been a producer and press agent, I asked Diane Janaver if Jackie had gotten on the show because of her husband, or had been asked on because of her hit book. "Oh, yes," replied Diane. "Must have been *Valley of the Dolls*. Yeah, I'm sure it wasn't because of Irving Mansfield. No, we didn't do favors for people, if that's what you mean. You know, you really can't afford to do that. Some agents would try, you know. They would say, 'We'll give you Lauren Bacall if you'll take two of these other people.' We can't do this.

"It's funny because I worked on an interview show with Hy Gardner on NBC, and I think of Jackie Susann from that, interviewed around that. I can't really remember her on *Match Game*. She probably did it. If you have it on your list, I'm sure she did it, but I really don't have any memory of that."

Gloria Swanson
(March 27, 1899-April 4, 1983)

When booking celebrity guests for the show, Diane Janaver admitted, "You get them in various ways. Gloria Swanson, it seems to me I got through her agent because I'd become friends with this agent. I would read the trades to see who was coming to town in a few weeks, and I would call and say to the agent, 'I don't know if she'd be interested, but--' and then they'd say, 'Well, let me mention it to her and if she's interested, we'll put her in touch and you can explain it to her on the phone.' And that's the way it generally goes. So, she was interested. I remember she came to the studios and she had a rose in her hand, a long-stemmed rose that she carried along. She was very sweet, very nice, very tiny. Short, little. And she was fine. She enjoyed it, and everybody enjoyed looking at her!"

Dick DeBartolo admitted he was surprised when Broadway legend Ethel Merman appeared on *Match Game* before adding, "And the other person I couldn't believe who did it was Gloria Swanson. And she used to roam through the halls carrying her [signature] red rose. She used to guess such esoteric answers. I don't think she ever matched anyone in any of the shows she appeared on. She was very pleasant; and amazingly short. God! She must have been five feet."

Leslie Uggams

Leslie admitted to being something of a game show watcher. "Oh, *yes!*" she told me, "Yes, absolutely. I love all those things. *Password*, all those games. They were fun.

As for *Match Game*, she admitted, "I was only on it once*. There's not really much that I can remember about it," she laughed. "Well, I always loved Gene, he was like Peter Marshall. He knew how to rein everyone in, so it didn't get out of control with all these celebrities. We had a great time working together.

"Basically, television gives you visibility. When people see you they know that you're still in the business. It helps because if you're doing clubs or concerts as a singer, you are able to tell the audience where you're going to be, you know, so it was good for business, absolutely."

Mae West
(August 17, 1893 – November 22, 1980)

"We tried desperately to get Mae West," remembered Dick De-Bartolo."We called her management so many times and she kept saying no to us, which surprised us because we thought Mae would have a great time doing our show. Finally, her agent called me and said, 'Look...let me tell you why Mae West will never do your show. She's legally blind, and she only sees people in her living room, because she knows where all the furniture is, and she could correct the problem if she wore glasses, but she's too vain." As a result, sadly, both *Match Game* and *Hollywood Squares* were denied that crooning voice rife with *double-entendre*.

Betty White

"One of the most generous people was Betty White," remembered

*= In 1966 Leslie Uggams appeared on *Match Game* with Mitch Miller and again in 1967 with Dick Clark.

Dick. "She was so sweet." He remembers a time when, before a taping, Betty asked what he was up to; at the time, he had just written a book in conjunction with *MAD* Magazine. When, during the taping, Gene made small talk with Betty, he asked her," 'So, Betty, what's happening in your life?' and Betty said, 'Oh, not much is happening with me, but you know, Dick DeBartolo has a new book out.' And she plugged the book! And back then—an hour later, 'Standards and Practices' came and I had to sign a statement that I had not prompted Betty White to say that, or given her any money to say that. Back in those days everything was so politically correct. They were terrified about paying people off....But a celebrity going out and plugging something for somebody else? God!"

When I asked Betty if the first time she met Gene Rayburn was on her first *Match Game* appearance, she thought a moment and answered, "No, it was on—oh, gosh, I can't even remember the name of the show now. It was, again, a game show run-through. Rayburn and Finch were a comedy team, Gene Rayburn and his comedy partner—I don't even know Finch's first name—but they started, I think it was a Goodson-Todman show, they started some kind of a game. It wasn't a very good game, it was a question and answer. Maybe it wasn't even Goodson and Todman, but I was there as a guest. They did two shows in one day, and I was a guest on both shows. And that's when I met Gene, and we kind of hit it off right away.

"We just liked each other a lot, so then when Mark [Goodson] put *Match Game* together, he thought the chemistry kind of worked between us. So I was delighted every time. But again, when they were shooting in New York, it had to be only when I was back there. And then I married Allen [Ludden] and I moved back there, so I could do it more often."

Henny Youngman
(March 16, 1906-February 24, 1998)

"One other story comes to mind, about Henny Youngman," remembered Audrey Davis. "Somehow he was related to an aunt of mine on my father's side; she was married to my father's brother. And when I mentioned this to him, he kept calling me 'Cuz' throughout the commercial breaks and every time he saw me."

The Sports Legends

"The stars who had the most impact on the show, I suppose, were Joe Garagiola who was a good panelist, but he also used to bring us in sports people," Ira Skutch told me. "It gave the show a different flavor than most of the celebrity bookings. And we got to know Mickey Mantle, and Joe Peppator, and Whitey Ford—Whitey Ford did the show a lot—and others

A few sports heroes dropped in to play *Match Game* in May, 1966. From left to right, Tom Tresh, Mickey Mantle, Joe Pepitone, Mel Stottlemyre, Whitey Ford, Roger Maris, and Gene.

The always-alert and ready-for-action Gene Rayburn lying horizontal before WNBC-TV sportscaster Mel Allen, WNBC-TV Major League Baseball play-by-play announcer Curt Gowdy, NBC sportscaster Sandy Koufax, former New York Giants quarterback Y. A. Tittle, WNBC-TV sportscaster Kyle Rote, and Paul Christman, NBC-TV commentator for the American Football League games. Clearly, network affiliation explains how Goodson-Todman was able to secure these sports figures to appear on *Match Game*.

from the Yankees. Those were a real high point, because you never know whether those have much effect on the audience. There was no way to measure."

Forty-odd years later, Diane Janaver is still amazed at the notable sports figures who showed up to tape the show. "Mickey Mantle!" she exclaimed. "We had Y.A. Tittle, remember? The football player. You remember him? He was really big at the time. But the guys, Mantle and Whitey Ford, used to watch the show. They liked playing. We had them on separately as contestants, and then we also did three ball players against three other ball players one week. They had a great time. Great competitors, you know."

About Whitey Ford, Audrey Davis remembered, "Even though I was a Dodgers fan, I remember him as being nice and friendly."

"We did quite a lot of stuff with ball players, football and baseball players," said Jean Kopelman, "thanks to Joe Garagiola, who kind of opened up the concept of baseball players being able to talk. But we had Maris and Mantle on together, and they were just absolutely charming."

At lunchtime, the big-shots (that would be Mark Goodson and Bill Todman) dined nearby at the exclusive '21' Club, while the rest of the staff dined at the restaurant they privately nicknamed '22.'

"It's what we used to call Shrafft's," Jean explained. "But we didn't take Mickey Mantle there. Mickey Mantle went to '21.' The *rest* of us went to '22.' Most of the other celebrities would go there—Rayburn and me, and a couple of the other members of the staff. It would depend on who was there at the time. We would all go over to Shrafft's between—we'd do two shows in the morning and then we would have a break, and then we'd do a show after lunch.

"And all go over to '22'...except for Mickey Mantle. He went to '21.' It was absolutely amazing what happened when I took him there. Goodson said, 'I think we should take Mickey Mantle over to '21.'" He didn't even know—well, he kind of knew who he was. But Goodson knew as much about sports as my candlestick, and he never quite understood the whole thing.

"My favorite story of all," admitted Jean, "is my story about taking my sons and my husband to Yankee Stadium. And my sons were then around ten and eleven and red-hot Yankee fans—and still are. I mean, it's unbelievable. I—because the guys were on the show, Whitey Ford and all the other players at the time, they were all on—and I said, 'Could I bring my husband and my boys up. They'd love to see a baseball game.' And they said 'Sure.' So it was arranged and we got there during batting practice, and so I walk in with my husband and the two kids, and all these ball players look up and say, 'Hi, Jeanie!' And I thought my sons were going to have a heart attack, as well as my husband! And they were thrilled to death. Then, after the game, they were allowed to go into the locker room, which I was not, because I was female. And they all got the baseball bats and they talked to them.

"Whenever I had all these sports stars on, the boys had to come to the studio to meet them. I mean it was absolutely—you know. That was one of the perks of being *my* son.

"So, one of the times we had on Bart Starr of the Green Bay Packers and Don Meredith of the Dallas Cowboys. And at this point, the boys were divided. And I remember the older one marched in and went right up to Bart Starr and said, 'Oh, I'm a big fan.' And the other says, 'Well, I'm not. I like the Dallas Cowboys,' and went right over to Don Meredith. There were a lot of cute stories with the kids."

Going, going, gone...

In December 2003, two copies of Mickey Mantle's contract to appear on *Match Game* sold for $2,500 on eBay, the online auction service. Included was a letter from Sojourn Productions addressed to Mickey at the St. Moritz Hotel thanking him and stating that the shows were excellent ("--thanks to you and Whitey."), and indicating they were including a check for $649.10 for his appearances (after taxes). The air dates for the shows are listed as May 30 and 31 and June 1, 2, and 3, 1966 and the episodes were taped at NBC Studio 8H at 30 Rockefeller Center (the famous "30 Rock" building) in New York City.

The Feminine Mystique

How unusual was it for a woman to be producing television in New York in the nineteen-fifties and sixties?

"Pretty unusual," admitted *Match Game* producer Jean Kopelman. "There weren't that many of us. Goodson-Todman was very good about that, giving them a job. The only thing they weren't very good about was paying us. Theoretically, you had a husband—even if you *didn't*.

Theoretically, you therefore didn't need to earn as much money as men did, who had wives who didn't do anything. *Fallacious reasoning if ever I heard it*, but that was what they did. So we were in fact cheaper labor, but that didn't make any difference. If we were no good, it wouldn't have made any difference if we were cheaper."

When I pointed out this made her something of an early feminist pioneer, Jean scoffed, "Well, it makes me *early*. I wasn't really a feminist, and I wasn't much of a pioneer, but I certainly was *early on*." But other than the pay, she reported that working for Goodson-Todman "was marvelous. It was the kind of job where one felt, 'I should pay them.'

"I think a lot of it had to do with the Goodson-Todman kind of way of treating us. They did treat us with respect and they did treat us nicely. It was always fun. I don't know why it was always fun. There were all these jokes going on. I haven't heard of a joke in years! People were amusing and entertaining, and we laughed a lot, and there were rarely any real problems with people. They were happy to be working. Some of them complained a little, but really I don't remember any real sourpusses."

I asked Diane Janaver what it was like being a woman producer at the time. "Well, Jean, of course was a producer," she said. "I was an associate producer under her and the executive producer Bob Noah. Jean was a producer under him."

"A company in the early nineteen-sixties having women producers sounds so progressive," I told her.

"It was a different time, but yeah, it *was* pretty good." She continued, "Goodson-Todman was a terrific organization that way. Gender really didn't seem to mean anything. If they thought you could do it, they wanted you to do it. Well, again, I had Jean to fend for me, kind of, though I wasn't in contact with that many outside people. I was doing the booking and I had no problems with agents. I don't know about network personnel, I wasn't in touch with them that much. When I came out here [in the early 1970's to Los Angeles], you know, after all these things, I was producing a couple of shows by that time, it was okay."

"Jean was your shining example," I said.

"That's right," she laughed.

"Which makes you both kind of pioneers."

"Yes, we were," admitted Diane. "Yeah. We also had a good time, I've got to tell you.

And that's all that really matters.

The Producer:
Jean Kopelman
(April 5, 1927-May 26, 2004)

Much is made today of the fact that so few women rise to the rank of power in Hollywood (or, in this case, New York City) in this day and age; and yet, even in an earlier and more conservative era, there were a few women who succeeded in the business. Jean Kopelman was one of them, a pioneer. She produced the nineteen-sixties version of *Match Game*.

Ira Skutch described her in his memoir as "a short, slim, blonde woman in her late twenties. Energetic, forceful and articulate, Jean started with G-T in 1949 as a production assistant on *Beat the Clock* and worked her way up; a testimonial to her abilities. Although Goodson-Todman had many female employees, Jean was the first to become a producer. Jean's success helped overcome the management's reluctance to move women to the top, and a number of others, including Mimi O'Brien and Diane Janaver, eventually followed her lead."

Jean began her career at CBS back when they were still transmitting out of Grand Central Station. "The first show I worked on was Arthur Godfrey's *Talent Scouts* show.

"Well, I transferred from radio to television and I got down into television in '47, and I think somewhere between '48 and '49 CBS put on their first live programs from theatre, one of which was *We The People*, one of which was *The Toast of the Town*, and there was something called *Winner Take All*. And I was the production assistant to the director of two of those, *The Ed Sullivan Show*—it was *The Toast of the Town*, which became *The Ed Sullivan Show*—and *Winner Take All*. And that was

Goodson-Todman. And then they put me on other shows and I went to work as Gil Fates' production assistant. Gil was a CBS television producer, as opposed to Goodson-Todman who produced the show, but they didn't know anything about television, so that's why we were doing that.

"Gil produced *What's My Line?* for them and *Winner Take All* and *Beat The Clock*, all of which I worked on. And then Gil left to do *The Faye Emerson Show* and I went to Goodson-Todman and asked them if I could come to work for them, and they said 'Yes, indeed.' And they made me the production manager and the co-producer of *Beat the Clock*, and that was about 1949, '50...First, I did *Beat the Clock* with Bud Collyer for years, and then we did *Number, Please* for one year. And then, I was pregnant with my third child. I proceeded to deliver her, and then there was nothing.

"And we were all sitting around the office and Frank Wayne, who was one of the writers and producers for Goodson-Todman—he used to write *Beat the Clock* with me and he ended up being producer for a number of shows for them. He walked in one day into an office which consisted of me and Bob Noah, and he said, 'Do me a favor. Take out a piece of paper and a pencil and write down your answer to this.' And he said, 'Name an animal.' All three of us wrote down 'elephant,' which I found was rather insane. Then he did a few more of those like 'Name a kind of pie.' And of course everybody wrote down 'apple.' We came to find out that in fact you could play this game with two teams of three people. And it was quite amazing what happened, how many times they matched, and how many times they really didn't match, and the reasons they didn't match. And so we all three of us played with this for some time, the three of us, Frank and Bob and I, played with this whole concept, and then we went charging in to Goodson, and basically that's how *The Match Game* was born.

"I needed an assignment and here was an assignment. And to put together a show—it took weeks and weeks of preparation and so forth before—we actually auditioned it for CBS and NBC and ABC. And the one who came in first with the highest price got it, and that was NBC. In those days we were pretty hot stuff."

Asked if NBC felt the need to re-tool the format at all, Jean replied, "No, they didn't do anything. They just sat there and smiled happily that they had gotten it from CBS and ABC! They were very happy. It was shortly after *Password* went on, and *Password* was an enormous hit. It was another Goodson-Todman game show. It meant money for everybody."

In addition to producing *Beat the Clock*, she produced the 1961 Bud Collyer-hosted *Number Please*, and then *Match Game*. "I had two husbands," said Jean. "My first husband I was married to from '49 to '59, and then I divorced him in early '59, and then I met my second one about three days after I got divorced. I had six months off for good behavior! So I had a second husband and I had these two boys, and they were about— five and six, and when *The Match Game* came on I had just had Elizabeth, which was '62. Elizabeth was an infant."

When I asked how she juggled a family and career, Jean replied, "Well, I had a wonderful housekeeper, and a husband who thought I was terrific, and that kind of stuff, so that really wasn't difficult. And it was easier in some ways because of tape, because we could tape ahead. For example, we could tape the whole month of August, so we all went away in August. We had a home out in Quogue, and we used to go out with the kids and spend the month of August out there. And we worked during the week, so there was no more working on Saturdays and Sundays. And it was all a lot of fun. It really *was* a lot of fun... I got to have my cake and eat it too."

How odd was it that, some forty years later we were discussing something that at the time was viewed merely as product? Jean replied, "Well, back then, it *was* just product. And furthermore, the whole concept of syndication came much later, and that turned out to be—everybody's making a fortune from syndication. I look at *Law and Order* every night on USA *and* TNT!"

Does she ever watch reruns of either the later *Match Game*, or other game shows on the Game Show Network? "I don't get it because I get just basic cable...I watch *Jeopardy* every night. I think *Jeopardy* is one of the great shows of all time. I remember I used to rush back from taping to watch [Art Fleming] do *Jeopardy*—the original *Jeopardy*."

The End of An Era

But all great things must come to an end, and Jean Kopelman's time with Goodson-Todman Productions was wrapping up.

"Having eighty-four hours a week, they went down to none," she said. "They had one on the West Coast [*Password* was the first Goodson-Todman show produced in L.A.], and there was some conversation about did I want to go to the west coast, and I said no, I just wanted to quit. I'd been working for twenty-four years and I wanted to see what it was like *not* to work."

When *Match Game* ended its run in 1969, Jean and her husband Mel retired, along with the kids, to Portugal where they spent more than two decades—and Jean discovered that even in Europe she couldn't escape her game show past!

"Nineteen years. We lived in a tiny little fishing village." When I asked the name of the village, Jean gave a flowery, beautiful name: "*Praia de Carvao*, which means 'beach of the charcoal seller.' Well it was gorgeous, just gorgeous. It was so backward, it was like living in the early 1900s. They didn't have cars, the men rode on a burro, and the lady walked behind carrying the mattress on her head. They didn't have electricity, they didn't have running water. We did, but most of the other people didn't. It took me a year to get a telephone!"

But Jean discovered that, even in Europe, her game show past would haunt her! "It was kind of amusing," she admitted, "because the first day I got there, I walked down to this little beach and there's this guy on the beach. And this guy—actually, his name is Harold DeWolff, and when we had this house in Quogue, we used to go play tennis. And suddenly, one day I'm on the tennis court and here is Harold DeWolff. Now, Harold had been a contestant on *The Match Game*! And so we saw him out there, we became friends—socially. And he said, 'Well, you know, it was because of my winnings on *The Match Game* that I could afford to buy the ring so

I could marry my current wife.' And the first day I'm in Portugal in this little village called Praia de Carvao, who should be on the beach but Harold DeWolff. And I said, 'You've got to cut this out!' And it turned out he had moved to Portugal even before I did! It was amazing.

"But it was a little tiny fishing village. There were lots of foreigners who lived there, so it was a lot of expatriates, I guess. I never thought of myself as being one, but that of course is what I was. There were a lot of Brits and there were a lot of Dutch, and there were lots of Danish and a lot of Swedes and Scandinavians. I was proficient in Portuguese—you had to be proficient in English or Portuguese. I mean, I was unable to do much of anything else.

"We did a lot of traveling and that kind of thing, it was fascinating. It was something that I'd always wanted, to spend a lot of time in Europe, so I finally got to do it. We spent summers in Italy and summers in England and summers in France, and went to Spain regularly, and basically went all over Western Europe.

"However, at one point very late on, somebody somehow got a license for a radio station in Lagoa, which was a town just above Praia de Carvao. And we were allowed to do broadcasts in English. So they heard that I used to do this, so I put together a radio show with quiz show questions and music and news and all kinds of nonsense, and we did it about two hours every night. And there were four of us that did that and that lasted about two weeks and I said, 'This is insanity,' and I quit.

"I was much older. I'd done live television; this was in many ways harder to do because they would leave us alone sitting alone in the middle of nowhere. None of us were basically engineers, and we had to run the radio station. You'd also screwed up everything, because, again, it was live, and from six to eight at night I was sitting alone in a radio studio. When you're doing television programs, there are people around. And here I was—basically we were left up there all alone. And we would each take a night. You see, it was just too hard. No money in it, and I thought it might be amusing, but it wasn't. It was amusing to put it together, but it wasn't amusing to do it.

"It was funny. When I married—well, my first husband got into television after I did, so those friends that we had all were in television. My second husband was not and I met a lot of people who were *not* in the television business and I was appalled at their language. I thought I'd heard every dirty word that was ever muttered.

"I don't know—I think that it's because they don't have fun at what at what they're doing. And I think that being in television is basically a lot of fun. And if you enjoy what you're doing, then I think you're a nicer person, and I think a lot of these people just do *stuff* to make money, and that's all there is to making money, as opposed to making money and having a good time. I do think the entertainment business—I'm not saying everyone in the entertainment business is a saint, don't misunderstand me—it lends you—you enjoy yourself more. And not enjoying yourself makes you perhaps crankier and maybe, a lot of problems with money, I don't know...The bunch we met in Europe— some of them were wonderful, but some of them were not to be believed. None of them were in show biz!

"Berlin was right. There is no business like it—at least there wasn't for me. I have only really very, very happy memories of it."

Review Questions

1. Between 1962 and 1969, Match Game was directed by <u>BLANK</u>.

a. Ira Skutch, Rozell Barnhard, and Gene Rayburn.
b. Ira Skutch, Jim Elson, Mike Gargiulo, and Rodger Wolf.
c. Federico Fellini, Michelangelo Antonioni, and Sam Peckinpah.

2. The problem with having Jayne Mansfield as a guest was <u>BLANK</u>.

a. She demanded Perrier water, champagne, and a pack of M&Ms.
b. She demanded Oson Bean babysit her pet chihuahua.
c. If she had to borrow your sweeater, you were likely getting it back stretched-out.

3. Match Game V.I.P.'s were treated to lunch at New York's famous '21' Club, while the rest of the staff dined at <u>BLANK</u>.

a. Delmonico's, feasting on steaks and lobster and champagne.
b. McDonald's, enjoying their Big Macs.
c. '22,' otherwise known as Shrafft's.

1. b., 2. c., 3.c.

Part II

The Apotheosis of Game Show Entertainment

1973-1982

"To me, Brett Somers, Charles Nelson Reilly, and Richard Dawson were like the cool adult friends that every kid wishes he had. To hell with my parents; I know that Brett or Charles would have made me a martini when I came home from school after a stressful day of sixth grade."

—Eric Szulczewski, on his website

6

The Caligula's Orgy of Seventies Game Shows

IT WAS THE GREATEST GAME SHOW EVER PRODUCED.

Okay, maybe that's a pretty bold statement, and maybe a lot of people will disagree with it (Sorry, Peter Marshall!), but it did become one of the most popular shows of its era—so popular, Brett Somers still got fan mail more than a quarter century after the show ended its run; so popular that reruns of the show were still out-rating the competition thirty years later.

When *Password* was sold to ABC daytime in 1971, it became the first Goodson-Todman game show to originate in Hollywood, and Howard Felsher was sent to the Coast as producer. Once the Goodson-Todman offices were set up in Los Angeles, it was only a matter of time before the focus shifted from producing out of the East Coast to the West; The Golden age of the sixties now gave way to a Platinum age in the seventies and eventually all of the Goodson-Todman shows were produced in L.A.

"The G-T West Coast operation grew apace," says Ira Skutch. "There was one week when Goodson-Todman aired twenty-five hours of programming; five hours more than the high-water mark of the Sixties." New shows were created, and old shows brought back and retooled—among them, *Match Game*.

Celebrity panelist Orson Bean joins Brett and Charles, Gene, Lynda Day George, Richard and Patti Deutsch as contestants Skip Robinson and Annette Bistikoff look on.

"I imagine the impetus to revive the show came from Jerry Chester, who was the driving sales force for the company," continued Ira. "The changes were done under Mark's guidance and leadership, and [were] a group effort as was most of the product of the company." In another departure from the original show, the title of the show was changed after 1973 to reflect the New Year—from *Match Game '74* all the way up to *Match Game '79*.

The Rules

Match Game '73, as the show was now called, was somewhat altered from the original format; the object of the game was still to match answers, this time with a panel of six celebrities. The first of the two contestants chooses from an A or B joke question. Gene Rayburn reads the question aloud and the six celebrities, using magic markers, 'fill in the blank' on a small card. Rayburn then asks for the contestant's oral response to the question, and one by one Rayburn polls the panel in search of matching answers. The second contestant tries to match the panel with a second question, and additional rounds follow until one contestant has accumulated six matches. To make this task more difficult, in the subsequent rounds the celebrities he or she has already matched abstain from answering questions. The first contestant to match six celebrities gets to play the two-stepped end game for up to $5,000 (later upped to a possible $20,000). In case of a tie and/or they were running out of time, Gene had the contestants play 'Sudden Death', in which he read off a short phrase ("BLANK Texas") and the first contestant to match a panelist (with answers such as "Austin" or "Dallas") won.

In the first step of the end-game—the 'Bonus Round'—a contestant had to find the most popular answer to a blank that was handled by audience survey (the core of the idea behind *Family Feud*). The most popular answer was worth $500, the second $250, and the third $100; that number was multiplied by ten, and one final match had to be made between contestant and the celebrity of their choice (usually Richard Dawson, until his departure from the show in 1978) to win that dollar amount. Later, a spin of the 'Star Wheel' determined the celebrity they had to match, and featured certain spots on the wheel that would double the money being played for.

The Pilot

Asked about the pilot episode, Ira Skutch says, "As I recall, the show had been pre-sold at the run-through that we did at our office. It went very well and was scheduled to go on the air. One sidelight: Jack Klugman asked us to book his wife, Brett Somers, as she was really antsy about getting work. It turned out that he did us a much bigger favor than we did

Gene Rayburn photographed on the Match Game set during taping of the pilot episode. The seating arrangement for the contestants on the turntable and the mechanism dispensing the questions would be reconfigured.

him, as she became a mainstay on the panel and was most important to the success and longevity of the program."

"Gosh, I don't even remember the pilot," says Kay Henley, celebrity coordinator throughout the show's popular run. "Of course I did work on it as well as many other pilots, some that didn't sell. If memory does serve me correctly, I think *Match Game* was pre-sold as it had been out of New York City originally. We just did a pilot(s) to work out the kinks."

The pilot was taped on stage 33 of CBS Television City on May 19, 1973. Built in 1952 on the former site of Gilmore Stadium, the studio is now considered an historical landmark; Elvis Presley taped his appearance on *The Ed Sullivan Show* there in 1956. In fact, the stages at 7800 Beverly Boulevard have been home to *The Twilight Zone*, *The Sonny and Cher Comedy Hour*, and TV specials featuring Doris Day, Bob Hope, Frank Sinatra, George Burns...The list goes on. Stage 33 was where *The Carol Burnett Show* was taped, and where *The Price Is Right* was and continues to be taped.

The pilot was shot with a celebrity panel now expanded to fit six in a two-tiered arrangement seating three and three. There were only slight differences in the set between the pilot and later episodes. The Super Match end game was called the Jackpot Match, and some of the questions were the old format fill-in-the-blank or 'name something' questions. But the turntable delivering contestants to the set was in place, as were the shag carpeting and flashing lights. Gene Rayburn was flown out to California to reprise his hosting duties.

Mark Bowerman, who began as a CBS page and later worked directly for Goodson-Todman, says, "My first day working as a page was the first day of the pilot for the *Match Game*. I was assigned to answering the stage phone. I remember that they completely changed the format of the show overnight. I had only passing contact with Gene and some of the panelists."

The pilot for *Match Game '73* featured a celebrity panel made up of Bert Convy, Arlene Francis, Jack Klugman, Joann Pflug, Richard Dawson, and Betty White. It took a few weeks for the show to find its rhythm, helped out by Jack Klugman's request that the show hire his wife Brett Somers, in order to give her something to do.

Ira Skutch points out that while the show was sold before the pilot, that "did not mean that it would have gone on had it been a disaster. The panel was made up of the best names and game players that we could book, as you can see they were people who had done our shows before." The panel featured the talents of Richard Dawson, Jo Ann Pflug, Betty White, Jack Klugman, Arlene Francis, and Bert Convy.

Skutch continues, "First, there was Richard Dawson. I had booked him regularly on the panel of *I've Got a Secret*, and he was so effective that he was the first person we thought of when assembling the panel for *Match Game*. Marvelously witty, he also supplied sex appeal, and was a large contributor to the show's success. I worked joyfully with him for the first four years of the run."

"Jo Ann Pflug was an actress," said Kay Henley. "She guested a lot on TV in shows like *Love, American Style, Love Boat* and other shows. She was an adorable brunette, tall [and] shapely, had a cute speaking voice, and I think she was married to Chuck Woolery for a while."

"Mark Goodson approached me, a wonderful man," remembered Jack Klugman. "I did a lot of their talk shows, *He Said, She Said...*" Though he agreed to do the pilot and appeared a number of times on the show over the years, he had no interest in being a regular panelist. "The questions seemed so childish and silly, toilet humor. The answers were so obvious, but you couldn't say that on television at that time." Though he finally agreed to shoot the pilot and a number of additional episodes, he had no desire to become a regular panelist; game shows are for actors publicizing their latest project, he felt. "You make five hundred bucks for the day, whole day. They tape a week's worth of shows. You don't make any money."

Betty White and Arlene Francis were game show royalty, having both appeared on countless Goodson-Todman programs over the years, and Bert Convy had been acting in TV and movies; the following year he would begin hosting Goodson-Todman's *Tattletales*.

The Celebrity Panel

"*Match Game* was an advantageous marriage of a comedy-game with an ideal emcee and a winning celebrity panel," said Ira Skutch. "Putting together a panel is like casting a play—each member has a different role to play, and the collective chemistry must be just right. Gene Rayburn instinctively knew how to encourage the panel to participate, while at the same time keeping tight control."

Richard Dawson was there from the beginning. Charles Nelson Reilly and Brett Somers both joined the panel beginning the third week of *Match Game '73*. Although each missed a week here or there, for the most part thereafter they were the three permanent fixtures until Richard permanently left *Match Game* to host *Family Feud*.

"We cast them carefully, the way a Broadway director casts a play," said Mark Goodson. "It takes a lot of trial and error, but when we get our 'family,' when a panel is finally working, each member possesses his or her own problem-solving talents that blend with and complement the personalities of the others."

The Seating Arrangement

Maxene Fabe, in her excellent 1979 book on game shows, analyzed the mechanics of the formula:

"*The Match Game* carefully arranges the seating of the celebrities according to the ability of each to provide entertaining chitchat. In the lead-off seat on the top-tier to the left sits a male guest celebrity, whom producer Ira Skutch tellingly refers to as 'the new kid on the block.' (At other times this seat is occupied by semi-regular panelist Gary Burghoff). Seated to the right of the 'new kid' are two of *The Match Game's* regular panelists, strong-willed and acerbic Brett Somers and fey,

> Gene: "Clara created the world's most unusual balloon. She made it by pumping helium into her BLANK."
>
> Patti Deutsch: "Her late husband Carl."

sophisticated Charles Nelson Reilly. If the response of the 'new kid' to a question is not quite entertaining enough, Brett and Charles can together improvise something witty to ease the conversational flow down to the second row. There, to the far left, sits 'the sexpot,' as Skutch calls her, the pretty starlet who, like the 'new kid' above her, is not apt to be as strong a player. She, however, can be bailed out if necessary by the show's anchor, its ablest player, Richard Dawson. In the last seat sits another 'strong' character, a woman celebrity with an offbeat imagination whose function on the panel is to conclude with an original remark. Semi-regulars Patti

Deutsch, Marcia Wallace, Betty White, Joyce Bulifant, and Fannie Flagg all work well in this position."

Brett Somers put it a bit more succinctly.

"You know that first seat down in the bottom row? That was always called 'The Dummy Seat,' and one week I came back to do it before I started doing it on a regular basis. They put me in The Dummy Seat, and I went, '*Excuse* me? The *Dummy Seat*?' because they always put the ingenues there, who were doing a series."

—And couldn't always be counted on to give a *definitive* answer. Brett continues:

"And of course the last seat, the Fannie seat, the Patti Deutsch and Joyce Bulifant—that was the hardest seat, because by that time everyone had said everything. Betty and Marcia and Fannie and Patti too, they were all good at it. They were all good on the last seat. But it was a tough seat."

"They used to cast those shows," says Orson Bean. "Certainly that was true of *The Match Game*. It was cast like a sitcom. It was also true of *To Tell the Truth*: there was the kind of high-falutin' Kitty Carlisle on my left, and there was—I used to call her 'Peggy Cass, the ward-heeler's daughter.' So there wasn't just the game, there was a combination of the game and people who kind of worked well together. Nowadays you don't see that much anymore. They don't really cast them with that in mind. Being a good panel is a very minor skill, but a specific one. There aren't a lot of people that can do that. In the old days there were talk shows with Jack Parr. There were people who were gifted in conversation, whereas that doesn't exist anymore. They're not really drawn out by the conversation."

"Of course, a game show's definition of a celebrity may not be everybody's," reasons Maxene Fabe, who adds, "Game shows have been a special sanctuary for the second-banana, the star whose career peaked early yet who was too good an ad-libber, too clever a conversationalist, too nice a person, really, to be allowed totally to vanish from public view. Put those celebrities to work playing a game, intersperse them with someone trendy, whose TV movie of the week or new series was coming up, or whose act was rolling into Las Vegas, and it might do something for the game show's ratings."

For the most part, taping days during the run of the show featured little backstage drama. The host, panel and crew members got along for the most part—better than most TV 'families.' We'll discuss the few 'bumps in the road' later on, but for those readers looking for dirt—sorry folks, there just isn't much to report. Except in rare cases, everyone got along; even when they didn't, they still respected one another enough not to make it obvious. The show looked less like a competition than a party because that's exactly what it was. The fun didn't have to be played up. Gene Rayburn was quoted as saying, "We'd tape two or three shows, then take an hour off, have a little lunch, a little vino, sit around and gossip and tell some jokes." And that's exactly what they did.

> "Charles Nelson Reilly characterized it perfectly one day when we were sitting around in the dressing room during the lunch break. He said, 'This is not a job; it's a social engagement.' And he was right."
> —Gene Rayburn

A lot of trial-by-error goes into producing a game show, and any show undoubtedly evolves from the first episode onward—and the way it most obviously evolved was in the nature of the questions. "Name a kind of muffin" wasn't going to cut it in the hip, changing world of the 1970's.

In his memoir, Ira Skutch remembered, "*Match Game* was a moderate success in its original form; now it was a smash. The key change lay in the titillating questions, each of which contained a blank. We carefully constructed them to be little jokes which sounded funny when read, and provided further amusement as the participants gave their answers.

"Perhaps our biggest laugh came with: 'The Burbank fire department doesn't have a hose. Whenever there's a fire, the men stand in a circle and

BLANK on it.' The audience giggles after the first sentence and roared after the second. The merriment continued as the contestant and panelists split their answers between 'Spit' and 'Tinkle.'"

In 1979, Maxene Fabe reported, "Four professional joke writers are employed by Goodson-Todman as consultants to write *The Match Game's* unique questions. According to producer Ira Skutch, 'The fellows, Dick de Bartolo, Joe Neustein, Patrick Neary, and Elliot Feldman, sit around and make up questions singly and together. Then they come in for a conference and go over them. We then throw some out, rework them, and polish them. What these questions are, are actually little jokes within themselves. But it is a very narrow, specific joke form. You have a joke where the punch line has a hole in it. The questions have to be wide enough to allow the possibility of a match. They also have to be constructed so they don't have to many elements in them. Take the example of 'The millionaire Japanese dwarf came to the United States and bought a BLANK.' There you have too many elements that can affect the answer. The question should lay a field for funny or amusing answers, but not so wide that there is no chance for a match.

The material we have selected is then tested around the office to see whether the answers we think we're going to get are actually the answers we do get. Then we arrange the questions to avoid conflicts in subjects. Even while the show is on the air, we are constantly doing last-minute checks for new conflicts that might arise."

The Definitive Answers

To the untrained eye, clowning around seemed high on the list of priorities with the panel, but wit was valued above all else. And the competition could get heated when it came to coming up with the 'definitive answer.'

Gene and the rest would make much about being clever enough to think up the 'definitive answer.' Technically, there were no 'right' or 'wrong' answers; your goal as a panelist was merely to match the contestants, thus winning for them as much money as possible. But since the show was like a party captured on videotape, and all parties feature parlor games—well, the competition could get pretty heated to prove oneself the wiliest wit. Gene read off the queestion: "*Vito said, You hear what happened to the Giovanni brothers? The Godfather made them into BLANKs'*"

Answers given by the panelists ranged from the mundane to the predictable: corpses, anchors, pizzas, meatballs, bookends. All were mentioned, and at least half were logical answers. But after the panel gave their answers, Gene pointed out the key word 'brothers.' According to Gene, the Godfather made the Giovanni 'brothers' into 'sisters'—the *definitive* answer. Of course, the party atmosphere aside, the point of the show *was* for the contestants to win money, and not all contestants were going to come up with a 'definitive' or even witty answer. It wasn't called the *Match* Game for nothing, so the panel had to judge the contestants' likeliest answers for themselves and know when to answer with wit...and when to answer like a nitwit.

Gene read off the following question: "*The cannibal said to his wife, 'I'm not very hungry tonight, dear. I think I'll just eat a BLANK'.*"

Answers ranged from "leftovers" to "toe" to the definitive answer (courtesy Richard Dawson): "lady fingers." Brett gave what was probably her most eccentric response ever, written on two cards: "A small child or a pizza," explaining to Gene, "Sometimes us mothers have to go *crazy*!"

As the questions evolved, recurring characters began to pop up in the questions—among them Dumb Dora, Ugly Edna, Weird Willie, read by Gene in a variety of character voices.

After a while of course, the audience started getting into the act. When Gene began a question with, "Dumb Dora is *SO* dumb," the audience (of course) responded with "How dumb *IS* she?"—at first encouraged by Gene although after awhile, and especially when Gene was pressed for time, the charm of it began to wear thin.

A set photo of the sign for *Match Game PM*.

Match Game proved so popular that a nighttime version of the show, called *Match Game PM*, was launched in 1975 and ran until 1981. Game play for the most part was unchanged; however, since it aired only once a week, "there was a change in format so that each week was a complete package unto itself," says Ira Skutch. "This was done so that the shows could be bicycled to the stations rather than having to make a copy for each outlet. It saved much money."

That wasn't the only difference; since the *PM* version aired in Prime-time, the questions—and answers—became racier, pushing the envelope as far as what was acceptable on American network television.

The daytime version was still running and still a hit. "That's why we're using 'PM' in the title," Ira Skutch explained in a 1975 interview, "to differentiate it frrom the daytime show. It's also why we called the daytime show *Match Game '73* when we revised it. We wanted to differentiate it from the old, original Match Game. Having the yea in the title also seemed to have a ing to it, so we'll just keep changing the date every year. And hopefully it will go on to be the *Match Game '78, '85, '92,* and so on!"

But as with all great things, the 'golden age' wasn't to last. In 1976, Richard Dawson was hired to host *Family Feud,* and did double-duty working on both shows before finally leaving *Match Game* altogether in 1978 (see chapter 18) under less-than-pleasant circumstances. The show suffered a ratings hit with that one, but prior to that came an even bigger blow: CBS Head of Daytime Mike Ogiens made the decision to switch *Match Game's* time slot in November 1977 from the afternoons to 11am. (Here's a great piece of gossip, courtesy Curt Alliaume's website: Ogiens was also a former staffer at Chuck Barris Productions, allegedly fired because he threw Barris out of a costume party he and his girlfriend were hosting because Barris came in street clothes).

Many of *Match Game's* biggest fans were students who couldn't watch the show in the mornings; coming home from classes, they could catch up on the latest in adult humor and witness Brett and Charles' latest antics. The network soon realized its mistake and moved the show back to 4 pm six weeks later, but the ratings continued to decline (as ratings for *Family Feud* continued to soar) and the show was cancelled in April 1979.

Without missing a beat, Goodson-Todman immediately launched a syndicated daily first-run edition which ran an additional three years

"And Now, A Word From Our Sponsors..."

Over the years a lot of companies sponsored the show, with Johnny Olson reading their names off just before the credits ran.

Do you remember these? Samsonite Furniture, U.S. Borax, Dentyne Gum, Colgate-Palmolive Co., Turtle Wax Inc., Bordahl, Elmer's Glue, Gum-Out...and yes, that game show standby, Rice-O-Roni, "the San Francisco Treat!"

(airing on many stations in the same time slot it had been in before) with the only change being the contestants each played two games, retiring after that regardless of how well they did.

I asked Brett Somers if the cast and crew knew on the very last taping day that is was indeed the last day, and if there was any kind of wrap-party. "Yeah," she said, "we knew it was going to be the last day of the show. I think there must have been, but you know, I don't remember. We must have had some kind of party...."

Either way, the party—sadly—was over.

The Long Skinny Microphone

Every icon has a trademark, whether intentional or not. Initially, Gene started *Match Game* with a small skinny microphone; Then came the long, skinny microphone, a Sony ECM-51 Telescopic microphone.

According to Patrick Neary, "The telescoping microphone that Gene used, I learned later, was of Gene's own invention some time back, possible to the original show."

Gene stopped using his ECM-51 in the last couple of years of the show for the same reason Bob Barker later discarded his: because it kept breaking, probably from age and usage.

Review Questions

1. Whether Peter Marshall agrees or not, *Match Game* was arguably <u>BLANK</u>.

a. Not nearly as much fun as being hit by a Mack truck.
b. Produced by Aaron Spelling as a vehicle to showcase his daughter Tori's questionable thespian talents.
c. The greatest game show ever produced.

2. According to Brett Somers, the first seat at the bottom row of the celebrity panel was called <u>BLANK</u>.

a. Clara.
b. The Dummy Seat.
c. The Elaine Joyce Memorial *bergere*.

3. According to Maxene Fabe, game shows have always been a sanctuary for <u>BLANK</u>.

a. Second-bananas.
b. Kukla and Ollie, but not Fran, much to her consternation.
c. Betty White.

Answer: 1 c, 2 b, 3 a.

7

The Elizabeth Taylor of Game Shows

Go ahead and mention *Match Game* to anyone, and chances are the first names they will mention are Brett Somers and Charles Nelson Reilly. Gene Rayburn may have been the host, and the show may have had quite a memorable parade of celebrity panelists over the years, but no two people made a greater impact on the show (Mark Goodson and Bill Todman notwithstanding) than Brett and Charles. "The preeminent comedy duo of the seventies" is a typical description of the two, and not an inaccurate one at that. Viewers tuned in week after week to watch the pair banter, argue and laugh as only two best friends can.

In doing research for this book, I came across a number of biographical details from several different sources that, when I asked Brett about them, have since proven to be less-than-accurate. (The spelling of her name, for instance: "It was always one 'm.' I've been a member of The Actors Studio since—somebody looked it up and said it's 1953—and they've always had it 'Brett S-O-M-E-R-S,' it's always been fine, and then one year they started sending things spelling it wrong—'S-O-M-M-E-R-S.' Don't ask me why, Ashley. Deliver me from modern technology!")

Here then, in her own words, is Brett's story.

"I'm from Maine—Portland, Maine. I was raised there all my life, until I ran away from home when I was eighteen. I had $75, I got on the train and came to New York, and said, 'I'm going to be a famous actress.' Put a white streak in my mother's hair.

"Well, I got various terrible jobs and then finally I went to drama school and began to work a little bit and I made a living in live television. You know, a lot of summer-stock in places like New Jersey and Pennsylvania and, you know, all those marvelous places, and then I finally got into live television. I did a play in New York called *Maybe Tuesday* that Lucille Kallen wrote and Mel Tolkin, two of the original writers for Sid Caeser. They were wonderful, and it was a very funny play. And if they hadn't had Paul Stewart, who didn't know his [BLANK!] from a grape, it probably would have run for a season! Why you would hire an old left-wing, serious-minded—Do you remember—everyone has seen *Citizen Kane*. He played the servant in *Citizen Kane*, the guy who showed the voice around. You know, the man servant. Paul Stewart. He always played bad guys in movies. I said to him once, 'You can say hello, how are you, but you cannot tell me what to do on the stage.' He just—you have to nail those guys. He finally got fired—fortunately for one and all. But it was too late! We saw maybe Tuesday, opened Wednesday, and closed on Saturday. Absolutely true.

"I did all the major [television] shows in New York at the time, which was *Robert Montgomery*, and *Philco* and *Kraft* and *Studio One* and *Mr. Peepers*, and you know, you name a show in New York, and I did it. And you made very little money, but I was only paying $63 a month for a two bedroom apartment."

Brett married actor Jack Klugman on June 10, 1956. "I met Jack in New York," she said. "In New York at Actor's Equity. And he was a friend of a very good friend of mine, and we became friends, and then ultimately started dating and got married." Love at first sight? I asked. "We started out just as good friends and then eventually we started going together and got married."

Brett had been married once before, and had a daughter, Leslie. That marriage ended in divorce. After she and Jack married, they had two sons, David and Adam. "Adam is the one I used to talk about on the show," she says. "'Adam, come home!'"

Regarding the kids, Brett told interviewer Michael Portantiere, "I think they were sort of embarrassed by the fact that I was on TV. When my older son, David, was a teenager, he went to Washington D.C. on a school trip. At one point, all of the kids were watching *Match Game* in a lounge at their hotel. David walked through the room and heard them saying, 'That woman is really funny!' He said, 'Uh-huh, yeah,' and kept right on going. He wouldn't admit that I was his mother for love or money! Another time, I went to pick up my younger son, Adam, at school. He was at the American Academy [of Dramatic Arts] and I went there to see what the hell he was up to, because he hadn't been answering my phone calls. He came down the stairs, saw me, turned around, and bolted. He wouldn't come down again until the lobby had been cleared. I said, 'You know, I'm a television personality. It's not like I'm a famous hooker or something!'"

Her television career flourished in the mid-fifties with guest turns on dramatic shows like *Kraft Television Theatre*, continuing into the early-sixties with roles on *Ben Casey*, *Naked City*, *The Defenders*, and *The FBI*.

Of her early television career, Brett told an interviewer she had done "live television, which is the scariest thing. Jack [Klugman] says, 'That was great fun'. I tell him, 'You forgot the time you burst into tears'. I'll never forget it: He came to my house one night for dinner, and I said, 'You look a little down'. He said, 'No, I'm fine, I'm fine', and then he literally burst into tears. I told him, 'You're having a nervous breakdown from doing live television!' The pressure was so great. I never thought it was a good time, but I did manage to pay my rent. Of course, my rent was only $63 a month..."

In 1971, in an exercise in method acting, she began a memorable recurring role on *The Odd Couple* as Oscar's wacky, acerbic ex-wife

The caption on this 1955 photograph reads, "Pretty Brett Somers, who made one of her first television appearances on KRAFT TELEVISION THEATRE, returns to TV's longest run when she appears in the comedy 'It's Only Money' Wednesday, September 14, at 9 PM (EST) over the NBC-TV network. Miss Somers has just completed a series of summer stock engagements, in 'Sabrina fair' and 'Picnic' in Pennsylvania, Massachusetts and New York."

Blanche; Oscar, conveniently enough, was played by Jack Klugman (Irony would later play a hand when the couple separated). In 1973, Somers appeared as Perry Mason's secretary Gertie on the short-lived CBS drama

The New Perry Mason. But it was *Match Game '73* that made Brett Somers a household name.

By most accounts, Brett came to be a regular panelist on the show almost by accident. In an interview in 1996, Gene Rayburn told David Hammett, "We wanted Jack Klugman (Brett's husband), and he kept turning it down, until finally he said he'd do it if we booked his wife as well. She ended up being 100 times better."

Brett had instant chemistry with Gene and the other panelists, and ended up staying for the next nine years. "Brett was a wonderful person," Gene told David Hammett. "There was all that wonderful chemistry with Charles; it made the show work." Kay Henley says, "I think I brought her in because I had booked her and Jack Klugman together. She was fabulous. Poor thing—they ragged on her mercilessly but she was such a good sport."

"You want to know how I happened to get the job?" asked Brett. "Jack and I were living in Connecticut and he was doing *The Odd Couple,* and I did things like *The Defenders* and *Naked City,* you know, shows in New York. And once in a while I would go to California. I think I did *Have Gun, Will Travel* or something. So any way, we were going to California. He said,

> Gene: "At the grand finale of the Hawaiian festival, King Kamehameha always BLANKs into the great volcano."
>
> Brett: "You know what I wish?"
>
> Gene: "What?"
>
> Brett: "I wish Jack Klugman would jump into the great volcano!"

'What are you going to do when you get there?' and I said 'Well, I don't want to do a series because my children are young and I want to be home.' And I said, 'And film, you know, nobody's asked me.' And so I said, 'You know what I'd really like to do?' Because we used to do this show called *He Said, She Said*. You remember that? Well, anyway, we used to do that. And whenever we did it, of course, everyone else was being very nice. And of course I would say things like, 'Well, one day Jack had me over the hood of a car, and he was choking me, and a woman came up and asked for his autograph...' So they would get all kinds of mail whenever we did the show. And so I said 'That's what I want to do. I want to do a game show where you don't have to be smart. You don't have to do anything, you can just be like I am in the living room, and have a couple of drinks and entertain people.' And he said, 'Well, *good luck,* dear.'

"And we went out there in June and in the middle of August they called and asked if Jack and I could do the show, and I said, 'Well, Jack is out of town.' And they said, 'Well, could you do it?' and I said 'Sure.' And I did one and got very good response, and then two weeks later they—and I don't think at the time they were exactly sure how they were going to do the show. I don't think they planned it was going to be this humorous. They really weren't. And Gene Rayburn was the greatest straight man in the business and was wonderful, because he would go along with anything. And so then they called me back again.

"And finally they called and said, 'Well, would you do the next thirteen?' and I said 'Sure.' So then Charles Nelson Reilly began to do it. And Charles was doing it one day and I said, 'Charles doesn't have any socks on,' and it was really kind of a turning point. And Charles raised his foot, and of course he *didn't* have any socks on. And it sort of, out of that came this sort of relationship. And they began to get funny people like Fannie and Betty White and Marcia Wallace. Now, they *always* had Betty. And it began to be a really kind of funny show.

"And Charles was the best. There was great chemistry between Charles and me and as a result, we would have a wonderful time. And sometimes I would do something really outrageous and Charles would say—they'd just cut to him, and he'd just look out. It was great. We had great, great fun.

"You know how we met? We were both taking a flight to Los Angeles, and I of course knew who he was, and I guess he knew who I was, and he was hilarious on the flight. And that was the first time I met him, and I never saw him again until we started doing the show. But he's wonderful—I love Charles.

"Sometimes I tune in late at night, because, you know, we're on, and I'll be channel surfing looking for a movie or something 'cause I don't go to bed 'til like three o'clock in the morning, and I'll tune into *Match Game*. And there is Charles, and I laugh just as hard today as I did then.

"One day, some woman got up and said, 'Mr. Rayburn, what do Charles and Brett do for a living?' Of course, at one point I did the new *Perry Mason* show, which lasted thirteen weeks. And I used to turn work down. I would do *Love Boat* and, you know, David Janssen's show because he was such an adorable, sweet, wonderful man. You know, I would do *some* things. But most of the time I went, 'I've *got* a job. I work every other weekend. I work four days a month!'

"The easiest money I ever made, I can tell you that. It was perfect for me because I really don't like to act. And I'd have people call and say, 'Do you want to do it?' And I'd go, 'I've *got* a job!' I never asked for it. I turned down so many—and now I'm sorry. I could have a *much* bigger SAG pension if I had said 'yes' to a lot of things I said 'no' to.

Gene (To Brett): "I'll blow your wig off! oh—you're wearing your own hair!"

"Someone said, 'Why is it so easy for you?' And I said, 'Listen, I grew up with a father who said, 'We don't need all that' when you tried to tell a story. And he would give you the 'speed-up' signal, long before the days of live television. And they said, 'Where did you learn your timing?' and I said, 'At my father's knee!' That's where you learn it, boy. You learn to be fast, funny, and out, and I think that something like this was being back in the living room in Portland, Maine.

"It was wonderful, it was great fun. I just talked to Fannie yesterday. Did she tell you the story about—we were always thinking up these things

Best friends: Marcia Wallace and Brett after a performance of Brett's one-woman show in New York City on July 28, 2003. Photo by A. Ashley Hoff.

we thought were going to be hilarious. Once, we said, 'Gene, we're not going to be in our seats'—and Gene was wonderful, he'd go along with anything—'We're not going to be in our seats, and when you pull the curtain, we'll come down.' So he pulled the curtain. 'Where are the girls?' And Fannie and I had raided the costume room and got all these freaky old things and hats and crap. God, what we used to wear! And we had all these terrible, sort of 'Fifties' hats and these 'Sixties'—but everything looked fine. And we said, 'We just came from Allen Ludden and Betty

White's wedding!' And we thought that was going to be hilarious. Well, hon, it *died*! They took us seriously. And there was total silence. We thought it was funny. No one else got it, and we're standing there with egg on our faces. Charles saved our asses! He came over and said, 'Ladies! Ladies! We'll have the warm bath, and your nurse companion, and you'll be fine.' And oh, it was just terrible! I mean, we just didn't know what to do, it was so awful. But we were always doing things.

"Fannie was terrible," continued Brett. "She was always up to no good. Once we went to—what is that famous restaurant? It finally closed—on Beverly Boulevard? Chasen's, that's the one! So one night Betty had been talking and she said, 'Have you ever noticed how people ask you for your autograph, but then they say do you have a pen or a pencil?' She said they never have a pen. She was having dinner at Chasen's with Allen her husband, and Carol Channing and her husband, I guess, and so Fannie

> "Let me put my glasses on so I can hear you better."
> —Brett

and I pulled up in front of Chasen's and said 'We won't be long,' and ran into Chasen's. The *maitre'd* knew us and we said, 'We just want to see Betty for a minute,' and we ran over and we said, 'Oh Miss White! Miss White! Can we have your autograph? Do you have a pen with you?' Well, Carol Channing just looked at us like we were crazy people, like we should be put in the UCLA psychiatric ward. Well, we just thought it was hilarious.

"Carol Channing was like, 'Who in God's name are those people?' Betty was laughing and having a good time; we fled! Carol I don't think had a clue who we were. Thought we were deranged fans, I'm sure.

"One week—it was really wonderful!—Do you remember—well, you probably don't, you're too young—when Patty Hearst got kidnapped? And they had all the guys who were these people who kidnapped her, The Symbionese Liberation Army? Peter Falk's mother was in town; Charles

Nelson Reilly said, 'Now come'—whatever her name was—'Come on over! We always have a great time. You'll come at dinner time. We always have a fabulous time and you'll feel a lot better, and your back, and we'll have drinks and everything.' And she came over and we were all riveted to the set as we watched, you know, those people try to get into the—she was like, 'Thanks for asking'. We were just, 'What the hell is *happening*?' So she [was left out since] we were all staring at the set."

Brett was the one panelist who never had to be reprimanded by the show's celebrity coordinator Kay Henley for tardiness on taping day. "I was the one person," Brett told me. "I was always on time, I was always early...I was always there, maybe ten minutes, you know, fifteen minutes. First of all, I lived like eight minutes away. I lived up in Holmby Hills, so, you know, it was snap, crackle and pop and I was there. And then I moved down into Beverly Hills; it was closer—I could've hoofed it. So I was always early, because that's who I am. I had a father who said, 'Oh, it's one minute past five, I guess they're not coming,' and he would leave; *very* good training growing up, being on time. So one day I came in on time and Kay said, 'I just called you!' I said, 'Yes, I'm on time.' She said, 'I know, but you're always *early*!'

"I was once late meeting my son because I missed the train. He thought I was dead. He said, 'Mother, I thought you were *dead*!' because I'm compulsively on time, and I take a dim view of people who are not. And that's also training from when you did live television. And film—boy, you'd *better* be on time!

"There was a girl—I can't remember her name—she was a lovely girl, and I was doing a movie—Oh *God*!—with Ann-Margret called *Bus Riley's Back in Town*. And the girl was under contract to Universal and she never went anywhere, she was always late. Oh! Her name was Mimsy [Farmer]. And I would say, 'Darling, you've *got* to be on time.' And she would never be on time. She was always late; she didn't care about her career. She was darling and I liked her very much, but I know that part of the reason [she was let go] was 'time is money' in television."

Ira Skutch couldn't remember a time when someone on the show suffered stage-fright, but Brett said, "Oh yes, one woman [contestant], once; very sweet, warm, very nice woman. And you never know how you—she absolutely just froze, and I knew—you could tell, it's not that she was dumb; she just had no idea she was going to freeze up when she got on the air. And she wrote me the sweetest letter and said, 'You were the only one who was nice to me!'

"But I felt so sorry for her. You could see that she was just struck dumb with terror. She was able to do it, but you know she didn't last long and people sort of picked on her. But I just really felt so sorry for her because I could just tell. I thought that but for the grace of God, could be any one of us. She was just—oh, poor—that was the only time it ever happened. And you'd get people who'd come on the show, and I always told them, 'This is the easiest money you're ever going to make in your life.'"

> Brett: "It's so *hot* in here..."
>
> Charles: "A woman your age, it's hot *everywhere!*"

I asked Brett about a number of celebs who did guest shots on the panel. "Jack Carter was alright, I guess. I don't remember him much. He was a comedian. They don't relate to people. He was okay, I guess." And Orson Bean? "Oh, Orson was fun. He didn't do the show much—he did it early on..." Lee Meriwether? "Oh, I loved Lee, she was great."

When I asked about one popular comedian, Brett deadpanned, "Is he dead?" "Nope," I replied—and then she laughed.

"Oh, well, he's probably still working. Oh, he was fine. I mean, there were some people you know you just love, like McLean, and Anson Williams was very fine. There were other people, you know, who don't make such a—you know, they did the show, it was fine, you said hi, they said hi, but you never sort of established a rapport."

Billy Ingram points out that "by 1975, Klugman and Somers' messy separation smeared the tabloid headlines just as Brett was gaining her own fame on *Match Game*. Any sordid revelations that came out in the press about her Hollywood marriage only solidified Brett's image as a 'liberated '70s woman.'" However 'messy' their separation at the time, the two remain on good terms today, and according to Jack, "talk all the time."

Various sources say the two are divorced; others say they are merely separated. Brett set the record straight: "We are still married...He's a good guy. Listen, I like him...He's a good guy, and I still see him, and he loves his kids and his kids love him. And he's very—he still gives me money. His lawyer said, 'Well, you don't have to give her money anymore.' And he said, 'Well, you know, I mean, she's the mother of my kids! I mean, you know.' He still gives me a yearly stipend, which is sweet."

So there you go—not divorced, merely separated. And amicable. Another myth de-bunked. In another interview years later she told Michael Portantiere, "We haven't lived together for—God, I don't know how many years. But neither of us will ever get married again. Jack is a man who should never have been married, but he's very dear and I love him."

> Gene (Reading a question): "A letter to Dear Abby: Dear Abby, How can I tell when the honeymoon's over?—"
>
> Brett: "*I* know when the honeymoon's over!"

"You know, I still get mail *every* day," said Brett. "I don't get a lot, but I will get—I'll get three or two fan letters every day. And about eighty-five percent of it is from guys. I get letters from fourteen year-old boys, or forty—Like I got a letter today from somebody who said, 'My wife and I have enjoyed you so much.'

"Unfortunately, they finally tracked me down, and my address is on the internet. I've been with The Gage Group [Talent Agency] which—if they had to depend on me, they'd go into bankruptcy!—and they were always marvelous about forwarding my fan mail. And then finally it got on the internet about a year and a half ago.

"One night—Oh, *Christmas*!—I'm sitting here reading or something, and all my doors were open. I live in the country, right? And I thought, 'Gee, it's pretty chilly.' And I got up to shut the door, and two guys were standing there. 'We're sorry, we didn't mean to frighten you.' And they found my house. They could have been serial killers. They just happened to be two very sweet guys who happened to be in the neighborhood, but it was very scary. And I have a friend who says, 'Well, you've *got* to get a post office box.' Well, it's *way* too late now, I tell you!"

One of the luxuries of writing a book like this is that you actually get to sit down with interesting people and ask them the questions you've always wanted to ask, no matter how deep or inane. So without further ado, here are...

Some Not-Frequently-Asked-Enough Questions (and Brett's Answers)

Brett was known for wearing her trademark big sunglasses on the show. Were they worn because the studio lights bothered her eyes?

"No, I wore them because I was blind!" laughed Brett. "And I always had a pair [of sunglasses] I guess. I just started wearing them because sometimes I would forget my real glasses, and I thought that the dark glasses were better, easier. I just started wearing them and people started noticing them. I never thought about it. So, I think I started the big sunglasses craze of the seventies, because I used to have to go and get men's glasses. And I always wanted to wear big glasses, long before it became fashionable."

So Brett Somers and Jackie O. started the sunglasses trend, eh?

"Oh, long before that! I mean, this was in the early sixties. And I would go to the doctor and I would say I wanted bigger frames, so I said, 'Show me some men's glasses.' So I would get men's frames, which were always larger. But I always—I thought if you wear glasses, you didn't wear those rag-tag [small ones]. I [recently] had glasses made, and I had to use some old frames that I had when I did *Match Game*, because it's very hard to find big frames."

Speaking of fashion—

"Yes, I wore wigs!"

Okay, on to the next question: who was the most fun to work with on the show? When the question was posed, Brett was stumped.

"Well, Charles of course, because he was so—they were all so—It's hard to say. Marcia and I—and Fannie and I, and Betty—Fannie and I had some great fun and we used to pick on each other...It would be hard to say. I liked so many of the people who did the show, and it was such fun. And they always had the guy who sat next to me was some young leading-man type who was on a series. And Charles would just make my life a living hell. 'I suppose you're going to the *prom*, Susan? With *Anson*?' He was wonderful.

"It's hard to say. Everybody had their own individual thing."

Here's one she's never been asked before: every now and then on the show, Brett would exclaim, 'Good gravy Marie!' Where in the world did this unusual catch-phrase come from?

"I don't know, I really don't! ...I guess I said it instead of '[BLANK] you,'" she laughed. "You have to watch your language, you know."

So Brett—can you cook?

"I'm famous for my one-dish chicken dinners. I don't believe people should spend time in the kitchen. I have several things I do. I have a shrimp dish I do, several chicken dishes, a scallop dish which is from Maine, and I do a *Coq-au-vin*. And those things I do well, but I'm not somebody who bakes their own bread or anything like that."

So Jack didn't marry a cook, eh?

"Of course I did SOME cooking. And then we had a poor woman who worked for us called Julie Gray...And she worked for us for years, so I sort of got out of the habit. But Jack's a pretty good cook."

Are you left-handed or right-handed?

"I tend to be ambidextrous because I'm left-handed. I broke my arm when I was twelve, so I learned to write with my right hand. And I do things—I iron with my right hand—not that I iron all of the time. But I do a lot of things right-handed. I've always used my right hand with no problem at all."

When is your birthday?

"July the eleventh."

So you're a Cancer—very thoughtful, reflective people.

"That's right, and great nest-makers, which I am. Well you know, wherever I go, if I go to a hotel, I get plants and flowers. I have to bring my own books. I have to fix it all up like I have my own nest. And my house—you know, I live in a converted barn, and...[when friends come over they say it's comfortable]. And even though I think astrology is silly, there are certain things that are basic in certain people."

Anybody suffer from major guilt if a contestant lost a round?

"Oh, I did. I always felt guilty when anyone—but most of the time they chose Dickie [Dawson], who was really good at it. But I just felt terrible, oh God, just felt awful if they didn't win...I think everybody felt bad."

Do you ever watch reruns of the show?

"Once in a great while. I rarely have ever seen it all the way through. It's fun to watch the people you knew.

"You know who is a big fan of the show? Eydie Gorme. Big big big fan. I love Eydie, she's great. They were here not long ago. I saw them when I went back—'Oh, now you're on three times a day, I watch you every day.'"

So, Brett—satisfy our 'Where are they now?' curiosity. How are you doing?

"Oh, I'm doing fine. I've been doing a little directing...I belong to an organization called The Theatre Artists Workshop, which is a group of people, professional actors, similar to The Actors Studio. So we do things, and then we have playwrights, so I directed several one-act plays. One had nine people in it, and I went, 'Oh shit! No wonder they didn't ask me to direct *My Fair Lady*!' Nine people on this tiny little stage, but it came off very well. I had a good time. They're actors who have moved up here, you know. James Noble is a member, and Kier Dullea and his wife actually started it about nineteen or twenty years ago. I moved up here a year after they started, so I've been with them about nineteen, eighteen years. It's been nice. Keeps me off the streets."

And today?

"I'm working on an act. Now that I'm a hundred-and-six I'm working on an act, and I sing and dance. Well, I don't actually dance. I do—what they call—I can't even remember, my mind is gone, Ashley!"

"A cabaret night club act?" I offer.

"That's right!"

A la Marlene Dietrich?

"That's right!" she laughs. "That's the one!"

And by chance, if you happen to give her a call, be warned: she's not a morning person.

"I don't go to bed til three o'clock. Oh, God, I cannot! I would be thrilled to be able to. I would like to be one of those people that says, 'My gracious, the news is over!' turn out the lights, and go to sleep. It will never happen. Oh, I can't! It's just terrible. I was always up, I was always the last one. I was in my house, when I was growing up, the last one to turn out my light. And I was always a nighttime person. I went into the right business, I thought—and then you get into film and it's all over. You've got to be up at the dawn's crack."

An Evening with Brett Somers

On July 7, 2003, Brett began a limited run of her one-woman-show in Danny's Skylight room on West 46th in New York City. An intimate cabaret space seating sixty, Brett was shocked when seventy-nine people crowded into the place on opening night. She was further shocked when,

Brett, flanked by Marcia Wallace and Jack Klugman, poses for Walter McBride's camera onstage after a performance of her one-woman show on July 28, 2003. Photograph by A. Ashley Hoff.

in succeeding weeks, the show sold out (*I* could have told her that would happen)! One funny side note: when she went to make a reservation for Jack Klugman to see her onstage when he was in town, she was told the show had sold out. "But he's my *husband*!" she howled. In the end, Jack did indeed get to see the show, along with Brett's best pal Marcia Wallace. Afterward, the trio posed for publicity shots.

An Evening with Brett Somers was described on Brett's official website as "a musical memoir of a life in and out of show business. The act contains hilarious and poignant moments of romance, marriage, career, and of course, *Match Game*. The show is written by Ms. Somers in collaboration with Mark Cherry, who also serves as musical director/arranger."

I asked Brett if Charles or Fannie had yet seen her show. "No," she replied. "They're all on the coast. Marcia Wallace saw it. My old husband saw it. Well, Jack was there, and he said, 'I didn't know you could sing.' 'Well, there's a question about that.' Anyway, he saw it. He loved it. A nice man... I wish Charles would come to New York to see my show. I saw his *twice*!"

Review Questions

1. Prior to doing *Match Game*, Brett Somers had a prolific career doing <u>BLANK</u>.

a. Three sailors and a jockey, but *never* your husband!
b. Naughty things in that motel room in Encino
c. Just about every TV show shot in New York

2. If you are dining with Carol Channing and a couple of fans make a scene, chances are <u>BLANK</u>.

a. Carol Channing is bad news
b. Brett and Fannie had the night off
c. You should head over to McDonald's because Chasen's is off-limits from now on

3. Whatever else can be said about Brett Somers, she was always <u>BLANK</u>.

a. Down by the docks waiting for shore leave
b. On time at the studio on taping days
c. Giving Audra Lindley a run for her money in the muu-muu department

Answers: 1 c, 2 b, 3 b.

8

The Life of Reilly

A popular episode of *Saturday Night Live* featured a skit spoofing TV host James Lipton's *Inside the Actor's Studio*, in which Alec Baldwin portrayed Charles Nelson Reilly (a caricature sporting ascot and big glasses) as a guest discussing his 'illustrious' career with the obsequious Lipton—and all he talks about is his great body of work on game shows ("I didn't see it," is CNR's only comment on the skit). Sadly, this is most peoples' perception of Charles, and the great irony is that he in fact *does* have a great, multifaceted and enviable career that extends far beyond the game shows with which he is so closely identified.

In a profile for *The Advocate* in 2001, Alonso Duralde put it best: "The name Charles Nelson Reilly may inspire eye-rolling over memories of the poncy, pipe-smoking '70s game-show guest—but he may well be one of pop-culture's most misunderstood figures. After all, Reilly is considered by many—including his close friends Julie Harris and Roberta Peters—to be one of his generation's best theatre directors. He won a Tony award in 1962 for originating the role of Bud Frump in *How To Succeed In Business Without Really Trying*. His students have included Lily Tomlin, Bette Midler, and, currently, opera sensation Rodney Gilfrey. And, one might add, his television ubiquity as a flamboyantly gay man in the supermacho '70s counts as a quiet form of revolution."

A photograph of Charles taken in the late sixties for his role as Claymore Gregg on the TV sitcom *The Ghost & Mrs. Muir*.

Despite one NBC executive's comment that Charles would never be accepted on television, he was a popular fixture on Dean Martin's comedy specials, here dressed as The Jolly Green Giant for a comedy skit involving Martin.

When I told Betty White what a prolific and multi-talented man Charles was, she agreed. "He is that, and a delightful man," she said. "I'm trying to remember where I first met Charles. I think probably out here [in Los Angeles], but we've become such good friends, we're still good friends. And what I always find interesting about Charles, he's so antic and so funny, but oh, he's so clever. When he directed Julie Harris in *Belle of Amhearst*, I just thought it was magnificent. It was just incredible, and what he brought out—not that she didn't have it herself—but he managed to keep it so fluid and delicate, it was just a theatre experience I'll never forget. And I had trouble attributing that wonderful direction to my silly friend."

Alas, Betty is not the only one afflicted by that trouble. "When I die, it's going to read, 'Game Show Fixture Passes Away,'" lamented Charles. "Nothing about the theatre, or Tony awards, or Emmys. But it doesn't bother me." That's what Charles may claim, but his actions suggest otherwise. His official bio lists virtually every credit on his resume and every award and honor he has received—except for *Match Game*. (The Sid and Marty Kroft masterpiece *Lidsville* didn't make the cut, either.)

His career as a performer began in the Bronx, where he was born and raised. "I made my own puppet shows and I put them on in church, and my mother would kick them in," joked Charles. "Years later, when she loved *Kukla, Fran and Ollie*, she said, 'Whatever happened to that puppet show you used to have?' I said, 'Ma, you kicked it in.' But I was always nuts."

Like many actors, he got his start as an actor in Summer stock. "Oh yes, all through New England. Newport, Rhode Island, is where I started in 1950 with Zasu Pitts. And she was funny." He studied under legendary acting teacher Uta Hagen. "In my play, there's a scene where I play Miss Hagen reading the list of new pupils. And the list goes something like, Geraldine Page, Jason Robards, Frank Langella, Hal Holbrook, Orson Bean, Peggy Cass, Jerry Stiller and Anne Meara, Barbara Barrie. Oh, that wonderful comedian—this is 1950—the man from *The Carol Burnett*

Show, Harvey Korman. And everybody became famous, the whole class. And it was free—if you didn't have the three dollars, they let you in anyway, because they were trying to start the school, you know what I mean? They were building the school, so they had to get some bodies in this broken-down loft on Sixth Avenue."

The acting classes paid off. "My first big break came in *How to Succeed in Business*," he said. "I was an understudy in *Bye, Bye Birdie* and played a small part. I understudied both Paul Lynde and Dick Van Dyke, and I played for Mr. Lynde every Thursday night because he had a contract with *The Perry Como Show*, which was live. Gene Rayburn I met in *Bye Bye Birdie*. He replaced Dick Van Dyke, and that's where I met him.

"But I got *How to Succeed* because my friend Bobby Morse recommended me, and they didn't want me because they wanted another type altogether. But they couldn't find what they were looking for in someone who could sing, dance and act—not that I can do all that, but I fake it well. He recommended me, and I went and I auditioned, and they were thrilled! They ran up to the stage, 'At last we've found you!' and all that stuff. And they wrote the part for me, and they made the part different than they thought it was going to be. And I won a lot of awards for that, and then from that, it was easy once you get started. And then I went to *Hello, Dolly*.

"I was two years in that, I had a two-year contract. I had to sing for Gower Champion. Jerry [Herman] recommended me, so I had to go sing for Gower Champion on the stage, a ballad, and I was perfectly awful. And Gower said to Jerry, who was sitting in the back of the theatre, 'Do you want to hear any more?' And Jerry screamed from the back, '*Noooooo*!' But I got the part anyway.

In *Hello, Dolly* he sang a duet with Eileen Brennan. "*It Only Takes a Moment*. They always play that wherever I go anyplace. When I walk in, like it's *God Bless America* and I'm Kate Smith. And it's very funny because there's only one song I'm famous for, so they don't have to worry about, 'What should he play when he comes?' There's only one song. One-shot artist."

C.N.R: Unsung Gay Rights Activist

As a young actor with Broadway experience, Reilly was told by one NBC executive to stick with theatre because (he said), "They don't let queers on television." (By one account this person was found dead years later, murdered by a male prostitute). Nowadays, of course, Charles is in rerun heaven. "I was told years ago that I would never be allowed on television," he told one reporter. "Now I had to try to find out who you have to [BLANK] to get off!"

In fact, one could argue that troupers like Charles Nelson Reilly pioneered the fight for gay rights on the battlefield that mattered most: on television. Chuck and his peers swished from guest shot to guest shot on sitcoms, making themselves at home in America's living rooms and inspiring a lot of laughter—*with*, not *at* them—while winning over middle America.

> **Gene (To the panel): "You're a beautiful, gifted gay bunch!"**
>
> **Brett: "Not all of us!"**

"Ruby Dee and Ossie Davis are activists; they're the first ones to march down the street," Charles told *The Advocate* in 2001. "But I'm more like Marian Anderson, who was a great black singer and never said a word about the fact that she was black—but [being] a black woman in a gorgeous gown and very good jewelry, accompanied by a man on a Steinway in Carnegie Hall, was her way of doing it."

But in the end, of course, Charles was welcomed with open arms on Television.

The *GREAT* Hoo-doo!

"I came to the West coast for two reasons. First of all, I didn't have heat or hot water til I was thirty. We were very poor, and so we never had heat or hot water, you know what I'm saying? Then when I was thirty, I was living in The Village on Sullivan Street in what they called a converted building, and the building went to steam heat. So at thirty I had my first radiator. And I came out to California to make a pilot film of *The Ghost and Mrs. Muir* in the late sixties, and it was eighty degrees and it was February. Oh, it was fun, and they were very nice to me. *The Ghost and Mrs. Muir.*"

The show lasted two years and after *The Ghost and Mrs. Muir* ended its run, Charles was hired to do a couple of Sid and Marty Kroft kids shows.

"Oh, God, yes," he said of *Lidsville*. "I played the Hoo-doo. And I was in Sardi's years ago, and it was four o'clock in the afternoon, and a birthday party was just breaking up for a little girl, maybe seven, eight years old or younger. And I was next to the table and I said to the waiter, 'I'll have a Manhattan on the rocks in a stem glass and no cherry.' That's all I said. 'I'll have a Manhattan on the rocks in a stem glass, no cherry,' and this little girl came over and said to me, 'Are you Hoo-doo?' I said, 'No! I'm the *great* Hoo-doo!' And she recognized my voice just from ordering a drink. And I thought, that's the power of those. Kids really get into this.

"And that was hard because the makeup was two hours every morning, and then you'd go home and you'd still feel it was on your face, you know? And the other one I did was *Uncle Croc's Block*, which went into oblivion."

And then there was a little show called *Match Game...*

"Charles Nelson Reilly was and is a fun and funny guy," said *Match Game* celebrity coordinator Kay Henley. "We met when I booked him in the fifties or sixties when I was working at Andrews-Yagemann Productions. I introduced 'Chuck' to Tim Helgeson who later researched and put together the play *The Belle of Amherst*. I went to the opening with Charles when it opened here at that theatre on Vine. It's a different name now—if it's even there! So I brought him into the Goodson-Todman fold and he was one of the best things that happened to our show, if ya ask me! He never let us down, and though he may not admit it, he had a ball every time we taped."

Ira Skutch recalled, "I first met Charles when we were doing *I've Got a Secret* with Steve Allen in 1972 and he did a guest shot with us one night. And when we started *Match Game* I booked him on the second week because I knew he'd be good at it. And he was so good we just kept him on. I can't remember if we booked him the second or third week."

Charles was, said Ira, "a true professional; dependable, and concerned for his fellows. Although he's had a long and distinguished career and is respected by all as an actor and director, he knew the *Match Game* was good for him, so he was good to *Match Game*. His zaniness and unfailing good humor brightened both the show and our dinner breaks. Sometimes he panicked us when he was late for his studio call, but he always appeared before his introduction on the air."

Charles was almost never at a loss for an answer—or at the very least, a funny one. On one show, Gene read off the following: "Kojak said, 'You won't believe this, baby, but when I put on my wig I look like BLANK'." While answers ranged from "a woman" to "Cher" to "Paul Newman" to "Rock Hudson" (with Brett quipping, "I wear my *own* hair now!") Charles gave the best response: "Well, there were so many answers I said, 'I look like *hell*.'"

> Gene: "Hey, did you hear that Lonely Lenny married an inflate-a-date, life-size girl that you blow up? Nine months later she gave birth to a BLANK."
>
> Charles: "I said a premature inner-tube."

"He was so dear," remembered Brianne Leary, who became friendly with Charles after she appeared as a celebrity panelist on *Match Game*.

"Yeah, I really liked him a lot. He probably wouldn't remember me at all, but I liked him a lot. Yeah, he's really brilliant. I mean, again, he's one of those people that are really underestimated because, you know, he's gay and he's flamboyant, or he always played the comic and they don't understand how brilliant he was."

"I never wanted to have a career of any importance 'cause I was a teacher," said Charles. "And that's what I always did and that's what I love to do, and that's the only thing that gives me true gratification is to be a teacher. And I worked very hard, so I'm a very good teacher. And I've got something in my house a pupil sent me years ago. It's a cartoon of her coming out of a basket, and she wrote on it, 'I've gone to school a long time, but you're the first teacher I ever had.' And so that means more to me than anything. So I never could work at important jobs because I was always teaching. I'd start a new term of twelve weeks, and then I'd get a call for maybe an important television part, and I couldn't do it. Because I would not have the substitute teacher if they paid to study with *me*, you know what I mean? So I couldn't do that. So then word gets around that I just do game shows and I'm never available because I teach. So what? I never cared if I worked. It wasn't important.

"But the *Match Game* root comes from my friendship with Mark Goodson. Peggy Cass and I got fifty dollars a week in the fifties—Can you believe this? We were very young—fifty dollars every Sunday if we call in at four o'clock, I think it's CBS, in case someone could not do *What's My Line?* In other words, it was live television. If someone was sick, someone fell in a bathtub, or someone's airplane couldn't get to New York in a storm, we had to call at four o'clock every Sunday just to tell where we were. By then they had all the actors in the studio anyway, but we had to check in and we got fifty dollars a week, which was a lot of money. And so that's how I started my association with Mark Goodson, and I worked for Mark Goodson for like forty years. So I was never thinking of myself as doing *game shows*; I was just thinking of being with this friend.

"Mark Goodson was an extraordinary friend, and I had the honor to speak at his funeral. It was very beautiful. And he lived in New York on

Beekman Place, and I could go there any time I went to New York and stay in these guest rooms and have a car. I mean, how do you meet that every day, you know what I mean? You could stay whenever you want, and I did, but then I didn't overdo it, 'cause you could get used to Beekman place and the free limo. But he was that kind of a person. So I didn't think of myself as game shows, I think of it as working for my friend who truly put me to work.

"He was extraordinary," continued Charles. "And he had this old limousine, this big one that kept breaking down, and he had to keep getting it fixed. It was gorgeous. It was a big Mercedes-Benz and it would break down on the freeways or the street, and he would have to wait until they put the hydraulic back in the windows, the hood was put down, or some [BLANK!] thing, and he would go nuts thinking that anybody that drove by might have an idea for a game show. And so he had to get a better car, because anyone whizzing by could have an idea for a game show ahead of him.

"When he lived here [in Los Angeles], he had an immense suite at the Beverly Hills Hotel. *Immense*. Immense, gorgeous, with artwork you wouldn't believe. And I live up the street from the Beverly Hills Hotel, and lots of times I'd be driving up toward my street and he would be behind me in the Rolls-Royce. And he would drive the Rolls-Royce right up to my bumper, so I would look and all I would see was the 'RR' and the grate of the car, you understand? And that meant to come to the hotel and have a drink. We did that a lot. If I looked up and felt a bump—he would bump into me!—and I would look up, I would just see the grate of the Rolls-Royce in the mirror, and that meant 'Just go to the hotel, I'll be right there.' And we did that for *years.* "

The Preeminent Comedy Duo of The Seventies

Form their first appearance together on *Match Game*, Brett Somers and Charles Nelson Reilly hit it off immediately. With their chemistry, I asked Brett if anyone ever thought she and Charles were married. "Oh *yes!*" she replied. "Oh, whenever we did a commercial, some lady would get up and say, 'Mr. Rayburn, are Charles Nelson Reilly and Brett Somers *married*?' People always thought we were married."

When I suggested they do a bus-and-truck company production of *Who's Afraid of Virginia Woolf?* Brett laughed and said, "Oh, I could never have learned those lines, Ashley. I could never have learned them."

The Battle For Center Square

People who aren't up on their game show personalities often confuse Charles on *Match Game* with Paul Lynde, the center square on *Hollywood Squares*. ("I was never in that," Charles told one reporter who had made the mistake of asking what it was like for him to do *Charlotte's Web*. "That was Paul Lynde. That's always in my biography. I never got anywhere near *Charlotte's Web*, any more than I did *Apocalypse Now*!") Granted, there *are* similarities: both men cultivated witty, sophisticated personas. *Out Magazine* once described Paul Lynde as 'the gay icon who made the world safe for sissies,' and the same could be said for Charles. Both were gay, yet hugely popular with their respective audiences.

> **(From *Hollywood Squares*)**
> **Peter Marshall: "Oh, Paul, what would we do without you?"**
>
> **Paul Lynde: "Replace me with Charles Nelson Reilly!"**

"I'll tell you how amazing it is," says Peter Marshall, host of the original *Hollywood Squares* and a friend to both men. "In those days, homophobia was rampant; still is, but more so then. He [Paul Lynde] had more love letters to him from women than I did, and I was pretty cute then. He got all the mail. And he was so obviously gay. Who cared? We didn't care. He didn't care. And the network didn't care.

"And Charles. If you look at how flamboyant he was on *The Match Game*, I mean, nobody was campier than Charles. But see, where Paul was awfully mean at times, it was never that way with Charles. Charles was the sweetest man I know. I've never known a nicer man in my whole life than Charles Nelson Reilly. I mean, on my seventieth birthday, we had a big party and he was there. I got some film on him...and he handed me The Obie Award for Overbite of The Year; He had a whole plaque made for me. And he's just a dear man and just one of my favorite people in the world. I think I'd rather spend an evening with Charles Nelson Reilly than almost anybody I know. He's so kind."

An Apple For The Teacher

"It's funny, every time I direct a play in New York, I get nominated for a Tony, but I never get another job. So I have to always begin again because 'He's from game shows.' But I get a kick out of it because I never wanted a famous career anyway; I just wanted to be a good teacher, which I am. But the problem is, nobody wants to study. See, I'm a teacher of a craft that nobody's interested in buying.

"I was directing a play in Florida a couple of years ago. And I go to this Italian restaurant where this wonderful waitress—played by Mercedes Ruehl; she looks like her, Italian woman, she's very funny—and she was upset because a friend of hers went to California, to Hollywood six months ago, you know what I'm saying? And she's trying to be an actress and she's not getting anywhere, and she's very upset, and she said, 'She's doing the right things, she's making the right contacts, she's meeting important people, she's networking, and nothing is happening. Is there anything she could *do*, you think?' And I said, 'Well, there's one thing she could do, I don't know if she wants to do it, but there's one thing that people used to do.' And she said, 'What's that?' and I said, 'Read a play! Read a *plaaaay!*' I mean, it makes me crazy, and kids want to study, and they want to study six weeks and then have a showcase and have important people come so they'll be famous right away. In the Hagen school,

Berghof, you were not allowed to have any kind of member from the profession come and see us. The tickets were carefully screened. It was not about getting a job, it was about learning to be an actor.

"Well, there's a *craft*. Do you want to go to a doctor that never took a *lesson*? I mean, the incision would be very interesting. I mean, it's the same thing. And I don't go to the theatre because I know everything, I saw everything, and I get upset. Do you know what I'm saying?"

Along with the teaching, he regularly directs theatre and opera across the country. "I do a lot of work in opera," he admits. "I love opera." He did voice-over work in the animated movies *All Dogs Go to Heaven* (1989) and *Rock-a-Doodle* (1991), and made memorable Emmy-nominated appearances as author Jose Chung on the cult TV show *X-Files*. He was nominated for a Tony award as director of the Broadway play *The Gin Game* starring his friends Julie Harris and Charles Durning. And he wrote and starred in his own one-man autobiographical show, *Save It for the Stage: The Life of Reilly*, which played to packed houses from coast to coast.

Save It For The Stage! The Life of Reilly

"Did you see his one-man-show?" Marcia Wallace asked me over lunch one day. "I thought the story about the makeup running at the Kansas City Civic Light Opera in the summer was the single funniest thing I have ever heard in my entire life. Brett and I went together, and we sat in the front row. Brett was doing something with her fingers or shoes or something, and Charles came to the edge of the thing and just stared at her, and pretty soon she goes [gives startled look], and then she falls down laughing. She laughed and laughed and laughed."

Critics complained during the run of his one-man show that Charles did a lot of name-dropping, but I like his response to that accusation: "I got a review today in *The New York Times* that says I do nothing but drop names in this play. That's what they all say. Burt Reynolds and I have been very close friends, he has been my best friend for *forty-six years*, and I think I can drop his name now."

CANON THEATRE
BEVERLY HILLS · CALIFORNIA

CHARLES NELSON REILLY

"Save it
for the
Stage"...
The Life
of Reilly

Theatre program (signed to the author, "For Ashley, Thank you for visiting me, Love, Charles Nelson Reilly") from a performance of *Save It For The Stage*.

Joyce Bulifant sides with Charles, calling him "funny as can be. I just loved to listen to Charles. He's just so funny, such a funny person. Such a *talented* person, my gosh! Did you see his one-man show?"

"I did," I said proudly. "I saw it twice."

"Yeah, I thought he was wonderful. Oh, he's incredibly talented, my goodness."

On my birthday, May 21, 2002 a friend took me to see Charles perform his one-man-show at The Canon Theatre in Beverly Hills. The show was great, very long, over three hours, but I could have sat through another hour. After the show we stuck around, along with a handful of other fans, and the stage manager told us Charles would be with us shortly. About ten minutes later the stage manager returned and ushered us all downstairs into his dressing room, where Charles had opened up the bar, offering us drinks and conversation (Charles drank a Manhattan, I had a glass of Chardonnay). It was like something out of *All About Eve*, without the malice. Charles asked everyone about themselves and was a gracious host. It was a wonderful taste of Old Theatre Tradition and a wonderful birthday.

Review Questions

1. Charles Nelson Reilly's first big break came when he co-starred in <u>BLANK</u>.

a. Cincinnati
b. *How To Succeed at Business Without Really Trying*
c. A bus-and-truck version of *Who's Afraid of Virginia Woolf?* co-starring Brett Somers as Martha

2. Every time Charles directs a play in New York, he gets nominated for a <u>BLANK</u> award.

a. Oscar
b. Tony
c. Overbite of the Year

3. People who aren't up on their game show personalities often confuse Charles with <u>BLANK</u>.

a. Brett Somers
b. Wolfgang Puck
c. Paul Lynde

Answers: 1 b, 2 b, 3 c.

9

Richard Dawson

Before Richard Dawson grew up to became a dashing presence on television, he was born Colin Emm on November 20, 1932 in Gosport, Hampshire, England, a small, struggling coastal village about seventy miles southwest of London. His was a loving but poor family, and as the war in Europe brewed and bombing began in London, young Colin and his elder brother John were sent from their seaside town to live in the country with friends. However, he and John were beaten by their guardians ("Our parents never did that," he remembered) and they ran away, returning to the poverty of Gosport. This shattered childhood obviously had a great influence on the protective way Richard later dealt with his own children.

The war cut short his education after two years—which also had great influence over the way Richard self-educated himself—and this, coupled with the family's poverty, led to Richard's very adult decision to lie about his age, run away at the age of fourteen, and work as a merchant seaman. As Richard later put it, "I looked around at the other blokes who had families young and never left town. I wanted more."

As Mary Ann Norbom put it in her 1981 book, *Richard Dawson and Family Feud*, "Despite his youth, Richard was already a tough-minded, independent sort...He held his own admirably in his first few rows, and it wasn't long before the hardy stomach-puncher was the main drawing card in shipboard boxing matches. During the three years he lived at sea, Richard won close to $5,000 in the ring, he estimates. He did not make much more than that in wages."

Almost eighteen, he began work on land as a waiter. One day he passed a small theatre on his way to work. As Richard later recalled, "A rep company, called The Barry O'Brien Players, was requesting people to sign up for auditions," Richard recalled. "I realized there were about eighty ingénues on the list, but only about half a dozen young men. I told my brother that showing up for the auditions would be a good way to meet girls. I wasn't even thinking about auditioning until John bet me five pounds that I wouldn't have the nerve to do it. So to win the bet, I signed up for an audition."

With no experience and no formal—or even informal—acting training, he had no choice but to pay attention to the other actors auditioning, all of whom had prepared monologues.

"I didn't know any plays, but I once had a teacher who recited Shakespeare. I didn't know any Shakespeare, of course. What I did remember, though, was the noise of it—the way Shakespeare sounded."

And so on the spot, he faked it—or attempted to. "*Henry the VIII*, Act Two," he announced as he strode the boards, and let loose with what he hoped sounded like a convincing Shakespearean monologue.

"Mr. Dawson, what are you doing?" called out the company manager, and when Richard replied that he didn't honestly know, he asked, "Then why are you doing it?"

"Because I want to become an actor," said Richard. And then he heard the words that would change his life—and the lives of many game show contestants:

"I may be able to help you."

Richard was hired by the theatre company, and recalled that "we did five plays a week...After two years of traveling with the company, I had one suit, one shirt, and one pair of shoes. There were no stars in those companies. We all got the same salary."

In time he decided to make the transition from actor to comic, and as he remembered, "I wrote to a major English talent agency, identifying myself as a big Canadian comedian. I told them that I was in England on a holiday and wouldn't mind a job if they would line one up. By return mail I received a six-week contract—without an audition."

"It was for forty-five pounds a week, which was exactly fifteen times what I was earning as an actor. I received the contract on a Friday and was told to open the following Monday at a musical hall in Plymouth. It was all incredible, especially since I had no material."

"Frightened almost to death," as he put it, he put together something resembling an act, some jokes and the song *Georgia on My Mind*. Monday night he reported to work, took to the stage, told his jokes which garnered no laughs and announced his song to the indifferent crowd.

"I was standing there waiting for the mike to rise so I could do my song," he said, and recalled what happened next. "I waited and waited. Suddenly I felt a strange sensation in my right leg and heard the audience laughing. The mike—it was one of those long, thin ones—had gone right up my trouser leg. I lifted my leg to try and get it out, but the mike just kept coming. There I was, standing on the stage with my leg up in the air. The audience was howling. They thought I'd planned it."

"You've never been on a stage before, have you?" shouted the stage manager, and after Richard confessed the truth, he turned Richard over to a ninety-year-old comedian named Billy Bennett, who trained Richard and helped the budding comedian succeed over the ensuing weeks of the engagement. Richard later asked the manager why he hadn't thrown him out then and there.

"I could see they didn't hate you," he replied.

Eleven months later Richard was invited to play the London Palladium, one of the most prestigious theatres in Britain, and over the next two and a half years he played in some of the most exclusive British clubs. In the summer of 1958 while performing at The Stork Room in London, he met a ravishing blonde actress named Diana Dors. He said she was "a vulnerable, sweet frightened girl" and he "fell madly, hopelessly in love" with her. On April 12, 1959 while in New York for an appearance on *The Steve Allen Show*, they were married in singer Fran Warren's apartment. They had two sons, Mark, born in 1960, and Gary in 1962.

Peter Marshall recalled, "I knew him when he was 'Dickie' Dawson, came over from England, married to Diana Dors. I used to hang with him all the time. Dickie Dawson. Had really an English accent in those days, and I always thought he was terrific at what he did."

The couple was separated in 1964 and when the divorce became final three years later, Diana signed custody of the boys over to Richard. As she later recalled, "It was the most heart-wrenching decision I ever had to make, but I knew they were better off with Richard. He loved them so and had provided them with such a solid home life. How could I ask the courts to let them come away with me? To take them from everything and everyone they were growing up with? To what? Besides, I knew Richard would never try to prevent me from seeing the children. I also had to consider Richard's feelings. His wife had already left him. I could not take the children from him, too."

"I went into a fourteen-month-long funk at the time of the divorce," admitted Richard. "I absolutely wallowed in self-pity. People looked down their noses at Diana for leaving me with two young boys. But it was an act of sheer kindness. I don't know what would have happened to me without them." He still continued to send Diana flowers for every birthday and kept photos of her and the boys on the wall, and over the years Richard and she kept an amicable relationship; the two maintained warm ties until Diana's death in 1984 from cancer.

Meanwhile, Richard seemed to find solace in work. As his career blossomed, he would appear on television shows like *The Dick Van Dyke Show*, and *The Outer Limits*, but ironically enough it was World War II, the very war that had so devastated his childhood, that would return to bring him success in two separate projects. The first was *King Rat*, a film based on the James Clavell novel that dealt with "the corrupting influence the battlefield had on soldiers," as Mary Ann Norbom put it. The second may have been a bit odder.

A situation comedy set in a German POW camp would seem like a hard sell on audiences, yet TV director Ed Feldman was preparing just such a show, titled *Hogan's Heroes*, concerning a group of Allied POWs—American, British, French—operating an underground intelligence network from behind Nazi lines.

"When Richard came in, I saw him as a leading-man type as well as a comic," said Feldman. "Although he was primarily known as a comic, I had seen him in *King Rat* and he was very good in that. He had this one marvelous scene in particular where he was very heroic walking into a Japanese POW camp all alone. Consequently, we tested him for the Hogan role. Again, he was quite good, but Richard still had a very noticeable British accent then and that's why I decided against him. I wanted Hogan to be an All-American, Middle-American type. I went with Bob Crane for the part." Richard was given the role of Corporal Peter Newkirk. His fellow prisoners included Ivan Dixon, Larry Hovis, and Robert Clary. Werner Klemperer played Colonel Wilhelm Klink, and John Banner played Sergeant Hans Schultz.

"To be honest, when Bob Crane and Richard started, they were not very good actors," confessed Feldman. "They didn't have that much experience, nor did most of the cast. The only real actors we had at the beginning were Ivan, Werner, and John Banner. The rest were entertainers, as opposed to actors.

"What I mean about Richard is that he could do stand-up comedy. I had seen him do routines and he was very funny. But that did not make him an instant comic actor. At first he started very slowly, but he grew a great deal during the show's run. He became a good actor who could handle almost anything you gave him."

Robert Clary agreed that Richard was very interested in self-education. "He learned all about cameras," said Clary. "He knew everything that was going on in movies and television. He knew who was on top in the music industry. He knew when films had been made and by whom. He knew the history of various acting careers. When we were rehearsing a scene, he was always very inventive. He would look for, and find, ways to improve on the scene. What it adds up to is that Richard worked very hard on his acting. He wanted to be a success at it, and he improved tremendously over the years."

Feldman continued, "In addition, each man came into the show at the right time in his career," and he explains, "It gave them security. It gave them a base to jump off into other things. It was a good schooling for their acting abilities. We also had one heck of a lot of fun doing it."

According to Feldman's account, Richard's presence on the set was a major asset. "Richard helped hold the unit together. We had seven distinctive personalities, all with talent. You can't have them all going at one another's throats. You can't have them all in business for themselves. But Richard was always there mixing with everyone. He was always fun. Always up. Always extremely bright. It was a natural humor and it helped keep everybody's spirits up.

"That was a consideration he would give to others," continued Feldman. "He was not always interested just in himself." His consideration and thoughtfulness are characteristics that will always stand out in my mind about Richard.

"There was that and something else about Richard, which he shared with Robert Clary. The two of them were never late one day. It was amazing. I always thought, well some day they'll be off somewhere when

> "As a celebrity panelist, Richard Dawson's clearly doing something right. On *Match Game*, the former star of *Hogan's Heroes* was single-handedly responsible for giving away over three million dollars!"
> —Maxene Fabe

we need them. It never happened. They were always there on time. They always knew their lines. Most of the guys were good about it, but those two were exceptional. In all the years I have been in this business, I have never seen their reliability duplicated. The funny thing was you didn't expect it from a guy who looks like Richard and acts like Richard. He comes on with this devil-may-care approach; like he's just there to have a good time. In the entire time we worked together, I can only remember him having one bad day, and that had to do with a problem Diana Dors was having in England. He was very concerned about it."

When the series ended in 1971, Richard joined the cast of *Rowan & Martin's Laugh-in* as a regular until the series ended in 1973. He had appeared as a panelist on game show pilots like *I've Got A Secret* A, *Royal Flush* and *Cop Out* (which were never picked up by the networks), and *Celebrity Password*. Then came the pilot for *Match Game '73*. While on *Match Game* he continued to work on other TV series and game shows (*The Odd Couple, Tattletales, McMillan and Wife*), even hosting the game show *Masquerade Party* in 1974 while simultaneously appearing on *Match Game*.

But it was another hosting gig that came along during his *Match Game* years that would change his life forever...

(To be continued...)

Review Questions

1. Richard Dawson's real name is <u>BLANK</u>.

a. Colin Emm
b. Eulalia T. Bibbens, Esq.
c. Russell Crowe

2. In 1959, Dawson married a buxom blonde actress named <u>BLANK</u>.

a. George
b. Marilyn Monroe
c. Diana Dors

3. Prior to *Match Game*, Richard co-starred in a TV sitcom set in a <u>BLANK</u>.

a. Car rental place in Jersey
b. Parallel universe inhabited by Fellini-esque denizens of the underworld
c. German POW camp

Answers: 1 a, 2 c, 3 c.

10

A Kaleidescope of stars

The list of stars (and quasi-stars) who appeared on *Match Game* over the years as semi-regular and guest panelists is a long and varied one. Most of them have fond memories of it, but a few of them have no particular memory at all! Here, we come face-to-face with some of the memorable personalities who graced the panel—some for years, some for one brief, shining moment...

Orson Bean

Vermont-born Orson began his career with a nightclub act in New York and performed in early television (*Playhouse 90*, *Studio One*, and *The Kraft Television Theatre*), on Broadway (*Will Success Spoil Rock Hunter?*, *Mr. Roberts, Nature's Way*, and *Subways Are For Sleeping*), and in films (Otto Preminger's *Anatomy of a Murder* (1959), *Innerspace* (1987), and *Being John Malkovich* (1999). The free-spirited Orson has a reputation for being a bit eccentric, but he is in fact a very down to earth, friendly and level-headed guy.

In his memoir *Too Much Is Not enough* he wrote, "Life isn't frightening. Life is a game show where people who have fun are the

Gene Rayburn, Orson Bean, Brett and Charles.

winners." Sound advice for contestants playing on game shows as well as those playing in the game of life.

"Every four or five weeks, I flew to L.A. to appear on *The Tonight Show*," he wrote in *Too Much is Not Enough*. "While I was there, I'd knock off a week's worth of *The Match Game* or some other panel show, then fly home and we'd live for the next month on what I'd earned. I had, as I used to say: 'Enough money to last the rest of my life, provided I die a week from Thursday'."

"I was just kind of on and off *The Match Game*," Orson told me in an interview for this book. "I was never a regular, although I could have been. I had been a regular on *To Tell the Truth* for six or seven years. At a certain point I picked up stakes, took my family, and moved to Australia, and Mark Goodson never really forgave me for that. And so I came back a year and a half later, and the producer of it wanted me to be a regular; they had an open seat, but he said Mark said, 'No, he can guest, he can be a recurring, but not a regular.'

"When I did do it, it was fairly frequent," he continues. "You know, I loved sitting next to Brett up there, and Charles Nelson Reilly. When Johnny Carson retired, they had a Top Ten List of most frequent guests. I guest hosted the show over a hundred times back in the days when it came out of New York, before it became a big deal. And then I guested when it was out here with Johnny just under a hundred times, and when they had the list of Top Ten most frequent guests, I like to tell people that I was number six—just under, you'll pardon the expression, Charles Nelson Reilly. But we used to have a lot of fun doing the show."

Bart Braverman

Bart has been acting since he was a child, even appearing as Giuseppe on *I Love Lucy* in 1956 in the classic *Lucy Gets Homesick in Italy* episode, as well as shows like *Have Gun Will Travel*, *77 Sunset Strip,* and *Rawhide*. His career took off in the seventies and he continued to work regularly through the eighties and nineties; today he is happily retired. One bit of trivia fans may not know about: Bart was diagnosed with epilepsy when he was twenty-eight. When he began suffering the symptoms while he was on *Vega$,* he joked that he "thought it was because of all the drugs I did in college!"

Asked about the show, he says, "I never watched *The Match Game*. I'm not a big game show person, except for *Jeopardy*. The Mrs. and I watch *Jeopardy* every night. I probably got on *The Match Game* after I started doing *Vega$* through my publicist Larry Frank, who was Bob Urich's publicist and my closest friend. He used to go down there with me. Not that it was necessary, but we were having a good time. It wasn't so bad, being in my early thirties and being a celebrity, after twenty-something years of anonymity. Remember, I'd been working since I was five years old. Anyway, it was not an altogether unpleasant experience.

"Among the people I met: Jamie Lee Curtis was very sweet, and of course very sexy. Her father, who was on my show, was an icon of mine during my entire youth, so it was difficult for me to imagine her with her clothes off, but I struggled; Charles Nelson Reilly, Gene Rayburn and Fannie Flagg were very funny; Betty White is a treat for anyone, but I had known her when I was younger.

"Fans can be pretty strange. I've had people come up behind me and whisper, 'Eh, she's-a my birthday, too,' which is one of my lines for the *I Love Lucy* I did in 1956. That's a few years ago, you know what I'm saying? So, yes, fans do occasionally say things about seeing me on *Match Game*. When they do, I smile and say, 'Thank you.'

"That's pretty much all she wrote. Sorry I can't remember more, or stranger."

Foster Brooks

(May 11, 1912 – December 20, 2001)

Foster Brooks was an actor and comedian who began his career in radio and local television before moving with his family to Los Angeles in 1960 and moving on to television and nightclub appearances, most famously as his "loveable lush" character, rooted in his own early drinking problems (which he conquered in 1964: "A fellow made me a $10 bet I couldn't quit," he remembered, "and I haven't had a drink since. At the time I needed the $10.") but it made his career.

His was the kind of boozy character that would show up in an episode of *Green Acres* mistaking Arnold Ziffel, a pig, for a U.S. Air Force lieutenant. Brooks was a regular on *The Dean Martin Show* and featured in Martin's famous celebrity roasts. On one memorable episode of the syndicated *The Steve Allen Show* in the late sixties, Allen introduced Brooks as an important movie producer, whereupon Brooks stumbled out, fooling some of the other guests on the show, drunkenly recounting highlights from his illustrious career, which included editing movies for television—such as the epic *The Three Commandments*.

Foster Brooks. "No one knew what a truly great man he was," *MatchGame* celebrity coordinator Kay Henley remembered of him.

Match Game celebrity coordinator Kay Henley remembered Foster Brooks warmly. "He and his wife Teri were so wonderful. I went to Foster's service and learned so much more about his personal life. No one knew what a truly great man he was. They used to have a Christmas party every year and I *soooo* looked forward to going. I still have the liquor decanter in Foster's likeness that he gave out one year. "

In 1978 Wilbro, Inc. brought out a series of celebrity-themed liquor decanters, the first of which (appropriately enough) featured Brooks. Kay Henley cherishes hers to this day.

"At that time, his was the only one made of a person still living. What a thrill that it survived the quake, " she said.

Dr. Joyce Brothers
(October 20, 1927-May 13, 2013)

For over thirty years Dr. Joyce Brothers, who was a New York State licensed psychologist, was considered the dean of American psychologists and certainly the most visible and recognizable in her profession. A noted columnist, author, business consultant, wife and mother, she got her start in TV game shows before co-hosting NBC's *Sports Showcase* and appeared in countless TV and film appearances as herself.

"Well, *The $64,000 Question* was on the air and they let you choose your category," Dr. Brothers told me. "And so I wrote to them and said that I was a teacher at Hunter College and a teacher at Columbia University and that I was doing research for UNESCO and I would love to be a contestant, and they called me and said, 'Take a cab, we'll pay for the cab, come over.' So they did and I was able to be on that show and I won $64,000 twice and did a lot of game shows after that, but I also had a show of my own show at NBC for many years, and then in syndication by ABC for eight years."

As a result, she gained national attention as a quiz show celebrity, winning both *The $64,000 Question* and *The $64,000 Challenge* in the category of Boxing. I just had to ask: why *Boxing*?

"If I had said I was an expert on classic literature it would have been ho-hum time," she admitted matter-of-factly. "So I looked for something that would be as different from me as possible. And I narrowed it down to boxing and to plumbing, and boxing seemed more interesting. You can't learn all there is to know about art or literature or music, but these were finite subjects, so I could memorize everything, which I did. Later, *Twenty-One* got into trouble with Charles Van Doren, but *The $64,000 Question* was never in question."

After winning the *The $64,000 Question*, her career in game shows flourished. I asked how she ended up on *Match Game*. "Well," she said, "they just called me because they had seen me on the air, and I seemed like

Fannie Flagg was a special guest co-host alongside Dr. Joyce Bothers for a special week's worth of episodes of Dr. Brothers' talk show *Living Easy*.

an interesting contestant. And so they called me, and I did it, and it went well, and so it continued."

I asked if she met Gene Rayburn prior to doing the show. "No. Never," she replied, then added, "He was a very nice man." I asked if she had met Dick De Bartolo or Johnny Olson before doing the show, and she said, "No. You know, I met them in terms of being onstage or backstage and so on, but I didn't know them before."

"You made quite a number of appearances on *Match Game*," I observed.

"Yes, well, I've made quite a number of appearances on *most* shows," she laughed. "I enjoyed them and apparently they enjoyed me."

Asked if she considered herself a big game player she replied, "Yes, in fact, game person and also a writer of stories. My friends and I would play games—not games so much as acting out a story, and I would write it. My mother and father would pay ten cents for my sister to be involved because the ones who did the show were older kids than she. They were older than I, but they were my friends. So my mother and father paid us ten cents for my sister to be part of our play, and so I always made her a tree."

I found that funny. "You were quite the entrepreneur early on," I laughed. I asked if there were any funny incidents that happened on the taping days, and she replied, "Not really. We just did the shows and went our ways. Unless you're doing a regular show day after day it's rarely that you get to do anything more than just be there, enjoy each others' company, and then all part ways and go about doing what you needed to do."

Was she a game show watcher or fan? "No, I didn't have time to watch. The only time I would watch is if I got a call to be on a new show that I hadn't been on before, and then I watched to see what the format was."

Later, Dr. Brothers appeared as a celebrity panelist on the seventies version of *Match Game*. "Yes, and it was always fun to travel to L.A. and get to know people there, too."

As a player, what were the differences? "Well, there was less pressure. You knew there was no way you could prepare for it. You didn't have to study...I was just having fun. And improvisational fun is more fun than having to study hard."

"What was your favorite show to do?" I asked.

"There wasn't a particular one. I just enjoyed doing game shows and loved when they invited me back. It meant that I did well."

Joyce Bulifant

"Oh, I always loved Joyce," remembered Brett Somers. "I always teased Joyce, but she was a good kid. I used to make her life a living hell, but she always shared a dressing room with me and we always had great fun. She's great."

"*Every time Joyce tells a dirty joke, it sounds like a nursery rhyme.*" -Betty White

"It's very interesting," Joyce (probably best known as Murray Slaughter's wife on *The Mary Tyler Moore Show*) began when I asked how she started with game shows. "My very first television show that I did was *so* long ago with George DeWitt, and I did a show called *Name That Tune*, the very first one, [of] which Amadent was the sponsor. Somebody approached me in New York—I was going to the American Academy of Dramatic Art and someone saw me on the street or in a television audience and they asked if I could try out for *Name That Tune*, which I did, and I was on that show and that got me an agent. So I guess my very beginnings were on that game show."

"Were you a big game watcher or game player at the time?" I asked.

"*Not at all.* But I knew music—that is, the old songs. I don't know the new songs at all," she laughed. (Actually, that makes two of us.) I asked how she got the gig on *Match Game*.

"Um, I think it was probably my PR person. I was doing a series or several of them at that time, and I had a PR person...And they asked me just to be a guest, which means you sit on the lower panel on the right side; all the way over to the right is where a guest goes. And after I did a week of those shows, they asked me to move to what they called the funny seat. Or the dumb blonde seat, in my case.

"I also was bleeped a few times. I don't know if they ever got on the air, but I remember the first—I think the first time I sat in that, not the guest seat but the recurring seat, which is where Betty White and Patty Deutsch and the crazy ones of us sat, was that. I said to Ira, the producer, he was behind the camera, and I said, 'Is it alright—?' The question had been, 'The midget dentist, in order to fill a lady's cavity, had to stand on her <u>BLANK</u>.' And I said, 'Is it alright to tell a true story?' and Ira's shaking his head yes behind the camera, and I said, 'I mean, are you sure it's alright? It was in the *Chicago Sun Times*, are you sure it's okay?' It was on the front page, and he kept shaking his head yes it's okay. I said, 'It's about a dentist. You're sure it's—?' 'Yes, it's okay.' So I said, 'Well, there was a dentist who raped a woman, and the headline said, "Dentist fills wrong cavity."' And I heard all these bells and things go off. But the audience laughed. And it *was* a true story."

I asked if she got into any trouble. "No, they just asked me back," she replied. "Then another time I *know* I was bleeped, Gene said that to fill in the blank, it was, 'The head undertaker was upset with the assistant undertaker because when he buried Mr. Smith his <u>BLANK</u> was hanging out of the coffin. And I called Gene over and I said, 'How stiff *was* he?' The bells went off then, too. But I kept getting invited back.

"It's amazing, and people stop me *all* the time, and they ask, 'Why do I know you? How do I know you?' The most obvious things are *The Mary Tyler Moore Show* and the movie *Airplane*, and they'll say, 'No, no, it's *Match Game!*' And a man stopped me the other day and he said, 'My wife is dying of cancer, and the one time, her happiest time of the day is to get to see you on *Match Game*.' And you just think, 'My goodness, that's just *wonderful*.'

"One time I was doing *Vanities* in Chicago, the play, and it was a *blizzard* out. And I was talking to my agent and he said, 'Joyce, I don't want you to do any more game shows.' He said, 'It's not good for you. You are an *actress*. That's what you do and you are getting to be known as a game show person, and that's not good, and I don't want you to book any more.' And I thought, 'Well, okay.' There I was, doing a play and feeling very much the actress, and I walked out into this blizzard on my way to the theatre, and this woman stopped me in the snow, an elderly lady. And she said 'Hey!' and I said 'Hello.' And she said, 'I know you. What is it you do for me? Do you work at the grocery store?' and I said, 'No.' And she said, 'Do you work at my cleaners?' and I said 'No.' And she was being very forceful, and I had just had this conversation, I didn't know *what* to say, but she was just sure that I worked—She said, 'Do you go to my beauty parlor?' and I said, 'No, I don't.' And she went 'Oh!' and she just sort of threw me aside and walked briskly away, and I kind of laughed to myself and walked along. Because often if you say, 'No, maybe you've seen me on television,' people will say, 'I don't watch TV.' And I was walking along thinking about that. All of a sudden, she came up behind me, turned me around, grabbed me and hugged me, and she said 'I just figured out what it is that you do for me!' And I said, 'What?' And she said, 'You make me *laugh*!' And that was it. I said, 'I'm going to keep doing those game shows.' Because, to me, that was the most important thing you could do. Oh, it just made me so happy.

"You know, that to me was worth everything, and I called my agent and said 'Well, guess what, I'm gonna keep doing game shows.'"

"What was your agent's reaction?" I asked.

"Well, he couldn't stop me. He said, 'It's your choice.'

"It was always wonderful to go into the dinner break. I think everyone looked forward to that. First of all, Charles was *hysterical*. He was more fun and said the funniest things that you just—Of course, I couldn't allow my children—it would be a weekend and I had a lot of children. I had five stepchildren and three of my own, and I would bring them down to the studio from time to time. But when dinner came I said, 'Now kids, you

have to understand that you can't *eat* with us"—she laughed at this—
"because it was usually pretty naughty, raunchy conversation, but so
funny. So I really looked forward to Charles' stories.

"And there were a lot of people," she continued. "I mean, I admired so
many people who were on there."

I asked her favorite person on the show. "Oh, gosh, that isn't a fair
question. It's like asking a mother 'Which is your favorite child? Which
one do you love more?' You love them all but you just love them
differently, and that's how I felt about the panel. But as I said, I was
mesmerized by Charles and his timing and his brilliant mind. Not that I
enjoyed him more than anyone, I just looked forward to hearing his sense
of humor and his wisdom and his jokes, and so I guess he stood out in my
mind so much, but I totally enjoyed everyone for different reasons."

Gary Burghoff

Actor, painter, jazz musician, and inventor (he holds patents on a
fishing pole, a device attracting fish to a fishing boat, and a lever used to
lift a toilet seat), Gary Burghoff holds two other distinctions: he was the
only actor who appeared in both the film and hit television versions of
M*A*S*H, playing the character Radar O'Reilly in both, and in real life
Burghoff was an acting student of fellow celebrity panelist Charles Nelson
Reilly!

"Gary Burghoff what a doll he was, " remembered celebrity coordinator
Kay Henley. "One problem with him was he was always late. I truly think
that because he worked on *Match Game* so many times, we broke him of
that bad habit. I'd call him in the AM day of taping and remind him—
he'd still be late. But as time went on he really did start showing up on
time and sometimes even early. "

Carol Burnett & Friends

One of the benefits of taping *Match Game* at CBS Television City is
that other TV programs taped there, too. And occasionally rehearsed

there, too. One day in early 1978 Carol Burnett and Vicki Lawrence, trailed by Tim Conway and Jim Nabors, took a break from a rehearsal and wandered into Studio 33 (the same soundstage where *The Carol Burnett Show* was taped), surprising Gene and the studio audience.

"We just think this is such a pretty set, we thought we'd come on!" quipped Burnett, as Richard Dawson gathered her in a mock-passionate romance (while Gene did the same with Tim Conway).

A delighted Gene invited the group to play a round and had Ira Skutch provide some extra pencils and paper. As the group hunkered down on the orange shag carpeting (just like so many kids in front of their televisions at home were doing) and settled in, Gene read off the question. "Gloria said, 'My husband the bomber pilot is always practicing. He even yells "Bombs away!" when he's BLANKing.'" The contestant timidly answered "Going potty," Gene guffawed when he read Jim Nabors' card and said, "Well, you can't--" then said to the cameras, "Jim Nabors said 'tinkling'" (one wonders what potential *non-euphemism* he *actually* wrote down) while Carol wrote "Wee-wee." Vickie was a match as well with "Tinkling while a deadpan Tim Conway held up a blank card and shrugged, "Well, I figured he was constipated," to much laughter from the panel and studio audience.

Joan Collins

Yep, before she became TV's most beloved villainess on *Dynasty*, our Dame Joan was a guest panelist on *Match Game*. I recently sent a last-minute interview request to Joan's personal assistant and caught up with Joan herself at a book-signing for her latest novel (Okay, so I stood in line with everyone else waiting to get my book signed, but hey, she didn't have me thrown out when I asked her about *Match Game*!) over at Book Soup in West Hollywood.

"I really don't remember it," she confessed. "I had gotten the fax yesterday. I really don't remember it *at all*! I have *no* recollection. When was I on it?"

"1975," I replied.

"Are you *sure*?" she gasped in utter amazement. "Who was I on with?"

Like many celebrity panelists, Joan Collins used her moment in the show's opening to send a private message written on one of the cards (this one to her son and daughter).

"Scoey Mitchlll, for one," I responded, but his name didn't ring a bell. The names Brett Somers, Charles Nelson Reilly, and Richard Dawson all drew equally blank stares. When I mentioned that she had also appeared around the same time on Goodson-Todman's *Tattletales* with her then-husband, she replied, "I *vaguely* remember it." Then she laughed, grabbed her new husband Percy's hand, and said, "We don't talk about *other* husbands!"

Bill Daily
(August 30, 1927-September 4, 2018)

When asked about *Match Game*, Bill Daily, the comedian most famous for playing the role of Major Healy on *I Dream of Jeannie* and Bob's neighbor Howard Borden on *The Bob Newhart Show*, remembered, "It was wonderful. Of course, Gene was a good friend, so, you know, that helped. And everybody was dynamite. Charles Nelson Reilly is the funniest man that ever lived. Betty White, I got to be [on the show] with her a lot. We were good friends. I hated her because she was funnier, quicker, and smarter than I was. She'd always get the joke ahead of me. Very smart, very bright. It was fun. It was just *fun*."

Bill was present for one of the funniest *Match Game* moments when a contestant named Ginger Morris went up head-to-head against guest panelist Robert Walden from TV's *Lou Grant*, and gave a very unexpected answer. Of Gene, Bill remembered, "He laughed so hard he couldn't go on with the show. Stopped taping. I was laughing so [hard], the panel, we were crying, *we could not go on*. And they played this on the network!"

"It was 'Cuckoo BLANK.' What's 'Cuckoo BLANK?' Cuckoo clock! Everybody, I saw everybody write 'Clock,' 'Clock,' 'Clock.'

"...So Gene Rayburn's standing there. He puts the mike up to her, she knows it right away. He said, 'Cuckoo BLANK.' She said, 'Cuckoo, Fran and Ollie.' Gene just went to the floor! I mean, Cuckoo Fran and Ollie?' ... "It was over. We never recovered, by the way. And we're laughing at this woman who lost twenty thousand dollars! We thought of maybe 'Cuckoo bird,' but 'Cuckoo clock' was it. 'Cuckoo. Fran and Ollie.' Boy, that was a good one."

Patti Deutsch
(December 16, 1943-July 26, 2017)

Patti has done a ton of voiceover work for cartoons and commercials but is probably best known for two things: appearing on *Rowan & Martin's Laugh-In* (along with fellow *Match Game*-er Richard Dawson) and giving what are undoubtedly the most esoteric answers ever delivered by a celebrity panelist on *Match Game*. This last bit of notoriety makes Patti somewhat controversial among fans of the show.

Bart Braverman, Brett, Gene, a somewhat disgusted Charles, Bill Daily and Fannie Flagg seem bewildered by Eva Gabor's answer.

"I suspected this," admits Patti, "but I never really knew it until, like a couple of months ago, I saw Ira Skutch. And he said to me, 'You know, Mark Goodson never *got* what you did. He always said, 'Why do you use her? She never matches anybody.'" And I could understand the civilian population thinking that way, but a) I was always within the realm of possibility—it wasn't just fruit loops—and b) by the time you got to the sixth chair—and it was known as 'The Dummy Seat'—it was essentially over. But the fact that *he* didn't get it...I mean, he was always distant anyway, but I always sensed that he was a little put off by me.

"I guess it was Ira that said, 'Oh, just never mind, go about your business.' No, I don't think anybody ever said that to me. But somehow I kept doing it.

"One time it did backfire. I was auditioning for something, I don't remember what it was, but the casting director—I walked in and she looked at me and she said, 'You know, you cost me $5000.' I said, 'I beg your pardon?' And she said, "I was on *Match Game* and you didn't match. And you would have been a match and you cost me $5000.' So a) I knew I wasn't going to get whatever it was I was auditioning for, and b) don't try to explain it...Just get out alive! But that's the only time it backfired, although I know people on the websites get a little pissy from time to time. But—it was thirty-five [BLANK] years ago! I mean, come on! The baby is thirty, he just bought a house, he's been married for two years in September. Get over it, I say!

Speaking of Patti's son, she told me, "He was on *Match Game*. He was almost two and they brought Gary Burghoff's little girl—show-off!—and Max. And when Max got married, [for] the rehearsal dinner I put together a video and I got the show of him on *Match Game* to embarrass the bejeesus out of him in front of all his *very sophisticated* friends and bride-to-be."

"I went to school with Gene's daughter, so it was like a summer job at first, working for my friend's dad, before I realized, 'No, you're up there *with* him, you're not working *for* him.' I think the thing that was really cool about the show was the camaraderie. I mean, people really played with each other and for each other. On *Hollywood Squares* there was a lot of defending your box. It really was a fun way to spend a Sunday afternoon.

"I don't think I watched it in the sixties...I'm not exactly sure how I fell into the game show world, except that when I was living in New York and working at The Upstairs at The Downstairs—oh, God, this is so weird!—Bert Convy was working at The Downstairs of the Upstairs as a shingle, and I was upstairs with the revue. And then my husband wrote a play that was being produced off-Broadway and they cast Bert in the lead. Bert, besides doing his gig at Downstairs at The Upstairs was also doing game show run-throughs as the host of game shows that they were trying out in people's offices at Columbia-Screen Gems. So he got me as a fake celebrity. I would get five dollars to do game show run-throughs, and then go to Upstairs at The Downstairs and do two shows there, and then I would go to The Improv to work out with the Ace Trucking Company. I mean, you'd get home at three, four in the morning. And then do commercials the next day? Bizarre! So it was Bert Convy, somehow, got me involved with game shows.

"Very rarely would you have a prom queen or somebody that just couldn't get with the program. But most of the time it really was fun.

"Charles of course was ridiculous. And I see him at Whole Foods every once in awhile. It looks like he's following his basket. I'm not sure he's got the strength to push it, you know, it's like it has a life and he'll go along with it. And he's just the cutest, funniest, most demanding person ever. Did you see his show, his one-man show? Brilliant. I mean, offstage he was an old man following his basket, and onstage he was King Lear. He's just remarkable. And he was our captain, pretty much. And Brett was Auntie Mame and the Jewish mother at the same time. She was a cool bean. And Richard was Richard. I did *Laugh-In* with him and still didn't know him.

I mentioned I had recently spoken with Betty White and Patti replied, "Wow, one of my idols. Did she say '[BLANK]'? She and Allen Ludden used to make the worst jokes—I mean things you wouldn't hear in a Vegas lounge at a late show. And it was *fabulous* because he looked like the professor and she was *Betty White*. But Betty White was, oh, was just fabulous. The two of them were great. Great, great people. Bright, funny. Very cool, and it was doubly cool because it was Betty White who would say, you know, '[BLANK].' I mean, if Brett said it, *okay*.

"The one thing that I would have liked to have been able to do was to have done the show *with* Fannie or *with* Betty or Marcia, but I understand why I couldn't. There's only one dummy seat. But that's okay, I'm proud of The Dummy Seat, Godammit. I think I did it proud."

Fannie Flagg

Born Patricia Neal in Birmingham, Alabama (she changed her name for obvious reasons) she became a popular stand-up comedienne best known for her hilarious impersonation of Lady Bird Johnson. In NY theatre she did *Patio Porch* and *Come back to the Five and Dime, Jimmy Dean, Jimmy Dean* and played the lead in *Best Little Whorehouse in Texas*. Her film debut was in *Five Easy Pieces* with Jack Nicholson in 1970 and she went on to appear in *Some of My Best Friends Are, Stay Hungry* (with Jeff Bridges and Melanie Griffith), *Rabbit Test* (starring Billy Crystal), *Grease*, and wrote the screenplay for *Fried Green Tomatoes* with Carol Sobieski.

Fannie had appeared on the original version of *Match Game* (Audrey Davis worked on the NBC version and reported that even then Fannie was "terrific. Funny and sweet. Gave us all autographed comedy albums of hers. Still have it!") and was brought back to be a semi-regular panelist on the new version—and ended up as one of the most popular. "I had done *Match Game* in New York before it came to Los Angeles," she recalled. "I guess they liked me on the show, and Mark Goodson, the creator and producer, was a friend of mine. He had married a lovely lady I knew from my hometown of Birmingham, Alabama."

Asked her favorite memory of the show she replied, "My favorite memory was basically, I would have to say, every day. We would film five *Match Games* in one day, a lot of people didn't know. We'd go in on a Saturday, we'd film three shows, and what would happen in between shows, we would go upstairs, change tops, come back down like it was another day, but it really wasn't. And they'd change audiences. So we'd do three shows and then they'd take a big dinner break. We did not eat with the contestants, but we did eat with the crew. Just a lot of fun.

"Well, the dinner break was about two hours, and Brett Somers and Charles Nelson Reilly and Richard Dawson would hit those marinis, and on Thursday and Friday Charles' toupee would be here, here...

"But my favorite memory was literally every day. [It] was just great fun and everybody got along on that show, it's just terrific."

"As the show did well, I noticed that people recognized us more and more. I remember getting a lot of fan mail but alas no bonuses, gifts or

"Actually, I think it's fascinating, we're the only show that has Edward Albee writing the questions," Fannie joked, referencing the *Who's Afraid of Virginia Woolf?* playwright.

perks. But we did get a fruit basket each week which was nice." She added, "Most of my fan mail mentioned they loved the way Brett picked on me."

Despite her post-*Match Game* career as the bestselling author of novels like *Fried Green Tomatoes at the Whistle-Stop Cafe* and *Welcome to the World, Baby Girl!*, Fannie, like Joyce Bulifant and Bill Daily, is dyslexic.

"I was, am, severely dyslexic," she revealed in a 2002 interview. When I asked her if being on the panel and writing down questions on cards in a short period of time ever posed a problem for her, she replied, "No. My misspelling of words was part of the joke."

However, working as a celebrity panelist help her solve the mystery of why she had trouble with math and spelling. "When I was doing *Match Game* I was thirty, maybe twenty-nine or early thirties. At that point I still didn't now what was wrong with me. And I had been doing *The Match Game* for about a year and this school teacher somewhere in the Midwest wrote me a letter and she said, 'Oh, I notice you're dyslexic,' and I didn't even know what the word meant. And I looked it up, and then I went to get tested. And that was the first time that I knew what it was...People thought you were just stupid, you know?"

While she regularly appeared on shows like *Candid Camera, Harper Valley P.T.A.*, and made guest appearances on shows like *The Dating Game* and *Hollywood Squares* in the sixties and seventies, in the eighties Fannie turned to writing, including the best-selling *Fried Green Tomatoes at the Whistle-Stop Café*, which earned her an Oscar nomination for her screenwriting debut. Not bad for a girl who couldn't read or write!

Debralee Scott told me, "One time Fannie Flagg, Brett Somers and I went to Joe Allen's and we made a bet with each other to see who could get the most business cards from our table to the ladies room. Fannie Flagg won."

"Was she wearing one of her infamous t-shirts?" I asked.

"I don't really remember, but I know she won. She came back with the most cards."

Fannie told me long after *Match Game* ended its run, she still kept up with "Brett and Charles and the producer Ira Skutch." the affection was mutual. "Fannie's one of my favorite people altogether," declared Ira. "She's wonderful—and a very good writer, too." When asked if he had known Fannie prior to her doing the original *Match Game*, Ira replied, "I don't think so. I think that's where I first got to know her. That was in New York, and of course she did the show out here frequently. Semi-regularly."

As for the lady herself, asked if she ever caught any of the reruns of *Match Game*, Fannie replied, "Yes, I did and I thought the shows held up very well. It is nice to have a reminder of such happy times."

I had to ask Marcia Wallace if people ever confused her with that *other* fabulous redhead, Fannie. "All the time," she admitted. "In fact, the other day, yesterday, I was walking up the stairs to Trader Joe's, somebody said, 'I love your books.' And I just say 'Thank you' now. First, I was recognized as Fannie Flagg, then there were ten years or so when she was recognized as me, and then it went back the other way. ("That's okay," quipped Patti Deutsch, another redheaded panelist, when asked if she had the same problem. "When I was on *Laugh-In* I used to get James Farantino's fan mail. We've *never* figured *that* out.")

"The Bette Davis story is fabulous," continued Marcia. "Didn't I tell you that? I did seventy-five *Merv Griffin* shows, and one day there were back-to-back shows, and Bette Davis was on the other one. So I thought, 'Oh, oh, I have to meet her!' So I'm hanging around the lobby, some guy comes out and says, 'You want to meet her, don't you?' I said, 'Oh, please, oh please, oh please!' And he goes and he whips the door open and he says, 'Miss Davis, Miss Fannie Flagg!' And she said, '*That's* not Fannie Flagg. I don't know *who* it is, but it's *not* Fannie Flagg.' So Fannie of course loves that story.

"That's a great story, because Fannie has told me in the sixties they said, 'Aren't you Fannie Flagg?' In the seventies and eighties, kind of, they said, 'Aren't you Marcia Wallace?' And after *Fried Green Tomatoes* they started saying to me 'Aren't you Fannie Flagg?' And of course I'm thrilled, I'm thrilled. I mean, we're both redheads. That's it. But there must be something. Maybe it's the *Match Game* connection."

Fannie and Those T-shirts

Fannie became known for wearing her trademark t-shirts, some bedecked in rhinestones and sequins, others sporting the images of Woody Woodpecker, Charlie Chaplin, Popeye, Superman, and the Confederate flag. Once, Richard Dawson was given a t-shirt so he wouldn't look so drab next to Fannie—it said "Fannie Flagg wears falsies."

"This is a running joke," laughs Fannie. "Here I'm trying to be a serious author, and there I was sitting there on network television with fried eggs on my—I don't know." But fans loved the t-shirts—and so did the other panelists.

"Weren't they heaven?" says Brett. "I just loved it. Then she was going around saying, 'I don't want to be noticed, I don't want anyone—,' and then she has these big flashing t-shirts over these big tits!"

Says the fabulous redhead herself, "I bought a few, then people began to send them to me. And that's why I wore them, because people sent them in, and people wanted to see them on television. My favorite was the one with the two fried eggs. I gave them away for charity."

"Oh, I know, weren't those heaven?" continued Brett. "I just saw those the other night. I was channel surfing, and when I came in, there was Fannie with the two fried eggs. I just totally forgot about that. They were great. *She* was great."

Eva Gabor
(February 11, 1919?-July 4, 1995)

Of the fabled Gabor sisters (Zsa-Zsa and Magda, along with mother Jolie, made up the infamous family) Eva was the most beloved. A cabaret singer and figure skater in her native Hungary (she was born in Budapest February 11, 1919 but some sources cite 1921—none of the Gabors were too good at math when their ages come under scrutiny) she emigrated to the U.S. and appeared in films and on Broadway in Rodgers and Hammerstein's *The Happy Time* in 1950, but is best remembered as Park Avenue-loving farm wife Lisa Douglas on *Green Acres*.

Brett Somers remembered, "When Eva used to do the show, she'd say, 'Oh Brett, what are you looking at?' and I'd say, 'I'm looking for the scars where you got that facelift.' And she'd say, 'Oh, Brett, you are so terrible!' She had the most gorgeous skin. She came in one day and she said, 'Oh, Brett, darling, look!' And she had her eyes done and she was, I don't know, her late forties. She looked fabulous! You know, they just didn't wrinkle, those old Hungarians...They all had this.

Bart Braverman, Brett and Charles, Eva Gabor, Bill Daily and Fannie join in the mayhem with Gene in the first syndicated episode of *Match Game*.

"Marilyn Monroe had it. There is a picture at The Actor's Studio, just a picture [taken] at Lee Strasberg's house...one of the acting sessions. And you are riveted by the fact that Marilyn Monroe was there. And I'm telling you, you would have thought she'd been specially lit. Well I knew she hadn't been, there was no such thing. Those people with that great, great skin. I've always wanted a copy of that picture, because it was so wonderful to see her, you know? She just stuck out like a sore thumb, and those Gabor girls were the same."

"You know," Joyce Bulifant told me in the midst one of our conversations, "someone that was really fun to work with was Eva Gabor. She was very sweet to me. She was so funny, though. She always teased me about how I dressed, and I tend to be more the Peter Pan-collar type person, and she was always coming around and pulling blouses off my shoulders and putting her jewelry on me and trying to jazz up the way I look. And she was very cute about it. She wanted me to go to Europe with her on a trip and I wish I'd done it. It would have been fun.

"I did play tennis at her home once and that was really interesting because on the way down to the court there was a makeup table just like you have in the studios, and she would sort of check all of her makeup before going on the tennis court. And on the court, waltz music played, so when you played tennis you could hear waltzes. And the ladies I played with all did those moon shots into the air. That was *very* interesting. But she was very sweet, very warm, and certainly wanted to do a makeover on me."

One question, just out of curiosity: Did Eva Gabor speak English better 'in life' than when onstage? "No, actually she spoke that way all the time, if I remember," said Joyce. "I don't think I remember her going in and out of that."

Brett Somers agreed. "It was about the same. I loved Eva too. She was great, a very down to earth person and really nice. 'Well, you've got all those rich guys, and you've got all the jewels.' 'Dahling, trust me, *I* paid for the jewels!' Yes she did! Very nice. She was terrific. She'd arrive all made up and she was there. 'Whaddaya *really* look like in the morning?' I would arrive, you know, with my scarf on, somebody to do my hair and my makeup. But she always arrived made-up and ready to go."

Greta Garbo

(September 18, 1905 –April 15, 1990)

In one memorable episode, Fannie Flagg dressed up in sunglasses and a wide-brimmed hat pretending to be "special guest" celebrity panelist (and movie legend) Greta Garbo. "The show was fairly free-form with the celebrites making up their own business," explained Roger Dobkowitz. "The Greta Garbo act was rather funny. A staff joke that kept going around after *Match Game* became such an enormous success was that

Greta Garbo was going to come out of retirement to be a celebrity on *Match Game*. This was as close as we got!" While Garbo was, in fact, a fan of *Hollywood Squares* (even going so far as to write Paul Lynde a fan letter!) she never came out of her fabled retirement to appear either on *Squares* or *Match Game*.

Monty Hall Wins a "Zonk"

(August 25, 1921-September 30, 2017)

While the *Let's Make A Deal* host never formally appeared on the *Match Game* panel, he made an indelible impression on the show.

Patti Deutsch played a part in one of my favorite *Match Game* moments when Gene read off the question: "The bank teller said, 'I think there's something wrong with this dollar bill. Instead of a picture of George Washington, this one has a picture of George BLANK.'" While answers ranged from George C. Scott to George Burns and George Raft, Patti said, "I couldn't think of another George, so I said 'Monty Hall.'"

(Oh, by the way, while we're on the subject—Washington was a U.S. President, right? This was the seventies, right? The definitive answer would have been George *Jefferson*).

"This actually has a story," Patti revealed to me. "When in doubt, when I couldn't think of anything, I would always say either Monty Hall or Richard Nixon. And Richard Nixon makes obvious sense, but *Monty Hall*?

"I was on the Johnny Carson show, probably when I was on *Laugh-In* and had just moved out here, so I was discussing the differences between living out here and living back East. And I said, 'Out here, people list themselves in the phone book, not only their name, address and telephone number, but their credits. For instance, Carl Reiner,' and I gave an address and telephone number and I went 'Writer, producer, actor.' I did a whole list. And then I did somebody else and a whole list, and then I went, 'And Monty Hall.' [Pause.] Well, when you're new, you don't think anybody's really watching...Well, apparently he *was* and he got pissed off. And he said to somebody, 'Just have her up here to do run-throughs and never hire her!'

"I thought that was so funny, getting so angry about something so silly and inconsequential. So it was my prerogative to get back at him for getting back at me. I never went up there for any reason because I had heard what he was doing. So that's where 'Monty Hall' came from. It is *odd*, I mean, that it would have a backstory. And he's probably forgotten it by now, I'm sort of thinking. But not me."

Elaine Joyce

Dick Martin remembered Elaine Joyce well. "Oh yes, yes, I knew her. At one time she was going with Bill Bixby, and so we double dated a few times. Now she's married to Neil Simon. That's wild! Good for her."

We can assume Elaine always had a thing for writers. Brett Somers dished (just a little) when we discussed some of the other panelists. "Well, there was Elaine Joyce," she told me, "who ended up having an affair, *little did I know*, with J.D. Salinger! His daughter wrote a book. Now who knew that Elaine Joyce..? There she was having an affair with J.D. Salinger! Oh yes, evidently it was not a rumor, but it was true. Who knew?" She added, "You know, I was never really that friendly with Elaine. I was always like, 'Hi there,' but—and Charles of course I adored," she said, changing the subject.

Maybe Brett wasn't Elaine's biggest fan, but *Match Game* writer Elliot Feldman confessed to having a bit of a crush on her prior to working on the show. "And when you finally met Ms. Joyce," I asked him, "what was she like?"

"Oh, I—you know—she was nice, you know," he answered sheepishly. "I don't think she knew," he chuckled.

Jack Klugman
(April 27, 1922-December 24, 2014)

Born in Philadelphia, Jack has worked with some of the biggest names around. On Broadway, he co-starred with Ethel Merman in the original production of *Gypsy*, and in movies co-starred with another legendary singer. "Judy Garland—I did her last movie," Jack told me. "I loved her, because she saw *Gypsy* about nine times, and she loved it. We became good friends.

"I learned more from Brett than anyone else. She studied at The Actor's Studio for years. Back then, they'd get up and do scenes from *Henry V* that took two hours. People would examine a penny for twenty minutes. I asked Brett, 'What's the most important thing you learned at The Actor's Studio?' She said, 'To get an aisle seat.'"

While his resume includes film and theatre credits, Jack is best known for his TV roles as the irascible, curmudgeonly divorced slob Oscar Madison on *The Odd Couple*, and later as crime-solving coroner *Quincy*. But—along with wife Brett Somers—he still found time to appear on a few Goodson-Todman shows.

"I've done a lot of their game shows," Jack told me. "*He Said, She Said*. Brett and I did a lot of those, *He Said, She Said*, because we were always arguing, and other games we always played all the time. We were doing them a favor in those days.

"Today, I did *Hollywood Squares*. It's like it's a big deal! I mean, they were very nice. Henry Winkler is now producing *Hollywood Squares*, and he's one of my dear friends. And it's like, [years ago] we were doing them a favor and they begged me to do it. And Brett would deny it, because she doesn't know it: Goodson and Todman—Mark Goodson—asked me to do the show, and I did it once [the pilot], and he said, 'Will you do it again?' I said, 'I'll do one, but you've got to give Brett a shot at it.' And that's how she got on, and they liked her and they did it and they used her. But she said no, that she got it on her own. *Bullshit*, she did *not* get it on her own, whatever she said. But she *held* it on her own. She was *great* on that show, she and Charles Nelson Reilly. Great."

While Brett triumphed on the show, being a regular panelist held no special appeal for Jack. "I was doing a series then," he pointed out. "See, I was doing *Odd Couple* then, and then had a year off. In '75 we stopped

Odd Couple and then in '77 I did *Quincy*. So I was only off for a year. I didn't want to do that stuff, you didn't make any money. You do five episodes, you make fifteen hundred bucks for that, that was it. There wasn't any money. And I didn't really get—and they were terrible. They were 'blank,' and all these double-entendres. But I think one of the better shows, *Password*, was best. *Password* I did all the time. I loved that show because it was really competitive, and you really had to use your head. I was pretty good at that game."

Ira Skutch observed, "Brett Somers we got because Jack Klugman did—I think he did the first week, second week of the show. I know he did the pilot. And he did it a couple of times after we started the run. And after the show one night he said, 'Would you do me a big favor?' And I said, 'What's that?' He said, 'Book my wife on the show one week. She's driving me crazy. She wants to work.' I said 'Sure, I'd be glad to.' Of course, she turned out to be wonderful and we just kept her on. Next time he was on he said, 'Oh, you saved my marriage!' I didn't save it for long, though!

"I ran into Jack, oh I don't know, three or four months ago. We went to The Cinegrill to see Lorna Luft, and Jack was there. So I went over—I hadn't seen him in years—and we talked and said hello, and we were very glad to see each other. I said to him, 'I was looking forward to seeing you. I wanted to tell you I did you a favor once that turned out to be the biggest favor you'd done us.' And he said, 'What was that?' I said, 'Well, you asked me to book Brett, so we booked her as a favor to you, but it turned out it was more of a favor to us.' And so we chatted, and he thought that was very funny."

The Landers Sisters

Okay, let's get this straight from the beginning: Audrey and Judy Landers are NOT twins. Judy is two years younger than Audrey.

"I was not a game show watcher growing up," admitted Judy. "I was into music and comedies, but I really didn't watch game shows growing up at all."

"No, I don't recall that we were," agreed former *Dallas* star Audrey. "I really don't. I mean, I was acting my whole childhood and through my teens, and we were never real game players actually."

"I got started doing game shows when I was on a television series," said Judy, who was a regular on *Vega$, B.J. and the Bear*, and the Wayland Flowers & Madame vehicle *Madame's Place*. "I think the first one was *Vega$*, and then the game shows would call the television show if we would be interested in being on the show. Sometimes they would go through the television show itself, and then sometimes they would try to reach us directly."

When I asked her favorite game show to do, Judy surprised me by replying without hesitation, "*Match Game*. Really. I loved *Match Game*, it was always so much fun, and it wasn't a pressure kind of a show like *Pyramid*, you know? It was a lot of fun.

"There was the most interaction, I think, between the guests and the host and the audience and whoever the contestant was. There was much more interaction in *Match Game* than there was in other game shows. In *Hollywood Squares* you were in this box, you know, and you really couldn't speak to anybody. It was just more relaxed and there was room for some improvisation. And Gene Rayburn was such a great guy, such a wonderful sense of humor.

"I never had a bad experience on *Match Game*. Everybody was always very friendly. It was a very relaxed atmosphere. You'd get there, they always treated you great, with wonderful gift baskets in your dressing room, and the green room was always full of friendly people. And you didn't have any—on some shows they go over things ahead of time, but on *Match Game* it was so relaxed, nothing was scripted, everything was just improv.

"And of course you always did a week at a time. And the thing that was so much fun about *Match Game* was that you do a show, then you go back and change your clothes, and they always had the *Match Game P.M.*, and that was so you could get dressed up. That was the more formal show, and I loved that. So there was one show where you were allowed to, you know, get really glamorous.

"The *Match Games* I did, I never remember a bad experience, or anyone being angry or pulling a star trip. Everyone was always very happy. It really was. It wasn't phony at all, it was real. Everyone enjoyed themselves doing that show."

"Well, it's funny," said Audrey. "During those years I was doing a lot of game shows, and I had done many appearances on *The $100,000 Pyramid* and *Password Plus*, and I was a real whiz at those kind of brainy games. And every time they asked me to do a *Match Game*, I always felt insecure, because my sister was always so funny, just naturally, you know? And so for me, the *Match Game*, odd as it sounds, I was always more nervous doing that than I was doing the *Pyramid*."

"Because of the improvisation involved?" I asked her.

"Well, also just that in my heart of hearts I was just more serious, and I always felt that I was never funny enough, you know what I'm saying? My sister was great at it, and so I always felt, 'Well, gee, I'm just not naturally that funny.' If they'd asked me serious, brainy questions, okay, I'd feel comfortable. But just to be funny, I was always very insecure about it."

Yet they were both very proficient at game shows, I noted. "Yes, we were, it was funny," said Audrey. Then I asked Audrey for her favorite game show to do. "My personal favorite?" she said in surprise. "Oh my goodness. You know, I really did love doing all of them. I thought they were lots of fun, and *Match Game* was probably the least stressful. It was a silly, fun, just pure entertainment, so in that sense I really did love doing the *Match Game*."

Peter Marshall and Jim MacKrell

Even hosts of *other* game shows had funny *Match Game*-related stories.

"One of my mentors, who helped me when I began as a game show host, was Peter Marshall," recalled Jim MacKrell, host of *Celebrity Sweepstakes* and *The Game Game*. "And I've known Peter for years and really hold him in high regard. And one day Peter decided there was a wonderful little French restaurant on Ventura Boulevard, and the two of us decided to lunch, and I'd only been doing the game show a month, month and a half—*Celebrity Sweepstakes*. And I was getting used to the fact that somebody could actually walk up and know my name. And so Peter was kind of putting me through the ropes; the old vet that had been around forever was trying to put the new kid through the ropes, so to speak, on primarily how to handle the public when they recognize you, what to do.

"Well, here we are sitting in this French restaurant on Ventura Boulevard and enjoying some outrageously expensive lunch, and a lady approaches and said, 'Oh, my God in heaven, my two favorite game show hosts at the same time!' At which point Peter, bless his heart, reached over and tapped me and said, 'You'll have to get used to this,' and said, 'Yes, how are you?' And she said, 'Oh, my goodness! Jim MacKrell and *Gene Rayburn*!'"

Dick Martin

(January 30, 1922-May 24, 2008)

With all those studs parked next to Brett week after week, I just had to ask if there was anybody with whom she wanted to run off to that little motel in Encino.

"I always thought Dick Martin was adorable," she confessed. "Dick Martin is the sweetest, dearest, most adorable man, and has the cutest wife who ever lived. I used to love it when Dick Martin did the show. He's funny, smart, he's great. He's *great*!"

Dick spent the better part of the 1950s and sixties as Dan Rowan's comic foil in stand-up comedy, but it was on *Rowan & Martin's Laugh-In*, one of the biggest hits of the late 1960s, that their stardom was attained. After *Laugh-In*, Dick hosted two game shows, *The Cheap Show* and *Mind Readers*, and also became a much in-demand sitcom director ("We were counting it up the other day," said Dick, "and I had over two hundred shows. I was a television director and never did break into film. But I did an awful lot of shows, and I was twenty-two years doing it.")

And then there was *Match Game*.

"Did a lot of those, and did a lot of *Tattletales*," said Dick and when asked his favorite, he replied without hesitation, "Oh, I loved *Match Game*. I just loved that. It was fun. They were all fun. They pretty much let me—I'm sure they wouldn't like to talk about this but they pretty much let me book *Tattletales*, because I just wouldn't go on unless I could have Bob Newhart and his wife, and Anthony Newley and his wife, you know, certain people, like Steve and Eydie. And so we all knew each other and it made the game like a half-hour comedy show. You can't get too much funnier than those shows.

"It was just the fact that we all knew each other and everybody *knew* we knew each other. And you could cut in on each other's questions, and it was fun."

Dick had fond memories of Gene and the gang. "I remember when he did *Bye, Bye Birdie*," remembered Dick. "I knew him well. *Very* nice man. Brett was a Broadway or legit actress that I met there, and Charlie Reilly I knew before and after. I'm just crazy about Chuck. And I did a lot—*lot*— of them with Betty White. I knew her before and worked with her quite a bit on a lot of other shows. We played man and wife on a couple of shows. I don't even remember what they are now.'"

Eva Gabor earned his admiration the night she injured herself. "Yeah, Eva sat next to me, and I was there the night she hurt her foot. She slid as she was walking across the floor. She hit something and boy, she hurt herself. And she went on! She kept going and finished the show. Boy, oh boy!"

Dick gave one of the funniest answers on the show, in my opinion. Gene read off the following: "The 19 year-old girl said, 'I just came back from Niagara Falls where I honeymooned with my 102 year-old husband. I spent the entire two weeks BLANKing.'" For the record, three celebs said "sleeping," but Dick had Gene and the rest of the panel rolling in the aisles with "shucking oysters." When I reminded him of his answer, Dick laughed and said, "I'd forgotten that. Oh, God, that *is* funny."

Dolly Read Martin

"Dick and I did *Tattletales* through Goodson-Todman, and that was a great show," remembered Dolly, who is best known for starring in the cult classic *Beyond the Valley of the Dolls*. "Then we did *Super Password*, or *Password Plus* or something, and Dick got me a T-shirt that said "Game shows are my life." And I just loved doing them. I was an actress when I met Dick and I went with him to the show one time, and who was it? It was Ira—he said, 'Would you like to do one?' and I said yes, and he had me try out for it, and I loved it. I love winning money for people, and I love to give it way, and that's why Dick's scared I'm going to give out money away.

"I was so young! Oh, my gosh, when I look at the reruns and I think, 'That hairstyle was good—no, not that one.' So it's a good and bad thing when you see yourself in reruns like that. Now I've got all these wrinkles and everything and it's—Oh, never mind, we won't talk about that.

"We were all having such fun. It was just as though we were at our houses playing a game, because nobody was trying to one-ups-man-ship anybody else. It was totally from the top of our heads. I remember one time I couldn't think of some answer and it just made sense that the answer was 'Blank'. I'll never forget, Gene looked at me and he said, 'Dolly...' and I said, 'Well, it just made sense to me at the moment.' I think that was awful but *I* went blank."

"Did anybody else answer with 'blank'?" I asked.

"No! Wouldn't that have been nice? Then I wouldn't have felt so dumb!" And she gave a hearty English laugh.

"I just have wonderful fond memories of them...When we did *Tattletales* that was hysterical too. We'd get very raunchy on that, it was wonderful. Double *entendres* and all, it was wonderful.

"I like to play poker. Barbara Sinatra, who lives ten doors away from us here, when she comes to town in the summertime a group of us get together and we play every Sunday. And it's *so* funny, and we all have a wonderful time and drink and cavort, and it's just wonderful. In fact, Frank never played, but he used to get popcorn and he used to come in and throw the popcorn at us and say, 'This is an illegal game with money being exchanging hands! I'm calling the cops!'

"But I've always loved games. Dick and I used to play Backgammon together, but he threw the Backgammon set at me one time and he said, 'You are the worst player but you keep getting double sixes! I'm not playing with you anymore!' I'm just very lucky. When I came to America from England, I played Roulette. The crown prince of Saudi Arabia, Prince Fahid, at that time was in England, and another friend of ours and my mother, we all went to the casino, and I won $6,000 on Roulette. And he was showing me his [system]. But anyway, that's how I came to America. I gave $3,000 to my family and I lived on $3,000 in America. But I was a Playmate in 1966 for Playboy, the first English Playmate, so that's when I first fell in love with America and decided to come back, and because of playing Roulette I was *able* to come back."

And then she added, "I'm very lucky."

Lee Meriwether

"I started *Match Game* during—I don't remember the dates, but it was in the seventies because I was on *Barnaby Jones* and did a lot of game shows. I remember Mark Goodson being a white haired, tanned, very handsome gentleman. Bill Todman I don't remember meeting. I have no memory of him whatsoever. I loved the panelists and of course Gene. There were several crew members that were really super folks; I mean they were just so nice and pleasant. A gentleman by the name of Ira Skutch was involved in getting me on the show as well. He was a producer and he was also a director on a play I did here in Los Angeles early on..."

Ira recalled, "I worked with Lee Meriwether on the first professional thing she did, when she became Miss America. We had Bess Myerson.

Philco sponsored that the first year it was on television, and that was the year that Lee Meriwether won. And so as part of the tie-ins, they made one of the television sets they called 'The Miss America set.' And we used to feature that on the commercials. That tied in that promoted the contest, and of course the contest promoted *Philco* that way. And so we hired Bess Myerson, who had been a Miss America, to be the spokesman or one of the announcers or whatever you call it, on *The Playhouse.* Jay Jackson was on all the time and she was on also. And then after the contest was over she came on with Lee Meriwether. We introduced Lee Meriwether on the show, and she said something, and we were friends all through the years. We used her on *Match Game* quite a bit, and I used to run into her at Theatre West and other places."

"Oh, it was good," continued Lee, remembering her *Match Game* experiences. "I loved it, I had great fun. And I don't keep in touch really with any of the people. I see several of the actors on occasion, but nobody that I'm, you know, close contact with. And memories, they're all pleasant. There was one time where they had to re-tape a section I did but it was just words were confusing, and that was all that I really remember. No, it was great fun. It was a chance to be on national television in a different venue than *Barnaby Jones.* It was great, great fun, I loved everybody."

Ethel Merman
(January 16, 1908-February 15, 1984)

Despite being the reigning Queen of Broadway, not to mention having appeared on game shows like *Hollywood Squares* and the original *Match Game*, "Ethel Merman was made to audition for the show," remembered Fannie Flagg, "a fact that *enraged* Brett and I, so we went in the office and played the game with her hoping she would not know it was an audition. But she did know and afterwards sent Brett and I a set of beautiful expensive pearls that I am sure cost more than she made on the show."

"The First Lady of musical comedy!" exclaimed Brett in near wonderment. "But, you know, that's show business. But she was fine with it, she was amazing. Fannie and I were upset, but she didn't seem to be upset with it. 'Oh, okay.' We were sort of pretending that it wasn't really [an audition]. She got it. She was no dope."

When I asked Joyce Bulifant if anyone with whom she appeared on the panel ever knocked her socks off, she replied, "Well, I thought that Ethel Merman—I just couldn't get over how sweet she was, and she told a story one day. She talked about being a candy striper and aid at the Roosevelt Hospital, and how somebody had come up to her, and she had her nametag on and she said they said, 'You even *look* like Ethel Merman.' And she said 'Well, I am.' And they said 'No, I mean you really do look like her. It's ama—' And she said, 'But I *am*. Look at my nametag.' And they said, 'No, but I mean *the* Ethel Merman.' They just kept going on like that. And I just thought that was such a nice thing that she volunteered to do that, and it was a fun story."

Scoey Mitchlll

"I gotta ask you this," I confessed to Scoey, "and I feel kind of embarrassed asking it, because I've seen it spelled a couple of different ways—"

"Three Ls," he said, obviously used to people asking how to spell his name correctly. He laughed and said, "People ask me, 'How'd you get your name? You know, how'd you get the three Ls?' I always say, 'Oh, we had a dumb massa.'

"I did *Tattletales* first, I believe. My wife and I did *Tattletales*, and I guess it's just sort of a natural progression, you know—you do one Goodson-Todman game show, you end up doing them all. And I did *Tattletales* and then I did *Match Game*. And it wasn't a big booking or anything, and I don't know how many times I did *Match Game*. A few

The Love Boat doctor Bernie Kopell joins Brett, Charles, Marjorie Wallace, Scoey Mitchlll, and character actress Edie McClurg on the celebrity panel.

times, quite a few times. We had big fun on that show. I liked *Tattletales* best. (He laughed)

"I like games. I wasn't a game show watcher *per se*. I was a comic, so being a bit witty they felt that I would do well on *Match Game*. And of course, we had a pretty good group there [and] I knew most of them. A lot of people I didn't know, only through the business, but I knew Betty White and Dickie Dawson, Charles Nelson, you know. So being a comic and a bit acerbic, they thought I could do well on that show and they booked me and I guess they liked me 'cause they kept booking me back.

"But I had a good time. Well, first of all, I got to know most of the people on a personal level, you know, especially the regulars there. What I liked about it, they usually put compatible guests together, people that you could play off. Because they knew I was going to say something about the other people on the show, so they made sure they booked people that could trade lines with you, and so forth. So they did nice bookings and I just had a lot of fun on it. I think it was the most popular of the shows.

"It's hard to do a game show now, I think. The public is just—we've let them in on all our secrets, you know? I remember when my mother came out here, this was back in the seventies also, and my mother came out to visit me and everything, and I had her doing all the touristy stuff. My wife took her around all the touristy stuff and the Universal tour, and when she came home, I said to her, 'Did you enjoy it?' She said, 'Yeah, yeah, it was nice, it was nice.' She says, 'It's just, I'm not as fascinated anymore.' She says, 'Now I know when he falls off the building, he's not really falling off the building, he's falling into an air mattress, you know?' And we've just given all our little secrets away and they don't think we're as good as we used to be when they didn't know. We've killed the mystique. And the same thing with game shows now. They know all the tricks, they know all the answers, they know—you know, 'cause everyone's in show business now!

"I think that *Match Game*, a show like that, it's a very simple format and they never know who's going to say what. So therefore I think that's part of the fascination, too...But I still like *Tattletales* best!" he laughed.

"I never salted opinions away in case I was going to write a book someday. I just went there, I did the job, I guess I got along with everybody. And it was a game show, and it had a game show atmosphere, which I think was very helpful. It was a Goodson-Todman production, and those guys had been in the business since television started, so it was a smooth-running production *as far as I know*, you know what I'm talking about?

"And everybody that I know—I'm thinking of Paul Alter and Ira Skutch and them—they weren't 'excitable' people, which is helpful on a set when the 'bosses' are level-headed. So it really created a nice atmosphere, and Goodson-Todman treated us nice. You know, they fed us good, you know? You'd take that dinner break and there was decent food to eat, you know, and stuff like that. So I think it came from the office onto the set where everything was—'Come on, we've done this before, we're going to do the same thing today that we did yesterday.' There shouldn't be any hassle. But I enjoyed all those game shows. I did *Squares* and *Password*, and I can't even remember all those shows back then. But back then you had a daytime schedule, and those shows were as important as the other productions were to primetime. They were pretty first class *I* thought, for game shows."

Richard Paul (June 6, 1940 – December 25, 1998), graced the *Match Game* panel while starring as the town mayor in the sitcom *Carter Country*. Later he recurred as the mayor of Cabot Cove on *Murder, She Wrote* and twice played the Reverend Jerry Fallwell: in a TV movie and in *The People vs. Larry Flynt*.

Burt Reynolds
(February 11, 1936—September 6, 2018)

When the original *Match Game* aired on NBC, Burt Reynolds was just another up-and-coming young actor then working here and there on various television series. By the time the show was revived on CBS,

Reynolds was a bona-fide movie star, one of the biggest of the era. He was also a close friend of Charles Nelson Reilly, and by that point, of Gene Rayburn.

During one taping of the show Burt found himself in the halls of CBS Television City, and decided to drop in to the set. Gene had just gone to commercial break, and went to the edge of the stage to answer a few audience questions. Suddenly the audience heard him loudly exclaim, "Excuse me, sir! We're taping a TV show!" The audience was shocked to discover Burt Reynolds moving toward the stage, as he and Gene greeted each other warmly and ccarried on a brief conversation, even as the show faded in following the commercial break. Realizing the cameras were rolling, Gene provided a hasty introduction and Reynolds graciously announced, "I got my start on this show, and I just wanted to come back and say hello. You know what I mean? I've always loved you and I've always respected you."

Then he acknowleged his close friend Charles Nelson Reilly by saying, "I wanted to come over here and see Charlie, because Charie was so great on the Tonys. Wasn't he brilliant on the Tonys?" (Charles appeared on the 1974 Tony Awards presentation and poked fun at his own supporting-actor status in the Broadway shows *Bye, Bye Birdie, How to Succeed at Business, Hello, Dolly!* and *Skyscraper* before launching into his big number *It Only Takes a Moment* from *Hello, Dolly!*) Burt's visit perfectly illustrated the spontaneous moments that brought magic to *Match Game* tapings.

Nipsey Russell

(September 15, 1918 – October 2, 2005)

In closing one episode of *Match Game '75*, Gene Rayburn announced to the cameras, "We'd like to close with a thought for the day, friends. Something pithy and full of wisdom. And we call on the poet laureate, Nipsey Russell." Whereupon Mr. Russell recited, off the cuff:

"The young people are very different today,
and there's one sure way to know:

Kids used to ask where they came from,
now they'll tell you where you can go."

The multi-talented actor, comedian, dancer, and poet started his career onstage in nightclubs and by making comedy albums before his 1957 appearance on *The Ed Sullivan Show* led to appearances on *The Tonight Show* (then hosted by Jack Paar) and a supporting role on the classic sitcom *Car 54, Where Are You?*

But Nipsey Russell will forever be remembered for his many appearances on game shows. His quick wit and brilliant improvisational skills made him the "poet laureate of television," able to make up limericks and poems on the spot, which made him a talk show and game show favorite.

In 1964 Russell became the first black performer to become a regular panelist on a network TV game show when he joined Goodson-Todman's *Missing Links*, hosted by Ed McMahon. He worked variously as a celebrity panelist on Goodson-Todman shows like *What's My Line?* and *To Tell the Truth* (and throughout its various seventies and eighties runs on the Bob Stewart-created *Pyramid*), as well as the pointedly appropriate poem-themed game show *Rhyme and Reason*, hosted by Bob Eubanks. His hosting skills were put to use on a couple of game show pilots before he was tapped to work on two separate runs of Barry-Enright's *Juvenile Jury* and Sande Stewart's *Your Number's Up*.

Soupy Sales
(January 8, 1926 – October 22, 2009)

Comedian Milton Supman, better known as Soupy Sales, began hosting his legendary kids' TV program *Lunch With Soupy Sales* first locally in his native Detroit before the show was picked up nationally.

Elliot Feldman recalled, "*Lunchtime With Soupy* was the best kids show ever. I met Soupy once when I worked on *Match Game*. I told him that I was a Detroit Birdbath and he didn't want to hear about it. Back then he was more interested in being a panelist on a Mark Goodson game show." (Soupy called all of his fans Birdbaths. "Well, you look for different things in doing a show, different gimmicks," recalled Soupy. "I came up with the thing of 'Birdbaths.' I said, 'Birdbath...you're a Birdbath.' ...And all of a sudden it caught on and we started the Birdbath Club.")

"A few years after that I met his two musician sons," Feldman continued. "They were only impressed when I told them that I'd sneak into my parents living room to watch Soupy's late night show."

Debralee Scott
(April 2, 1953-April 5, 2005)

Debralee Scott freely gave her birth date to me, something rare among actresses: she was born April 2, 1953 in Elizabeth, New Jersey. While her film credits include *Dirty Harry, American Graffiti*, and *Police Acadamy*, she is best known for her TV roles as Rosalie 'Hotzy' Totzy on *Welcome Back, Kotter*, as Cathy Shumway on *Mary Hartman, Mary Hartman* and *Forever Fernwood*, and as Donna Pescow's kid sister on *Angie*. Debralee had that sarcastic New York sense of humor which made her really down to earth and fun to talk to. So on a rainy New York day, we conversed as she did laundry and baked a blueberry pie. In fact, at the time she was studying at the French Culinary Institute.

"I actually started acting just because I wanted to do game shows," she joked. "No. Well, you know, I really loved game shows. I really liked sort of intelligent game shows. Like I was one of the top female players on the *Pyramid*, and I liked the *Match Game* because it was sort of funny...I liked Password a lot. So I liked word games. I also liked the fact that—one reason I liked doing them was that people then called me by 'Debralee Scott,' and not 'Cathy Shumway', because they got to know my real name versus just my character name on *Mary Hartman* and *Angie*. And my characters on both those shows weren't the brightest bulbs in the sign, so it made me feel good to show that I was sort of intelligent on these game shows, and that I wasn't just some stupid actress, and that I was actually very smart. So that's why I started to do it; plus I really, really liked it. I really liked, you know, helping people to win. I ran into some person here in New York at one point, and I won him like, I don't know, $20,000 which allowed him to go to law school. And now he's a lawyer. I'm like, 'Give me your card! In case I need one! *Hello*!' I also ran into a guy that I lost money for, but he wasn't too mad at me. But I'm a game player, I like the competition and I love working."

When I repeated Jack Klugman's observation that on *Password* you used your brain and *Match Game* was more of a 'social' game show, she said, "Well, yeah, that was. The *Pyramid* was also one that you had to really not only use your brain more but, I always made sure that, like, I understood where the people came from because you really have to sort of base clues on where they're from. Meaning like one time I had, it was like 'a pawnshop' is what the clue was. And I said 'Three Brass Balls' because you knew the person was from New York and he'd know that three brass balls means—it's what hangs outside a pawnshop. You didn't know that, did you? You're too young."

She didn't recall having watched the show before appearing on it, and when asked how she ended up as a guest panelist on *Match Game* she said without hesitating, "Kay Henley called me. I also had a manager—Judy Thomas at that time—and she was pretty much hired to get me on game shows and like all the talk shows, and that was her primary function. I think she finagled or talked to Kay, who I still—I talked to when I was in L.A. a little while ago. She's such a sweetheart.

"We did have a good time on that show, and I moved from 'ingénue' to the other, to the last seat. I started out in the ingénue seat and then I moved over to the Betty White seat. But I loved, you know, Betty White and Brett and I got along fabulously."

Who was the most fun to work with on the show?

"Richard Dawson," she replied without hesitation. "I don't know. He just had this kind of quiet sense of humor, and I sat next to him a lot, so we would sort of have in-jokes and write to each other, and I just thought he was adorable. I just liked him a lot. I mean, I liked everybody but I felt like I was friendlier with Richard than anyone else on the show, just because we sat next to each other, yeah, and shoot the shit. And he hosted *The Tonight Show* and requested me on *The Tonight Show*, so I did *The Tonight Show* with him.

"I remember two questions that we did. 'Little Johnny, when he picks up a seashell, he hears not the ocean, but <u>BLANK</u>', and I said 'his mother-in-law.' And then it was 'Santa on Thanksgiving, he stuffs turkey with <u>BLANK</u>', and I put 'chopped elves.' Well...it was sort of fun. The meter of the show was, you could do comedy the first part, and then you had to get down and get serious."

"Were there any negative effects from doing the show?" I asked.

"No, I can't think of one. It was so much fun. I have tapes of it, so I watch it—somebody taped it for me. I mean it was a good time had by all."

Like so many others, Debralee suffered a loss in the September 11, 2001 terrorist attacks on the World Trade Center. "The unfortunate thing was I was going to get married to a Port Authority police officer who died in the World Trade Center," she said matter-of-factly. "My fiancé was a Port Authority officer and he went down to help, and the second plane hit the second building. But they found him, so at least his mom, who lives above me, who I take care of, you know, could put her son to rest."

As for what she was up to at the time we spoke, Debralee informed me, "I'm taking cooking classes. I don't know what I'm going to parlay that into. You know, it's my other passion besides acting...I don't know. Maybe I'll meet a cute chef, we'll open a bed-and-breakfast in Vermont, and you can come and visit."

Sadly it was not to be. Debralee Scott passed away on April 5, 2005 at the age of 52.

McLean Stevenson
(November 14, 1929-February 15, 1996)

When Richard Dawson left the show to focus on his hosting duties for *Family Feud*, McLean Stevenson was brought in and more or less groomed to take Richard's spot on the panel. Robert Sherman explained,

McLEAN STEVENSON

An early headshot of McLean Stevenson.

"McLean had done *Tattletales* and *Password Plus* and always brought the right combination, where he played the game really well but he was incredibly funny while playing it well. But when he appeared on *Match Game*, one of the things we noticed was that he had the same knack for anticipation that Richard had. He could anticipate questions and see what the writers were going for and give us exactly what we were hoping for. And he was outstanding at filling a lull and making everything more fun. So we thought McLean would be a good choice to fill that gap and be our new Richard."

"I loved McLean," said Brett Somers. "He came on—they told him he should wear a tie. He came out one day at the top of the show and he just had a tie on and a pair of pants, no shirt. He said, 'Do I have to wear a tie?' and they said, 'Well...' So he came out in a tie.

"But boy was he sorry he left *MASH*. He said, 'I've made a lot of mistakes in my life, but leaving *MASH* was the biggest mistake I ever made.' He was great fun. I loved McClean. He always made me laugh."

Charlene Tilton

Dallas star Charlene Tilton appeared on both *Hollywood Squares* and *Match Game*, and when I asked her about working with Brett and Charles, she admitted, "I don't remember them *at all*. I mean, I only did the show a few times. I really don't remember them at all...It's kind of one of those things—you go in for the day and you leave, you know? And at the time, *Dallas* was such a huge show and we were so busy. I think one season we did like thirty or thirty-two [episodes]. A lot of that stuff is kind of just a blur."

John Travolta

What? You say you don't remember John Travolta's appearance on *Match Game*? Well, there's a reason you don't...

"When *Welcome Back, Kotter* was a hit, I tried to get Gabe Kaplan and the boys," explained celebrity coordinator Kay Henley. "Mr. Kaplan was unavailable, but John Travolta, Ron Palillo, Bobby Hegyes, and

Robert Pine, Brett and Charles, Dolly Read Martin, McLean Stevenson, and Fannie share a moment with Gene.

Lawrence-Jacob Hilton [were available]. Anyway they came into the office. We always asked the celebs to come in and play the game so we would know if they could play the game. Of course the day they came in most of the young girls came to my office to get a glimpse of 'Barbarino.'

"After they were shooed back to their offices, we had the boys come into Ira's office where there was a long conference table and we played the game with them. I have to say that we were really disgusted with Travolta. He was such an ass and every other word out of his mouth was [BLANK]. I realized that he was just a kid, but still, it was a disappointment. The more he acted up, the more the other boys did, but Ron and Bobby could play the game and we did use them—Ron more than once. And Bobby even did *Tattletales* later on."

Marcia Wallace

(November 1, 1942-October 25, 2013)

Marcia (like Bill Daily) gained fame as a supporting cast member of *The Bob Newhart Show*, playing Carol Kester, the wacky receptionist. She has appeared on countless sitcoms and commercials and game shows (including the 1990-91 version of *Match Game* with Charles Nelson Reilly) and is the voice of Bart's teacher Mrs. Krabapple on *The Simpsons*.

"I don't remember," Marcia told me when I asked how she got booked on *Match Game*. "I was on the Newhart show and they were looking for people on shows, and they made you come in and play the game. But I was good at games, and I played the game and they called me. And then the first time they called me, I don't think I did all that well, so they didn't call me again for quite awhile. But once they did...they wanted to sign me, but I was doing *Hollywood Squares* a lot. So there was a little rivalry there.

"Later on when you got a name for yourself, even if they hired you, you still had to go in and play the game. I did a lot of pilots. They would just do pilot run-throughs in front of the network. I was a very good *Password* player. I won a lot of money. People still come up and say, 'You won me ten thousand dollars on *Password*.'"

Marcia indicated she never saw the original sixties *Match Game*, and I asked if she had ever been a big game show watcher. "I hadn't been at all," she admitted. "I was very good at word games like *Password*. I was okay at *Pyramid*. I'm terrible at card games. But of course the most fun was things like *Squares* and *Match Game*, where they wanted you just to be funny and have a good time."

Match Game holds a special meaning for Marcia because she met her best friend while working on the show: Brett Somers. Brett herself recalled the start of that beautiful friendship: "Marcia did *Match Game*, and sometimes I would share my dressing room with some people; like I always shared it with Betty White. So I shared it with Marcia. And I said, 'If I seem a little removed and aloof, it's nothing personal. I just separated from my husband.' And she said, 'Well, that's okay. I just got out of the loony bin.' And we became best friends. We've been best friends for—oh, God, she could tell you how many years. I just talked to her today, as a matter of fact. Oh, she's doing great. I talk to her two or three times a week."

The feeling is mutual. "She's just an amazing woman, just amazing," Marcia said of Brett. "She's my son's godmother, you know. When he was thirteen, some girl—he paged me—and he said, 'Mom! Mom! How old do you have to be to get head?' I said, 'EXCUSE ME!?' And it seems some twelve year-old girl had made him an offer he couldn't refuse. So unfortunately, Brett was in the house at the time. 'Auntie Brett, how old do you have to be to get head?' She said, 'How old are you?' He said, 'Thirteen.' She said, 'That's it!' Stay away from my child, you're a terrible influence!

"Then one time Mikey—she was sending him letters in camp, and I said, 'Brett, Mikey can't read your handwriting.' So she [wrote], 'Dear Mikey, I am sending you a dollar. Your mother tells me you can't read my handwriting. Can you read this? [BLANK] YOU. Love, your Auntie Brett.' Well, he showed it to everyone, and of course I got a call from camp. He said, 'Look at my Auntie Brett! Isn't she funny? Look at my Auntie Brett!' He thinks she is hilarious.

"Well, she *is* Auntie Mame," Marcia continued. "She's his Auntie Mame-Brett. She is a hilarious, loving, one-of-a-kind madcap. And let's be honest, *Match Game* wouldn't have been *Match Game* without Brett and Charles by a long shot. The seventies *Match Game* was very much like a cocktail party; because Brett watches herself and says, 'What's the big deal?' But she just was chatty, and Charles was chatty, and they had this relationship, and 'Darling' and 'Sweetheart' and 'Susan' and 'Vincent.' And everything he said, she fell down laughing. Brett is one of a kind, they both are, and it was magic what they had, absolute magic."

Marcia, Marcia, Marcia

Though it's off-topic, I just had to ask Marcia Wallace about one of her early acting gigs: playing the saleslady who sold little Jan Brady the infamous black wig she wore to Lucy Winters' birthday party in a very special episode of *The Brady Bunch*.

"That was my first job on television," said Marcia, "and it's kind of famous. *Brady Bunch* fans really, really love that show. But that was then. I had more hair, and people always think I wear a wig, so it was perfect that that was what they wrote into it. I'm sure I was hired for my masses of hair that looked like a wig! My very first job and I loved it. And to this very day, thirty years, thirty-five years later, people still come up and say, 'You sold little Jan Brady...'

"I get a lot, too, because I did another one that I barely remember, but it was the Davy Jones episode. I had no scenes with him, but he was a very hot guy in those days."

Don't Look Back!

Life hasn't been all laughs for Marcia Wallace. In 1985 she was diagnosed with breast cancer, and has been lucky enough to beat the disease. Single until her forties, she married in 1986 and has a son; when her husband Denny developed pancreatic cancer, she acted as caregiver during his illness. He passed away in 1992, and Marcia has been a featured speaker and lecturer on the subjects of fighting breast cancer and acting as caregiver to family members who are ill. She has written about her experiences in a memoir titled *Don't Look Back, We're Not Going That Way*.

"This has given me a new lease on life," she says. "You know, after sitting in your house waiting for someone to come along and tell you that you're too old—I've got a book. I wrote a book! It's a good story and people are liking it.

"Now Charles gets some credit for my book because Charles, after every one of my Christmas letters, he's been calling and saying, 'You have to do a one-woman-show, you have to write a book.' And he was going to direct a one-woman-show, but then he got his own. And I believe I sent him a [copy of my] book, because I said, 'Alright, get off my back, here it is. Here's the book.' Probably didn't even read it...

"Brett read it. Brett goes back and forth. Brett is a terrible snob when it comes to *literature*. She says, 'I read three books at a time. I read a work of fiction, a biography, and a work of *literature*.' So she's alternated between 'You're going to have a bestseller' and [with polite disdain] 'Oh, yes, yes, yes, *that book*.' But what she does always is give me credit for, you know, the way I have of hanging in there and selling myself. I always said, 'With your talent and my drive we could rule the world,' because she *fell* into that *Match Game*. She's fallen into everything she's ever done."

The Patron Saint of All Game Show Contestants: Betty White

TV Legend Betty White has earned a special place in game show fans' hearts, as Jim so readily testifies. After appearances on Goodson-Todman shows like *What's My Line?* in the 1950's, she entered the Goodson-Todman family—*literally*—when she married *Password* host Allen Ludden in 1963.

Betty White grew up in Hollywood. "I was born in Oak Park, Illinois, which is a suburb of Chicago. I was born in the Oak Park Suburban Hospital. On one side of the street was Oak Park, and across the street was Chicago. But my folks came out here when I was a year and a half old. I always say, 'I don't think California was a state at that time.' But I say that to young people now and they look at me and they say, '*Really?*' so I've stopped using that joke."

Her late husband Allen used to tease her about her showbiz roots. "That's right," she laughed, and imitated him: "'She's a veteran of silent television,' 'pioneer of silent television.'" But he wasn't far off base: though her first paying gig in television came in 1949, her first actual TV appearance took place a full decade before, when she was just out of high school. She took part in an experimental telecast of the operetta *The Merry Widow* shot in a building in downtown Los Angeles. Wearing

Betty White in her usual spot in the sixth seat, parked next to Richard Dawson.
Photograph taken from a proof sheet found in Gene's collection

thick, heavy pancake makeup and blinded by the hot, bright lights, she made her debut.

"Yep," she remembered. "That was *interesting*. A hundred and fifty degrees, and it was upstairs over a Packard Showroom; it was an automobile showroom. We did the show upstairs on like the fifth floor and it was shown downstairs in the showroom where the parents and people like that had to stand around the cars and look at this crude little monitor. But it was a start—it was my first television."

When I said, "I guess it really *was* silent television," she laughed and replied, "It was as close as you can get!"

I asked Betty how she first got involved with *Match Game*, and she replied, "Well, I lived in California, of course, and Allen and I fell in love. He lived in New York, and I wasted a whole year we could have been together by saying no, I wouldn't marry him. I didn't want to move to New York, but I did make several trips back there. He was doing *Password* at that time. Originally I was invited—I used to do *The Jack Parr Show*,

In one memorable episode, Richard Dawson imitated Brett (while wearing her eyeglasses) while Betty White imitated Charles also while wearing his own cap and glasses. Brett and Avery Schreiber were amused. (Taken from a proof sheet found in Gene Rayburn's estate.)

and every time I was in New York I would do Jack's show. And Mark Goodson kind of got wind of that, so he invited me when I came back, would I do *What's My Line?* and some of the other game shows. So when he started *Match Game* he invited me to be kind of a semi-regular when I was in the vicinity. And it was such fun because *Password* and *What's My*

Line? and all those were very different kinds of shows, but *Match Game* was so silly. And Gene Rayburn, who was the original host, was just as silly as anybody on the panel, so it made it great fun."

Anyway, Betty had a ball on *Match Game*. "Oh, they were wonderful," she said of her cohorts. I asked her favorite people to work with on the show. "Oh, Richard Dawson was great and good fun. Charles I think was my favorite because he was so antic. He never called me anything but 'Cynthia.' I never called him 'Charles' in my life; he was always 'Victor.' Don't ask me why. But when you've been with game show nuts, you're playing games on and off screen.

"The most fun was our meals together. We'd break after the third show and have a meal, then come back and do two more shows. And it was those meal breaks that got us all going and had such fun. It was just marvelous. People used to say, 'Do you drink at those meal breaks? What is it?' No, we just giggled and laughed and scratched together, and got to know each other so well we'd know what the other guy was going for. It was great fun."

For Betty White, being a staple on game shows had its benefits. "It was like stealing money," she admitted. "My mother and father and I—I was an only child, and growing up we used to play games around the breakfast table. And my father, when I started doing so many different game shows, said 'For all those years you gave it away, and now you get *paid* for playing games?' He said, 'I don't understand it.' And it *is* like stealing money, because you go in and you do five shows with delightful people and call it a job. I never thought it was really what you might call *working* for a living."

We talked a bit about the differences between the later versions of *Match Game* and the classic seventies version. "I think they played it a little straighter," said Betty. "They were trying to play the game, but they lost some of the edge by losing some of the fun. In the early games— remember the end game where you had to pick the word with three clues? Well, one day we had <u>BLANK</u> willow. Well, you can imagine, with that crowd onstage, what happened. And it happened to be weeping willow, tit willow, and pussy willow. Between Gene Rayburn and Charles Nelson Reilly and Dickie Dawson, it was what we *didn't* say that was kind of fun, rather than what we *did* say. But you have to have people who trust each other and love each other a lot so that you can banter back and forth."

"And it was just one of those games that if you enjoyed playing, you could relax and really take part. If you came in a little stiffly or tried to *listen* to what you said—you had to go with your first impression. If you listened to what you said, it got awfully kind of planted. So you didn't listen, you just let your mouth go, and hoped your mental editor would keep you straight.

"And the toughest spot to be in was number six, because by the time they'd get down to number six, everybody had said as much obvious—it was not an easy game. It looked like the easiest game in the world, but to keep it fresh or fun you had to kind of try to work *with* others as a team rather as opposed to just working for yourself."

That fits in line with what Jim Colucci, author of *Golden Girls Forever*, the ultimate celebration of Miami's most famous fictional lanai, told me when I asked him for the key to Betty's appeal as a *Match Game* panelist.

"Before *The Mary Tyler Moore Show* and *The Golden Girls*, Betty was best known for her prowess on game shows—the woman is brilliant! And yet, she also has such a quick wit, and can deliver a double-*entendre* perfectly. So when Betty would appear on *The Match Game*, I would wonder: which part of her brain will win out? Will she go for the joke answer, or the smart one for the win? Luckily for contestants and their bankbooks, Betty's generosity of spirit—or more precisely, her famous competitive nature—would always win the day."

During the course of my conversation with Betty, a 'friend' of hers was barking in the other room. "Oh, a man has the temerity to pull his truck up in front, and Nikita has to announce everybody that goes by. He's my golden retriever. He's nine. He'll be ten in January." Betty's reputation as an animal lover is not underestimated: "Well, that's half my life. My life is divided—half animals, and half show business, the two things I love best. You can't ask for anything better than that."

At last it was time to go, and I thanked Betty for her time and her graciousness, and wished her luck with her future projects.

"Thank you," she replied. "I'm having a wonderful time. I just finished a movie for the Hallmark Channel, and I'm going to take it easy for a little while because it was a four week shoot and I was in every blinkin' scene! It'll be out in November. I'm tired is what I am, but you know the next job that comes by, I have no willpower; I'll just say yes."

The Brett-Betty White 'Feud'

Consider the following exchanges between Brett and Betty:

Brett: (to Gene) "Now don't yell at me, I'm almost finished."
Betty: "You've got that right....She's got about one good year left."

Brett: "I just want Betty White to know I killed seven flies on the way here."
Betty: "She *talked* them to death."

Brett: "I'm the first one finished!"
Betty: "You were finished a long time ago, sweetheart!"

"They were the best of friends," said Ira Skutch.

And yet, there were times when Brett Somers and Betty White traded barbs worthy of a *Dynasty*-era Krystle-and-Alexis catfight! "I don't know," Betty confessed to me, "because I didn't watch *Dynasty*! But we had lots of fun with it, and of course, nobody ever took anything seriously. We liked each other very much."

I asked Brett Somers if she felt people took their insults seriously. "I don't think so. I loved Betty, you know. Betty is the nicest—she is the epitome of the word 'nice,' and man, she's faster than the speed of sound...You know, she comes across as 'Okay,' and everything, but—you can't top her, boy. You can try but you never will top her. She's really wonderful. I love Betty. And we always shared a dressing room. Because there were certain people...like Marcia Wallace always shared my dressing room, and Fannie and Betty, and people like that. Other people went down the hall. Because I had my own bathroom and my own dressing room and that was nice. But we always shared. We'd hang out and scream and yell and shout."

Initially when asked about Brett, Betty replied, "Oh, Brett was a piece of work. We used to dress together in the dressing room to change, because we'd do five shows a day, and you'd change wardrobe between each show, and I was the only one she'd allow to dress with her. And she never said a nice thing to me like you do if you really like somebody! You know, you don't dare say something nice to them, because we were great friends, but we teased each other unmercifully. So she was a very strong lady, and not a very positive one. There were a lot of things she didn't like, but it made her very funny on the show, and she *thought* funny."

....And Our Vote For Most Incongruous Guests Ever: Kukla And Ollie (A.K.A. Burr Tillstrom)

(October 13, 1917-December 6, 1985)

Dwight Whitney put it best in a 1970 profile for *TV Guide*:

"There was a time way back there in the pre-hippie 50s when Oliver J. Dragon III, an incurably romantic hand puppet with one tooth and soulful button-eyes; his bulb-nosed little friend Kukla; and their zany 'Kuklapolitan' pals were as big with the short-pants set as Santa Claus or the giant Popsicle. *Kukla, Fran and Ollie*, on which a whole generation grew up, was the Old Vic of children's TV shows, and Ollie its Sir Laurence Olivier."

Behind every great puppet, there is a great and talented puppeteer, and Chicago-born Franklin Burr Tillstrom was an integral part of the historic

Gene and Helen Rayburn posing with old friends Burr Tillstrom, Fran Allison, and a couple of friends on the set of *Kukla, Fran and Ollie*.

Kukla, Fran and Ollie, one of the first programs to be regularly broadcast on television. Having worked on the beloved children's show out of the University of Chicago, Tillstrom and radio star Fran Allison's unscripted conversations drew an *audience* of kids as well as adults such as Thornton Wilder, Robert E. Sherwood, Leland Hayward, Lotte Lenya and Kurt Weill, Lillian Gish, and even John Steinbeck. Despite its popularity, the show went through its ups and downs, disappearing for a few years before being revived in the 1970's.

So, how did Brett Somers, for one, like working next to puppets?

"That's right! They were on the show!" exclaims Brett. "I don't even remember, I've got to tell you. Well I must say, I just treated them like they were real people, you know...I never felt uncomfortable."

Review Questions

1. When Bart Braverman was just a kid, he appeared on an episode of <u>BLANK</u>.

a. *I Love Lucy*
b. *The Edward Gorey Comedy Hour*
c. USA's *Up All Night* with Rhonda Shear and a really dirty movie cut to ribbons

2. Gabor beauty secrets include <u>BLANK</u>.

a. A paper bag
b. An alleged eye-lift and great skin
c. Slapping a police officer

3. According to Fannie Flagg, her favorite T-Shirt featured <u>BLANK</u>.

a. Two fried eggs.
b. Mickey Mouse being arrested for slapping a police officer.
c. Her phone number.

Answers: 1 a, 2 b, 3 a.

11

How To Catch a Star
(Even If They Aren't Falling)

Everybody wants to know how to get a star's attention, right? Let's find out from someone who succeeded just how it can be done. Kay Henley worked as celebrity co-ordinator on *Match Game* throughout its popular run in the seventies, and worked closely with the stars and their representatives.

"I had taken my grandmother to see *Beat the Clock* starring Dennis James," said Kay, explaining how she got involved with the world of game shows, "because she watched it every day. After the show was over, Rick McClun gave the audience members forms to fill out to be contestants. I filled out a form and was called to be on it. After that, they called me to be a contestant on another show they were testing on KTLA (can't remember the name. I think it was *Show Me!*). Then I got called to be a contestant on *You Don't Say!* I had met Ralph Edwards at the *Beat the Clock* taping and he took us all out to a restaurant where during the conversation I heard Ralph was looking for a secretary. I was working at Don Fedderson Productions at the time, in the accounting office.

"I worked for Andrews-Yagemann Productions for ten years. Started as a secretary/talent coordinator—Ralph Edwards's secretary. Booked the talent on *You Don't Say!* starring Tom Kennedy. As time passed, Ralph asked me if I wanted to stay his secretary or become full-time talent coordinator as we had several shows on the air at the time and I of course said, 'Hey, I can always be a secretary. I'll stick with the talent coordinating.' Years later when I read in the trades that *Password* was coming to L.A., I called Allen Ludden and told him that our shows were all going and it didn't look like anything else was in the works, so if there's a chance, I'd love to book *Password*. Allen put in a good word for me and I had an interview on Friday and began working at Goodson-Todman the following Monday. *Password* was the first show of Goodson-Todman's in L.A.. The fun part was: Rita Moyes was the Associate Producer and she and I had worked together at Andrews-Yagemann since I first started on *You Don't Say!* Also, the director, Stu Phelps [and] John Harlan. So the three of us left Ralph Andrews and went to work for Goodson-Todman. Rita Moyes had already been hired because she worked on *Password* in New York.

"I stayed with Goodson-Todman for nine years as talent coordinator but I left there on a Friday and worked for them the next day as a stand-in on one of the other shows (I forget which one). I continued to work for Goodson-Todman off and on for about three or four years in different capacities. I had left Goodson-Todman because I wanted to try my hand at acting and I told Mr. Goodson that. I told him I didn't want to regret not trying and he was very understanding. Normally when someone left G-T, they were never heard of again. But Mr. G. was very good to me and I will always appreciate that fact.

"A typical day for me in the *Match Game* office at 6430 Sunset Boulevard: I spent a lot of time on the phone, contacting agents, managers and public relations people, making offers for celebs.

"I called them all, but found the publicists were the most understanding and more interested in the exposure than the dollars involved. Most of the agents I dealt with have gone on to other things or passed away. If I knew the celeb, would call direct. I spent much of the time on the typewriter: once a celeb was 'booked,' I'd type a memo and pass it on to the producers. Then I'd make up a three-by-five card with all the info on the celeb, plus the tape and air dates. I'd type up contracts and send to the contact or celeb. Contact AFTRA to make sure the celeb was paid up. Get a photo if I didn't have one on file. I'd type a letter to the celeb regarding what colors not to wear, how many changes of clothing to bring and a general reminder of the time and place. Notified all that needed the names; i.e. graphics at CBS, Production Manager, and so on."

"What was the criteria by which you picked celebrity panelists?" I asked.

"They had to be able to play the game a little, have [a] fun personality and depending on who the other celebs were, be known to our audiences. As time passed, we kept most of the same people, rotating them each week and bringing in a new one when we found ones that fit our show.

"We tried to get 'bigger' name celebs for *Match Game PM* but usually stayed with the tried and true. I think we ended up taping six shows a day and one would be a *PM* or maybe three and three. I know they got a few more bucks for the nighttime show (Don't ask how much, I don't remember).

"There were many stars that I tried to get but the reps would say they wouldn't do a game show, or they were too busy, or they were going out of the country, and on and on. Needless to say, I tried every major star that I felt there might be a chance of getting, both on TV and in the movies. Also, begrudgingly, many I knew never would appear on a game show. I gave a lot of reps good laughs asking for them. Often I would get direct phone numbers and call. Ninety-nine percent of the ones I spoke with directly were very courteous in turning me down. I'd read *Celebrity Bulletin* to see who was in town and even call them at the hotel where they would be staying. Unfortunately I can't remember who I spoke to anymore. The stories that stick in my mind are from Andrews-Yagemann Productions because I was new at it then (Like chasing Danny Thomas into the men's room at NBC, trying to get him to guest on *It Takes Two* with his wife. Or calling Charleton Heston at home to guest on *You Don't Say!*). Although I was and still am star-struck, by the time I was booking MG, I just called or stopped whomever on the street and made a fool of myself asking but was a little more mature then, so that's maybe why my mind is a blank when it comes to names of those people.

"I have to interject this: many times I would campaign for stars, drive the producers nuts bringing up their names over and over. Sometimes I would win but many times I wouldn't. It broke my heart not being able to bring in so many of the *You Don't Say!* people and all the people I had worked with at A-Y.

"We taped on Stage 33. When we taped early, *The Bold & The Beautiful* and *The Young & The Restless* would be going too. Our stars usually wouldn't have time to go visit and I doubt they would. *MG* wouldn't be taping at the same time as *Price is Right* because we both used the same stage. *Feud* taped at ABC. *Tattletales* taped on 41 but I don't recall a conflict; the producers were the same and managed to have the schedules made up accordingly.

"On tape days I'd be at the studio to make sure the dressing rooms were open, basket of fruit in the rooms, etc. Then I'd greet the celebs as they came in, helping carry their wardrobe, showing them where the makeup people and hairdressers were located, etc. Once they were settled, I would take them to makeup and hair and keep tabs on them so they'd be ready when the stage manager needed them on stage. I'd be in the booth with the director during the taping and then ran back down to see if anyone needed anything (sodas, water, whatever) and get all of them changed and back on stage before the next show. We started doing three shows on one day and two the next but as time passed went into five shows in one day. That seemed best for all concerned. It also, in some cases, made it easier to get a 'big' name celeb. Big in the sense they had a recognizable name and/or were in a series. We would have a dinner break between the third and fourth shows. We always had a catered meal in one of the rehearsal halls.

"I was glancing over my lists to see if anything came to mind about *Match Game* celebs. I'm sure there must have been problems but they had to be minor or I'm sure I'd remember them. Only one thing that happened that irritated me and shocked me as well. One day I was late in getting down to the Artists Entrance to meet one of our celebs from NYC. As I was waiting for the elevator to go down, the door opened and she came out with all of her 'stuff' and just dropped it all in front of me and walked off to the studio. I picked up the clothes and bags and ran after her trying to apologize but she was miffed and didn't get over it until the break. I had never seen her behave like that before so I was very surprised. We worked together again after that and she was fine. Guess she had had a bad flight or something. Who knows?

"We never knew what to expect until the star would come in and play the game. On rare occasions when the star was considered important enough by the producer, to not have to come in and play, it usually ended up being not such a good show. So many of the stars thought that they could play the game because they thought it looked easy on TV. What they didn't realize was that if they weren't clever and funny, the show would suffer. I doubt if they understood even after they appeared. Needless to say they weren't asked back.

"One of the most exciting shows was when Ethel Merman guested and after the shows, Brett Somers and I took her to Chasen's. She was a lot of fun and really nice and a time I will cherish.

"Arlene Francis was another one I was happy to meet, having seen her on TV for so many years. I picked her up at the airport and drove her to the hotel. She was such a lady and wouldn't even let me help her with her bags. The day she left, she gave me a pin she was wearing, a horse with diamonds (faux) and emerald eyes. Just took it off her lapel and said she wanted me to have it to remember her by. I still have it.

"I loved country music, so when Minnie Pearl guested, I wore an outfit in her honor. A friend who was one of the stars of *Hee Haw* [George

Lindsey—'Goober'] had sent me a pair of overalls, with donkeys and chickens in yellow and red, like the ones some of the cast wore on the show. They were large and I wasn't (at the time) so I took them to a dressmaker and had her make them into a jumper. Sounds weird, but it turned out to be very cute. I wore a red t-shirt under it. Big straps with buckles, like farmers would wear in the field. Anyway, Fannie Flagg saw what I was wearing and talked me into letting her wear it on the show. It was hysterical. Fannie is very endowed (not me) so we had to pin it around the top so it would fit. In any event, it went over big with Minnie and we all had fun about that.

"One guy that was a friend and one of the most naturally funny guys I've ever known was Alfie Wise. He was a friend of Burt Reynolds, too. Anyway, I knew Alfie when he was Ralph Wise, a page at NBC. You could always tell he'd been by in the hall at NBC, because of all the people falling down with laughter from his comments. He played the short cop with Jackie Gleason in one of Burt's movies and later was in a short-lived series with Lou Ferrigno [of *The Incredible Hulk*] playing paramedics or something. He also had a side line making jackets which he sold to many shows. His shop was on Riverside next to the *Now, Voyager* bar.

"I would even wear his 8x10 pinned on the front of my shirt. Finally they let me book him. I think he did a good job, they didn't. To tell the truth, I think Alfie, knowing how tough it was to get him on and how long it took to get him on, put pressure on him so he was nervous. But even then he was good and they should have let him come back again!

"In going over the list and comparing it to my schedules showing all the people, it warms my heart remembering them; and saddens me when so many are gone now. I still think of 'Deac' (Richard Deacon) every time I go into the cupboard and see his cookbook.

"Aside from my memory going, I was working on other shows at the same time as I was on MG, so some of my memories conflict, as we used some of the same stars on the other shows too.

"I just thought of another actress that came in to play the game. All the guys were hot to meet her because she looked gorgeous and sexy in her photo. When she came in, they didn't recognize her. She almost didn't get booked but because she played great and was clever and funny, we hired her.

"So many 'Where are they now?' names. So many passed away. So very, very sad."

Why Do Game Shows?

It's pretty obvious why the show would want celebrities to make appearances on the panel, but what's in it for the celebs? Jack Klugman was quick to point out that. unless you were a regular, you didn't make much money.

As Betty White pointed out, the game shows sometimes brought people together, building friendships that have lasted for over a quarter of a century; Betty still keeps up with Brett and the gang. Said Fannie Flagg, "Brett and Charles, myself and a few others were very close and did socialize. Brett and Charles are still two of my best friends although I do not see them as often as I like." Asked who amongst the MG troupe she still keeps in contact with, she replied, "Brett and Charles and the producer Ira Skutch."

When I mentioned Kay Henley to Dolly Read Martin, she exclaimed, "Oh, Kay! Oh, I love Kay. You know that we still exchange Christmas cards, Kay and us, and we look forward to it every year. And she's such a doll."

"Nowhere else," said Nipsey Russell, "can an entertainer attain the same instantaneous recognizability with the public as on a game show. On television, your face is there in a person's living room for a full minute at a time, far longer than in a movie close-up, and at a far more intimate range than in a nightclub. That allows people to develop a warm feeling toward you that is absolutely impossible anywhere else."

Patty Duke mused upon the same idea. "When you walk down the street and a total stranger sings a 40-year-old theme to you [theme to *The Patty Duke Show*], you go, 'Someone was paying attention.' I love it! Strangers nod and smile or call out 'I love you.' What a nice way to go through life. Other people don't even say 'excuse me' to other people, and a total stranger is sending me love vibes."

"Many of the celebrities who participated did so because the atmosphere on the show was so conducive to their enjoyment," observed Ira Skutch, "both on stage and during the breaks between the shows."

"You know what a game show does for you?" asks Brett Somers, rhetorically. "It gets you a cab in New York City. It gets you a good table in a restaurant. Those are the advantages. And all the hookers know you! I was walking up Eighth Avenue one night, and this girl—she must have been seven feet tall!—she leaned out of this big, white limo, and she said, 'Hi Brett! I love you! I watch you every day on *Match Game*!' And obviously her pimp was driving the car. You get *maitre d*'s, cops, cops who work the night shift. A friend of mine used to get so mad. The cops would stop me and they'd go, 'Brett! Aw, gee whiz,' and then they'd let me go, and she's go, 'God damn it!' It pissed her off. Great advantage.

"Once I was on my way to the airport. I'm trying to get a cab in New York to Kennedy, and the cab driver pulled over and the guy said, 'Get in.

Where are you going? You're going to Kennedy?' And he saw I had a suitcase. I said, 'Could you get me?' He said, 'Get in. I'll give you a lift!'

"So it has a lot of advantages. I never dogged *Match Game*. I always had a good time doing it, I loved Ira, I loved Kay; there were a lot of people that were very sweet. It was fun. It was the kind of fun it looked like, and that was because of the atmosphere that someone like Ira Skutch created, you know? And people didn't say, 'You can't do this, and you can't do that,' they just let you go. And they didn't try to make it more than it was; you know, when you do *Hollywood Squares*, they give you a joke. Well, I'm not good at that. I'm either funny on my own or not. As a result, *Hollywood Squares* isn't the kind of fun to do that *Match Game* was."

"It was Kay, who was always a dear friend and really helped my career a great deal," remembered Pat Harrington, when talking about how he ended up a guest panelist. He added, "All these game-show things were kind of fun."

But doing the game show circuit has its drawbacks, no doubt about it. Not everyone feels it, of course, but Betty White notwithstanding, there has always been something of a stigma attached to celebrities appearing on game shows. "You can't do anything else once you do game shows," Charles Nelson Reilly once told an interviewer. "You have no career."

Fannie Flagg disagreed. "No negative effects that I know of. And I have a lot of people come to my book signings and tell me they loved *Match Game*."

Brett was sympathetic to Charles' plight. "Because he has this career, he's directed, he's directed opera, he's done all these things. And how do people know him? *Match Game*!" She continues, "He's just like, 'I have no feeling—.' But—gets you a good seat in a restaurant, cab drivers recognize you, pick you up, now I'm for that! No qualms."

Character actress Teresa Ganzel, who appeared later on the ill-fated *Match Game-Hollywood Squares Hour* and often played on the various *Pyramid* shows says, "My agents just started getting phone calls requesting me. I truly did game shows because I loved doing them. I was making really good money (unlike now!) so it wasn't about that. I simply thought they were a blast to do. I have always loved playing games at parties....I got a huge kick out of meeting the celebrities and used to love having game show fans come up to me and tell me how much they enjoyed seeing me on an episode of *Hollywood Squares* or whatever. Many times people would say that watching the *Pyramid* show, for example helped them learn the English language, which I found a surprising benefit of game shows.

"I remember eventually my agents as well as a few casting directors told me I had to stop doing the game shows. They said I was coming across too much as a 'personality' as opposed to an actress. They said it was getting harder to get me auditions for certain things because I was getting over-exposed on those shows. In retrospect I fear they were right. But at the time when I would be asked to go play a game for a day I'd think what could be more fun. However I think it is smarter to do them if you have had a long running series and are already so closely identified with one particular role that you are not risking anything career-wise.

"The truth is that if I were ever lucky enough to be on a series again I probably would go right back to the game show circuit! I probably didn't learn my lesson because they were so much fun!"

Orson Bean, a forty-year-plus game show veteran says, "Well, the drawback was, if you did enough of that stuff, you got to be known for that. People didn't know that I was on Broadway for twenty years from like 1952 to 1973, one show after another. You got a reputation as 'just a game show person,' or being 'famous for being famous,' you know, that kind of stuff. And, you know, that hurt. And it didn't at the time, but after the fact, it took me quite a while to be considered for serious roles. But I didn't care much because it was fun."

A wide variety of celebrities graced the *Match Game* panel, starting with this crew taping the first episode following the pilot: From left, Michael Landon, Joanne Pflug, Richard Dawson, Gene, Vicki Lawrence, Anita Gillette, and Jack Klugman.

Review Questions

1. Perks of the job of celebrity coordinator can include <u>BLANK</u>.

a. Filling in as host when Gene Rayburn takes the day off.
b. Chasing Danny Thomas into a men's room to get him to come on your show.
c. Making sure the coffee is made *just right*.

2. Brett Somers claims that one of the perks of doing game shows is <u>BLANK</u>.

a. Your marital woes will end up on the cover of the *New York Post*.
b. It insures Jack Klugman will never speak to you again.
c. All the hookers know you.

3. What does Teresa Ganzel say is a surprising benefit to wtching game shows?

a. It wins you a refrigerator.
b. It helps people learn the English language.
c. You can learn the retail price of a box of Rice-a-Roni.

Answers: 1. b., 2. c., 3. b.

12

Well, Somebody Had To Play The Game, Right?

Well, somebody had to play the game, right? I mean, that's the whole point of the show, isn't it? And of course somebody had to book those contestants, too. Diane Janaver was associate producer on *Match Game* in New York before moving to Los Angeles. "I left Goodson-Todman when it was over," she said of the New York run of *Match Game*. "I came out here to work for Dinah Shore. Dinah paid my way out here, my husband and I came out, and I worked for her out here. And then Goodson-Todman came out with the *Match Game* out here, and they already had a celebrity person working for them because Kay Henley had done *Password* and she had the contacts. So she did what I'd done on the old show with the celebrities, and they asked me to come and do contestants. At that point Dinah was going off the air, and the timing was just perfect."

And so Diane moved from booking celebrities on the show to booking the contestants. "Doing contestants was a whole completely different thing," she said. "First of all, after the quiz scandals everyone was very

Occasionally the contestants got a little overzealous, even for a seasoned pro like Gene Rayburn.

careful. Everyone was very separate. So we could not go near the celebrities or the staff....When you'd go to the studio, they were kept separate. They couldn't even go to the men's room or the ladies' room by themselves. They didn't want to take any chance of anybody cheating about anything, so we had to be very careful that way. We had our own area."

Brett confirmed that there was no fraternization between the contestants and panelists. "No," she said, "the contestants were not allowed to speak to *you*. If you went by and said, 'Hi, darling,' [it was alright]. They were told not to speak to the panelists."

Diane continued, "I knew Brett from kind of being around, but as I said, the contestants had to be so separate from those people that I really didn't see them very much on show day. When I came out here I did *I've Got a Secret* out here, before *Match Game*, and I booked Richard Dawson as talent on that syndicated *I've Got a Secret*, and he was great. Booked him for one shot and then we kept him on for the whole series. And then from that, and since I knew him, put him on the show. I knew Richard, and I know Charles—I still see him occasionally."

Getting contestants was easy. "The show became very popular," continued Diane. "We had a lot of people write in. We really didn't have to do anything else. There was a plug on the show saying 'If you want to be a contestant, please drop us a letter, or call the number,' and we'd give that on the air." (Fannie Flagg told me, "I was happy to see a Southerner on the show. But as I recall most of the contestants were from Southern California.")

Diane continued, "I had an assistant. What we used to do was to call in groups at a time. I think we'd have twenty-eight people, and we would look at people ahead of time, and they would come in and they would sit around the edge of a good-sized room, and they would fill out a contestant card giving us basic information about themselves, and also whatever shows they might have been on, because there was a restriction. It would have to be a year...before you could come on to play a game show. We got that information and then we took their picture, a Polaroid picture, for their card. And then we would come in and I would explain, you know, the game and the rules, and we would play the game. And in playing the game, you'd get a good idea of what people can do, first of all how well they can play it. It's a simple game but some people couldn't quite do it. And secondly, you could get an idea of people and their reactions. We looked for outgoing people. We looked for a general fun-loving attitude, kind of a sense of humor. But we couldn't take people who were too shy or too straight, because if they're shy, we used to bring them in a group of that size just to know how they would react in front of an audience. If they were too shy and retiring there, we knew they would just fall apart when we got to the studio. So mostly it was that kind outgoing thing, that out-going feeling that you go from people, and it started with—I had my assistant come in to do pictures taken and I would always be because getting two people to stand up in the middle of a room you can get an idea of their attitude and how they are. Then the game playing session.

Gene: (reading the Super Match) "BLANK sour."

Contestant: "Whisky sour."

Gene: "All the winos in the audience *love* your answer."

"You wanted people who could, if a panelist did say something to them, who wouldn't just be frozen, who would be able to answer. And occasionally we would pick someone because they had an unusual something about them. I don't know why, but what comes to mind...a man that we had and his occupation was he painted chickens. I mean, you can see what the panel would do with *that*!"

"He painted little porcelain chickens, or he painted real live chickens?" I asked.

"No, he painted pictures of chickens," she laughed. "Yeah, well, who knew at that point? They had pictures of him [in their minds] out in the

Ready to roll! The contestants were seated at twin consoles on a turntable which, upon gene's introduction, delivered them onstage. Snapshot taken in 1975 by Greg Kleinman for *Broadcast Programming & Production* magazine.

barnyard with his little spray can painting the chickens! But anyway, sometimes we would go for something like that.

"I had a thing when they'd come to the studio. I had to do a whole briefing with them. One part of my briefing was the words you cannot say. One of the contestants at one point who wanted to be a comedienne—you know, we couldn't use actors. We never did. That would give them an unfair advantage. But a lot of people, before they joined AFTRA, came on the show. They were here in California because they wanted to be actors. Kirstie Alley was one of our contestants. I guess you knew that. Brianne Leary. Sure, I remember her. Yes, yes, yes, she was cute.

"But I had a list of words. One of the contestants who wanted to be a comedienne asked me if she could have the rights to use that as part of her act. You know, this thing about words you cannot say on television. So I don't know if she ever did.

"And every time something like this would come up in a room, you know, some contestant would say, can you say something, and my list would grow. I remember saying, 'Please do not say the word *urinate*. If you want to use that word, you have to say *tinkle*. The *Match Game* word is *tinkle*, the *only* word you can use. Do not say *fornicate*, we say *make love*. Please do not use *lay* or *laying* when you're talking about making love, we say *make love*.' God, it's in my brain.

"And also we would pull in more people than we expected to use so that there would be a choice, in case anybody did get [stage fright]. Often people came a second or a third time before they got on the air. So by that time they heard the list so many times...

"I remember one really cute lady who actually froze out there, and she just froze. The turntable came turning out and Gene would introduce the contestants, and when he introduced her she could barely remember her name. Then we went to commercial, and I was there, and Gene said to me, 'Is she okay?' and I said 'Yes, she's going to be fine. She's a funny lady.' 'She's not going to throw up on me, is she?' 'Gene! No, she's not going to do that, just watch.' She won like fifty dollars, and Gene said, 'What are you going to do with your money?' And she said, 'Well, I'm going to buy a house, and a car,' and she started this whole list of stuff. She was fine. She was funny and even in her nervousness she was fun. She was not one of those people you feel sorry for. She was an animated, nervous person, and it's funny, it worked out great.

"I think it is also that initial thing when the little platform used to turn out. If they could just get past that first thing of lights, they were okay again. And again, if I was concerned about them, I would make them come back the next time."

> "Do you know how many polyesters they had to kill for this suit?"
> —Contestant

Some contestants did the show for the sheer fun of it, some to just get on television. Some may have figured it was one way to get Richard Dawson's attention. But let's face it—most of them did it for the prizes!

"Goodson-Todman had a prize department and it went through them," said Diane. "People filled out and signed a release right there, and when they got off they signed a release for the prize. They got it within three or four weeks. Usually when we told them how long it takes, it was about four weeks, and they would get back the check or whatever prizes they won."

"Did the contestants get to take a copy of the home game with them on their way out?" I asked.

"No, we didn't have those in the studio. The thing we had, we had sweatshirts with '*Match Game*' on it. Everybody got a sweatshirt, a red one with white print or a white one with red print. They were great. I stole a bunch of them for myself. I would take those home."

> "That's very inventive...Most creative losing answer we'll probably ever have on this show."
> —Gene (To a contestant)

The show isn't totally heartless; in a case where a young lady didn't win anything (in the Super Match, the line was *"Split BLANK,"* she went on her own with "Split ends" and lost), Gene gave her a reprieve—for every celebrity she matched, she'd get $100. They broke out an easy one: *"Dumb Dora doesn't want her son to get spoiled, so she keeps him in a BLANK."* The contestant answered with the obvious, "Refrigerator." She ended up matching all six celebs and won $600.

After *Match Game* ended its run, says Diane, "I went on to another show. Goodson-Todman was good about that and often—well, it was to their advantage to that too, of course. I can remember this back in New York—well, no we did it out here, too—you'd be working on a show and another show would come up. They would say, 'Would you like a little extra money?' You know, it was a *lot* of extra money, but it was still cheaper for them than hiring, getting new office space, getting new office equipment, and hiring all new staff.

"I think I went off to something called *Child's Play*, and then after that, I was producing a show called *Blockbusters*, which was a Goodson-Todman show. It was Ira's show, as a matter of fact, and then I produced, co-produced, *Super Password*. There was another show called *The Better Sex*. It was done in '77, that I think came just before *Child's Play*. *The Better Sex* before *Child's Play*, and then *Blockbusters*, and *Super Password* after. Yeah, that's right. Goodness!"

A Few Memorable Contestants

The Host and Panelists weren't the only stars who appeared on *Match Game* over the years; and it just may surprise you to know that a handful of contestants on the show went on to bigger and better things and become celebrities in their own right.

Brian Billick

There was Brian Billick, who was named head coach of the Baltimore Ravens in 1999 and led the team's 34-7 Super Bowl XXXV victory over the New York Giants. In 1977, Billick was a contestant on *Match Game* (along with fellow contestant Marla Marshall) while he was coaching at the University of The Redlands. Brett flirted with him mildly, and he good-naturedly took some ribbing from Richard Dawson when his answers failed to make the grade. Brian shook it off, as any pro-football player is trained to do. He needed six celebrities to match for the win, and five matches to stay in the game, but Lady Luck wasn't on his side. Gene shook Billick's hand and Brian was spun off as the celebs waved goodbye. The final score was Marla 5 to Brian 0. Billick lost that game, but I think the Super Bowl win more than made up for it.

Jenny Jones

Talk show hostess and comedienne Jenny Jones was a contestant in 1981, using her married name of Jenny Wilburn. Game shows were pretty good to Jenny—she was a winner on the game show *Press Your Luck*, and was the first female comic to win on *Star Search* in 1986. "A friend of mine had appeared on *The Price Is Right* television game show," she wrote in *Jenny Jones: My Story*. "Having been there herself, she told me I'd be perfect for the show. Her advice was that I not wear a bra, as she was convinced that's why she was chosen out of an audience of over two hundred people.

"'I can't go braless on TV,' I thought, not because I thought it too racy, but because I was ashamed of my body.

"'You can take a bra with you in your purse and then put it on in the restroom before you enter the studio,' she countered. 'They pick people while they're standing in line.'

"I took her advice, feeling a little guilty about the switch, but it worked. They told me to 'come on down!' and I won $13,000 worth of prizes, including an MG midget sportscar, a recliner, a barbecue, waterskis, a bikini, and $6,000 cash."

Well, that was Jenny's account of her initiation into The Goodson-Todman Hall of Fame. "Still eager to concentrate full-time on my comedy," she continued, "I decided to try another game show.

"I knew *The Match Game* liked bubbly contestants, so I went to an audition and bubbled my way to a spot. *The Match Game* was hosted by Gene Rayburn and featured six celebrities: Betty White, Charles Nelson Reilly, Brett Summers [sic], George Kennedy, Barbara Rhodes, and Bill Daly [sic]. Gene would read a partial phrase, and both the celebrities and contestants would fill in the blank. The match that won for me seems amazingly simple. Gene said: 'Day-old *blank*.' When Betty White and I wrote down 'Day-old bread,' I was $5,500 richer and able to quit temping and finally get serious about comedy."

Of course, Jenny traded comedy for hosting her long-running TV talk show, *The Jenny Jones Show*.

Kirstie Alley

Long before she gained fame on *Cheers*, Kirstie Alley was a *Match Game* contestant, and from the very beginning, she had star power. "I just remember thinking at the time that Kirstie Alley reminded me of Lauren Bacall," said Diane Janaver. "It was something about her look at that point, reminded me very much of that. Her eyes were very green, and she was a pretty girl, no doubt about that. I had a wonderful picture of her on the card that she filled out, a Polaroid that we took, and she was terrific looking, but what happened was, after her year was up I referred her to *Password*, which she did. But the woman doing *Password* had taken a very fuzzy-looking picture of her for her card, so I gave her my good picture as a courtesy. So I can't provide her picture. Isn't that great?"

Oh, well. Kirstie won some money on the show back in 1979 and a dozen years later had a reunion of sorts with Brett Somers at The Emmys. "Isn't that funny?" exclaimed Brett. "Kirstie Alley came up to me—I was with Marcia [Wallace] at the Emmys, and Kirstie Alley was up for an Emmy, and I don't know how it came out but she said, 'Well, if I don't win, I'm going to kill myself.' And I said, 'Don't worry, you're going to win, hon, don't worry about it.' And she said 'You know, I was a contestant on *Match Game*!' I said, 'You're kidding!' And she had been a contestant I guess when she was very young. And she *did* win the Emmy that night.

"I think she's a marvelous actress. I loved her on *Cheers*. She has a wonderful quality. She has a very individual quality, very interesting quality, I think."

Brianne Leary

Brianne Leary holds the singular distinction of having appeared as both a contestant *and* a celebrity panelist on the seventies version of *Match Game*.

"I just auditioned," admitted Brianne. "I was seventeen or eighteen, I was really young...Come to think of it, Alan Bersky—he was a stand-up comedian at the time, then he turned into a manager. And his brother, I think, was in the army and then a contestant. And I was working as a waitress and his family said call, or whatever, go. And I went. You know, you go and audition, or you go apply, and then they interview you, put you in a room. And I thought, 'Well, this could be a fun way to make some money.' You know, working as a waitress is not easy."

Had she seen the show before she ended up as a contestant? "Oh yeah, I think I saw it, probably seen it. Yeah, I think it was a bit of a cultural phenomenon, wasn't it?

"I think I got a letter or something saying I was going to be a contestant, and then I guess I was on. And you know it was nine hundred years ago! I remember specifically I missed the big question... I guess I could have won the big money, I think five or ten thousand, the bigger money. And the clue was 'Parson <u>BLANK</u>.' I don't know if you need that, 'cause I don't know why that sticks in my head. And I didn't know what a 'parson's table' was. I think I said 'parson's pear' or something. Why I remember that after five hundred years, I have no idea.

"It was a fun, goofy time. And I remember thinking, it was extraordinary because I needed the money desperately because I was trying to make money as an actor, and I wasn't really doing that well. I think I'd just been in town for a year, and I remember thinking, 'God, it's so amazing I got chosen to be on the show and I won all this money.' I remember that. And I think I bought a washer and dryer with it, as glamorous as that is. I got sick of the laundromat. And I bought that, I paid taxes, I bought something for my mom, you know, the usual. For some reason, I had sort of a charmed life in that way. I'd be in L.A., and I got work so soon, no training, and not an enormous chest and all that. It was extraordinary, especially at that time. It was like the first thing that, like a lucky charm, kind of happened, and then I got work."

Her career took off when she appeared on *Black Sheep Squadron* and later on *CHiPS*, and as an irony, she returned to the show as a guest panelist, "like, the next year, or year later, because I was on *CHiPS*...I was a little bit savvy at that time. You know, I was really young, twenty. I hired my own PR people and it was Larry Goldman and Stan Rosenfield. That's what PR people did at that time; once you were on a series, you sort of did that roulette of game shows, *The Battle of The Network Stars* and all that kind of stuff. The PR people sort of did that."

Apparently, nobody on *Match Game* remembered she had been a contestant before, but she had fun as a panelist and liked working with the others. "I loved Charles Nelson Reilly. In fact we sort of became friends. He would invite me over to his house a couple of times when he had parties. And Brett Somers had that scraggly voice like, 'Yeah, kid, how old are you? What are you, a fetus?' You know, that kind of thing, but she was terrific. I just liked her so much. And I think Richard Dawson was on the panel when I did it. I only did it a few times, I think. But I don't really remember much of Richard Dawson...mostly I remember Brett and Charles."

In the days since they won big—or didn't!—on *Match Game*, the contestants have gone on with their lives, getting married, raising children, working their jobs, and occasionally catching glimpses of themselves in reruns.

Brian Billick went on to win The Super Bowl, Jenny Jones went on to become Chicago's *other* TV talk show queen, Kirstie Alley starred in *Cheers* and *Veronica's Closet*, became a *Fat Actress* then slimmed down.

> **Gene:** (To contestant) "You're a policeman? Where do you police at?"
>
> **John:** "Huntington Park."
>
> **Gene:** "Huntington Park? (To celebrity panel) Are you going to get the right answer for the policeman?"
>
> **Brett:** "No, I'm going to stay out of Huntington Park!"

But while the aforementioned contestants may have been more celebrated in their respective fields, Brianne's story is possibly the most fascinating of them all.

At the time we talked, Brianne had just returned from Afghanistan. "I was there during the Battle of Tora Bora," she says, "and I was covering it for CNN. And when I came back, Robert Altman optioned my story. I wrote a piece for *O Magazine*. I just finished writing a treatment-slash-bible for him based on my experiences over there. And then I was approached by a literary agent, so [I'm] finishing up the book proposal now.

"The basic genesis of the story is, I was working as a co-anchor for Fox on *Good Day, New York*, and I was basically doing the entertainment stuff. And then September 11th happened and I thought, you know, I want to do something more than entertainment things. And ironically, I'd covered the Soviet occupation of Afghanistan in 1985 as a print journalist. There were people I'd met back in '85 had suddenly gotten into positions of power, and so I was able to get exclusives and report on Afghanistan a lot of people hadn't. I mean, very few people really, this time around in the media, had ever been to Afghanistan.

" Anyway, so that's how all that happened. So I left my contract at FOX, my agent screamed at me, and I went to work for CNN strictly as a freelancer.

"I had a wonderful little munchkin TV career, and I was really young, and it was terrific. But when I got to Pakistan, I was in Islamabad, and unbeknownst to me, I guess they celebrity-searched me. In fact, I know they did because I went to the computer the morning I arrived. One guy said to me, 'You were on *Love Boat*?' and I kind of went, 'What are you talking about?' I swear to God this happened! I went to the computer that morning, it was like six in the morning in Islamabad, and I had just walked out of my contract. And I went to the computer to email people home because I left so quickly, and my name popped up on 'celebrity search.'

"Can you imagine how it must have felt? I went, 'Oh my God!' And everything I had ever done, *Battle of The Network Stars*, and *CHiPS*. And then I thought, 'Oh my God,' like all of a sudden you were doomed because they thought, 'Who the hell is *she*? She's with FOX Entertainment, and CNN has sent her over to go to *Afghanistan*?

"So that was funny, so we laugh because my career is kind of goofy and none of it really makes much sense. Some people just took me at face value and they were terrific, and once they realized my connections because I'd been to Afghanistan before. None of them had, even the well-seasoned people. Um, that was fine. But there were a couple of people who didn't want to give me any kind of respect because I'd been on *CHiPS* or *Love Boat*, you know? And they just thought I was a bimbo, so it was interesting. It certainly made writing the book that much more fun; makes the story more interesting, but funny. People like to peg you in a certain way, and you can never escape that.

"One of the things that was kind of the genesis of my going back to Afghanistan was because FOX didn't let me do anything serious, and the quote about that from my executive producer was 'Brianne, you're hired to entertain, not educate.'

"That was the morning I sort of had an epiphany and I knew I had to leave FOX no matter what. I had to get to Afghanistan. Kabul is falling and I'm the only one that can point to Kabul or Islamabad on the map, and I'm having to give the other anchors, you know, tell them what's what, but I'm not allowed to talk to anyone about it. My assignment was to launch the Girl Scout Cookies, and I was live with little girls dressed like 'Thin Mints.' I'm like, 'Little girls at this Girl Scout Cookie launch, I'm the only one who knows how to pronounce Kabul, it's falling, what is wrong with this picture?' I wanted to kill myself!

"Robert Altman has optioned my story and I've been working with him, which has been extraordinary. I mean, I have been having meetings once a week with him—he's a riot—and then the book thing. So, my goal is not to dance with any more cookies; as long as I can pay my bills, no more dancing with cookies.

"So we'll see. So if you see me dancing with cookies again, you know I just had to pay my mortgage."

Review Questions

1. <u>BLANK</u> will help you get selected to be a contestant on a game show.

a. Using the words *lay* or *laying* when you're talking about *making love*.
b. Reminding the contestant coordinator of Lauren Bacall.
c. Being outgoing and having a fun-loving attitude.

2. Coach Brian Billick <u>BLANK</u>.

a. Lost *Match Game* and won the Superbowl.
b. Lost *Match Game* and won *Password*.
c. Lost *Match Game* and lost his shoes.

3. Brianne Leary says <u>BLANK</u> will insure you are included in the trivia annals.

a. Dancing with cookies on a slow news day on *FOX News*
b. Appearing on *CHiPS* and *The Love Boat*
c. Having Oprah Winfrey's home telephone number

Answers: 1 c, 2 a, 3 b.

13

Slide It, Earl!

Just who WAS that man in the 'Super Match' box?

Fannie Flagg: *"I think it may have been a man named Earl."*
Brett Somers: *"Earl? I never really knew Earl that much. I mean, I knew him, but I was not privy to his life, his love, his—all of that. No, I remember Earl, but I can't tell you anything about him."*
Kay Henley: *"Oh, 'Earl the Pearl.' I can't recall his last name. It's probably on the credits. Earl was inside the box where the Bonus Round was. That was the place where it had spaces for three answers and the winning contestant would pick three celebs to help answer the puzzle. When Gene said, 'Slide it, Earl,' Earl would slide the board out to reveal the answers. He was on camera a few times, great guy."*
Ira Skutch: *"Earl was a CBS prop man. Don't remember his last name, but he was regularly assigned to Studio 33 when the show was there."*

Well, Earl's true identity may be lost to posterity for the moment, but that brings us to the subject of the present chapter. Sure, everyone recognizes Brett and Charles, but far too few people know about the people behind the scenes who made it all come together. At the end of every episode of the show, a list of credits known as 'the crawl' would whiz

Just who was that man in the "Super Match" box? Gene Rayburn (before the end game was renamed) and stagehand Earl Wilson's usual work assignment on taping days.

by, far too fast for most at-home viewers to read. The full listing of credits, known as 'the long crawl,' ran only once a week due to network regulations.

Except for the crew, most of the production staff worked out of the Goodson-Todman Production offices, at 6430 Sunset Boulevard in Hollywood—that is, when they weren't at the TV studios on taping days. According to Kay Henley, the *Price is Right* offices were located on the fourteenth floor, while the *Match Game*, *Family Feud*, and *Tattletales* offices were on the tenth. "Someone was on the fifth for awhile," says Kay, "maybe that was accounting or storage or something. Most of us had our own office. Wait a sec—at first I was in an office with Patricia Fass Palmer (now a producer). She was Ira's secretary. Ira was alone in his office.

Bobby [Sherman] had his office. I think Joel, Joe, Elliot shared a big office. Later it shifted around; Ira had my office, Paul Alter [of *Tattletales*] had Ira's and I had a small office alone."

The fun of 'musical chairs!' Anyway, here we will meet some of those unsung heroes of the television world and learn just what the heck it is they did!

The Director: Marc Breslow
(July 5, 1926-December 1, 2015)

When Marc Breslow passed away in 2015, he was remembered not just as a top-flight director shaping some of the most beloved game shows on television, but as a vast repository of knowledge eager to share the wisdom of his experience.

"Marc was a very nice man," remembered Roger Dobkowitz. "When I arrived at [Goodson-Todman Productions] he sort of took me under his wing." Randy West had a similar experience when hired to work on The Price Is Right. "When I first started on *Price*, he became a good friend of mine, and helped me learn the ropes of working in television. Besides *Price* and *Match Game*, he also directed specials, parades, and other shows." His technical skills were honed to such a degee that it was said that he could (and did) watch a Dodgers game *while similtaneously* directing the show. Breslow's talents can be witnessed in a series of *Match Game* outtakes posted online displaying episodes of the show overlaid with the audio track of his direction to the on-set camera crew and sound booth technicians.

In a rare interview he gave in 1975 to *Broadcast Programming & Production* magazine, Marc Breslow described the challenges he and his colleagues faced in binging *Match Game* to life on the small screen.

"We went though all kinds of growing pains to get it to where we are right now, where everything is smooth and running like a freight train," he explained at the time. "But it was difficult to work out how everything was going to get accomplished...to have indication lights and determine how they are going to be triggeed, the bells, buzzers, how we cleared the

Match Game's Director Marc Breslow

Above, a rare shot of *Match Game* director Marc Breslow in action. Below is a fuzzy snapshot of the director's booth. Both photographs were taken in 1975 by Greg Kleinman.

audience match board, working out the camera shots...all the mechanics. But now that it's all worked out, and everybody knows their jobs, we'll just come in, light up the set, check out the electronics and mikes, see if the fly-in sign that indicates $5,000 o $10,000 is working, and run though a little bit of the game with stand-ins. Taping the show is no longer complicated."

The dawn of the new millennium brought a certain coldness to game show sets. *Who Wants to Be a Millionaire?*, *The Weakest Link* and *Deal or No Deal* boasted dark, foreboding surroundings in which contestants sat or stood under a single spotlight looking as if they'd be hauled off for execution if they gave a wrong answer. Seventies game shows, by contrast, were brightly lit, 'happy' sets where the act of competing for money looked fun, not like punishment.

"I think we've gone through a period of every set looking like what we call 'early pinball,' with flashing lights everywhere. But I still like chaser lights, because to me it's 'gamey.' With all the lights on *Match Game*, it's kind of a razzle dazzle effect to give a feeling of excitement and variety. Game shows geneally have patterns that repeat, repeat, and repeat...so anything you can do to create variety is desirable. Even if it's just changing colors."

He went on the explain how the U-shaped set provided convenience and efficiency in shooting the show using five cameras. "Because of the six stars, and with Gene and two contestants, along with all of the boards and everything that happens, five cameras were necessary.

"Looking at the set, camera 1 is far left, camera 2 is left of the center, camera 5 is center—way in back of the audience, camera 3 is right of the center (again on the stage), and camea 4 is furthest to the right. So we've got the cameras shooting in opposite directions across the stage. Cameras 3 and 4 shoot right (camera left) and 1 and 2 shoot stage left (camera right). 5 shoots right down the middle.

"Basically, camera 5 will work the wide shots coming in and out of commercials. It will do the opening, and will give us kind of protection shots left and right. 5 will also always take the shots going into the 'head-to-head' match. Camera 3 basically handles Gene Rayburn. He takes the contestants, and follows Gene over to the stars, and stays on Gene and the stars when they're giving their answers. Camera 4 generally stays on the contestant, because the contestant is listening to what the stars are saying

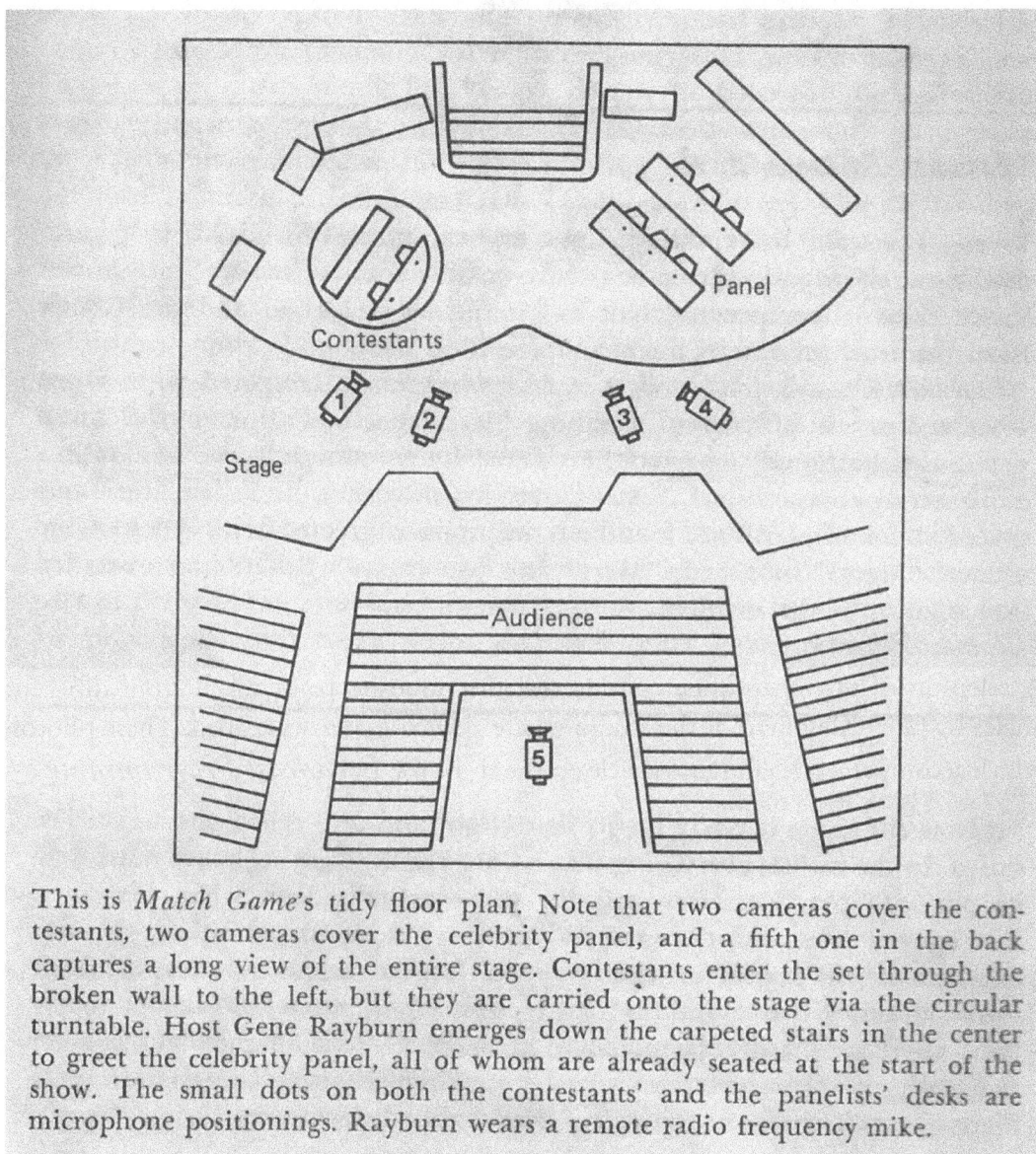

This is *Match Game*'s tidy floor plan. Note that two cameras cover the contestants, two cameras cover the celebrity panel, and a fifth one in the back captures a long view of the entire stage. Contestants enter the set through the broken wall to the left, but they are carried onto the stage via the circular turntable. Host Gene Rayburn emerges down the carpeted stairs in the center to greet the celebrity panel, all of whom are already seated at the start of the show. The small dots on both the contestants' and the panelists' desks are microphone positionings. Rayburn wears a remote radio frequency mike.

The illustration above appeared in a feature article on *Match Game* in the September-Osctober, 1975 issue of the trade magazine *Broadcast Programming & Production*. It was later reproduced with the description above in Maxene Fabe's seminal book *TV Game Shows*, published in 1979 while the show was still airing.

A selection of rare snapshots, on this and the opposite page, taken from different angles by Greg Kleinman of the studio where *Match Game* was taped. These photos, which accompanied Kleinman's article on the show for *Broadcast Programming &*

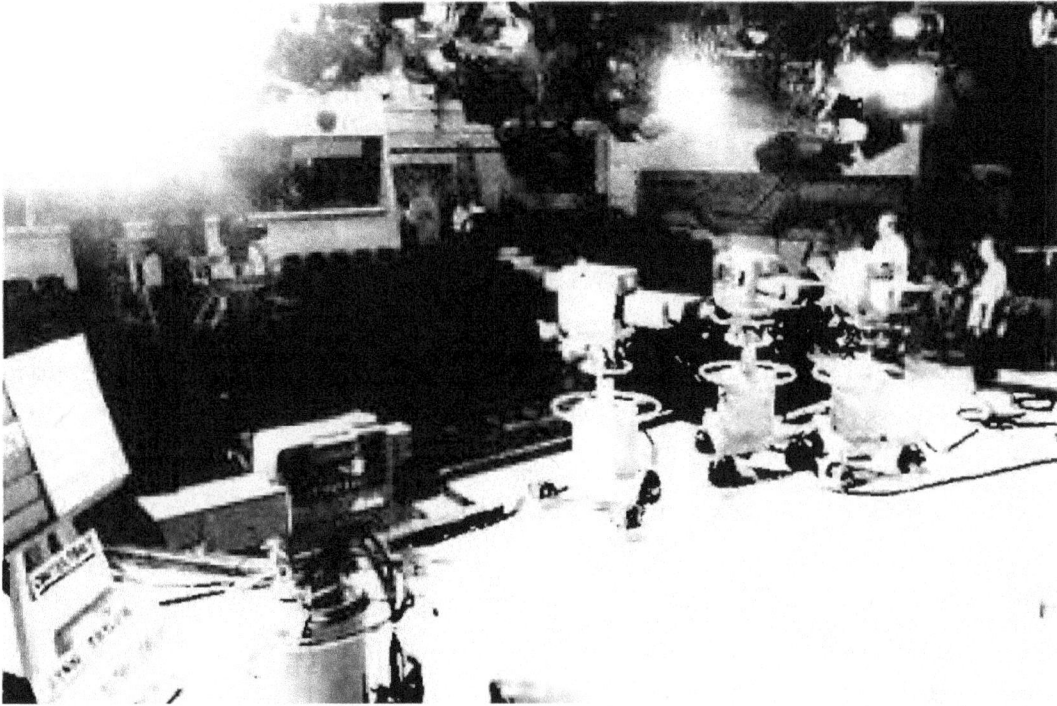

Production magazine, provide clues as to what the contestants, panelists and studio audience saw and experienced behind the scenes.

basically follows that pattern all the way through, and it hasn't really changed. The only thing that has changed is the speed of the shooting. The cutting has gotten much more rapid and the show has become very flexible and wild. Because of this, each camera has the flexibility to do anything he wants. Sometimes Gene will run to the top of the audience and kiss someone, so whoever can grab the shot, 2 or 3, can take it. It's become one of the fastest shows to direct that I've ever been involved with."

Breslow indicated that he was trying to bring out what he termed a "third dimension" through his direction of the show. "Instead of a two-dimensional job of just the joke and hearing somebody laughing, I'm trying to pick up the people who are actually reacting to it," he went on to explain. "That involves trying to pick up the stars when they're [delivering] their jokes and lines, get the reaction shot, see them kind of enjoy what they've said. I'm not hanging on to any one thing for too long...but taking the 'meat out of the nut' on a particular line. Then I'll go for another reaction to that same line...a laugh, somebody else reacting to or enjoying it, and getting back to the star, who maybe is going to give another line. It's trying to anticipate what is going to happen and move fast on it and when it does happen. So when I say 'three dimensional effect,' I'm trying to say that this is not just a game, but a lot of people having a lot of fun. Let's see all the fun that is happening. Fo example...when Avery Schreiber is a guest on the panel, he'll do little takes on every question. Sometimes he'll just hit his head and not say anything, but those are the kinds of reaction shots I'm trying to anticipate. It's something you develop a feel fo after a while, and it makes it easier once you've leaned the patterns of the people you'e working with. Having three regular members on the panel helps.

"Another aspect that adds dimension is something that we developed on *The Price Is Right*. On that show, the audience plays a very big part, and we've brought some of those ideas now to the *Match Game*. The contestant is playing the game, but his brother, cousin, mother, or uncle is out there in the audience dying for him. We miss that extra dimension unless we go out thee and show that person playing along with the game. We're finding there's a while half-a-show out there."

He continued, "Studio 33, as far as I'm concerned, is the best stage. It's where *Match Game*, *Price is Right*, and *The Carol Burnett Show* are taped. Fom a director's standpoint, you're standing at the helm of a ship. I stand looking though glass with the audience down in front, and I can see eveything that is happening on stage. It's got the best of all worlds...the stage is raised slightly, so you've got a television set, and it's like a theater. Some of the sets were designed specifically for that stage and could not work anywhere else."

The audio aspects of the program posed some difficult situations during tapings. The sound engineer would control the in-studio's PA. with a Shure M63 Audio Master mixer. Microphones used on the program wee generally Sony ECM51 condenser units. Often, ten microphones were used on the set, along with additional backstage and audience microphones, a potential feedback hazard with the P.A. system. "We were very lucky to have a guy named Jerry Martz who knows how to ride those mikes so well, and get such a vibrant sound out of the P.A. without any feedback. And there are a lot of mikes...two with the contestants, Gene has a mike and a stand-by mike, there are six mikes on the panel—one for each celebrity, Johnny Olson, the announcer, has a mike, and there are at least four additional audience mikes hanging for reactions."

Because of all the ad-libbing that went on during the show, editing was occasionally necessary. "Sometimes it gets a little racy, but we never bleep anything*. It looks worse if somebody's mouth is moving and they're not saying anything, and you always know that something has been deleted. So we ty to make edits very clean and replace anything that has to be replaced, or just lift it out entirely. The editing is not difficult because

*=A rare exception ocurred three years later on *Match Game P.M.* when Marcia Wallace gave an answer to a question requiring a great big obvious "OOPS!" sign covering her censored response.

shots are constantly going back and forth. When you edit, all you really need is a change of shot, and there is quite a bit of that.

"If the shows ever goes ovetime, which is very rare, it's usually because the stars are taking extra time in writing out their answers. Right there we can edit out a lot of dead air. If we end up short, killing time at the end is not a problem either...with six stars you can ad-lib all the time you need. But geneally we're not faced with timing problems. We've got it down enough to a formula where it almost always times out as we go along."

Here Come Da Judge! Here Come Da Judge!
Ira Skutch
(September 12, 1921-March 16, 2010)

After graduating from Dartmouth College in 1941, Ira Skutch spent a year working with producer Alexander Cohen in the production of Angel Street, in which he simultaneously made his Broadway debut and farewell in the non-speaking role of a English bobby. In the Spring of 1942 he switched to radio as an NBC page. When World War II wound down, he transferred to the newly formed television department as a stage manager. By 1948 he was directing and producing four programs a week.

Sstarting out as a freelance, he became commercial producer-director-writer for the *Philco Television Playhouse*. In 1954, Lennen & Newell, a Madison Avenue ad agency, hired him as a producer. In 1957, he escaped the clutches of the ad world by joining Goodson-Todman Productions, where he seerved as producer, director, and vice-president until 1983, and logged over 10,000 episodes of such shows as *I've Got a Secret*, *Beat the Clock*, *Play Your Hunch*, *Password*, and of course, *Match Game*.

"The show was almost entirely a pleasure to work on." said Ira, who not only produced the seventies version of *Match Game*, but acted as the show's only judge. "The staff and crew were composed of really fine people, mostly with a good sense of humor and an enthusiasm for the project. Particularly outstanding were: Robert Sherman, the head writer and associate producer, is inventive, witty, caustic, and indefatigable; and

Diane Janaver, who was in charge of the Contestant area, is among the ablest and most pleasant people I have known in the business. They remain friends to this day."

His having also directed the first run of *Match Game* on NBC, I couldn't help but ask which version Ira preferred. "The second one, the seventies version," he replied. "I don't know if you've been watching it. About a year ago I moved to a new apartment where they've got DIRECTV, and I've been watching the show from time to time on the Game Show channel. I was very amazed to find out how well it stood up."

I asked how his duties differed, as producer of the West Coast *Match Game*, as opposed to director of the East Coast show (for instance, while directing he was always in the control room on taping days, and as a producer he was always out on the set just off-camera). "Well, as a producer you're just responsible for all of the material that goes on the

A rare snapshot taken by Greg Kleinman of *Match Game* producer Ira Skutch. Having worked for Goodson-Todman since 1957, Skutch worked his way up to vice-president at the company, along the way contributing to classic shows like *Beat the Clock*, *Tattletales*, *Concentration*, *Missing Links*, *Make the Connection*, and *I've Got a Secret*.

show, overseeing the writing, doing the editing of the questions. A lot of questions are not so much written as re-written, like most things. And booking who was to be on the show, and also the contestants.

"Diane Janaver was in charge of the contestants of the seventies show, and she would bring people in and she and I would sit and play the game with them and interview them, and between the two of us we would pick all the people who went on. And then you were also dealing with the network and with Standards and Practices, schedules and budgets and anything else you can think of.

"One of Goodson's good virtues was that when he put you in charge of a show, he let you run the show. And he would check it from time to time and make comments if anything was wrong, or send you plaudits if everything was good. But the running of the show, the money, everything, was in your hands. And so you did it and he relied on those people, and the result was that he got good results."

The Producer: Robert Sherman

"Please make sure that you give credit where credit is due when it comes to Robert Sherman," *Match Game* writer Elliot Feldman told me. "A lot of people tend to take credit for his contribution." Robert came by his game show savvy naturally; his father was Allan Sherman, and despite his father's hot-cold relationship with Goodson-Todman Productions, Robert Sherman excelled in the business.

In his memoir, *I Remember Television*, Ira Skutch wrote, "My closest associate on *Match Game* was Bobby Sherman, son of the co-creator of *I've Got a Secret*, Allan Sherman. After the demise of *The Herb Shriner Show*, Allan had gained nationwide fame for his album, *My Son the Folksinger*, and Bobby was equally creative. A short, dark-haired, vital young man, with a keen feel for comedy and for language, when *Match Game* began he functioned as associate producer and head writer. Together, we sharpened our writing and editorial skills--homing the questions, keeping them crisp and colorful, yet concise and clear.

"The two of us also developed a number of new games. The most successful, *Blockbusters*, enjoyed a year-and-a-half run on NBC daytime, with the superb Bill Cullen as emcee."

Even in his formative years, young Robert was fascinated with electronics and gadgetry. His cousin Terri Leamy remembered, "When he was four years old he had wired a doorbell and light in a little log cabin. I don't know how he did it." Allan Sherman was a brilliant, creative man, but his son observed, "My father was smart and mechanical and inventive, but even at age eight I knew electricity and he didn't." Yet this created odd opportunities for father-son bonding. The elder Sherman enlisted his son's technical abilities when he was creating new game show ideas to pitch, such as one called *Matchmakers*, and Robert crafted a buzzer for a desktop prototype demonstrating the gameplay.

Robert Sherman recalled, "It was to be played by a celebrity panel. There were two big visual game boards and what they were trying to do was match up clues from each board that related to each other somehow," such as a picture of an engagement ring and a photo of the oft-married Elizabeth Taylor. Sadly, *Matchmakers* never found a buyer.

Robert sherman entered what had become the family business, having far better luck with Goodson-Todman Productions than his father did, working as a producer on classic shows like *Match Game*, *Tattletales*, *Super Password* and *Password Plus*. In his memoir, Ira Skutch wrote, "The first person I knew to buy a computer, Bobby has an inquisitive mind, geared especially to statistics. He said, 'Have you ever added up how many shows you've directed and produced?'

"'No.'

"'Let's do it.'

"I went back through the years, and the total came to more than 10,000 episodes. The nine years of *Match Game*, in California, accounted for more than 2,000." Not bad for a man whose father was fired from the same television production company!

Roger Dobkowitz

Roger Dobkowitz wrote his Master's Thesis on TV game shows and had the foresight to send copies of it to various producers, one of whom passed it to Mark Goodson. Suitably impressed, Goodson called Roger to set up a meeting. It was scheduled, and Roger, then living in California, drove his car across the country to attend the meeting.

Between the intelligence displayed in his writing, his driving three thousand miles to meet with Goodson, and his natural charm, Goodson naturally hired "the kid," who would rise in time to produce *The Price is Right.*

"I got involved with *Match Game* because I worked on the pilot show," Dobkowitz explained to Greg Palmer. "Mark Goodson did not hire new people to work on pilots. He used people working on other shows; after the show sold he would then hire people to staff the show. Since I was single and had a lot to time on my hands, I asked to work on *Match Game.* It taped on weekends and since the director was also the one working on *Price,* I realized there would never be a conflict of tapings.

"My job on *Match Game* was cue cards* on stage left (camera right). I would write the responses given by contestants and hold them up to remind Gene what the contestant said (not too difficult of a job!). I would also have to hold up the warning of 'Must Match' to Gene to let him know when a positive match was critical for the contestant (that required concentration!) When they played the audience match, I would have to write down the three suggestions that the celebrities gave...I ran into problems here because there were words I couldn't spell sometimes ('lingerie' and 'lieutenant' were problems!) and Gene would make fun of me, which I didn't mind because I usually got on camera during those moments.

"I really enjoyed working on the show," Roger explained. "I would actually look forward to it! The atmosphere on the set was one of

*=Roger Dobkowitz added the following "historical note": "Until the sixties cue cards were not called 'cue cards,' they were called 'idiot cards.'"

'anything goes' Everyone seemed to have fun and nothing was ever taken too seriously. And it is true...the celebrities did drink during the dinner break and the last two shows of the day were always a little more wilder. Most of the antics did get on the air, because back in those days of television editing was never severe. Marc Breslow, the director, and Mark Goodson did not believe in creating an artificial game show where it had to be edited a certain way (as in today's shows). Most everything was left in. Occasionally a little bit had to be edited out for time restraints. Unfortunately, this editing rule changed during the last few years of the show. Suddenly the producer (Ira Skutch) felt the chit-chat and antics during the 'writing' time had to be edited out and the game advanced. Personally, as a staff onlooker, I felt that the show was harmed by this and never really recovered.

"Another thing I felt harmed the show badly was when Richard Dawson left. For whatever reason, the studio audience loved him. They would always respond to him far more than any other celebrity on the show. During the head-to-head match, the contestant almost always chose Richard. The other celebrities didn't really like this and (I supposed) complained to the producer. Thus, the wheel was introduced. Richard did not like this and this is when the animosity between Richard and the producer began. Later, when Richard was a hit on *Family Feud*, was when he felt he could leave the show. This was another blow to the show... it was not the same without Richard.

"The other thing that harmed the show was the introduction of lazy writing. The staff started recycling questions from the past which started to take away the fresh look of the show. I am a big believer in *not* repeating stuff; even though it is hard to write because one might think 'everything has been done,' there is always something new to write. Jay Wolpert on *Price* made me realize this when he said he didn't want to repeat [a] showcase. I remember telling him that everything had been done and I didn't think anything new could be written. Well...he forced me into creating and thinking up new stuff (even though it was hard) and I learned a valuable lesson...there is always something new!

"Thus...editing, exiting of Richard, and lazy writing resulted in the cancellation of one of the biggest hits in daytime TV."

The Set Designer: James J. Agazzi

Admit it—you're just *dying* to know about the set! I know—I was, too. So, I managed to track down James J. Agazzi, who designed the iconic look, replete with all that great orange shag carpeting! He shared his story with me, and told me how he got into the world of game show set design.

"I left Joliet, Illinois to attend UCLA where my field of study was Theatre Arts, eventually obtaining my BA in Theatre, specializing in design for the stage. I followed this when I completed the MFA program focusing on Design and Direction for the stage. Two weeks after graduation I was supervising the set up of a Bob Hope special at NBC."

Agazzi would work over the next several years at each of the three major networks working as an Art Director for TV shows and specials starring Danny Thomas, Bob Hope, and other big-name stars. He ended up woking at CBS as Assistant Art Director on *The Bill Cosby Variety Hour*, co-starring Lola Falana. "When it was close to being cancelled," Agazzi explained, "I was asked to take over the Art Director job for the *Price Is Right*—which made me a full time Art Director. That was also my introduction to the Mark Goodson 'family.' As long as the job was done to his liking, Mr. Goodson was quite loyal to his staff. I spent the next eight years or so a part of that family, while maintaining my responsibility to *The Price Is Right*, I began to design pilots for other Goodson productions, including *The Match Game*."

"As the *Match Game* was not the typical game show at the time—it was initially a fairly low budget effort. Yet, I had to fill the stage with a set and came up with the large 'donut' look—which was economical and filled the space. The mere fact that the space behind the celebrity panel was not a solid wall was what sold Mark Goodson on the design. He found that a 'new' approach. They were hollow plywood structures, 'gussied' up by using a heavy textured surface treatment which added visual interest and helped the lighting designer keep them from looking flat. The addition of mica chips was just a little bit of old-fashioned glitz. Later editions of the show—when a nighttime version was put on the air as well as a daytime— strobe lights were added and the cyclorama lighting became darker—all of which was considered more of a nighttime look.

"Much of the look was left to me to pull together—subject to Mr. Goodson's approval. I submitted a color scheme that was not being currently used for a game show—royal blue, cream and orange (shag carpet). In description it is a little garish, but used in broad, bold strokes, it still achieved a certain style and taste level that appealed to Mr. Goodson, who was personally a very stylish and tasteful man.

"Each production required presentation of ideas, design and treatment at a meeting of the Goodson Productions staff, a large group of producers and show runners, all of whom were encouraged to present their opinions. I rarely had a difficult time getting my ideas and designs accepted. Quite often I had a secondary design ready, should my first design be rejected." (Sadly, he didn't remember what alternate set design he came up with if the orange shag carpet had gone over with a resounding thud. Oh well.)

He continued, "Each time *The Match Game* was reincarnated it reflected decisions and choices that had been set during production of the first edition. The 'donuts' allowed lighting that previous solid walls somewhat prevented, giving the panel a more glamorous look. It may have been the first show to gently curve the seating arrangement of the panelists, who were supposed to interact as part of the charm of the show. The curvature of the platform helped create an intimacy between them without constantly throwing them into profile when interacting, unlike the flat stacked 'boxes' of *Hollywood Squares* which totally prevented any comfortable relationship between panelists, forcing them to only relate to the camera.

"Early on I recognized that the problems of camera placement, revelation of answers to audience, camera, and contestants, lighting accessibility, etc.—all crucial 'behind the scenes' elements of game show production—were never a given, but constantly in a state of flux. Thus I tended to make my set designs a combination of movable elements to accommodate necessary changes of position once the set was first set up on stage."

In 1978, the set underwent a transformation, and the 'donuts' were replaced with a criss-cross pattern. "The redesign of the set was done by James Agazzi, as was the original," Mark Bowerman confirmed, then added, "It was just a redecoration of the original framework. Nothing was actually changed as far as the [foundation] of the set goes."

Agazzi himself told me, "Through and into the late 1970's, the physical set up became a standard. Changes were primarily cosmetic, but even then there was always a visual reference to the premiere production which enhanced the 'family' feeling the show projected. I think I preferred the nighttime version because it was a little more glitzy."

James later designed the set for the 1990-1991 version of *Match Game*—we'll talk about that one in a later chapter—but, "I was not involved with the 1983-1984 [*Match Game-Hollywood Squares*] combo production," he says. "In fact I may not have ever seen it."

Over the years, James was Production Designer for such shows as *Hart to Hart* and *Paper Dolls* and a wide variety of made-for-TV movies, gaining nine Emmy nominations and winning the coveted gold paperweight for his design work on *Moonlighting*.

Making a transition in creative outlets, he wrote and directed the award-winning short film, *A Window That Opens* (2000), described on the city of Joliet, Illinois's official website as "a poignant study of three generations of women enduring the changes wrought by having to say goodbye." According to James, "My venture into filmmaking reflects having turned a corner, so to speak. It is something I have always yearned to do and have finally taken the opportunity. Currently I have been writing feature length scripts, and hope that it is something that will bring creative satisfaction and fulfillment."

Theodore 'Ted' Cooper

(November 11, 1920-December 5, 1999)

A former Broadway designer named Theodore Cooper served as 'Creative Consultant' on *Match Game* and other Goodson-Todman shows after he was hired by the firm in 1950. While James J. Agazzi was the designer of the physical set of the show, and Marc Breslow figured out what the cameras would show on the screen, Cooper and his team were involved with figuring out all the logistics.

Working from the game rules given to him from the Production staff, Cooper and his staff figured out details such as how the show was to be scored, where the game's mechanical and electronic elements were to be positioned, both in and out of camera range, and how many people it would take to operate them. It took months to perfect and hundreds of thousands of dollars to make it all look effortless. Cooper had to figure out how the results of a poll should be revealed, and how the answers to the next polls could be gotten swiftly into place without slowing things down. With the help of production assistants and stagehands, and computer technology, all the elements came together.

Mark Bowerman, who worked closely with Ted Cooper at Goodson-Todman, shared some of his memories of working with the man: "I was the only other person to work with Ted. We shared offices for over eighteen years. Teddy was an innovator, inventor, artist, scientist, designer, and was never too proud to share his gifts with others. Love is family, and his work."

An L.A.-area native, Bowerman himself got a job as a page-usher at CBS and in 1974 was hired by Goodson-Todman as a Production Assistant on *The Price is Right* and as "Executive Office Gopher/Mailroom Boy/Xerox Key Operator". As he relayed, "My luck came in a man called Edward Theodore Cooper, a.k.a. Teddy. He discovered I possessed the ability to cut a straight line in cardboard with a knife. I was immediately elevated to the position of 'Teddy's Assistant', whenever duties on my assigned show allowed."

By 1979, "My job as Stunt Coordinator on *Beat the Clock* comes to an end, and with that I begin a new era at Goodson-Todman Productions. I was made 'Permanent Teddy's Assistant', a position I enjoyed enormously. Ted and I worked together in the department he called 'The Department of Everything Else'. He would say, 'We don't do game material, contestants, talent, or sales, we do everything else!' Everything visual did cross our desks and we had enormous creative input from development through the on-air product. We often designed and built prototypes of game mechanisms which reduced engineering time during set construction. In addition to what you *saw*, our behind-the-scenes involvement had us coordinating all the vendors and supervising the set construction and graphics production. Our involvement from the development stage on, led to problems being solved during the early stages of construction which saved time and money for the production. That combined with the ability to accomplish seemingly impossible changes to set requirements overnight made our contribution highly valued."

While they helped coordinate and fine tune the games, Mark says, "Ted and I rarely did the actual designs for the sets."

"I worked, as did Ted, at all three networks as well as at some local stations when producing some of our syndicated shows. Goodson never had his own scene shop. We contracted with the network or independent shops for building of all our sets. We did indeed specify and/or approve microphones, lens compliments for cameras, communications devices between production and the various technical departments."

Bells and Whistles

So you want to know what wizardry allowed you to see Patti Deutsch holding up a card with "Please Laugh!" written on it through the lighted, revolving, orange thingie at the top of the show? Or allowed you to witness Charles posing *a la* Statue of Liberty through said same spinning doo-hickie (Just what *was* that thing called?) as Johnny Olson announced the celebrity panelists' names? By today's standards, game show special effects really aren't all that special, but just in case you gizmo buffs want to know how things were done...

"By the late sixties, the electronic breakthrough called chroma-key enabled game shows to superimpose one camera shot over another to produce such special effects as the split screen used on *The Price Is Right*. Chroma-key is also what enables stars to peer out of their 'secret' squares on *Hollywood Squares* and to wave goodbye on *The Match Game*." Or so explained Maxene Fabe in her excellent 1979 game show tome.

As for 'the crawl' listing the credits at the close of the show, it was shot by having one camera focus on a special monitor containing the moving names on videotape. That shot was then superimposed on a shot of the game show's set; or to be more specific, on views of the panelists caught mid-conversation, as viewed—*courtesy chroma-key*—through that revolving, light-bulb studded thingie.

Speaking of which, Rick Stern, whose first job for Goodson-Todman was stage managing *Match Game* at CBS in 1981, recalled, "We called the device the 'flipper board.'" It was developed by director Marc Breslow, who explained, "At the opening of *Match Game*, I felt that it would be good if we could somehow focus on the six stars of the panel, and pop them in some way. So I came up with the idea of what I call a 'flipper'...or a rotating board, and using chroma-key, as one side of the board comes aound, you see the face of one of the celebrities. As the board turns to the other side, you see the next star's face, and so on. After all the stars have been shown, the flipper turns once more and displays the [*Match Game* logo]. So I just saw all those crazy chaser lights, drew it up, took it to the art director, and we tried it...and it worked well."

Above, unidentified production assistants sounded the bells and buzzers, depending on whether answers given during the game were correct or incorrect, and operated the show's indication lights using the small console seen to the right. Below, from behind the studio audience a sound engineer mixed the in-studio PA system with a Schure

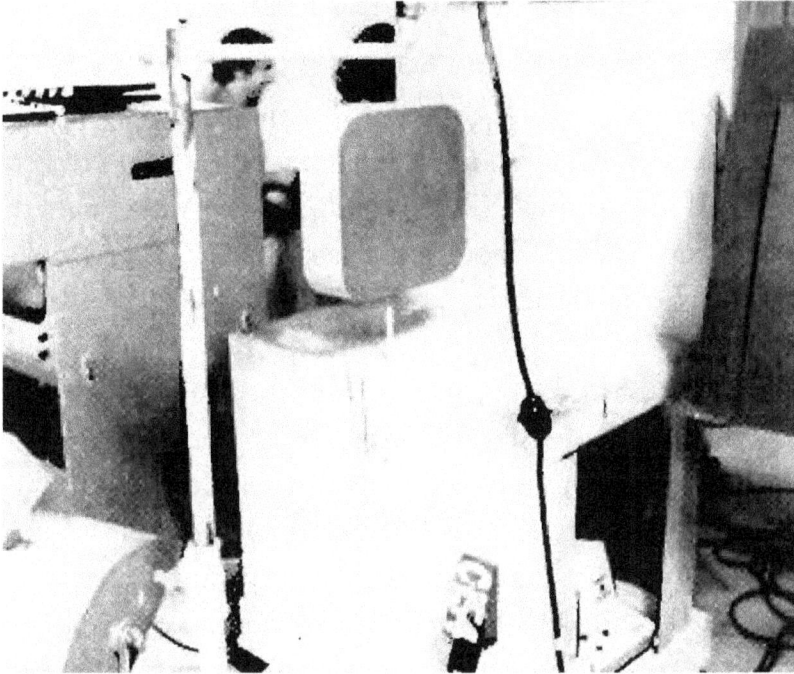

M63 Audio Master mixer. The microphones used on the show were generally the Sony ECM51 condenser units. Above, a side view of the chroma-key "flipper" board used in the opening and closing credits of the show. Below, the "flipper" in operation. These snapshots were taken in 1975 by Greg Kleinman.

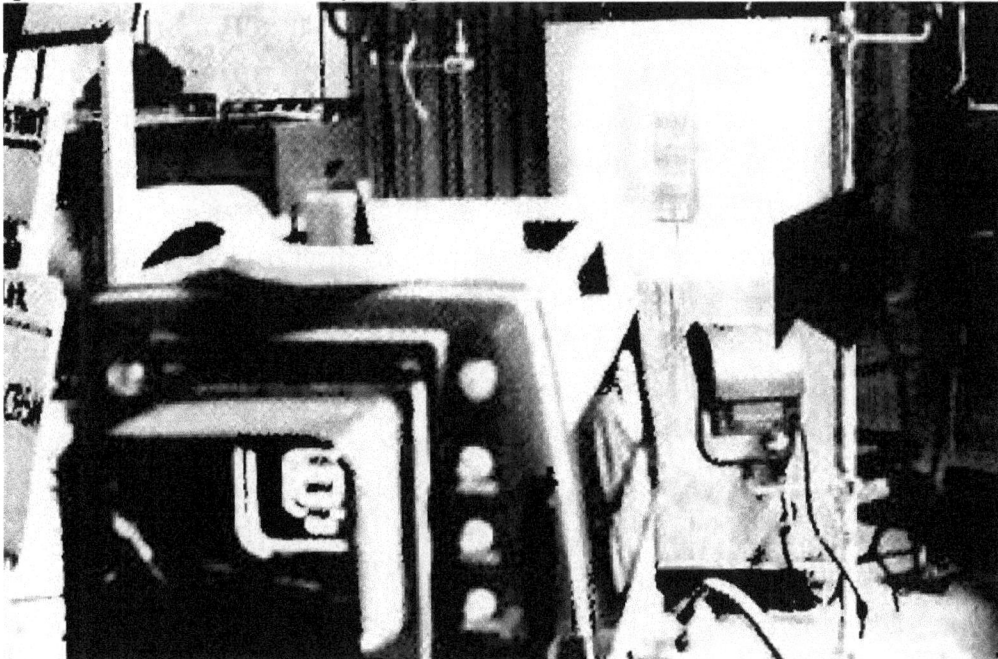

The Sound of Music:
Ken Bichel, Robert Israel and Score Productions

Brett Somers laughed when the *Match Game* theme music came up in one of our conversations. "I said to somebody once that, 'I think it was the *music* that made the show!' That wasn't *music*! What *was* that?" And together we 'sang' (rather like the sound the 'teacher' makes on the *Peanuts* cartoon specials) the *Match Game* theme song: "Mwa-mwa-mwa-mwa-wah-ah-ah-ah..."

Okay, the music has taken a beating over the years, but hey, it's catchy enough that you're probably humming it as you read this. The man responsible for this much-maligned little ditty is Ken Bichel, who worked under impressario Robert A. Israel, founder of the award-winning Score Productions, a company that provided the music for a wide variety of television shows. While working with Goodson-Todman Productions, Israel and Score produced the themes for *The Price is Right*, *Super Password* and *Family Feud*, and many more.

Bichel explained, "I was in the second year of my Masters at Juilliard in1969 when I got a call from the head of student placement that [electronic music pioneer] Gershon Kingsley was auditioning pianists to form 'The First Moog Quartet,' which he sought to fashion after the Guarneri String Quartet, at least in terms of gestalt and marketing. I could read anything, had a background in Jazz as well as Classical performance, I could improvise (Kingsley was an amazing improvisor) and I had a background in electronics as an amateur radio operator as a kid. It was a perfect fit. Prior to that I don't think there *was* any Synthesizer music *per se*, certainly not in any recognized commercial vein."

(Months later Bichel found himself performing on a Moog synthesizer at Carnegie Hall. Meanwhile, he and three other musicians formed the psychedelic rock band Side Show and the group was signed to Atlantic Recrods. In time Bichel became an in-demand keyboard player, later working with Peggy Lee, Judy Collins, Aretha Franklin, and Billy Joel, among many, many others. But all that came later.)

"I was fresh out of Juilliard, where I'd gotten my MS in '69. Because it required two liberal arts courses over two years, they had the temerity to call it a 'Master of Science' degree rather than the traditional 'Master of Music.' At the time, I had a record contract with Atlantic records and had become a pioneer with the Moog and other synthesizers. I came to the attention of the late Herbert J. Harris, the former percussionist with the NY philharmonic, under Leonard Bernstein, and the most powerful contractor in New York City at the time. Herbie took me under his wing, as he had so many other talented musicians, and became my music business 'Rabbi.' He took me to Score Productions to meet Robert A. Israel, the undisputed New York City king of television music production.

"Bob was a very astute composer [and] producer. He studied composition with Nadia Boulanger in Paris as a young man; she was the 'go to' pedagogue in those days. His famous, ubiquitous *World News Tonight* theme broke the mold, and has not been topped since.

"The only negative thing regarding his reputation was that anything written for Score Productions was a work for hire, and therefore did not accrue royalties for the actual composer. This bred a certain resentment among those of us who contributed to the Score library. Whether or not that was justified is a matter of opinion.

"On the other hand, I learned much from him in terms of production and integrity of quality. Bob never skimped on production costs and never settled for final product that wasn't top quality. I was on expensive sessions with him that he scrapped because we just weren't hitting the mark."

Bichel's first assignment for Score Productions was to work on the theme to the all-new version of *Match Game*. "The project was one of many on their production desk and they gave me a shot at it," he remembered.

"I was young. *Match Game* was my first commercial writing assignment and I didn't know the tradition of providing different themes to choose from, so I spent my time crafting the 'perfect' theme. An hour before we were to leave my studio for the presentation session, Bob's assistant came to hear my work. He then asked 'Where are the others?' '*What* others?' I responded, 'This is the *theme*!' Since there had to be more than one I spent maybe twenty minutes writing 'the throwaway.' It's been running for over thirty years." (Incidentally, in case you're wondering, Bichel's alternate 'perfect' composition was never used for any other production.)

"There was no collaboration on the theme," he continued, "and very little on the incidental cuts, which were based on mix-downs of the original *Main Theme* tracks with a bit of overlay here and there. The producers gave us a 'shopping list' of the incidental cues they would need, and these were constructed in the studio, rather than being 'composed' in advance."

Four other musicians joined Ken Bichel in the recording studio to cover the *Match Game* theme. Herb Barris worked on several tracks on percussion instruments. Two tracks of trumpets were recorded by "the amazingly talented Ray Crisara. Bass, I think it was Richard Nanista, but I'm not sure." Lou Volpe played guitar. "Lou is an internationally famous guitarist, still based in New York City," explained Ken before adding, "and myself, multiple tracks of synthesizer."

I had to ask just out of curiosity if there were ever any lyrics for the theme or if it ever had a formal title beyond *Theme to Match Game*. "So far as I know it never had any other title, and no lyrics that I'm aware of."

In retrospect the *Match Game* theme is one of the most recognizable and memorable in TV history, and "happy" music, on top of that. When I asked Ken his thoughts about that, and how he has or has not grown to appreciate or embrace it, he replied, "As a young opinionated Juilliard grad and Jazz aficionado I judged the piece rather harshly—the word 'disdainfully' comes to mind—especially since I wrote the piece as a throwaway. It's hardly a 'sophisticated' composition in terms of classical craft. However, having mellowed over time, I've grown to accept and appreciate this bizarre, archetypal, unexpected phenomenon. If something makes you happy, what could be bad?"

Mark Goodson

(January 14, 1915 – December 18, 1992)

"As Mark Goodson said, '*Match Game* is a game you can't *not* play,'" said staff writer R. Patrick Neary. "One thing that I think made Mark Goodson a better game impresario than anyone else was the depth of his ability to know his audience. With *Match Game* and most of his shows, you didn't need to sit in front of the tube the whole time. You could be busy doing a number of other thing, including housework, yet still play along."

"Mark was very hands-on," said Marcia Wallace. "I think it was fun to do because he came to the *Match Game* a lot. He came to the dinner between the three and three. For a long time we did six shows; we did the five, and then the syndicated nighttime. That went off before the daytime, didn't it? Or did it? Listen, you know a lot more than I do.

"Well, Mark was very formidable. I mean, I never felt close to him. Brett was very close to his second wife, Suzanne, or third wife or something." Audrey Davis, who worked on the sixties version of *Match Game* recalled, "He was one of the most intimidating men I had ever met. He was *wildly* successful, enormously wealthy, and the most beautifully dressed man I have ever seen in my life."

Despite his occasionally formidable appearance, Kay Henley regarded Goodson warmly. "Every Christmas Mr. G. would put on a big party at the Beverly Hills Hotel. Each staff, all crews for every show, all the celebs that had been on any of the shows would be invited. And we would have a wrap party on the stage with champagne, beer and canapés."

Ira Skutch observed Goodson while working on the seventies version of *Match Game*. "Maintaining a suite at the Beverly Hills Hotel, Mark spent half his time in New York, and half on the West Coast. For the first time, he and I began to develop a rudimentary social relationship, and we dined together occasionally. We never became truly intimate, but when his third marriage broke up, I spent many hours with him, helping him through the bitter period that followed."

Bill Todman

(July 31, 1916 – July 29, 1979)

For most kids the parental decree is a stern, 'No TV until you've done your homework." but when Lisa Todman was growing up in Scarsdale, New York, she would often hear her father's impatient, "Are you finished with your homework yet? You've got to watch this show!"

Of course, her father was Bill Todman, and he wasn't encouraging her to shirk her schoolwork so much as he was registering his excitement at his company's latest success.

Not bad for a John Hopkins University chemistry and psychology major who initially planned on becoming a doctor. Born Wilbur S. Todman in 1916 in New York City (he changed his name legally to William after his uncle William, for whom he was intended to be named, passed away), Todman grew up in an environment of accomplishment and privilege: his father was esteemed Wall Street accountant Frederick S. Todman, who wrote several books about accounting principles.

The summer before entering Johns Hopkins medical school, Todman took a job as a junior copyrighter at an ad agency in the CBS building in New York. There, he met CBS radio employees over lunch in the cafeteria, landing freelance work writing scripts. Eventually, he became head writer and director of *The Connie Boswell Show*, starring Boswell, a well-known jazz vocalist.

"He was always a writer," Bill Jr. (himself a producer) said of his father. "Even in college, he wrote plays, and for the newspaper. His creative calling got the best of him."

Why did game shows appeal to him?

"With the original group of programs, it was always answering questions," said his daughter, Lisa Todman. "He was like a sponge. No matter what the topic was, if there was knowledge, he was interested.

"He had a marvelous sense of humor, and he liked fun," she added. "That also drew him. But it was mainly answering questions—and you were probably out of luck if you thought you were going to beat him at it."

As Todman himself told *Sports Illustrated*'s Gilbert Rogin, "I'm primarily involved in being a sounding board. Basically, Mark's in charge of production, I handle the contracts, sales, economy, budget; the minutiae. we complement each other."

Bob Stewart, who created *To Tell the Truth* and *The Price is Right*, said, "Bill was the guy who would talk to the agents, to business affairs. The ability, in those days, to negotiate with the networks was a very special skill. When we approached them with an idea, there was a real open atmosphere. They welcomed us nicely. Once they showed an interest in something we pitched, Bill would come in and do the negotiations. He was very instrumental in that company becoming very, very wealthy. He was also a great guy to be with socially."

While numbers mattered to Todman, so did people. Mark Goodson was quoted as saying in *Sports Illustrated*, "Bill is kind, generous, somewhat dismayed by me. We have our own groups, but we are certainly friends. He would be the man I'd come to instantly in time of trouble. My tendency is to give a man a raise according to his merit. The way to get a raise from Bill is to need it."

"They wanted to expand their horizons; nobody wants to be pigeonholed," says Andrew J. Fenady, who produced a trio of western-themed TV programs with the duo. Todman was an avid reader and a western fan, and where the shows were concerned, "You could talk to him at any time," Fenady says "He was there if we needed something. And the Goodson-Todman accounting was impeccable. We never went over budget, and we made a lot of money from their honest bookkeeping. They were very, very fair-minded partners."

When the production company moved to California in the early seventies (and during the time the seventies version of *Match Game* hit its zenith) Bill Todman rarely came west, instead focusing on the company's publishing ventures. As the years went by, he withdrew more and more, and went into virtual retirement.

While it was Todman's expertise that expanded the team's horizons beyond television into ownership of newspapers, radio stations and New York real estate, it's the game shows which are his true legacy. He died during heart valve surgery in New York on July 29, 1979, two days before his sixty-third birthday.

According to Ira Skutch, there was no dedication of "In memory of" in the end credits of any of the shows. "Purchasing Bill's interest in the firm from the estate, Mark became the sole owner. The familiar end-of-show credit: 'This has been a Mark Goodson-Bill Todman Production' was changed to, 'This has been a Mark Goodson Television Production.'" The company continued to produce TV game shows, including several televised lottery games.

Mark Goodson passed away on December 17, 1992.

(And last but not least....EARL!)

Stagehand Earl Wilson, invited on camera by Gene during a round of the Super Match on an episode of *Match Game '77*.

Earl Wilson

Over the years, a number of crew members appeared on *Match Game*, whether seen bantering with Gene or being 'assaulted' with cue cards by him, but none made so indelible an impression as the all-too invisible Earl Wilson. During the Bonus Round on the show, Earl faithfully sat inside the Bonus Round Box, removing the boards to reveal the answers.

"I remember Earl," says Elliot Feldman. "Can't remember his last name. The only thing specifically I remember about Earl was that he told me Bob Marley and The Wailers were in the next set. They were doing like a— what was the name of that? It was a summer replacement show?— *Manhattan Transfer*. And Bob Marley and The Wailers were in the next studio, and he said the sweet smell of ganja came on...And I went running over there and sat in the audience while they were doing a technical run-through, and had my own private Bob Marley and The Wailers concert. Wow! That was amazing."

Mark Bowerman remembered "Earl Wilson—or 'Earl the Pearl,' as Gene used to call him. I believe I heard he had passed away, but I would not halt any search for him based on that rumor."

"I did have huge dealings with Earl," recalled Jay Wolpert, "but only in regard to *Price Is Right* because Earl was my prop man on *Price Is Right*. And Earl was a funny guy, a hard-working guy, got the job done, but he was funny as hell. He had—I think he had a trailer...he kept parked in the parking lot which was the butt of many jokes, a 'den of iniquity' that I think was more mythical than anything else. But he was a character, oh, was absolutely a character.

"I don't remember whether he was married or not, but I guess that he probably was. But like I say, I never saw this trailer, but there was always talk about Earl's trailer. He was a great guy."

Review Questions

1. On taping days during the 1973-1982 run of Match Game, Ira Skutch was always BLANK.

a. On the studio floor
b. In Earl Wilson's trailer
c. Flashed onscreen via chroma-key into the lighted, revolving thingie seen during the opening and closing credits of every show

2. According to Brett Somers, <u>BLANK</u> made the show.

a. The music.
b. The lighted, revolving orange thingie seen during the opening and closing credits of every show.
c. Earl's infamous trailer.

3. Crewmember Earl Wilson was best known among the crew for possessing a mythical <u>BLANK</u>.

a. Box of Rice-a-Roni.
b. Lighted, revolving orange thingie seen....Oh, you know the rest.
c. Trailer/Den of Iniquity

Answers: 1. a; 2. a.; 3. c.

14

Boobs, Booze, and Howard Cosell

Gene Rayburn once said that if you're ever stumped for an answer on the show, just answer with "boobs, booze, or Howard Cosell" and you'll probably match the panel.

"That's right!" exclaimed Brett when I mentioned it to her.

"That is funny," agreed Diane Janaver, "and almost true! Almost."

"Well, it *was* true!" thundered Brett.

When the original *Match Game* began airing, John and Jackie Kennedy were still in the White House and the show was as traditional as the era in which it was shown—an entertaining but dignified format. By the time CBS brought the show back in 1973, both John and Bobby Kennedy had lost their lives and Jackie had traded in her white gloves for a pair of dark sunglasses and a jet-set lifestyle. Likewise, American tastes had changed—for better or worse—and the questions and answers got funnier. And racier. And *Match Game* became one of daytime's highest rated shows (it was the number one daytime show four years in a row, from the 1973-1974 to the 1976-1977 television seasons).

Betty White, who appeared on the original NBC version of *Match Game* as well as the racier seventies version, recalled the difference in her memoir *Here We Go Again*: "Gene would read the questions, everyone would write their responses, then reveal them in turn. For example, 'cold blank' could be one of several things—cold water, cold shoulder, cold turkey; 'Blank clock' could be time, alarm, grandfathers, et cetera.

Howard Cosell.

Harmless enough in theory; however, giving six flaky show folk a stack of blank cards and marking pens is tantamount to handing finger paints to a troupe of chimpanzees. The endgame was an audience match—trying to match three answers collected from the studio audience in the warm-up before the show. There were three chances, each worth an increase in dollars. Somehow, the one that sticks in my mind was the day the question was 'Blank willow.' Maybe *you* can come up with something besides weeping, pussy, and tit."

"I suppose they went as far as they could without being stopped by the censors," says Kay Henley. "I can't remember if they had to check with them first....I didn't really pay attention to the writing. When the guys would come in and ask me questions, I'd say the first thing that popped out of my mouth. They either liked the answer or didn't. They usually tried the material out on all of us and went from there."

> "Speaking of 'bazooms,' Fannie, would you show us yours?"
> —Gene Rayburn

According to Elliot Feldman, "The original *Match Game* that was done in the early sixties was a completely different show. The material was pretty straight. It was like *Family Feud* material. 'Name something that's brown.' It was that type of thing. 'Brown <u>BLANK</u>.' There were no jokes. It was Bobby [Sherman] that decided to bring in jokes...Basically what we did was, we looked toward the Carson show at the time—at least, Bobby did when he was shaping the style of the show. And I joined about 2 years after the show started. And he looked at what they were doing on Carson. You know, it pretty much modeled the material after that. You know, Carson material was racy, but it was late-night. So essentially, it was bringing late-night sensibility to daytime television."

"Double-entendre was one of the principle mainstays of the show," says Ira Skutch. "Originally, in the '62-'69 series, the show used fairly straightforward material, i.e. 'Name a kind of pie.' Dick de Bartolo, the sole writer, came up with 'John always put butter on his <u>BLANK</u>.' When Rayburn read this, it got a huge laugh, although the answers were confined to 'bread,' 'toast,' 'potatoes,' etc. which got no laughs at all. When we did the pilot in '73, we got much saltier answers to the [blank] questions we used in the run-throughs and the pilot, so the plan was to use them more frequently on the series. They were originally slated in the first round, with straighter questions used in the second round in order to get more 'scoring,' but we quickly discovered that the laughs were more important [than] the score, so the straight questions were abandoned."

When the evening version of the show, titled *Match Game PM*, was introduced, it took the double-entendre to far greater lengths—pretty hot stuff for the period. What is interesting is that shows like *Hollywood Squares*, *The Newlywed Game*, and *Match Game* were known at the time for being racy—and yet, they got away with it!

I asked Peter Marshall, host of the original *Hollywood Squares*, why he thought this was. "Because what we did was so hip that if you didn't get it, you didn't get it," he responded. "And if you got it, you said, 'That's terrific.'"

How racy did *Match Game* get? On one infamous episode, Gene read off the following question: *"Bill the sports reporter said, 'I asked the baseball manager how the team was doing, and he said, 'We're holding our own.' When I went into the locker room, the*

Top 10 Fave Characters Appearing In The Questions

1. Dumb Dora
2. Weird Willie
3. The Mad Scientist
4. Dr. Frankenstein
5. Count Dracula
6. The Godfather
7. Old Man Periwinkle
8. Ugly Edna
9. Marvin the Martian
10. ....and of course Brett and Charles and Betty White and Allen Ludden.

entire team was holding their own BLANK.'" Brett Somers gave her most notorious answer *ever* when Gene came to her. "They were a sports team, right?" she asked rhetorically. "They were holding their own balls!"

According to Ira Skutch, "There was a representative of the CBS standards and practices department at every taping. We also supplied them with copies of the material, and discussed possibly questionable answers with them. In fairly short time, we had mutually developed a sense of what was acceptable, and we had very little friction with them throughout the run of the show."

So, the censors were always on the set?

"Oh, always," says Elliot Feldman. "Standards and Practices from the network, you know, kept an eye on us. And we would slip in—I wish I could remember some of the stuff. [After] writing fifteen thousand of these babies, it all kind of mushes together."

So a lot slid by, but was anybody ever censored on the show?

"Marcia got censored!" tattled Brett. "Marcia Wallace. She said—there was something about—"

The question Gene read was: "*Unlucky Louie said, 'My lousy luck! I went on a diet and I lost three inches. Unfortunately, it was off my* BLANK.'"

"—and they said feet," continued Brett, listing off some of the suggested answers. "And Marcia said 'genitalia' and they went, 'Cut! Cut! Cut! CUT!' Oh no, they cut it right then, said, 'That's it, now we'll go back and do this again,' and said, 'You won't be saying 'genitalia' or you won't be coming back!' It was so funny."

The final, edited cut of the show allowed Marcia to give her answer— with a big, *Gong Show* styled "OOPS!" covering her mouth and the card displaying her answer. The home viewers knew she had said *something* forbidden, but could only guess what naughty thoughts danced in her head.

"Hillary said, 'I don't trust that new doctor. He painted temperature marks on his BLANK and tried to use it as a thermometer.'"

"I mean, I knew I wasn't supposed to say certain stuff," Marcia said in her own defense. "It was a euphemism show, but there were a thousand questions that the answer was either 'boobs' or 'making whoopee.' So there was one, and you knew the answer they wanted was 'penis.' So I thought, 'Oh, I'm sick of all this innuendo. I know! I'll answer *medically*. They can't mind *that*. Why, this is a *technical* term!' so I wrote down 'genitalia,' and I show it to Dickie 'cause I'm so proud, and he goes [looks horrified], and I say, 'Well, how *rude*.' And then I whipped it up and bells went off and everybody's screaming and yelling, and that's when Ira came over and said, 'You get *one*. That's it. *One time*.' And I was truly shocked because I thought, 'It's a medical term, who can object?'"

On another occasion, Gene read off the following:"Suzy the senator's new secretary said, "I'm not much good at typing. The last time I tried, my BLANKs got caught in the typewriter." The contestant demurely answered, "breasts." He was told, as one of the celebs revealed his answer, "Here on this show, Jeff, we use the medical term: boobs." Brett launched into a story, telling Gene, "You know, Fannie used to type. You know what happened? Her boobs got caught in the typewriter!" and she held up her card, upon which was written "Boobs."

"Nobody ever pushed us one way or the other about raciness," said R, Patrick Neary. "Everyone was aware that there was a line that could not be crossed—but you could dance on it (the line itself), and that's essentially what we did. Sometimes we'd come up with a really good racy one and try it out on Ira in the writer meetings just for laughs, with no expectation that it would be selected.

"If a question seemed to have only one likely answer, and especially if it was a racier answer, then Ira would say it was 'too much on the nose.' In other words, while there may be some shock response, there's nothing really funny about, say, a body part. It's just a fact. But if you mess with a listener's mind by wording the question in such a way that the answer can

Gene read off the question: "Galdys said, 'I just played strip poker with Tony. On the last hand, Tony didn't see my hand. Instead, he saw my BLANK.'" Guest panelist Bonnie Franklin shows off the definitive answer in this pair of shots blown up from a proof sheet found in Gene Rayburn's estate.

just as likely be 'nose' or 'big toe,' then you get laughter as the response. Editorially speaking, too much standup comedy today is merely 'on the nose.' And, beyond adolescence, that's just not funny. And there's certainly no art in it.

"We came up with questions alone or together, worked on them together until they were honed. This is where I learned the precision of language—we often haggled about whether a certain question should be worded 'the BLANK' or 'a BLANK' because 'the' or 'a' led to very different answers. I use this appreciation for precise language to this day.

"I don't remember any of my own questions. The only one I can ever think of, and one that really is a model of a classic *Match Game* question, was Joe Neustein's. 'The Jolly Green Giant has a jolly green BLANK.'"

"I think the show was geared to be silly on the level of a twelve-year-old," says Fannie Flagg. "As I recall, one little old lady gave the real answer the question suggested without the usual words instead."

"What *The Match Game* gave to society is a mixed bag," reasons Orson Bean. "It gave the right to say things like scatological baby-talk like 'pooh-pooh' and 'tinkle' and all of these things. They were the first one to do that and kind of stretch the borders of what you could get away with saying. Like, 'So-and-so said, 'I'm afraid to go out because I might BLANK in my pants'.' And they would say 'tinkle' or what people called baby-talk, scatological terms. That began to spread, until you get to the point now where you can say '[BLANK]' on *NYPD Blue* and stuff. So, for good or bad, it was all funny and we enjoyed doing it, but it was one of the things that broke down the barriers, depending on how you look at it whether it's good or bad. It's either 'free.' or it's the 'decline and fall of the Roman empire.'

"Someone told me a funny story about that. There was a short-lived sitcom called *Carlucci's Department* with James Coco—you know who James Coco is?—and they were doing stuff like that, and this guy was a guest on the show, and he saw the producer coming out of a meeting with the Standards and Practices guy. And he was saying, 'You can't say 'caca.'' The line was, 'The whole world is caca!' He said, 'You can't say caca.' He says, 'But we said tinkle, we said, pooh-pooh, we said doo-doo.' 'I gave you two doo-doos and a tinkle in this very script, but you can't say caca.' He says, 'Take back the tinkles.' 'We gotta have the caca.'

"Auntie Brett, please explain Orson's answer to me."
—Charles Nelson Reilly

'Okay, well, I'll give you back one of the tinkles and the two doo-doos, but give me the caca.' And these were grown men with suits and neckties on! It was so weird, and it really came out of *The Match Game.*"

Of course, Orson made his own contributions to *Match Game's* collection of euphemisms, as when he was on the panel when Gene read off the following question: *"Weird Wilma said, 'You know that little old man who lives inside the refrigerator and turns the light on and off? Well, this morning I opened the door and caught him BLANKing in the Jell-o.'"*

While the contestant and other panelists gave the answers 'swimming,' 'sitting,' 'skating,' and 'sleeping,' it was Orson Bean—sitting next to Brett—who answered "tinkling."

Of course, sometimes the contestants took the show's naughty reputation just a little too seriously, as when Gene read off the following: "*Sid said, 'I read a really revised version of the Bible. In this one, the world is created in six days and on the seventh day Adam and Eve go to a* <u>BLANK</u>*.'*"

The contestant, in his quest to be cutting-edge, replied with "an orgy"—pretty 'with it' for the swinging seventies, but the practical-minded Gene was perplexed with the answer. "You've read the Bible, right? If there were Adam and Eve, how the hell could they go to an *orgy*?" But I liked it when Brett threw in, "Whatever gets you through the night, babe."

Oh, by the way—what was up with Howard Cosell?

Well, this may not explain why he was used in so many jokes, but it's a nifty anecdote anyway: When *Family Feud* began its run, polls were conducted among studio audiences of other Goodson-Todman shows to supply questions and answers for the show, and one of the questions, written by Mark Goodson himself, was "Name someone many people dislike."

The four answers most often given by the New York audience of *To Tell the Truth* were, in order, Richard Nixon, Adolph Hitler, the Devil, and sports announcer Howard Cosell.

"I didn't trust that poll," admitted Mark Goodson. "I had it taken again, this time asking one hundred people in the audience of *The Price Is Right*, three thousand miles away in Los Angeles. The results were Richard Nixon, Adolph Hitler, the Devil, Howard Cosell. I still didn't believe it. We then polled one hundred people by mail, in all parts of the country. For the third time, it was Richard Nixon, Adolph Hitler, the Devil, and Howard Cosell. Then I believed it."

The Writers

While the contestants and panelists were willing accomplices to pushing that envelope, the writers (A.K.A. *Editorial Staff*) were the real envelope-pushers.

I asked Elliot Feldman, one of the writers who worked on the show, what the editorial staff's daily schedule was like. "It varied. It varied personally. Initially it was everybody worked by themselves, coming up with a lot of material. Depending on how much material was needed....And the group meetings were like *The Dick Van Dyke* Show, very funny-people stuff. Bobby Sherman was like Buddy on *The Dick Van Dyke Show*. He was very funny, Borscht-belt comedian type of guy, like that. Joe Neustein is very funny; he's like a joke savant, he could pull it out of anywhere. His style is like a late-night-television—in the joke style. Then when Joel Hecht joined us after Patrick [Neary] left, you know, he had a very schmaltzy, New York kind of style; kind of that Borscht-belt style. It was very funny. It was a lot of fun. And for quite a while, after I was there a few years, they let me work at home."

Dick De Bartolo

Dick DeBartolo had been the sole writer of questions used on the original *Match Game* back in New York, and when *Match Game* was revived in 1973, Mark Goodson approached Dick and asked if he would be willing to relocate to the west coast to write for the show. But Dick was still writing for New York-based *MAD Magazine* (he's been there now for over forty years) and declined the offer. But they arranged for Dick to write questions in New York and send them to the West Coast. "I was at all the tapings when the show was in NYC," he told one interviewer. "When it went to California, Goodson let me write questions from NYC, because he knew I had to be here for *MAD*.

"It's so weird. [Recently] I was out at the Consumer Electronics Show for my other career as the 'Gizmo Guy,' so I was with a bunch of reporters. And we were talking about everything under the sun. 'Oh, I'm so addicted to the Game Show Network, I can't get enough of *The Match Game*,' this woman says. 'Well, for seventeen years, I wrote for it.'

"When it was in New York I was the only writer. When it went to California, obviously they needed writers right there. And I just sent my stuff every week. I used to mail it. We had what we called 'the pouch' which would just get Fed-Exed every day between Goodson New York and Goodson California."

"He would send stuff in [written on] three-by-five cards," explains Elliot Feldman. "While we were in the writer's meeting, we would either go through the stuff there, sometimes we'd put him on speakerphone, other times we'd just go through his work, you know. It was part of the session.

"I went out there once just to shake hands and stuff, but I really just—everything was done out there [in L.A.]," said Dick. "I came out for three months when Goodson had a summer show called *What's My Line?* It was a one-hour prime time show that interviewed people with strange occupations. So that was the only time I was out there for an extended time. I went out when they did the pilot."

As for *Match Game*, "I think that we just [wrote racier questions] for the nighttime show with the thought that they would probably go a little further in the nighttime. And I remember a question I wrote, and back then—but I did it as a *joke*. 'Unlucky Louie was so unlucky, when he went on a diet and lost two inches. But he didn't lose it from his waist, he lost it from his BLANK.' And there was hysteria as [the panel answered] 'nose,' 'hair.' Yeah, I think we tried to push the envelope, but I think we used to sometimes just send stuff we knew would never get on air just to see..."

"Did network executives ever veto any of the questions?" I asked.

"It never got that far. I know for awhile Goodson read them, but occasionally Bob [Sherman] would say, 'You know, we're thinking that we don't want White House questions.' They might just say, you know, 'Here's a category you might want to think about.' I never got any kind of memo or anything saying, 'Tone it down.'

"Actually, I thought Gene Rayburn was great. I mean, I liked the show. I loved the fact that it was the first game show where the contestants, and a lot of the celebrities, would say outrageous things about the contestants. I remember Brett Somers once braying, 'Do they not *screen* these people? Do they not *tell* these people what this show is about?' It was one of the funniest on-camera moments."

Elliot Feldman

"I'm originally from Detroit," said Elliot, "so I literally came into town with my life wrapped in black vinyl trash bags. And this was mid-seventies, very counter-cultural at the time—long hair, big beard. And I did everything they say you're not supposed to do, and that's actually show up in person and ask people for work. So I just knocked on a lot of doors, and eventually I wound up in a producer/director named Paul Alter's office. Of course I'd heard he was accepting freelance game material for *Tattletales*, which was a celebrity *Newlywed Game*. And so, to give you an idea of where I was financially at the time, I was making about fifty bucks a week writing those questions, and I said to Paul, 'Look, I can make it on seventy-five. Is there any other show that could use some freelance work?' and he said, 'Why don't you try writing up some *Match Game* material?' I said, 'Oh.'

"Well, most of my life I've been a cartoonist, and writing those *Match Game* questions was like writing a one-box cartoon with about eight different punch lines. So I wrote a bunch of them and got called in, and they said, 'You know, we like your questions. I want you to write another batch'. Wrote another batch, handed it in a day later, and then they called me in. And they brought me in, in front of all the guys—Bobby Sherman, Ira Skutch, Joe Neustein. Patrick Neary was writing at the time. Actually, he was leaving as I was arriving. Dick DeBartolo was in New York. And they said, 'How would you like to join the staff?' And that was it. They hired me right off the street, almost.

"Along the way as the show progressed, we added a couple of writers, and some left. Arnie Meissner, Maxine Nunes—I actually saw her last weekend—Abbe Schorow.

"Well, I wrote only for a short time with *Tattletales*...and they put me full time on *The Match Game* because it was the kind of show where the [question] seemed simple when you look at it, but it was extremely difficult to write because you're trying to be funny and you're trying to make material a play in the game. And so you're trying to work two different sides of your brain and stuff. So they put me on full time; I guess they needed the extra brain in there. So, that's about it. I've worked on quite a few other Goodson-Todman shows.

"When I was a kid, I remember vaguely the New York show. I was never a game show kid, which is kind of strange. I came out to Los Angeles to be an animator, and they were on strike...To be honest, when I was back in Detroit, right before I came to Los Angeles, I was kind of a closet fan of the show."

Gene: "Sheila said, 'I went to a plastic surgeon, and boy was he rotten. My new nose looks like my BLANK'."

Elaine Joyce: "I said 'Liver.'"

Gene: "And may I ask why?"

Elaine: "I had it for dinner."

The writers were present on the set on taping days. "Always," says Elliot. "Always. In fact, Johnny Olson, the announcer, would be on one side of the stage, to warm up the audience, and I'd be on the other side of the stage and telling them to quiet down for the Bonus Rounds or helping Johnny with the applause and all that stuff.

"We often ate with the celebrities in the Green Room. Most of [the regulars] ate in their own dressing rooms. Sometimes they'd stop by and say hello. A lot of times the guests would come in and eat with us. Like Zsa Zsa came in; she had a little poodle with her. And she took a plate full of food and she took one bite, made a face, put the plate down on the floor with the poodle, and we're all eating the food and watching the poodle have dinner just like us.

"Now, the writers had warm-ups for the technical people before the show started. So the writers sat in with the stand-ins on the set to do the warm-up test. And we did that usually for every show. Joe Neustein would fill in for Gene Rayburn, and I'd be one of the contestants, and one of the other writers would sit in and be one of the other contestants. And one of the SAG actors would be sitting in one of the panel chairs.

"We used to like to pull off gags during these run-throughs. One of them in particular, we had no idea it was being piped throughout the studio. And I was particularly notorious with the gags, and a lot of them were sight gags. It was Joe Neustein's birthday, and me and his girlfriend decided to surprise him. The day before, I went over to Frederick's of Hollywood and got one of those one-size-fits-all male panty girdles. It was flesh colored, so you could wear a bathing suit underneath, but it looks like you're naked. I took sweat socks and I stuffed them in the crotch area, so it looks like a Genoa salami, you know, big long thing. And it looked like I'm stark naked.

"So I'm sitting there and we have this turntable that went around with the contestants, and his girlfriend is sitting next to me, and she's got a birthday cake with all the candles all lit. And it looks like I don't have a shirt on. So they don't know. And then the thing spins around and Joe almost falls over and we sang *Happy Birthday*. And I said, 'Joe, since it's your birthday, I decided to wear my birthday suit,' and you know, I stood up and had this big schlong in my hand, and at the end was a three-by-five card that said, 'Happy Birthday Joe.' And the camera guy zoomed in on the card, you know, and everybody fell on the ground.

"The show started, and Ira comes running out saying the run-through was piped in all over the studio and that Gene Rayburn was ballistic and was absolutely going through the roof and he wanted me fired. And you know, I said, 'Ira, I'll never do that again. Gee, I'm sorry. I'll never do that again.' Right, who *wouldn't* do it again? Anyways—so I thought, 'Well, I'm out. I just got fired, what the hell.'

"The show's dress is about halfway through, and Richard Dawson's sons came over to me, and one is about eighteen and the other's about fifteen. They said, 'Our father saw what you did out there and was on the ground. He thought it was the funniest thing he ever saw.' I said, 'Well, Gene Rayburn didn't.' And they said, 'Oh, he didn't like it?' I said, 'No, he hated it. He wants me out of there.' So they went running back into the dressing room and told Richard Dawson I was about to get fired, and Richard interceded on my behalf. So anyways, I'm eternally grateful to him.

"Kind of a side note with that, a few weeks later there was a woman that was a sound engineer in the booth, and she was a friend of mine, and she was friends with all the *Saturday Night Live* people. And about a month later was the first Richard Pryor variety show, and the opening—she was on the ground floor for that gag, too—the opening sketch for that show was the one that got him into trouble. He was standing up, it was just him on the stage alone with the Frederick's of Hollywood one-size-fits-all panty hose, so it looks like he's naked, but instead of the schlong part it's blank like a Barbie doll. And that's when he got into trouble with it. And I've always suspected that it was a twist on what I did. I always thought it got back to them because she was friends with all of those people."

R. Patrick Neary

"Growing up, I'd never had any strong feelings about game shows one way or another, not even about possibly becoming a contestant. I certainly never had an inkling that I'd ever work on any television show. I would have dismissed such a thought as an unattainable fantasy."

Yet the fantasy was attained in a most unexpected, even storybook fashion. Raised in Scranton, Pennsylvania and Penn Grove-Carneys Point, New Jersey, he dropped out of engineering school and found himself needing a day job. "As luck would have it, I ran into friend (from grade school and high school) who said *The Mike Douglas Show* was looking for an usher, and suggested I check the bulletin board. I found the notice there and called. The next day, Friday the 13th, I went for my interview and was hired. They put me right to work that day—and my whole world changed. I worked as an usher (page) and after about six months was offered my boss's job (audience coordinator/house manager) after she moved on. I stayed there for three and a half years while continuing full time at [St. Joseph's College, now University, in Philadelphia].

"At that time, *The Mike Douglas Show* was the Number One syndicated program in the country. I met many young creative people there, many who later went on to Hollywood. One of them, Rick Rosner, later creator of *CHiPS*, called one night and wanted me to move to L.A. to work on *The Steve Allen Show* as a production assistant. Five days later I was living and working in Hollywood.

"After a couple of other shows, I was offered my first game show position as a writer for the CBS/Jack Barry production *Hollywood's Talking*, which wasn't a bad show but was cancelled after an 11-week run. Then came *Match Game*..."

He continues, "CBS quickly replaced *Hollywood's Talking* with Goodson-Todman's new *Match Game 73*. Word on the street was that there were no writing jobs available there, so I didn't even call. But a few weeks into the series, I got a call from Bob Sherman, with whom I'd worked at *The Steve Allen Show* and on some other projects, and we'd continued to be in touch. They were considering adding a writer, he said, and suggested I put together twenty-five to thirty sample *Match Game* questions.

"I did so that very night and went in to meet with Bob and with Ira Skutch, the producer. Bob and Ira seemed to think my questions were good. Ira asked me to wait while he took my page of questions up to the 14th floor. When he came back fifteen or twenty minutes later, I noticed that just three of the questions were circled. I didn't think that was a good sign, but Ira arranged for a typewriter and suggested that I take up residence temporarily with Bob Sherman in his office until they arranged a proper space. He never did actually say I got the job!

"'Oh, one other thing,' Ira said. 'We do a lot of shouting here, and we've already got someone named Pat (an associate producer), so what would you like to be called? How about Patrick?' That resonated with me immediately, and ever since that moment I've always strongly preferred to be called Patrick—never Pat, not anymore.

"I soon discovered why three good questions were enough. My sample questions introduced characters already known elsewhere in our culture, including commercials, comics, radio, movies, even literature. Until that time, the only characters used regularly were John and Mary. One of Elliot Feldman's and Joe Neustein's biggest contributions was that they came up with original characters.

"Although I didn't actually write for other G-T shows (in fact, most of them on the air at that time didn't require writing *per se*), we all contributed to shows in development in one way or another. I remember playing a contestant during an in-office run-through for *Now You See It*. In answering I mispronounced the name of the philosopher Goethe, but made the score. (I knew the answer but had never heard it pronounced. So much for book learning!) Everyone had a good laugh over that one. Another time, Richard Dawson was auditioning for a host position—it was in his contract that he be given the opportunity. I remember he surprised everyone—he was great! That of course led to his becoming host of *Family Feud*.

"I have never since worked with such a great group of people, and it was a number of years before I recognized just how good I had it there at G-T, and how rare a working situation that really is.

"Joe Neustein and I shared an office in the *Match Game/Password/Concentration* suite on the tenth floor at 6430 Sunset. *Price Is Right* and Mark Goodson's west coast office was on the fourteenth floor, where film writer-director Nancy Meyers (*Private Benjamin, Father of The Bride*, many others) was the receptionist at the time.

"Our office looked South over the entire L.A. basin. I miss that view! We worked from about ten am until six. Elliot joined the show sometime during my last year there and seemed to fit right in. But the office they had for him was also the *Password* word library which, unfortunately, was also windowless. But I never heard Elliot complain. Dick DeBartolo only visited our west coast office once during my time there, but he's an instantly likeable guy, and funny as heck. The other writers you mention were after my time.

"Most of our time was spent 'hanging out,' waiting for inspiration to strike, and you never knew when it would, whether you were in the office or not. We'd try new questions out on each other, then on other staff people to see if we got the answers (and reactions) we were looking for.

"Remember, we weren't writing novels. The way I thought of the writing task was that we had to paint a cartoon picture in the listener/viewer's mind, then add a caption that had a blank in the critical place in the punch-line. Hearing the question, your mind would automatically fill in the blank, and you'd laugh because two or more answers would pop into your head at the same time, especially if one of the answers was a bit risqué.

"Bob Sherman and Ira Skutch also contributed questions regularly, as Mark Goodson also did on occasion. A couple times a week we'd meet with Ira to review new questions as a group. We wouldn't just vote them in or out. We'd try to make them work, but if one didn't work we'd all agree on why. Ira would read the questions Dick DeBartolo would send in from New York. Then in another meeting before a studio weekend, on Ira's giant conference table, we'd lay out the questions and arrange them by show and grouped in sequence. We were careful not to overdo the racy ones. At one point I was told (but I forget by whom) that I was the one who came up with the 'funny' 'clean' ones.

"We'd also come up with the words or phrases for the Super Match. I believe the polls were completed by people waiting in line for *Price Is Right* or one or another of the G-T shows.

"There were no difficult parts of the job! It spoiled me forever, because now I know it's possible to do work I enjoy, make good money, and hang out with great people. (So why did I leave? That's what everybody asks. I'll get to that.)

"These shows were really 'live on tape.' It was very rare that a flub might require an edit in post-production. Generally they went out on the air exactly as they happened in the studio. There were monitors everywhere in the studio, so we instantly knew what the broadcast would look like.

On taping days, Patrick says, "We were all there on the set during the show. We had studio tasks, such as helping lead the applause, or holding cue cards during the Super Match. We taped the show in Studio 33 at CBS, alternating weekends with *The Price Is Right*. During the week, that was the *Carol Burnett Show* studio.

"During camera rehearsal before the taping, I was the host of the show, playing the Gene Rayburn role. This came to be one of my favorite parts of the job. The other writers and staff people would play the celebrities and contestants, and we'd do the show as if for real. We'd use the previous week's questions, but everyone would play for real, including ad-libbing and joking. It was a very creative bunch. The whole thing would take twenty minutes and we'd all get paid union scale for two hours minimum, since we'd had to join the union (AFTRA) for that purpose.

"At one point, Mike Ogiens, who was head of daytime programming at CBS, was in the studio during rehearsal and afterward asked if I was interested in actually becoming a game show host. I didn't take him seriously at the time, but later I wondered. I don't think he was kidding.

"Until that time, the history of my life had been characterized by shyness, so it was as surprising to me as to anyone that I volunteered to host during rehearsal. Ira had come into our office one day and said that he needed to find a replacement for Peter (the previous rehearsal host) before the weekend. My hand shot up and I said, 'I'll do it!' To this day, I don't know what possessed me to do that. But in fact I turned out to be pretty good at it.

"Everyone was friendly, including all the celebrities, though some were more likely than others to join us staff folks in the green room during the meal break. One of the rules in show business is to not necessarily disturb performers before or during a show, so we never considered it odd that some preferred their dressing room during breaks. I do remember Charles Nelson Reilly dropping by, and Gary Burghoff and his wife liked to eat with us folks. And of course Gene came by regularly, too.

"Nothing less than a life-altering experience could have made me even consider leaving *Match Game*, but that's exactly what happened. I've never shared this real reason with anyone connected with the show or even with my family, but here it is.

"Sitting on my couch one evening, I had a profoundly spiritual experience, which included having my entire life before my eyes in a blink. There'd been no imminent danger, I was just sitting there reading. Apparently I'd begun a train of logical thought that went popping off like a string of firecrackers, essentially around the idea that my surroundings were a pure reflection of myself, but it was hitting me in a progressively profound way. I'd been reading the Bible, Ram Dass, and P.D. Ouspensky/Gurdjieff, and several other spiritual books. The string of thoughts led directly to a brief but timeless moment in which my entire life passed by, chronologically and in complete detail before my inner eye but in literally no time, and I suddenly saw my relationship with the universe.

"It was years before I could describe what happened, and I told nobody about it—because I couldn't. I later learned that some people call this a 'peak experience.' I had long heard about some people having had their lives flash before their eyes. But I've ever heard or read about others having both experiences more or less simultaneously. In this clarity of mind I saw that game shows were fine but not something I should spend my life on. My spiritual 'seeking' shifted into a higher gear after this experience. But I didn't know how to explain it to anyone, and I did have concerns about risking ridicule.

"That was in March 1975. I decided then and there that I would leave television. I went in to the office the next work day, prepared to resign. Curiously, as luck or something would have it, Mark Goodson announced *Match Game PM*—and essentially doubled the writers' salaries! As for the workload, this meant that, to carry my weight, I'd have to write six good questions a week instead of five! So I then stayed for several more months until the PM show was established, partly because it would be unconscionable to leave at a critical time like that, and partly because I could bank the extra money.

"One of my brothers thought I must have been fired, because why would anyone leave a fun, easy job on the top-rated TV show? Goodson-Todman gave me one heck of a going-away party at The Magic Castle (an exclusive private club) so I'm pretty sure my departure was on good terms!

"Afterward, did some intensive volunteer work, and pursued creative speculation for television with a partner for a couple of years. I ended up at Ralph Edwards Productions on and off with several shows over several years. NBC's *Knockout* with Arte Johnson, *The CrossWits*, *Name That Tune*, then as Creative Consultant in program development....

"Why didn't I go back to G-T? I'm not sure exactly, but I seemed to remember that generally people weren't invited back after leaving. But more than that, I think I was embarrassed that I hadn't really succeeded at whatever my new thing was (volunteering, etc.), plus I no longer really cared for TV, in the sense that my heart was no longer in it. I'd developed values. I saw the immense power of TV and thought it was mostly wasted and sometimes perverted—increasingly so as time goes on.

"At Ralph Edwards Productions, my last title was Creative Consultant, working on finding or creating new programs. Trying to design game shows, I continually ran into a big problem: Every time I got to the heart of a human 'game' and tried to turn it into a game show, there was Mark Goodson's mark—he'd already been there. I didn't want to fashion a mere derivative, and Goodson had mined most of the originals: *The Price Is Right*, *To Tell The Truth*, *Match Game*, *Password*, *Beat The Clock*,

What's My Line?—all of these are derived from the 'games' of daily life in our culture."

"Am I surprised that people still like *Match Game*? Initially surprised, but not after watching it again. It really holds up because it's a classic, and because we all really did have fun doing it. And it's a classic because Mark Goodson designed it, and he was a true master. Goodson's description of what makes a good game was 'luck and skill in nice proportion'.

"I only have cable for internet access these days, so I'm unable to see the Game Show Channel reruns, at least not directly. When they first began running there, a friend at work taped a week's worth for me. I surely enjoyed watching that tape. I regret that I haven't been in touch with anyone from the show for a while, and I hope there's opportunity to do so. If ever there's a reunion, I'll be there!

Classic Match Game Moments

While the writing staff provided the fill-in-the-blank questions inspiring a wild array of offbeat answers, some of the show's best moments happened out of imporvisation and some sort of natural social combustion. There was the time Gene Rayburn, handsomely dressed in a gray flannel chalkstripe suit, found himself surrounded by Richard and Charles, both armed with pieces of chalk, who suddenly began playing an impromptu game of Tic-Tac-Toe, adding "x's" and "O's" to the fabric of Gene's blazer. And then there was the time when, while railing against the weeklong mini-series *Shogun* (based on the James Clavell novel and starring Richard Chamberlain, Toshiro Mifune and an all-star cast) Charles accidentally socked Gene in the jaw, knocking him temporarily to the floor before McLean Stevenson took up the mike and began hosting a round of the show. Or the time when Gene read off the question conccerning "Sally the stripper," who was tired of dating the musician who kept trying to tune her BLANK; while seeking a matching answer Gene commanded Betty, "Show us your 'G-string,'" prompting our Miss White to begin a striptease. Or that *other* time Betty performed a striptease on the panel (I'm sensing a pattern here about Betty). Or the time Gene spontaneously demonstrated some killer Disco moves as the sound department played the Bee Gees' newest hit, *Staying Alive* from the then-current box office hit, *Saturday Night Fever*. Or when Gene entered the set on roller skates. Or the time when Gene was interrupted leading into a tie-breaking question, so instead decided to climb up seats in the audience to reach the cameraman manning Camera Five..

The *Match Game* editorial staff was clever and talented, no doubt about it, and together, their writing talents "matched" perfectly with the host's and panel members' inborn sense of showmanship.

Review Questions

1. Gene Rayburn once said, if you're ever stumped for an answer on *Match Game*, answer with <u>BLANK</u>.

a. Boobs, booze, or Howard Cosell.
b. Larry, Moe or Curly.
c. Mary Wilson, Flo Ballard, or Diana Ross.

2. During one infamous blooper, Marcia Wallace was censored for answering with <u>BLANK</u>.

a. "Watergate."
b. "Brett's name is NOT Susan!"
c. "Genitalia."

3. When Mark Goodson polled studio audiences to name four things most people dislike, the answers invariably read <u>BLANK</u>.

a. Goodson-Todman's four most popular game shows.
b. Richard Nixon, Adolph Hitler, the Devil, and Howard Cosell.
c. Patti Deutsch, Patti Deustch, Patti Deutsch, and Patti Deutsch.

Answers: 1. a., 2. c., 3. b.

15

Dumb Dora Is Sooo Dumb...

Beginning New Year's Eve, 1962 until the end of the classic run of *Match Game* in 1982, Dick DeBartolo wrote thousands of questions for *Match Game*. After the show ended its run, Mark Goodson Productions (as the show had been renamed upon Bill Todman's death) closed up their New York offices. All the files were packed up and thrown into dumpsters. As he watched the boxes of *Match Game* questions being trashed Dick thought to himself, "I should take some of them as a souvenir!" So he stuffed a bunch in some envelopes and let the rest go off to the dumpsters.

After spending more than $85,000 in storage fees, Dick recently went through his storage space (otherwise known as "Dick's Gadget Warehouse") and came across a bunch of original *Match Game* question cards. So here, thanks to Dick DeBartolo's foresight, we present a small piece of television history—or at least, a few small three-by-five-inch pieces!

And—because it's my book—here is my personal favorite *Match Game* question. Don't ask me why: "Weird Willie is really weird. Instead of making obscene phone calls, he makes obscene BLANK calls." Five out of six celebs answered "house calls," but clever Marcia Wallace came up with the much more appropriate "bird calls." Now THAT'S weird!

2454

Complete this sentence with one word:

Hollywood turns out a lot of _____

movies.

A note on the back of the card above indicates it was used in the June 3, 1963 episode of the show featuring Rod Serling and Joan Fontaine as the celebrity guests. A note on the back of the card below indicates it was used in the February 17, 1965 episode of the show featuring Lauren Bacall and Abe Burrows as the celebrity guests.

10,055

Complete this sentence with one or more words:

Mary had a short circuit in her _____.

Complete this sentence by <u>finishing</u> the word:

John did not like to be disturbed

when he was _____ing.

21,196

While it was still a few years before network censors working on *Match Game* tapings would have to worry about questions conjuring up answers like "making whoopee" and using words like "boobs," Dick DeBartolo's questions still put the dirty minds of New York's *cognoscenti* to work in finding appropriate alternative answers, if not quite the euphemisms that would put the seventies *Match Game* on the network map.

WORD

JOHN SAID TO MARY: "I'VE HAD <u>ENOUGH</u>

OF YOUR ____ING."

Match Game 101

Complete this sentence by finishing the word 23,367
as you think your teammates will:

John told Mary all his _____s.

A note on the back of the card above indicates it was used in the March 7, 1969 episode of the show featuring William Shatner and Dina Merrill as the celebrity guests. Below, when *Match Game* was revived in 1973, the first questions used resembled those on the NBC version. But it wouldn't be long before Dick and the other writers introduced characters like Dumb Dora and Weird Willie and made sport of their antics.

46.

JOHN DIDN'T USE HIS _____ ENOUGH, AND
IT GOT RUSTY.

ddb 8/1/75

ON THE CAMPING TRIP, HARVEY SAID: "BOY

THE TELEVISION RECEPTION OUT HERE WAS

TERRIBLE UNTIL I DISCOVERED I COULD USE MY

_____ AS AN ADDITIONAL TV ANTENNA."

CAR, TIN FOIL, HAND, BODY

The nighttime version of the show, called *Match Game PM*, was launched in 1975 and ran until 1981. While game play for the most part was unchanged, since the *PM* version aired in Prime-time, the questions—and answers—became racier, pushing the envelope as far as what was acceptable on American network television.

ddb 2/27/76

THE PILLSBURY DOUGH BOY SAID: "I DON'T

KNOW WHAT'S WRONG, BUT I CAN'T SEEM TO

GET MY _____ TO RISE."

BREAD, MUFFINS, CAKE, ROLLS, ETC....

12/17/76 ddb

GENE RAYBURN SAID: "ON MY C.B. RADIO THIS
MORNING, I HEARD SOMEONE WHOSE HANDLE WAS
                                        LOT
'BIG MOUTH'.... IT SOUNDED AN AWFUL/LIKE
_____." 90

HOWARD COSELL, BRETT

There was *a lot* of ribbing done at Brett's expense in the questions, and at one point she blew her top at Charles and the writers for making her the brunt of so many jokes, though celebrity coordinator Kay Henley insisted, "Any 'ribbing' done between the stars was in fun and for the camera."

12/24/76 ddb

90

THE PRIEST SAID TO THE LITTLE BOY: "SON,
IT'S NOT NICE TO _____ IN THE HOLY
WATER."

PLAY, SWIM, WASH, TINKLE?

4/29/77 ddb

AUDREY SAID: "I DON'T MIND WHEN MY MARGARINE

TALKS...BUT THIS LAST PACKAGE OF MARGARINE

_____S."

SWEARS, SINGS

[signature: Rick Hurst]

"We came up with questions alone or together, worked on them together until they were honed," said *Match Game* writer R, Patrick Neary. "This is where I learned the precision of language—we often haggled about whether a certain question should be worded '*the* BLANK' or '*a* BLANK' because '*the*' or '*a*' led to very different answers. I use this appreciation for precise language to this day.

5/6/77 ddb

BARRY SAID: "I DON'T WANT TO SAY MY WIFE IS A

BAD COOK, BUT WE DON'T SERVE WINE WITH EVERY

MEAL....WE SERVE _____WITH EVERY MEAL."

BROMO SELTZER, STOMACH PUMPS, TUMS

```
                                        6/3/77 ddb

  AT THE BAR FRANK SAID:  "THIS IS THE WEIRDEST

  XXXXXX GLASS OF BEER I'VE EVER SEEN...IT NOT

  XXXX ONLY HAS A HEAD ON IT, IT ALSO HAS A

  _____."

  HAT, TOUPEE, FOOT
```

"Nobody ever pushed us one way or the other about raciness," said *Match Game* writer R, Patrick Neary. "Everyone was aware that there was a line that could not be crossed—but you could dance on it (the line itself), and that's essentially what we did."

```
                                        7/29/77 ddb

  KATE SAID TO THE OWNER OF THE PET SHOP:

  "I THINK THERE'S SOMETHING WRONG WITH

  THAT POINTER DOG YOU SOLD ME...HE POINTS

  ALRIGHT...BUT HE POINTS WITH HIS_____."

  TAIL, FINGER, PECKER
```

The Match Game Who's-Who Glossary

According to Robert Sherman, "We used pop cultural references in the questions quite a bit, but we were very careful about what we were referencing. Even though we had the highest audience overall, we also knew that a sizable chunk of our audience were women, so we were very careful to keep questions involving sports to a minimum. We also tried not to use references to rock music because male or female, the audience that watched daytime television wasn't an audience that knew rock music. So that was a touchy area, you had to know what you could write that the audience would want to play along with at home."

Not sure about some of the dated references to people, places or things found in some of those *Match Game* questions? Here's a guide to help you through some of the personalities mentioned from time to time on the show.

Suzy Chapstick

Olympic alpine ski racer Suzy Chaffee was a three-time world freestyle skiing champion who was the first woman to serve on the board of the U.S. Olympics committee. Following her racing career she acted and modeled, famously appearing in commercials as a spokesperson for ChapStick lip balm—hence her nickname, "Suzy ChapStick."

Billy Carter

William Alton Carter III (March 29, 1937-September 25, 1988), better known by his nickname "Billy," was the younger brother of former Georgia governor and U.S. President President Jimmy Carter. While his brother entered politics, Billy owned and operated a gas and service station in Plains, Georgia. In 1977 he endorsed Billy Beer, introduced by the Falls City Brewing Company, capitalizing on Billy's colorful image as a beer-drinking, Southern 'good ol' boy.' Known for his outlandish behavior (often brought on by his love of beer) he was occasionally used as a gag answer for Carter-era questions used on *Match Game*.

The Energy Crisis

The energy crisis of the seventies was a period when major industrial nations of the world, in particular the United States, faced substantial shortages and raised prices of petroleum due to an embargo imposed by members of OPEC, the Organization of Petroleum Exporting Countries, beginning in 1973 and running through most of the decade.

Euell Gibbons

An outdoorsman and a proponent of natural diets in the sixties and seventies, Gibbons authored a string of cookbooks starting with the 1962 bestseller *Stalking the Wild Asparagus* and starred in a famous 1974 commercial for Post Grape Nuts cereal in which he declared the cereal's taste "reminded me of wild hickory nuts."

Mrs. Olson

Character actress Virginia Christine (March 5, 1920-July 24, 1996) had a long career on stage, on television, and in films including *Invasion of the Body Snatchers*, *Judgment at Nuremburg* and *Guess Who's Coming to Dinner?* but she was most famous for appearing as spokesperson in a number of Folgers Coffee commercials as "Mrs. Olson," offering her specially blended "mountain grown" coffee to friends and neighbors alike.

Twiggy

Twiggy, whose real name was Lesley Hornby, was an English-born top fashion model in the late sixties, gracing the covers of *Vogue*, *Tatler* and other fashion magazines. Her thin build (which initially earned her the nickname "Sticks," then "Twigs," and finally "Twiggy"), large eyes and boyish haircut made her a sensation in the "Mod" era. Later she had a successful career on stage, in film, and on TV.

8/3/77 ddb

THE COWBOY SAID: "MY NEW WIFE IS WEIRD...
I TOLD HER TO <u>PACK</u> MY GUN, AND SHE PUT
_____IN THE BARREL..."

UNDERWEAR, MY TOOTHBRUSH, A SUITCASE

"If a question seemed to have only one likely answer, and especially if it was a racier answer, then Ira would say it was 'too much on the nose,'" observed *Match Game* writer R, Patrick Neary. "But if you mess with a listener's mind by wording the question in such a way that the answer can just as likely be 'nose' or 'big toe,' then you get laughter as the response."

3/2/79 ddb

LARRY SAID: "BOY DID I HAVE A WEIRD
EXPERIENCE LAST NIGHT. I <u>WALKED</u> INTO A
DRIVE IN RESTAURANT...AND SINCE I DIDN'T
HAVE A CAR, THEY HUNG THE TRAY ON MY
_____."

NECK, LIPS

```
(IRA: IS THE COMMERCIAL WITH JOE NAMATH
WEARING PANTYHOSE OUT IN LA?) Yes.


NOW THAT THERE'S A COMMERCIAL SHOWING JOE

NAMATH ACTUALLY WEARING PANTY HOSE, I WONDER

HOW LONG IT WILL BE BEFORE SOME COMPANY TRIES

TO GET HIM TO WEAR A _____.
```

Since they were working for television, the writers from time to time referenced in their questions characters in popular TV commercials, such as "The Pillsbury Dough Boy" and "The Ty-D-Bol Man.". When football star Joe Namath appeared in a commercial illustrating that Beautymist pantyhose could make anyone's legs look great, including his own, Dick formed a question (double-checking with Ira that the commercial was likely to have been seen across the country so contestants and panelists would 'get' it.

```
                                    ddb 2/27/76

   THE PILLSBURY DOUGH BOY SAID:    "I DON'T

   KNOW WHAT'S WRONG, BUT I CAN'T SEEM TO

   GET MY _____ TO RISE."

   BREAD, MUFFINS, CAKE, ROLLS, ETC....
```

DUMB DORA WAS SO DUMB, WHEN HE RICH BOYFRIEND

TOLD HER SHE WOULD SOON BE ROLLING IN THE

DOUGH, DUMB DORA COVERED HERSELF WITH

_____.

RAISINS, PIZZA SAUCE, FLOUR

When Gene began a question with, "Dumb Dora is *SO* dumb," the audience (of course) responded with "How dumb *IS* she?"—which Gene at first encouraged although after awhile, and especially when Gene was pressed for time, the charm of the audience participation began to wear thin.

DUMB DORA WAS SO DUMB, WHEN SHE HEARD THE

WALLS HAD EARS, SHE PUT _____S ON THEM.

EAR PLUGS, EARRINGS, EAR MUFFS

```
                                          9/2/77 ddb


   MILDRED SAID TO DUMB DORA:   "MY SON'S

   A SHRIMP....SO DUMB DORA COVERED HIM

   WITH _____."

   COCKTAIL SAUCE, BATTER, LEMON
```

In time, Dumb Dora was joined in her adventures by Dumb Donald, Weird Willie, and a host of other recurring characters. When a questions concerned Count Dracula, Gene would fashion an appropriately camp Rumanian accent as he read the question aloud to the contestants and panelists.

```
                                          7/29/77 ddb



      DUMB DORA WAS SO DUMB SHE THOUGHT

      "GREASE" WAS A MOVIE ABOUT _____.


      FRENCH FRIES, BURGER KING, ETC.
```

BARRY SAID: "I DON'T WANT TO SAY MY WIFE IS A

BAD COOK, BUT WE DON'T SERVE WINE WITH EVERY

MEAL....WE SERVE _____ WITH EVERY MEAL."

BROMO SELTZER, STOMACH PUMPS, TUMS

Gene (reading a question): "Tom said to Fred—"
Brett: "I already don't like this question."

THE GUARD AT THE BANK VAULT SAID: "PRICES OF

SOME THINGS ARE SO HIGH, I JUST SAW A GUY

PUT _____ IN A SAFE DEPOSIT BOX."

GASOLINE, MEAT, OIL

90

6/3/77 ddb

CATHY SAID: "BOY IS MY NEW BOYFRIEND DULL.
HE SAID HE WAS A GOOD MIXER, BUT IT TURNED
OUT HE'S IN THE _____ BUSINESS."

BAR, CEMENT, PAINT

6/3/77 ddb

LARRY SAID: "DATING A LIBRARIAN IS NO FUN
AT ALL.....EVERYTIME I START TO _____
SHE SAYS: 'Shhhhhhh!' ".

90

whisper sweet nothings, make love

15

Smoking and Drinking

"I have so many questions for you!" I confessed to Patti Deutsch when we met up for lunch.

"Do they involve drinking?" she asked me point-blank. She explained she had recently been approached by a particular cable channel putting together a program on funny game show moments. "All they wanted to know was about booze," she sighed.

The myth goes something like this: before going onstage, everyone in the Green Room would be swizzling up a storm, downing cocktails to either gain 'courage' or just loosen up, and the resulting antics that went on during the tapings were always the product of mildly drunken revelry.

Always?

According to Kay Henley they "never served cocktails on *Match Game.*" But Brett Somers admitted, "They had drinks. 'Whaddya want? We got it!' I always had vodka and club soda. Now where it *came* from, I didn't ask. I just always knew there was bottle of club soda, ice, and some vodka up there, and that's what I had. They used to serve drinks on *The Hollywood Squares.* Now, they don't anymore. People would just go on bombed! [On *Match Game*] we were always very circumspect, and nobody ever went on bombed."

This crowd didn't need to! Stone-cold sober they were a walking party. "I never saw anybody topple over the top tier," said Patti Deutsch. "I

"At Weird Willie's wedding the guests did not throw rice. Instead, they threw hay, because Weird Willie married a BLANK." While the contestant responded with "horse," Mel Tillis offered a different response. (Taken from a proof sheet in Gene Rayburn's estate.)

know people had a drink in their hand, but I don't remember people getting loaded. And I had enough trouble [sober]."

Jokes about drinking were commonplace on the show. Once when Brett was about to give a non-matching answer to a contestant who worked in a bar, she apologized, "I feel sorry about betraying a bartender; I feel such a *loyalty* to them."

"They also told you we drank on the show, didn't they?" Debralee Scott asked me. "They did it between lunch, you know? So if you watch the show, the first part of the week we're all sort of serious, but like Thursday and Friday and the night show—and if you ever watch the show and you see like Brett and Charles and Dawson and myself and other people [with] styrofoam cups? Not coffee. I'm telling you the truth. Nobody got blotto, but we just got loose and had fun. Nobody got sloppy, because we were still very professional. You had to be. Also, being an actor you didn't want to show—you never got that way. But you'd have one and you got a little looser, you got a little giddy, a little sillier. I think it did [add to the show] in a certain way because we just loosened up and got silly and that's what the whole show really was. It wasn't like—I would never do that on a *Pyramid* show or *Password*, you know, some show where you really had to be intelligent and smart. This was like comedy, you know? But nobody had more than one, nobody got sloshed or anything. At lunch we'd have like one little cocktail. Then it would just loosen everyone up and we would giggle."

"Especially this was on *Tattletales*, too," added Dolly Read Martin. "Especially knowing everybody, we would start having a little wine after the third show and it just got looser and looser. It was wonderful."

So there you go: Yes, drinks were served on taping days during the break. No, the panelists didn't have to be poured into their seats onstage during every taping.

...It Was Like How Everyone Smoked

When I asked Brianne Leary if anyone ever got blotto while she was on the panel of the show, she replied, "No, not that I know of, but on all those shows, everyone did! It was like how everyone smoked. Honestly, this is an interesting thing in working. I was like nineteen or twenty when I started working, and by that time I'd smoked a lot. And when I started *CHiPS*, the craft service guy just came up to me—and it would happen on every show that I did—'Well, what do you smoke?' And at the beginning of the week I'd have a carton of cigarettes in my dressing room. I mean, it was unbelievable!

"And every show that I'd done, and even the run-throughs like for the pilots I'd done, the comedies where you sit around the table and you rehearse, you know, you read through three days and then you get [it] up on its feet. And the amount of cigarettes! It was unbelievable. Everyone smoked, no one complained.

"I think Tony Randall was the first person to put a 'no smoking' ban on his set, because I know my girlfriend Lorna Patterson, who's a great friend to this day, did *Private Benjamin*. She was smoking a bit. She was doing a movie with Tony and she couldn't believe that no one was allowed to smoke on the set. And everyone smoked! And I don't think I smoked on the air [on *Match Game*], but I remember everyone smoking, yeah."

On one occasion, Gene read the following: "Smokey the bear didn't get much sleep last winter because there was a <u>BLANK</u> in his sleeping bag." There were a number of answers that were possible, but "Fire" seemed definitive...especially since Richard Dawson was smoking a cigarette during that round.

Ahhh, yes. Adding to the party atmosphere of the show was the occasional curl of smoke billowing up just to the edge of the television screen. Ashtrays were scattered about the set, and viewers would be treated to the sight of Richard surreptitiously sneaking his cigarette; and sometimes, out in the open. Charles made no secret of his pipe, and on more than one occasion could be seen puffing on a cigar. In fact, Ed Asner, Joan Collins, David Doyle, Alex Karras, Scoey Mitchlll, Bobby Van...the list goes on...all were caught at one time or another smoking on-camera on *Match Game*.

"They *asked* you to be surreptitious," Marcia Wallace specified. "And what was the other show I used to do all the time, with Peter Lawford? I forget what it was. I was smoking then, too, because I quit in 1980. And we all had cigarettes below, and we *weren't* supposed to get caught. We were supposed to wait until we were off the air, but many times we *didn't*. Brett quit a couple of years before me, but she was smoking, certainly the first six or seven years of that. She may have quit in '78. Dickie was an inveterate smoker, and Charles. But I think Charles did his pipe on camera, didn't he?"

He did indeed.

"I'd always hide a cigarette," said Debralee Scott. "I'd never have a drink in my hand. I really made a concerted effort for the most part not to do that. I think it's important. You are sort of a role model, you know, you're in the public eye so you should have some kind of responsibility with that."

"Oh, isn't that amazing?" Betty White asked me, about watching the panelists smoke on-camera. "And it looks so weird now."

"It's so weird to see people smoking and talking on television," agreed Patti Deutsch. "I guess the only saving grace was they weren't *selling*, like way back on *What's My Line?* or those guys."

Fannie Flagg just shrugged and reasoned, "People smoked back then."

"But if I were on that show today," Brett told me, "I would be like, 'There will be *no smoking*!' I'm like a reformed drunk. I used to be a smoker, and there's nothing worse than a reformed—Oh, I am the worst! I can smell cigarette smoke if I go down the street and I go by an office building. I go, 'What is that smell? Oh, that's a terrible addiction!' And they are now passing a law in New York. Oh, I'm so thrilled and happy! ...I was a true addict. I smoked two or three packs a day."

"Well, nobody smoked more than Brett when she smoked," admitted Marcia Wallace. "She used to say [when] she and Jack smoked, they used one match the whole day because they lit them off the other. They both just were chain smokers. And she quit, and Jack had had throat cancer and he quit."

Asked when she finally quit smoking, Brett replied, "About—oh, almost twenty years ago. I just...I went to the doctor, and he told me I had pre-throat cancer. And I didn't like him and I thought, 'You little [BLANK]!' But I quit anyway. He said, 'You've got to quit smoking.' ...And now I look at it and think, 'Who is that woman smoking on that show!?'"

Another reason helped color Brett's negative view of smoking. "I had a daughter, but she died," she said matter-of-factly. Her daughter Leslie passed away in 2001, long after Brett quit smoking. "She died of lung cancer. Talk about a big smoker! I was a big smoker, and I haven't smoked in twenty-five years, but she was a big, big smoker, and she got lung cancer. Terrible."

Well, at least (with the exceptions of Charles' pipe and the occasional shot of Richard, cigarette-in-hand) the panelists seemed fairly discreet about it.

"Well, we weren't being discreet *at all*," said Brett. "It's just that we weren't smoking. I would love to say we were being discreet, but we weren't. We were just, you know, we would smoke off the air. But now, I'm horrified to see myself smoke on the air."

Hardly anybody complained about the smoking on-set, as Betty White pointed out. "No," said Betty. "I've never smoked in my life, but you just took it for granted because so many people did. You thought, you didn't want to be a pain in the neck and complain. But it's awfully nice to breathe clean air now, not to mention what it does for the smoker." In time political correctness took over the airwaves. "I mean, Carson had to stop smoking on the air," Marcia Wallace pointed out. "*Politically incorrect*."

"*Everything's* politically incorrect," laughed Dolly Read Martin. "What *happened*?"

> Gene: (urging Brett to finish her answer) "Come on, Brett, light your light!"
>
> Brett: (pretending to be drunk) "My light's been lit for forty years!"

No Way To Treat A Lady

"Any 'ribbing' done between the stars was in fun and for the camera," claims Kay Henley. "I think I mentioned at one point after the show had been on for a long time, Brett finally blew her top at CNR and the writers for seemingly making her the brunt of so many jokes. I think they (the writers) laid off her for a little while after that. She never threatened to quit or anything, just became very sensitive for a while. Couldn't blame her!"

There was a LOT of ribbing done at Brett's expense. In one episode, Gene read off the card: "Brett is going to star in a new soap opera. It's called 'The Old and The <u>BLANK</u>less'."

Hmmm...How to answer *that* one? The contestant said, "reckless", a pretty good answer—better than most of the panel, whose answers ranged from bizarre to bizarre-er: "Sugarless" (like gum?), "hairless", "clothes-less", "truss-less", and the on-target "tasteless." And what did the lady herself give as her answer? Brett was a good sport, laughed, and said "The Old and The Nevertheless." It was a cute play on words—fitting, since one of the guest panelists was an actress on *The Young and The Restless*.

Of course, Brett wasn't the only victim of ribbing. "Most of my fan mail mentioned they loved the way Brett picked on me," reports Fannie Flagg.

Betty White knows a thing or two about being the brunt of a joke. Both she and her husband Allen Ludden made frequent appearances in *Match Game* questions, but she didn't take it personally. "Oh, that's the fun of it," said Betty. "You know, you only tease the people you like, and it was always fun. Johnny Carson was the classic one doing that. He would say, 'Betty and Allen went to a wife-swapping party and nobody would come.' It's a compliment, really, when people tease you."

That's the way Joyce Bulifant sees it. When I told her Brett spoke very highly of her ("And she admitted being so *mean* to you!" I informed her) Joyce replied, "Oh, I knew she was teasing. I *hope* she was teasing! Because she became a friend and at one difficult part in my life she was right there for me as a friend. She was very sweet, and she always teased me about living in 'the dreaded Valley.' She always called it 'the *dreaded* Valley.'"

What About Chocolate or Strawberry?

Coming up with acceptable euphemisms could be tricky, and *Match Game* sometimes tested contestants' and panelists' abilities to conjure them on the spot. And sometimes those answers proved to be, um, Freudian.

Gene read off the question: "Dumb Dora is so dumb—"

The audience took their cue with "How dumb IS she!?"

Gene: "—She's so dumb, when she was filling out the job application she came across the part that said 'sex,' and she wrote <u>BLANK</u>."

When revealing their answers, Ed Asner, seated next to Brett, said "I thought of Brett and wrote 'Often.'" The audience laughed, and so did Brett, who retorted, "I thought of Ed and wrote 'Seldom if ever.'" When Gene came to the end of the line with Patti Deutsch the downcast redhead admitted this wasn't going to be good. Citing being up all night with an ill and crying baby as her excuse she revealed her answer: "Vanilla." Groans and bewilderment from the studio audience and Gene, playing the stern principal, asked her to "report to my office."

"I just wondered if you got any brickbats thrown at you for that one," I said to Patti more than a quarter of a century later over lunch.

"No more than usual," she sighed.

Dyslexics of The World, Untie!

Celebrity panelists Fannie Flagg, Joyce Bulifant, and Bill Daily all have one thing in common: all three are dyslexic.

During one round, Gene read off the question: "Whenever Melvin hears organ music, he starts to skate. That's why he got thrown out of his sister's <u>BLANK</u>."

A popular answer proved to be "wedding," but Fannie, displaying the charming misspellings that would crop up from time to time, showed her card, upon which was written, "Furneal."

"Well, spelling was the worst thing for me!" admitted Joyce. "So it kind of helped to play up the 'dumb blonde' image?" I asked. "Well, I did it because if I couldn't spell a word and I knew that's what it should be, I had to make something up, not to be embarrassed. It was usually pretty silly."

Since she always played up the dizzy blonde character on *Match Game*, I wondered if people really thought that's what she was like in real life.

"Uh-huh," she sighed, indicating yes. "Except when I became involved in Dyslexian research. The people I met said, 'We always knew you were dyslexic by just watching that show.'"

"And I do remember one really difficult day for me when there was no way I could think of another word that I could spell. And I can't remember what the word was. I'm sure I drew a blank on it, but I had to put in the right word and I couldn't spell it, and I thought, 'Well, if I take it out really fast and show it to Gene real fast then put it back, then I'll be okay.' So he came over and said, 'What's our dizzy blonde have to say?' or something and I took it out real fast before anyone could see it, but I said the word, and he said, 'Oh, my God, she got it right!' and walked away from me, and I went—I was really perspiring. I thought, 'Oh my gosh, got away with that!' And then he suddenly turned and he said, 'Wait a minute, *how* did you spell that?' and my heart just sank. And he said, 'Let me see that card,' and I pulled it out and he showed it *to the world* on camera and everybody and made a joke about it, and I laughed 'Oh well, that's me.' But you know, it hurt *really* bad.

"And until I knew that I was dyslexic, I always carried that thought with me about how embarrassing it is, instead of being able to say, 'Well, you know, I'm dyslexic and I can't spell.' But at that time it wasn't something people talked about, it wasn't—I didn't even *know*. I just thought I was stupid.

"I did a play with Gary Collins, and then I was working with children in the Aspen area and doing theatre with them, and then just got so involved, and then in the meantime I wrote a screenplay that *almost* got produced, but that's a whole other story. I didn't *know* I could write before.

"The whole idea was to really get the word out about dyslexia. I did two documentaries that have played all over, all over the *world* actually. One was even translated into Catalan in Spain. And it's gone to all of the different organizations, and they play it at different conferences, and it's gone to schools, and it's in libraries. And it's a videotape, two musicals. So that makes me feel good. The word really got out that it's a learning difference, not a disability."

Flirting

Now, here's a tacky question: anybody ever get lucky off the show?

Brett was the first recipient of this question, and answered it in her straightforward manner. "I'm trying to think. Oh, I never really thought of that. I know *I* never did. I don't think so. Oh, that's very interesting. As far as I know, no…"

Well, maybe no one 'got lucky', as they say, but there sure did seem to be a heck of a lot of flirting going on—whether for real or for show. After all, it *was* the 'Swinging Seventies.'

But that brings us to another sensetive topic. In the "#MeToo" era, Gena and his ever-present Binaca breath spray, ready to greet the new ingenue in the 'Dummy Seat' with a kiss can be viewed harshly.

"He was a terrible flirt," Marcia Wallace said to me of Gene. "Oh, he was very bawdy and funny and flirtatious,"she continued, and when I remarked he always struck me as something of a gentleman, she replied, "No, you wouldn't find him gentle. He was a nice sweet man, but he was *funny*." She also added, "He adored his wife, his wife was great."

> Contestant: "Aside from sex, I love cooking and backpacking."
>
> Gene: "Well, anything that turns you on is okay with us."

"I think he was great." said Audrey Landers. "He always had a little twinkle in his eye. And he had this fun little flirtatious way about him that I think really came across well on camera. I enjoyed working with him."

"He was very naughty, very flirtatious, as you could tell, with all the ladies," said Joyce Bulifant. "But again, very sweet, lots of fun, but very flirtatious always. Sometimes you had to duck around him."

When I interviewed Debralee Scott, I asked her, "What was Gene Rayburn like?"

"A letch," she deadpanned. "He was! Well, he always like tried to—I mean he gave you a big ol' wet kiss. So I would hide in Betty and Brett's dressing room and they would say, 'She has a cold! Get away!' But no, you know, he was a nice man, " she soft-pedalled. "Really. A kind man. I mean, I didn't know him outside of the show. Brett and Betty and I would go out outside of the show, and I went to Charles Nelson Reilly's house a couple of times—who was a hoot."

Sometimes the antithesis to flirting occurred. After a game, the celebrity panel traditionally waved goodbye to the losing contestant as they were whisked away offstage via the turntable. During one episode Gene said to Charles, "You didn't wave, Charles. You didn't wave to Susan."

"I'm still in love with Carlotta!" exploded Charles, referring to the previous contestant. "I can't wave to every chick that comes by here!" Finally he relented, waved goodbye and called out "See ya' around, *chick*!"

Ya can't win 'em all...even on a game show.

That Motel Room In Encino

Speaking of which, Gene and Brett had a running joke that they would occasionally meet up in a motel room in Encino. "Just who came up with *that* one?" I asked. "I did," admits Brett. "I came up with that. We were just kidding around one day. 'Yeah, sure. That's not the way you act when we get out there in Encino.' And of course I said it, and we kept it up."

Hopefully, Helen Rayburn saw the humor in it all. During one episode, Brett stage-whispered to Gene, "Hon, did you make the reservations in Encino?" Gene's reaction was a sharp "Sssssssshhh!" and Brett called out to Helen that she was "Just kidding!"

"I loved Helen," said Brett. "She was great. Poor thing, she suffered from depression, but she was great." Hey, I'd be depressed too if my husband talked about shacking up in Encino with Brett Somers!

Diane Janaver kept the running gag in mind when she worked as contestant coordinator on *Match Game* in the seventies. "Occasionally we would come up with something that had to do with the show," she said. "One *perfect* one I remember: I don't know how many of the shows you've seen, but Gene and Brett used to hint around about after the show going to this little motel in Encino. Well, I got a man who *ran* a little motel in Encino! And he came on the show, and of course they were just *dumbfounded* when Gene asked, 'What do you do for a living?' 'Well, I run a little motel in Encino.' That was laughter for the next two minutes. It just happened that he had been a contestant on another one of our shows. I had seen him, and then I thought, 'Oh *boy*!' He's a good contestant *and*—well, you know. If you can tie the contestants into something, that's terrific."

Brett may have done a bit of pantomime flirting on the show (with Charles' *endless* ribbing about it) but sometimes it was Gene who did the flirting. *"All the Eskimo men stay away from Nanookla,"* Gene read off the card, *"because she has the coldest* <u>BLANK</u> *in Alaska."* The lovely female contestant answered with the definitive "Nose," and Gene pointed out that that was how Eskimos traditionally kiss—by rubbing their noses together. And with that he leaned in and rubbed noses with the pretty contestant.

Smooth, Gene, real smooth!

The Integration of TV Game Shows

It has always been my theory, lightweight view of the topic or not, that game shows helped pave the way for the Civil Rights Movement by introducing co-called 'ethnic' talent, performers, personalities, and their respective viewpoints into mainstream, middle-American homes on a daily basis....via the non-threatening medium of TV game shows.

When the breakthrough 'dramedy' *Julia* premiered in 1968, it was the first primetime series on American television to star an African-American actress. The star of *Julia*, Diahann Carroll, won a Golden Globe and Emmy nomination as Best Actress in a TV Series. But even before the first episode of *Julia* aired, ethnic talent such as Rita Moreno, Leslie Uggams, Barbara McNair, Dionne Warwick, and Flip Wilson had all already shown up as celebrity guests on the 1960's version of *Match Game*.

While marches were still going on in the South and race riots erupted in Watts, TV game shows (including *Match Game*) were handling racial integration in their own way, and—oddly enough—with minimal fuss. Was it a conscious effort on the part of producers like Goodson-Todman?

"I don't remember ever being pushed about that, you know?" said Diane Janaver, who booked celebrities on the 1960's version of *Match Game*. "We had Nipsey Russell. We used the best names we could find. We did have contestants who were black, and Asian-American contestants. I don't remember anything about racial things. I remember there was a thing at one point about handicapped people on the show, they wanted us to use handicapped people. I don't think there was any racial pushing."

"I must admit, if there was a tendency to be 'ethnic' I wasn't aware of it.," observed Audrey Davis, who worked on the sixties version of the show. "I just assumed celebrities were booked for their popularity, something to plug and someone the audience was would be interested in seeing playing a game as themselves.

"I have no idea if there were conscience discussions about integration. Same with the contestants, based on their ability to play the game and maybe because there was something 'kooky' about them which could be fun to watch."

"I guess we all just kind of felt the same way," continued Diane Janaver. "We wanted the best people we could find, and we didn't really think that way. There was a black fellow on our staff, Ken Abernathy, on the early version of the show. And then the names [of celebrities] that you mentioned."

By the time the show moved to Los Angeles in the 1970's, ethnic talent such as Esther Rolle, Jimmie Walker, Pat Morita, Della Reese, and Nipsey Russell were familiar faces on television, and all appeared as celebrity panelists on *Match Game*.

"First of all, I was on Mitch Miller," Leslie Uggams told me when we discussed her experiences on the old NBC *Match Game*, "which was on way before—in '61. I was on a show every week. I was on *Name That*

Tune as a kid, you know, which was a musical game show. So for me, I was out there way before Scoey was sitting on a panel game, you know. I was always breaking ground."

Racial Humor

One of my favorite *Match Game* moments occurred when Gene read off the following question: *"The bank teller said, 'I think there's something wrong with this dollar bill. Instead of a picture of George Washington, this one has a picture of George* BLANK*.'"*

When the pretty, young contestant answered "George Wallace," Scoey Mitchlll—the *perfect* recipient for *that* one—gave a fierce look, and exclaimed, "Had the old boy let me go to school, I'd have learned how to spell his name!" as he held up his card and matched her with the answer "George Wall*ass*". When I talked with Scoey, I reminded him of the "George Wall*ass*" incident, and he laughed and said, "I don't even remember that!"

I told him, "I wanted to ask you if you realized at that time—or realize today—how truly subversive and brilliant that really was."

"You think?" he asked.

"I really think so."

We talked some more, and then I said I had heard the rumor that GSN screened episodes of some of the old game shows for sensitive material, whether racial or whatever.

"Is that right?" he replied, then continued, "Yeah, well, nobody's got a sense of humor anymore. But see, I started doing television in a period where most black comics did racial material. I used to use that line in my act, 'If you don't like me, you don't like the six o'clock news, 'cause we're talking about the same thing.' And a major part of our act was on the race situation. So we kind of thought along those lines then, you know? That's why I probably didn't think 'Wall*ass*' was as brilliant as you do!"

"Well," I said as we were both laughing, "it definitely made a political statement!"

"Yeah!" he cheered, then added, "Well, I had a whole twelve minutes on George Wallace, you know? But I wish I'd thought about that. That could've gone in my twelve minutes."

Of course, over time, tastes—and the political climate—change. Some of the humor that was topical then seems, well, rather 'dated' today. And in the long run, maybe that's a *good* thing.

Banned In the U.S.A.

But apparently this 'racy' game show from the seventies is *still* making waves all these many years later. An article in the July 31, 2001 issue of *The New York Post* stated, "The Gay and Lesbian Alliance Against Defamation (GLAAD) is praising The Game Show Network for removing a *Match Game* episode from the mid-70's that first aired July 18 on GSN. In this episode of the often-racy, fill-in-the-blank show, host Gene Rayburn asked the panel, 'Doris just got married and found out that her husband was a "blank."' Guests Dick Gautier (Hymie from *Get Smart*) and his wife, Barbara, answered with: 'fag.'

> Brett: "Don't boo me! Please don't boo me! I'm a woman in my middle years!"
>
> Charles: "*That*'ll be the day!"

"Game Show Network is to be congratulated for removing gratuitously bigoted remarks, even from an old TV show, that aren't worth repeating,' says GLAAD spokesman Scott Seomin..."

Well, in *this* author's opinion, if the choice of vernacular is a bit...yes...*dated*...it is, at the very least, the definitive answer! And Goodson-Todman wasn't exactly a homophobic company: after all, one of their biggest stars was about as openly gay as you were going to get on network daytime TV! But there were other groups of people that might have taken offense to some of the questions—for instance, the overweight:

"In Fat Town, people are so fat ("How fat are they?"), the traffic signs don't say 'walk-don't walk.' Instead they say <u>BLANK</u>*-don't* <u>BLANK</u>.*'"*

The contestant said 'roll,' while Jon 'Bowzer' Bauman came close with 'Rock-don't roll' (appropriate for a member of the music group Sha-Na-Na). Bill Daily came up with "Run your buns off", and Brett, Gina Hecht, and Fannie all answered with "waddle-don't waddle." All were appropriate to the question, but the question itself wasn't exactly the product of a 'kinder and gentler nation.'

Of course, Fat Frieda, Ugly Edna, Old Man Periwinkle, Nanookla the Eskimo, and all those *Injuns*...pretty much every group or minority (or *majority*) was out of luck on this show. Yikes!

The Game Show Network reportedly pre-screens episodes of some of their old reruns with the result that some episodes do not air due to what is now seen as 'politically incorrect' humor. The racial humor can be particularly touchy if you watch some of the old episodes of *Hollywood Squares* and *Match Game*.

Episode number 376 of *Match Game '75* featured Greg Morris as the guest stud parked next to Brett in the upper tier of the panel. Morris was a black actor who appeared, prior to his stint on *Match Game*, in guest shots on everything from The Twilight Zone and The Dick van Dyke Show to *Mannix* and *The Six Million Dollar Man*, and would later move on to regular roles on *Vega$* and *Misson: Impossible*. During Gene's lengthy monologue explaining the contestant's response to the question, Morris pretended to fall asleep. Gene exclaimed, "Wake Up! Or we're gonna put you in the back of the bus!" Morris retorted, "No, you can't do that, 'cause I *own* the bus, baby!" Both were laughing and smiling throughout the exchange

Only an individual audience member can determine if they are themselves offended by the exchange. But it's clear that, in 1975, Gena and Greg Morris were simply bantering back and forth and harbored no ill feelings toward one another

Bottom line: should certain episodes of old TV shows be banned because they contain potentially offensive material? Well, it helps when viewing the shows, as with, say, when reading Mark Twain's *Huckleberry Finn*, to view it within the context of the time when it was written. Would disclaimers appearing before the program starts help warn viewers about an episode's contents? They weren't being insensitive on *Match Game*, they were just trying to get a laugh.

Let's just be glad we're all now in an era (supposedly) in which we are a little more sensitive and socially aware of hurting and offending others and try to avoid it in the present and future.

Review Questions

1. When Patti Deutsch was approached by a cable channel putting together a program on funny game show moments, all they wanted to know was about <u>BLANK</u>.

a. Brett's fued with Betty White
b. What Patti thought of rivals Fannie Flagg and Marcia Wallace
c. Booze

2. Celebrity panelists Fannie Flagg, Joyce Bulifant, and Bill Daily all have one thing in common: all three are <u>BLANK</u>.

a. Co-stars from The Bob Newhart Show
b. Dyslexic
c. Graduates of the Montgomery Wards Finishing School

3. Had <u>BLANK</u> not voted in favor of school segregation, Scoey Mitchlll might have learned to spell his name.

a. George Washington
b. George Jefferson
c. George Wallace

Answers: 1.c., 2. b., 3. c.

16

The Man Who Matched The Stars

"It's a shame Gene isn't around. He would love to talk to you," Marcia Wallace told me. But while Gene Rayburn passed away before I began researching and writing *Match Game 101*, he did play an active part in *another* game show tome.

Gene was quite proud of his career as a game show host. Fred Wostbrock co-authored *The Encyclopedia of TV Game Shows* with Steve Ryan. "Gene actually helped me put that book together," Wostbrock told Rayburn biographer Adam Nedeff. "When we were assembling material for it, he invited me to his home and showed me all sorts of photos, because he had saved everything from his career. And he told me stories and just enjoyed reminiscing. It made him happy that anybody wanted to preserve any kind of record of the work that he did." Brett Somers had her own copy of the book, which featured a photo of Brett and others gracing the *Match Game* panel.

(Opposite page) Gene's interest in needlepoint was the focus of this cover shot and the profile illustrated on the following page.

YOUR LUCKY NUMBER
RULES & DETAILS INSIDE

tv PREVUES

SEATTLE
Post-Intelligencer
THE VOICE OF THE NORTHWEST
WEEKLY tv MAGAZINE

DAILY LISTINGS • WEEK BEGINNING AUGUST 4, 1974

**Gene Rayburn
Of "Match Game '74"
Keeps Himself
In Stitches**
Page 2

Complex Study of Gene's (Life)

JACK RYAN

Gene Rayburn has a busy professional career that includes jetting across the country to handle his chores on NBC'S daytime game show, "The Match Game."

But unbeknownst to all of you Rayburn fans he has a hidden passion — needlepoint. He really doesn't keep it a secret, it's simply that few interviewers can pin him down long enough to question his particular hobby that would more properly fit a Little Old Lady from Dubuque rather than one of the glibbest men in the speak-for-a-buck professions.

But, then again, Rayburn is a master interviewer in his own right and it is possible that he has been able to fend off questions that edged too close to his secret.

Rayburn, by his own admission, has interviewed more celebrities than he can remember during his 11-plus years on NBC Radio's "Monitor" series. The only one who ever made him

Gene Rayburn:
A 'Needler'

nervous, he says, was "Julie Andrews. "I worshipped her.

"I saw her on stage in 'My Fair Lady' seven times."

Maybe what disconcerted Rayburn was the fact that Julie was getting ready to ask about his needlepoint.

Having let that secret out of the bag, let's drop another bombshell. Does anyone out there know he is also part-owner of a factory at Cape Cod, Mass., which manufactures a plastic bricking facing for use both inside and outside houses?

Howzzat for a two career parley — needlepoint and plastic brick facing? Where else would you read stuff like this. While I'm on the expose kick, I should just go on and tell you the name of Rayburn's first show business partner. It was Jack Lescoulie and the pair had a show on New York's WNEW called — are you ready? — "The Jack and Gene Show." (At this point you should be absolutely breathless.)

For the real trivia fans, we'll lay this one on you — if Jack Lescoulie was Rayburn's first partner, who was his second? It was Dee Finch and the show was called "Rayburn and Finch." Please don't ask me why everybody started using last names. Anyway, "Rayburn and Finch" was on the air for five years.

Rayburn broke into television in 1954 in New York on a locally produced show starring Steve Allen. It was known as "The Steve Allen Show," for obvious reasons.

Rayburn stayed with Allen when the show developed into the "Tonight" segment of programming. Prior to joining the network, Rayburn bumped around on radio stations in Newburgh, N. Y.: Baltimore, Philadelphia and New York.

He also had a bit part in World War II as a bombadier-navigator in the old Army Air Corps. The slender master of ceremonies has dabbled in acting, and played the lead in "Bye Bye Birdie," on Broadway for six months. He had a part in "Come Blow Your Horn."

His career in broadcasting started as an NBC page boy in New York in the dim, dusty days of the 1930s.

Just when his career in needlepoint began, I cannot say. Unfortunately.

"I didn't start out to be a game show host," admitted Gene, years later. "I happened to be pretty good at it and had a long run with it. But I would say to anybody starting out, don't stick to one thing. Try and vary your interests as a performer. Do different things. It'll make you a better 'whole' entertainer."

Ira Skutch had nothing but praise for the man. "Oh he was terrific. Gene was one of the least 'actory' people I've ever worked with. He went through an extensive period of analysis at one time, and he was one of the people it really took with. And so he did not have an inflated opinion of himself, and although he had ego—as you have to have if you're going to be a performer, because you have to have a very strong ego to force yourself to go out and appear in front of a lot of people. But it was never so bad that, so overweening, that [it would] drive you crazy like a lot of them are. So the result was that he was very un-temperamental to work with, and he was a very pleasant companion. We had a lot of good times together. My wife and I had visited him on the Cape a couple of times, and he came a number of times. We had dinner in New York a lot. Of course, out here I saw an awful lot of him because he was here by himself. His wife didn't come out very often. And even when she did, we all hung around together. I was one of his biggest fans."

"Gene Rayburn was the sweetest and the best straight man," Marcia Wallace told me, "and I say this as a woman who loved Peter [Marshall]. But Gene Rayburn was hilarious, kept it going, knew what to say, knew how far to go with the contestants. He did much more byplay with the contestants than Peter had occasion to do because of the way the game was set up. Gene had to do a lot more banter with the contestants. He never went too far, he never made anybody look foolish. He was smart, he was funny, he kept it going, and without anybody really knowing. There was nobody better, in my opinion, nobody better. I absolutely adored him. I only saw him once after that. We did a *Marilu Henner Show*.

"I can't say enough good things about Gene. He had an unbelievable instinct for dealing with celebrities, contestants, and like I said, he made

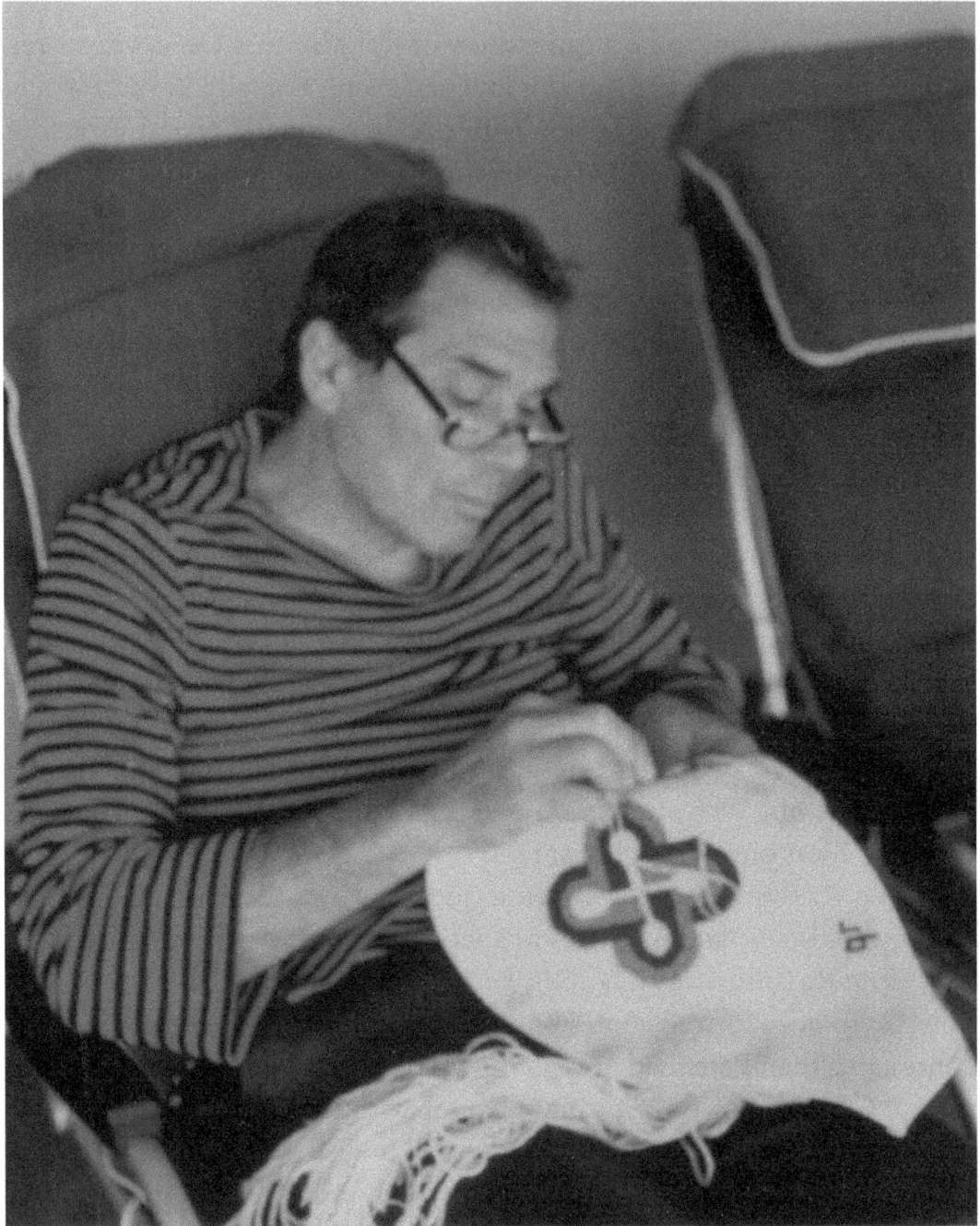
Gene doing needlepoint on a flight during one of his long commutes.

everybody look good. Everybody. I mean, when Brett was going through a very hard time, you know, it was a *very* hard time, and she still had to go to work. Gene really watched her back. Just the greatest, the greatest. I loved him. "

The West Coast Came calling

After the original *Match Game* was cancelled in 1969, Gene made guest appearances on *What's My Line?* and *To Tell The Truth*, and in 1972 briefly hosted *An Adventurer's Guide To Love* for CBS. But when the pilot *Match Game '73* was set to shoot, Gene was called to the West coast.

The new format was perfect for Gene's hosting skills and sense of improvisation. "Gene and I were very close," noted Ira Skutch. "We were really very good friends all through the years... And he was fortunate *The Match Game* came along because it was the perfect format for him, the West coast version. The East coast version he always felt a little constrained in. But this one gave full vent to all of his abilities. He was just wonderful with keeping order on the show.

"It's a very deceptive job, but it's very difficult to be the emcee of one of these shows, and anything with a bunch of personalities on it is doubly so. You're constantly walking the line between suppressing them so that they'll give their best, and letting them go hog-wild so the whole show flies apart. It's not easy at all. And to do it with good humor and without it being noticed at all don't realize that's what you're doing.

"Goodson always said that a good emcee had to be a good onstage producer, and that's true. You're reacting to what's happening, and you have to go with it, one way or the other, know when to let it go and when to stop it, when to push...And that was one of the few things that Goodson was very loose about; allowing an emcee to do that when he had a good emcee. He never had to tell Bob Barker what to do about anything because Bob Barker knows instinctively what to do onstage, and Rayburn did too. And a lot of the success of the show rested on his shoulders."

His ability to bounce back came in handy early in the show's run when he experienced one of the most famous gaffes in his career. "There was a very attractive young woman contestant on the show..." Gene recalled. "So in trying to keep her at ease, I was trying to compliment her on her beautiful smile and the beautiful dimples she had when she smiled. And so I looked right into her eyes and I said, 'You know, you have the most beautiful nipples I've ever seen. I mean dimples. I mean, oh boy.' I really wanted the earth to open up and swallow me right then and there because I was embarrassed."

Gene kept up a hectic taping schedule during the run of the new *Match Game*. The show taped every two weeks and on every other Friday, Gene would drive from his house on Cape Cod to Hyannis, then catch a plane to Boston, and then one to Los Angeles, arriving on Friday night. On Saturday and Sunday he would tape twelve shows (ten network and two syndicated), returning home on Monday. In a 1996 interview he told David Hammett, "Looking back, I should've moved to California while I was doing the show, but my wife wanted to stay in the East, so we stayed in the East. "

"Gene commuted to California from New York every two weeks to do the tapings; he flatly refused to move west," remembered Betty White. "I was on the *Vicki* show

What Becomes A Legendary Host...
Gene Rayburn's wardrobe (those stylish, three-piece suits) was credited alternately to Rubin Bros. International Fashions and to the John Weitz Signature Collection by Palm Beach.

with Gene and was very surprised when he told me, off-camera, that he came to regret that decision. Staying in New York had proved to be a bad career move, and he said he wished he had it to do all over again. What a secure, sure-footed bunch we all are in this strange line of work we insist upon pursuing."

The long commute on the planes gave Gene a new hobby: needlepoint embroidery. During one episode, Brett announced on-camera, "I would like to tell America that Gene Rayburn showed me his needlepoint in his dressing room. It's true; he *did*." Gene said his wife Helen got him started when she suggested they have a needlepoint show to raise money for a local charity. Gene made several covers for his tennis rackets and enjoyed the process. He often did needlepoint on his long flights from the East and back, and in his dressing room.

"I fly a lot, and you can read so much and then you gotta do needlepoint," he explained. On one episode of *Match Game '74*, Mark Goodson made a surprise appearance to show his appreciation to Gene for help for making *Match Game '74* the highest rated show on daytime television, and gave Gene a bag for his needlepoint."

Age and Finances

Match Game was a hit, but there was a downside to his success, most of it financial.

Says Peter Marshall, "He had a lot of bad things happen to him. I don't know if you know about this—I think it was a skating rink or something. He put all of his money into it and it burned down...There's a lot of stuff about Gene you should know about. Financial problems. And Goodson-Todman never paid him well. For as big a star as he was, he was—I think—vastly underpaid. I was kind of the first guy to make a lot of money because I kept saying, 'I don't want to do this,' and I would quit, so they'd pay me all this money...I couldn't have cared less, I could have gone back to Broadway...But Gene was never paid that well, and he'd always bitch to me about it."

After *Match Game* ended its run, age also factored into things. As Peter recalled, "Gene was supposed to come back to do another *Match Game* or some other show, and *Entertainment Tonight* said he's seventy on his seventieth birthday—and it killed the deal. He was so miserable about that, he called me about that. And I said, 'Well, that's stupid, you know, there's an age thing out there, so just roll with that.' And his wife wasn't well, and he's always had problems with his daughter, I don't know if you know anything about that."

A special game show reunion hosted by Marilu Henner featuring Gene, Jim Lange, Monty Hall, Marilu, Marcia Wallace, Wink Martindalle, Tom Kennedy, and Nipsey Russel.

As big a blow as it was to both his career and his ego, in time Gene did find other work to keep him occupied. In 1985 he hosted a revival of *Break the Bank*, but reportedly he was fired after thirteen weeks because the producers blamed him for the show's poor ratings; the experience was so unpleasant that he disliked talking about it. He fared better in 1989, hosting *The Movie Masters* on AMC.

"He spent some time with me in Chicago," remembered Peter Marshall. "I did the national company of *La Cage Aux Folles* at McCormack for about ten weeks, and he came in and spent a week with me; About '86. We hung out for about a week. He wanted to do that show so badly. I said, 'Go after it!' So he finally did it—I don't know where he finally did it.

Also, Gene replaced Dick Van Dyke in New York in *Bye Bye Birdie*, and I did the London company with Chita Rivera...He sang. He could—acting was great. As an announcer he was great, as a second banana he was great. He was wonderful at anything he did."

So Gene continued to find work—sometimes in the unlikeliest of venues. Howard Stern "watched *Match Game* every day of his life," Gene told an interviewer in 1996. "He booked me on his show just so he could meet me. We got along fine, even though I'm not a big fan of shock radio." In an odd role-reversal, Gene was one of the 'panelists' to Stern's host in the 'shock jock's' 'Homeless Hollywood Squares' parody, alongside such celebrity panelists as Jaye P. Morgan (of *Gong Show* fame) and 'The KKK guy.'

Helen Rayburn passed away in 1996. Al Roker and his wife ran into Gene on the street the following week, and the co-host of NBC's *Today Show* described the encounter in his online journal: "His face lit up and he called out, 'Al...Al Roker...How are you? Gene Rayburn.' He stuck out his hand and I shook it. He looked pretty good, that trademark smile that had the secrets of thousands of game

> "I would want them to know I had as much fun doing it as they had watching it. It was a great trip."
> —Gene Rayburn

show questions, answers and ad-libs behind it. I asked how he was, and suddenly his face darkened. 'Not so good,' he replied. Naturally, I asked what was wrong, thinking health or professional problems. He started to cry. Deborah and I looked at each other. 'My wife just died.' We each professed sympathy and condolences. He told us it had just happened last week. 'I can't talk anymore, but thank you for your concern. It was nice meeting you.' He turned, sobbing and walked away. We were both stunned. It was something we are both still thinking about today. The loss of one for the other, how suddenly in your later years you're alone, left to deal with grief, loneliness and pain." Roker later added, "I really do believe he died of a broken heart, that he missed his wife so much his health deteriorated until he could no longer be here, but instead be with her."

Brett Somers never met Gene until she began *Match Game* in 1973, but they became fast friends and even after the show was cancelled, they occasionally saw one another. "He and Helen came one night to visit, and we went to a concert. And I'd see him upon occasion, but for awhile he lived in Cape Cod and then he moved into New York and then I was out here [in Connecticut], so we would see each other occasionally. And then after his wife died I saw him a couple of times, but you know, he really was lost without her. And he died a couple of years after that."

Gene Rayburn died of heart failure at his daughter's home in Gloucester, Massachusetts on November 19, 1999, just two and a half weeks short of his 82nd birthday. His agent, Fred Wostbrock said it best in a statement he made after Gene's death: "He was the Frank Sinatra of game show hosts."

Review Questions

1. Gene helped Fred Wostbrock and Steve Ryan put together BLANK.

a. A car built from old soup cans
b. A sitcom about a retiring game show host
c. *The Encyclopedia of TV Game Shows*

2. Gene's attempt to compliment one contestant's dimples backfired when he inadvertently complimented her BLANK.

a. Resemblance to Brett
b. Resemblance to Howard Cosell
c. Nipples

3. Gene continued to find work, including appearances on BLANK.

a. Seinfeld
b. Howard Stern's Homeless Hollywood Squares parody
c. A bus-and-truck production of *Who's Afraid of Virginia Woolf?* co-starring Brett Somers

Answers: 1. c., 2. c., 3. b.

18

Richard, The Feud, and 'Tude

I asked one of the women who worked as a recurring celebrity panelist on *Match Game* for her impressions of Richard Dawson.

"Well, I think that the contestants adored him," she said in a very well-rehearsed voice, and then said with some hesitation, "and I just didn't know him that well."

Hmmm...There was a long pause, before I finally said, "That was very well put."

"Thank you very much," she laughed, knowing she was caught. "I was just asking my husband, 'How do I get around a Richard Dawson question?'"

"I don't think anyone was crazy about Dickie Dawson," Brett Somers told me, and when asked why, she replied, "It was just that he, he was a sort of—he would be funny sometimes, and he was a funny man, but you know, *we* were all just having a good time..."

And Richard apparently wasn't?

"Well, I think he was always sort of—well, he was nice, he was always, you know, *pleasant*. But I think he felt—and this is just pure conjecture on my part—I think he felt that this was something that was beneath him. I myself am *trash*! I don't think—I think it's just *swell*! The best job I ever

Gene and *Match Game* regulars, Richard, Brett and Charles in happier times.

had. I hate to act—it makes me crazy. So this was made for me. I just had to show up, do it, and take off."

Well, Brett Somers may not have been crazy about Richard Dawson, but audiences sure were. It was usually a given that during the Head-to-Head Match, nine times out of ten, the contestants would call on Richard to play the game, and about nine times out of ten they would match; He had a great knack for connecting on the same wavelength with players. If Brett and Charles were the most popular and funniest players, Richard was the best at the actual game. Moreover, it was clear that for any of his faults, Richard genuinely cared about the contestants, and genuinely wanted them to win.

"I would agree with you," said Jay Wolpert, a friend to both Richard and his sons. "He did care *very* much about the contestants and he was a wonderful game player. Richard is a tremendously talented performer. If you've ever seen footage from his comedy routine, his stand up—there's one thing where he wraps himself with the mike cord, which is just unbelievably funny. He is a remarkable, remarkable individual."

And, lest we forget, as a single, attractive man at the height of his powers...Well, is it any wonder the female contestants flocked to Richard for a thank-you kiss and hug whenever they matched?

Cathy Hughart Dawson, Producer on *Family Feud* (and, not incidentally, Richard's daughter-in-law), admitted in an interview for *E! True Hollywood Stories*, "He's very charming and always was, and a bit of a flirt, and he had a reputation as a ladies' man." On that same program, Mary Ann Norbom, the author of the 1981 paperback *Richard Dawson and Family Feud*, said, "There were always rumors that he was quite the ladies' man. He was certainly notorious for spending time at the Playboy Mansion."

Speaking of *chemistry*....ahem...sometimes even co-workers just don't quite have it.

"One week, Marcia Wallace came in," remembered Brett, "and she is my best friend in the whole world; and she came, and she did the show and she said, 'Why isn't Dickie Dawson speaking to you?' and I said, 'Isn't he speaking to me?' and she said, 'Haven't you *noticed*?' And I said, 'No! Are you sure he's not speaking to me?' and she said, 'Oh, you live in a [BLANK] *vacuum*!' He was evidently ticked off at me for something and I never even noticed! I just went on about my life. It's terrible to have to waste all that energy not speaking to somebody."

"He was a good guy," says Elliot Feldman. "Some people didn't like him, some people liked him. He was as big a star with the *Match Game* as Gene Rayburn, and he obviously *wasn't* a star. So that was a problem. It was time for him to get his own show. I liked him. He did me a great favor," says Elliot, referring to the time Richard saved Elliot's job.

As Robert Sherman related in Chapter Two, Mark Goodson wanted to create a new game show using the old 1962-1969 version *Match Game* questions—similar to the Super Match questions using audience polls. The team developed a new show called *Family Feud*. *E! True Hollywood*

Stories described it best: "A modern-media version of the dispute between the Hatfields and the McCoys; no guns here, just dollars and prizes in a show that is as wholesome as Mom and apple pie."

When the time came to audition hosts for the new show, Richard's manager and friend Leonard Granger approached the company. "He came to us one day and asked why we didn't try Richard out as an MC," said Mark Goodson. "He told us Richard was a bit unhappy that the opportunity was never being presented to him. I, the master of the cliché, said it seems that Richard's talents are so much that of a counter-puncher. He was the free-associating man. I didn't know if he could do it."

"Richard had guested on all of our shows and had always been very good," Goodson said as he pointed out, "He is an instinctively good game player. That did not necessarily mean, though, that he would be a good host. They are very different skills. I was skeptical, too, about how Richard would do within the rigidities of the format. He is such a free-associating thinker, and the format is so iron-clad. You can move away from it, but not too far. It always pulls you back."

"Richard was anxious to emcee a show of his own," noted Ira in his memoir. "We tried him out for several. No format was right for him until *Family Feud* came along. Because of the previous failures, Mark had given up on Richard as an emcee, but I insisted that he be given a chance."

"He was always plugging for Richard," Mark Goodson said of Ira. "He told me he thought that not only was Richard a great liberated thinker with absolutely no fogginess in his mind, but that he also had all the stuff that makes for a great host."

Goodson continued, "We tried him out and he was marvelous. After seeing Dick, we talked it over and decided he would be the best.

"We considered Richard's being from the usual game-show-host mold a big plus...but at the same time, it made us nervous. As it worked out, I think Richard is a key factor to the success of the show."

The audition may have gone smoothly, but shooting the pilot proved to be a different story. The taping ran overtime, and it was thirty minutes before the contestants reached the end game; questions and answers from the earlier rounds, not affecting the outcome of the score, had to be edited out.

"I was not happy with it at all," Goodson said later. "But when we played the tape over the wire to Fred Silverman in New York he said, 'I think it is the best game show ever to appear on the air.' I said, 'I thought it was just awful.' But I admit to being a notorious pessimist."

According to Ira, "His audition run-through was brilliant; the show was his. At first, all went swimmingly. *Family Feud* was well-received, Richard was embulient, and his performance reflected in both shows." *Family Feud* premiered on July 26, 1976 and was an immediate hit.

The Kissing Bandit

If Gene's trademark as host was the long, skinny microphone, Richard's on *Feud* was a kiss for each female contestant. According to Maxene Fabe, "The practice began with the very first show, when Dawson spontaneously offered a kiss on the lips to each female family member, a handshake to male contestants in greeting them. Though nothing about Dawson's manner was lecherous, there was a storm of protest from some viewers, and even some hate mail. The uproar refused to ebb even when Dawson explained on camera, "I'm a toucher. It's how we expressed affection in my own family, and it just comes naturally to me. My mother always said, you can't ever hate anyone you're on kissing terms with." Finally Dawson placed the matter in the hands of the viewers. He called for a write-in vote and promised to adhere to the verdict. The results were overwhelmingly in favor of Dawson's kissing: 14,600 to 704."

The show was a hit, but Richard, according to Chris Lambert, "did not handle fame well. While on camera he was the same, lovable guy that America had embraced, his ego was growing to gargantuan proportions."

Ira Skutch said, "Because high ratings are ephemeral, and nobody knows for certain where they come from or what makes them disappear, there's a deep fear of change, a reluctance to tamper with success. As a result, everyone catered to Richard and treated him with kid gloves. Then, as *Feud* became a bigger and bigger hit, Richard seemed to become infected with the same virus that had infected Robert Q. Lewis; the belief that he alone was responsible for success."

Ira is referring to the popular host and actor Robert Q. Lewis, who gained huge success early in his career—he had his own hit daytime TV variety show on CBS in the 1950s—and, as he himself later admitted, became impossible to deal with. After his star waned, he found to his surprise that fame is indeed fleeting, and couldn't get work. "Mark Goodson maintains loyalty to friends who find themselves in adversity," said Ira. "He stood squarely behind Robert Q. and for many years fostered his career in any way possible." When Merv Griffin left *Play Your Hunch* in 1962, Gene Rayburn replaced him as host; however, the ratings dropped, and after five weeks the network panicked and replaced him with Robert Q. Lewis.

> "If someone asks me what I do, I tell them: I play games, and they PAY me! Isn't that marvelous?"
> —Richard Dawson

On *Match Game*, audiences were used to seeing Richard joking around and in a great mood, but as he became more and more popular in the wake of *Feud*'s success, he became increasingly difficult to deal with on the set of *Match Game*.

"He was great in the beginning, but eventually he just stopped participating," observed Gene Rayburn. The producer would play backgammon with Richard to keep him up between shows. He seemed to withdraw more and more from the other cast members on *Match Game*, yet he projected his usual, warm persona on *Family Feud*. "These problems did begin after *Family Feud* became a huge success," said Ira Skutch. It soon became clear that Richard was simply disenchanted with *Match Game*.

It didn't help when the 'Star Wheel' was introduced in 1978 shortly before his departure from the show. Contestants consistently picked Richard to play with them during the Head-to-Head Match. But once the Star Wheel was added, the contestants had to spin the wheel and play with the celebrity whose name they landed on (the wheel also featured spaces potentially doubling the stakes to $10,000). But the introduction of this element to the end game was an obvious move into Richard's designated territory.

"Dickie saw himself as the star of *Match Game*," said Marcia Wallace. "And he *was*. And he got very upset, I think, when people didn't pick him, you know, for the final thing. And most people did. And there was one time—Brett probably told you this story. I got along with him great. I sat next to him until he left to do *Feud*. And I said, 'Brett, I don't think Dickie's speaking to you.' And she said, 'He's *not*?' She hadn't noticed. And he *wasn't*.

"She persisted in calling him 'Dickie,' and he didn't like to be called Dickie at that point. He was *Richard Dawson*. And I kind of understand that; you know, he was forty years old. But he was really a good player, and funny. God, it was fun. Then McLean Stevenson sat in that chair. Bob Barker, sometimes."

It all came to a head during the taping of one surreal episode when a subdued Richard refused audience requests to smile. It was in late spring or summer of 1978. The panel that day consisted of David Doyle, Brett and Charles, Elaine Joyce, Richard, and Betty White. Nothing on-camera seemed to provoke the taciturn mood, and the incident happened at the very end of the show just before Gene was to say goodbye to the audience:

Gene: "We have a request from someone in the audience. Will you repeat your request?"
Audience: "Give us a smile! Do it!"
Gene: "Now look at your friends out there screaming at you."
Richard: "What do you want me to do? 'Smile' or 'do it'? Say 'goodbye,' Gene."

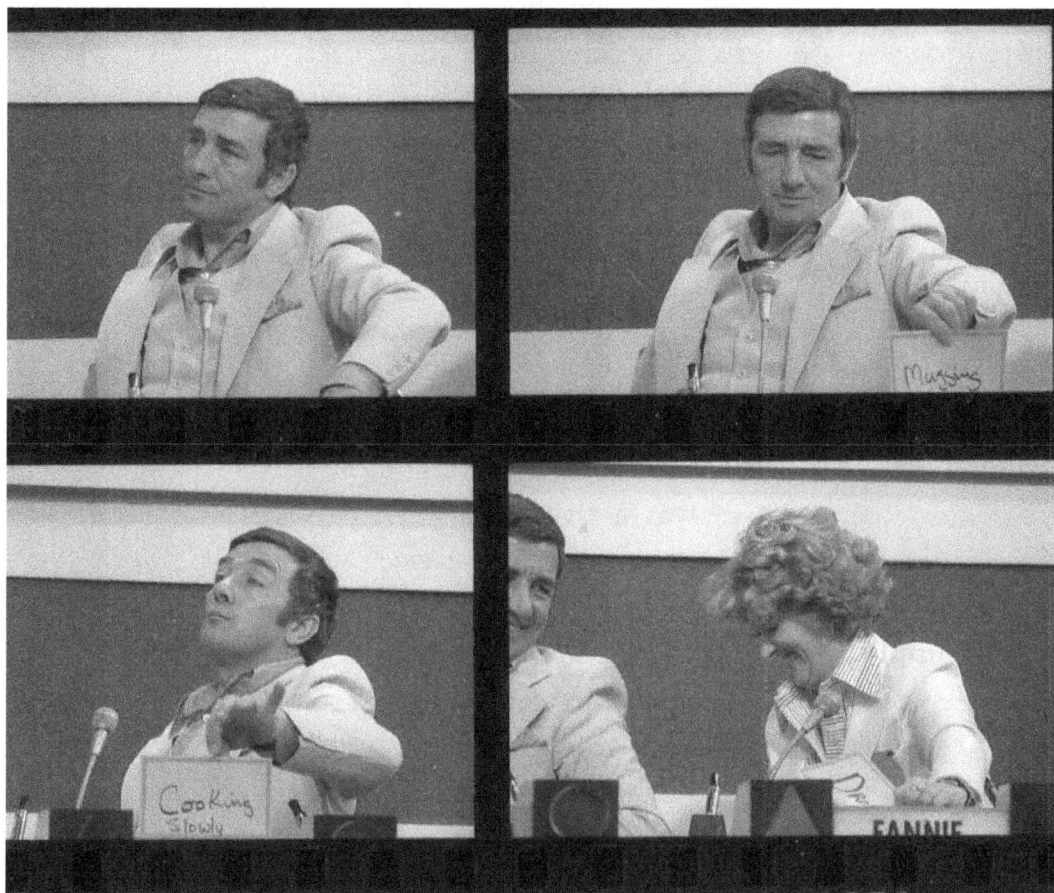

Richard and Fannie share a laugh during a round of *Match Game*. Photographs from a proof sheet found in Gene Rayburn's collection.

Gene: "I'm not going until you smile!"
Richard: "Alright." (To the audience) "We'll see you tomorrow on *Match Game*."
(Gene actually came over behind Richard and was trying to hold Richard's mouth open in a smile)
Gene: "I'm not going until you smile! Smile!"

It was a bizarre display, and when I asked about it, Ira Skutch said only, "The audience took this as the usual clowning around, the staff was disturbed."

Ira revealed in his memoir what happened next: "As Dawson became more successful on *Feud* he became more and more withdrawn at *Match Game*. Finally he was contributing so little and seemed so unhappy that we offered to release him from his *Match Game* contract. He accepted at once. At the end of the taping session, he left the studio without so much as a goodbye to anyone, even his fellow performers of five years standing."

Why would Richard Dawson, with his immense popularity on not just one, but two hit shows, behave with such seeming animosity?

For about a year and a half, Richard Dawson had reportedly been growing more distant on *Match Game*. With the success of *Family Feud*, Richard was putting in grueling hours doing tapings for two shows—or four shows, since there was a five-day-a-week network and syndicated *Family Feud* in addition to five-day-a-week *Match Game* with 1 syndicated *Match Game PM*. Moreover, after five years on *Match Game*, he was simply bored with the show.

Ira Skutch continued, "I haven't seen or spoken to him from that day to this. Several weeks after he left *Match Game*, I was told that, even though I never went there, he had insisted that I be barred from the set of *Family Feud*. He even had Howard Felsher, the producer of *Family Feud* exiled from the studio. Dawson's daughter-in-law became producer." His son Gary also served on the Feud staff.

In the meantime, *Family Feud* was still hugely popular with viewers—until 1983, when the syndicated version started losing viewers to a new show called *Wheel of Fortune*. The syndicated *Feud* was cancelled in 1984; the ABC daytime show died a year later with one of the most tear-filled goodbyes in TV history.

Whether Richard's closing speech came from the heart, or was merely played to the cameras made little difference; Dawson's reputation made it difficult for him to find work after *Feud* ended. However, he was cast in a memorable turn as an evil and vicious game show host in the 1987 Arnold Schwartzenegger film version of Stephen King's *The Running Man*; gossips unkindly suggested it was a case of art imitating life.

Mark Goodson had publicly stated that Dawson would again work for his company only upon Goodson's death and when *Family Feud* reappeared in 1989, Roy Combs was hired as host.

But Richard had other things on his mind at this time—notably romance. When a woman named Gretchen Johnson appeared as a contestant with her family on *Feud* in 1981, the two hit it off. In 1990 the pair had a baby girl, Shannon Nicole Dawson, and the following year Richard and Gretchen married.

Rumors of a comeback to host a new version of *You Bet Your Life* popped up around this time, but the pilot headed by Dawson went nowhere, and Bill Cosby ended up hosting the short-lived show. After Mark Goodson passed away and ratings for the Roy Combs version of *Feud* dropped, Goodson's son Jonathan brought Richard back for one more round as *Feud*'s host in 1994. Richard, now 62, was in top form, but the show sadly was not and was cancelled after a year.

Various sources described Richard as a semi-recluse. According to Cathy Hughart Dawson, "I see Richard pretty often and he's just enjoying his life. He's loving being with his daughter and his wife."

He passed away June 2, 2012 at the age of 79 from complications of esophageal

Not Such A Bad Guy After All

Over the years, a few unflattering accounts about Richard have tarnished his reputation a bit, but here's a quote from the early eighties to balance the picture a bit:

"He has been actively involved in the civil-rights movement and is vitally interested in the American educational system. When his only marriage ended in divorce, he was awarded custody of his two sons and subsequently raised them on his own long before it was fashionable for men to assume the responsibility of single parenthood."
—Mary Ann Norbom

cancer.

Whatever Richard Dawson's flaws offstage during his stint on *Match Game*, onstage he was the consummate pro, one of the fans' favorites, and though the show continued without him, there was always something missing in those later episodes. Says Kay Henley, "Ya know, I don't remember any problems with the transition, except that we missed him on *Match Game* and I think the other celebs did too."

(Richard Dawson may have left the show, but if you think this is the end of *Match Game*—think again!)

Review Questions

1. Richard was popular with contestants because <u>BLANK</u>.

a. He was handsome, charming, and an excellent game player
b. He took them all out for ice cream afterwards
c. He paid them to write all those fan letters

2. At first, Mark Goodson didn't think Richard was cut out to be a <u>BLANK</u>.

a. Game show host
b. Champion sumo wrestler
c. President of the Brett Somers Fan Club

3. Richard got mad when Brett persisted in calling him <u>BLANK</u>.

a. Flossie
b. Dickie Dawson
c. Every night at 2:30 am

Answers: 1. a., 2. a., 3. b.

Part III

Remakes, Reruns, and Reunions

Here and Abroad

"The concept of the game is negligible, the prizes insignificant, and yet almost as many people watch Wogan on *Blankety Blank* as listen to him in the morning. The sight of the lad himself in loose charge of one of the more unbelievably bad Quiz-shows on television is more than flesh and blood can stand..."

—Criticism of The UK's *Blankety Blank*
quoted by Terry Wogan
in his memoir, *Is It Me?*

19

Around The World With *Match Game!*

Ah, the great trade-off: The United States imports wine from France, oil from the Middle East, cars from Japan, and in return we export our finest television programs to far-off lands. Sound like an unfair trade? Well, Malaysia *does* seem to appreciate our reruns of *Baywatch*...

Of course, sometimes, instead of exporting the TV shows themselves we export the *idea* so that production companies abroad can develop their *own* TV shows. "Good ideas are good ideas, no matter where you take them," observed Diane Janaver. As a result, Goodson-Todman licensed their shows to foreign production companies and made a lot of money in the process.

"I used to travel all over the world teaching them how to do these shows in their own way," said Gil Fates, who handled Goodson-Todman foreign productions. "In other words, their own emcees, their own panelists, and where necessary, rule changes. And most of them are still going!"

There have been quite a number of foreign versions of *Match Game*. Gene Rayburn occasionally referenced *Schnick Schnack*, a German version of the show (the title literally means "Something, Anything"). In the early 1990's Germany aired another version of *Match Game*, this time called

Punkt, Punkt, Punkt (the literal translation is "Dot, Dot, Dot," approximating an ellipsis, and the closest translation of the show's title is "Blank"). It had a 150-episode run on satellite and cable network Sat. 1. The show featured the familiar six-seat celebrity panel and even had the Star Wheel. It was hosted by Mike Kruger, who later appeared on such shows as *Wetten, dass..?* and *Wir wird millionar?* (the German version of *Who wants to be a Millionaire?*).

During the mid-1980's The Netherlands had their own version, also titled *Blankety Blank*. Mexico had a version titled *Espacio en Blanco* ("Blank Space") hosted by Mauricio Barcelata, which ran for forty episodes in 2006. And for five seasons beginning in 2010, Canada had their own French-speaking version "à la Québécoise" in Montreal, titled *Atomes Crochus* (which roughly translates to "Things in Common") and hosted by handsome Alexandre Barrette!

But by far the most successful and popular foreign versions of *Match Game* were those produced in Australia and the United Kingdom. Read on...

Blankety Blanks

Dismissed by some critics as just a "smutty panel game" (sound familiar?), *Blankety Blanks* originally aired from 1978 to 1981 on the Ten Network in Australia. More like a comedy program with a game format built around it, it was bawdy, rude, and hilarious. Hosted by the irrepressible bug-eyed comedian Graham Kennedy (February 15, 1934-May 25, 2005), it became (like its U.S. and later British counterparts) a prime-time mega-hit.

The King

The best way to explain Graham Kennedy's status to an American is simply to state that in Australia, he was Uncle Miltie, Johnny Carson, and Benny Hill all rolled into one. Australian television began regular broadcast in 1956. The following year, Graham Kennedy's *In Melbourne Tonight* premiered, making the comedian a household name and pop culture icon. Kennedy's brand of humor was rooted in vaudeville, burlesque, and stand-up. Nicknamed "The King" during his heyday, he is still revered as just that...in fact, the king, the jester, and the rest of the royal court.

Anyway, someone got the bright idea of bringing a popular U.S. game show to Australian television. Graham learned of the project from fellow comedian-and-actor Bert Newton while both were panelists on *Celebrity Squares* (Australia's answer to *Hollywood Squares*). Graham asked about

Noel Ferrier and UglyDave Grey look on, from the top tier, as Grahm Kennedy has fun with Noeline Brown and Stuart Wagstaff.

the show and had tapes sent to him. "Then suddenly this plethora of game show ideas hit me," he recalled. "The ABC [The Australian Broadcasting

Corporation is Australia's public broadcaster] wanted me to do one, and Grundy's wanted me to look at others, but I knew the *Match Game* was the one the first time I saw it."

"When I went into television in Australia, which was in the early sixties," began *Blankety Blanks* regular panelist Barry Creyton, "Graham was already a national name in television [because of] *In Melbourne Tonight* and he vanished from television for a long time after this immense success that he had. He was someone who only did things he wanted to do, and he saw the *Match Game* here and he very much wanted to do that, thought it would work in Australia. And because he was known as the host of a television program, I think the initial thought from the network was, 'Why does he want to host a game show on television?'

"The difference that he saw was that in America it was done with the host as the straight man to all the personalities. Graham saw it the other way around: he saw all of the panelists as straight men to him. He saw I'm very witty, very funny guy, and sure, we all had stuff to offer, but mostly, you didn't get in the way of his gags. You simply fed him, you know, that was the point of it, the way he did it. And it worked perfectly for Australia."

Graham signed a reputed $1 million contract to host a new panel game show to be called *Graham Kennedy's Blankety Blanks*, produced by the Grundy Organization for Australia's Ten Network and set to air early in 1977. The show was rehearsed for weeks before going on the air.

"Graham was a perfectionist," recalled regular panelist Noeline Brown. "Not only did he want the show to work really well, he wanted the other characters who were going to work with him to work really well. He chose the panelists. We had become very close, personal and warm friends during the rehearsal period. We had a lot to do with the material. Graham had a lot to do with the material. It was a show that always looked like it wasn't scripted, but he had a certain amount of script. We had some lines we could use if we couldn't think of anything, but basically we had a good time and Graham was in total control. He is a total control kind of person."

The Rules

Game play was more or less the same as the American version, except for a top possible prize of $1,000 Australian Dollars in the head-to-head match. Contestants didn't win much, but it didn't really matter. As with the U.S. version, there were no 'right' answers—only a match mattered. And there was no 'star wheel' here.

The set was virtually identical to the *Match Game* set of the early seventies, as was the seating arrangement of the panel. "They had it set out, three above, three below, exactly the same set," said Barry Creyton. "I was always the first, at the far left, the first that he approached. Noeline was always next to me. We had a great association from way back in the sixties—in the theatre, on *Mayvis Bramston*, which was like *That Was The Week That Was, Saturday Night Live,* it was like that—it was satirical, political comment. The third in the upper row was a very low stand-up comic called Dave Gray. Then the bottom left hand corner was always the guest, whoever was the guest panelist for that week. They were the easy ones to get by—they weren't very bright, and they weren't very funny, you see. This was terribly, carefully worked out. And the center one was usually a regular. They would get a guest for the last—they would try somebody out for the first one in the bottom row. They tried all sorts of things, and I think after about six months it settled into pretty much what you see now."

"Cyrill Said..."

"I guess there was a writing staff," said Stuart Wagstaff. "I always felt that when Grundys bought the show from the U.S. they probably bought a great bundle of questions to go with it, although some were certainly written locally, and I know Graham K wrote a few himself." According to Noeline, Graham had writers but the panel did not.

Match Game questions featured a bevy of characters who regularly cropped up in questions, such as Dumb Dora and Old Man Periwinkle. *Blankety Blanks* featured a few characters of their own, namely Graham's campy, lisping character Cyril (for trivia buffs who care, Graham's middle name is Cyril). "Cyril said..." began Graham, and with an exaggerated pouting of lips and soft effeminate voice exclaimed, "Ohhh..." Suddenly Graham would throw in an aside, in his own voice: "He always starts like this." Laughter from the audience before he continued, "Ohhh, my friend Derek is so manly he picks his teeth with <u>BLANK</u>."

The End Gags

As with its U.S. counterpart, an episode of *Blankety-Blanks* might run short, leaving Graham and company to stall for time by filling up a minute or two of airtime.

"We didn't rehearse," admitted Ugly Dave Gray, who then added, "The only thing I had to have prepared was at the end of the show they didn't know if we were running a bit early, or whatever, so I'd have to have three gags ready: a little one, a medium one, and a long one. and tyhe producer would give [an indication of which story to tell.]"

The most popular were the Dick routines. At the end of the show, if there was time, Graham would engage panelist Ugly Dave Gray in the latest adventures of his friend Dick:

> Graham: "Dick was dining at the restaurant."
> Ugly Dave: "Dick was?"
> Graham: "Was Dick ever!"
> Ugly Dave: "Clever Dick."

> Graham: "How tall is Dick?"
> Ugly Dave: "Oh, Dick's about six foot seven.
> Graham: "Big Dick!"

"Graham was a master of vulturising off another comedian," remembered Ugly Dave Gray. "You would crack a gag, get a big laugh and then he would come in with another line for a bigger laugh."

Writer Gary Reilly said, "He knew the effect that was going to have. And he knew he would get material out of it. Graham would do anything when he got past an edge. But he was always in control and he always knew the effect that it was going to have. He could begin something and suddenly you could see him thinking, 'I can get 52 weeks out of this.' So he would start a routine and suddenly stop and say, 'I can't do this, I'm not allowed to.' And that line, too, would fastidiously be remembered, knowing that once embedded in his audience's collective consciousness, he need only mention it again for a laugh."

Improvisation was the name of the game on *Blankety Blanks*.

Ugly Dave Gray observed that Graham Kennedy "would rehearse to do other things, but as far as *Blankety Blanks* was concerned, he could see it was just a natural thing. No need. I used to arrive in a caran hour before the show and get ready, and I wouldn't see Graham til we were on the set. He didn't know what I was going to do."

In a situation similar to the weeks following the premiere of the original NBC version of *Match Game*, Ugly Dave remembered, "Actually, when *Blankety Blanks* first started, it was going downhill. After about eight weeks it was sinking and we thought it was going to get cancelled. And it was because we were playing the game and having the laugh secondary.

"And Graham said, 'I reckon we should alter it. I said, 'Yeah, why don't we forget about the game. Why don't we have a lot more fun and the game is secondary.' He said, '*Great.*' So he said, 'Anytime you want to interrupt me, you just interrupt, say what you like.' He said, 'I'll give you a free hand.' So, if you got contestants on and [one said], 'Charlie Bloggs is a builder.' 'Dave, he's a builder!' he said. 'Funny, my brother's a builder, and the other day—' And then I'd do a gag.

"And we started doing gags and the ratings went so high on Channel Ten...our ratings were equivalent to the other three channels added together."

Is it a match...?

In some cases there could be an element of doubt as to whether the word matches or not. And that's where Tony the Moustache Twirler comes in. He is, of course, the judge or adjudicator who decides whether the word matches or not by giving a thumbs up or a thumbs down signal. Nobody, but nobody, questions Tony's word. His decision is final.

Let's give you some examples of doubtful matching words. Take the following Blankety Blank:

SUSAN SAID, "MY HUSBAND IS SO MEAN THAT ON OUR IRON ANNIVERSARY ALL HE GAVE ME WAS A ———". The contestant's answer was AN IRON. Noeline Brown's answer was a PRESSING. In that instance Tony gave the thumbs down signal that this was **not** a match.

However, Tony gave the thumbs up signal for this Blankety Blank:

THE ADMIRAL SAID TO THE SAILOR, "I DON'T MIND A MAN TAKING HOME A LITTLE SOUVENIR FROM THE NAVY, BUT YOU SHOULD BE COURT MARTIALLED FOR TAKING HOME A ——".

The contestant's answer was ANOTHER SAILOR, and Stuart Wagstaff's answer was CABIN BOY. Tony judged that a match.

At the end of each Game, Peter, in his role of scorer, announces who is the winner — either the Champion or the Challenger. The winner is then entitled to go on and play SUPER MATCH.

A page from a souvenir booklet featuring *Blankety Blanks* questions compiled by Ali Ferguson and published in 1977 at the height of the show's popularity.

"Pull It, Peter!"

There were other parallels between the U.S. and Australian versions of the show. As in the case with Richard Dawson, *Blankety Blanks* saw a regular panelist go on to host his own game show when 'Ugly Dave' Gray later hosted *Celebrity Tattle Tales* (Yep, just like the American *Tattletales*). And *Blankety Blanks* had its very own 'Earl,' a stagehand called Peter behind the set whose task was to pull something. Kennedy dubbed him 'Peter, the Phantom Puller' and frequently instructed him to "Pull it, Peter!" (which seems somewhat naughtier than "Slide it, Earl!"). "Peter the Phantom Puller was a small stagehand," remembered Stuart Wagstaff, "small enough to fit inside the set—he varied according to the duty-roster."

"He made characters out of everybody that was involved in the show," Barry said of Graham, "even the cameramen, who became characters. He made a personality out of the voice-over announcer, who became well-known because of the show."

There was also (in lieu of producer and judge Ira Skutch) a chief adjudicator called "Tony the Mustache Twirler" (Don't ask), whose corpulent frame hovered just out of shot giving Graham the nod of approval or the shake of the head to dubious answers. "Tony Connolly (the Mustache Twirler) had been around a while," said Stuart Wagstaff. "I had worked with him before; he had been a cameraman on my *Tonight Show* out of Sydney and as I said, producer for Grundy on various game shows."

"Tony was the producer who would always go to pieces when he realized that something had been said that he'd have to cut," said Barry, "because it was much more difficult in those days to edit videotape than it is now. And we could see him on the floor, and Graham would say something totally outrageous, and you'd see Tony just shriek. I mean, just go to pieces thinking 'I've got to go into the editing room and I've got to cut this tape up and put it together again before it goes to air.' But such fun.

"I just remember Tony's face every time he would, say, drop a four-letter word or something, or do something totally against what was allowed on television at the time. And Tony was just—you'd see him sinking into the shadows. That's all I remember of Tony: just this terribly put-upon person who knew it was going to be trouble every week.

Trouble or not, *Blankety Blanks* was launched early in 1977 against the hit Aussie shows *A Current Affair* and *Willesee at Seven*—and quickly emerged victorious in the ratings. The show soon achieved a 41-rating in Sydney. "That," Graham announced with modesty, "would be the biggest Australian success in history." *Blankety Blanks* was so successful for the Ten Network that it was announced that Graham was signed to a contract, "the largest in Australian television history," and the Network took out a $1 million life and accident policy on him.

> "Welcome to the cleanest show on television!...No? All right, the second cleanest?...No?...Yes, it's dirty time again."
> -Graham Kennedy

He claimed that Goodson-Todman was astonished by the show's success. "The owners of it check on it periodically and they think it's sensational." According to Graham, they were unfamiliar with his previous work, "'Who is this man? Where had you buried him?' they keep saying. It has to be explained to them that I'm not exactly new at it...although new at game shows certainly."

As with *Match Game* in the U.S., *Blankety Blanks* got a reputation for being, shall we say, *racy*. "It was announced to the world at large that Graham Kennedy fondled my breast, which of course never happened," reported Noeline. She added, "Graham is really not naughty, certainly not 'dirty.' I've rarely heard him use foul language and there are words you just can't use in front of Graham. He is very proper."

"We were not directed to go in any particular way at all," said Barry. "They let us do what we wanted to do, and we tried to stay within the bounds of good taste.

"Occasionally he would drop a four letter word, and they were not acceptable twenty years ago on Australian television. They are *now*, of course. Everything is acceptable everywhere but in American network television, which I think is very cowardly." But as Barry conceded, "It was very risqué, much more than America is now. You know, Australian television gets away with a lot more, and British television with even more than that."

Noeline Brown admitted it was "bawdy from the start. Innuendo, double-*entendre*, very naughty. Ugly Dave and GK used to do a Dick routine at the end of the show that was pretty racy. I believe they did have a few complaints. GK probably read them out and used them to his advantage."

"But it's the advertisers they have to consider," explained Barry. "In Australia they were *desperate* to advertise on a show as racy as *Blankety Blanks* because it was top-rated. An in fact, when Graham did *In Melbourne Tonight*, he used to insult the people. This is in the days when they did live commercials on the show. And he used to advertise—I don't know whether you know this—shoes called Ron Merton's in Australia, very posh men's shoes. And their sales *soared*, they *skyrocketed*. And he started to insult every advertiser on the show. But I think it is a common fact throughout the world, generally speaking, commercial advertisers have no sense of humor."

One review summed the show up nicely: "He insulted the producer, chided the crew, complained about the format of the show, and bantered with the crew and the audience. He walked a fine line between naughty and offensive, and often goaded his panelists into the same."

The cavalcade of celebrities sitting on the panel included Noeline Brown, Barry Creyton, Stuart Wagstaff, Carol Raye, Noel Ferrier, and comic 'Ugly Dave' Gray. While their monikers may be unfamiliar in the

U.S. they were television royalty down under, each of them skilled in comic timing and clever double-entendre.

Noeline Brown Remembers...

When *The Mavis Bramston Show* premiered on Australian television in 1964, it made everyone connected with the show into household names, in particular Noeline Brown, who not only starred in the show but created the Mavis character.

"I was asked to be a panelist because I had done a lot of comedy for TV and theatre," Noeline informed me, "sketch comedy shows in Australia like *Mavis Bramston* in the sixties and *The Naked Vicar* in the seventies. And, yes, I had done some game shows.

"We all had to rehearse with Graham Kennedy over a week before we were actually chosen, to make sure he could work with us. I had met Graham once or twice before but had never worked with him. I admired him as did everyone else. He was Mr. Television, having done 124 years of *Tonight* shows five nights a week. He was brilliant. Stuart Wagstaff I knew, Barry Creyton and I had worked together for years doing music hall and revue, also in *Mavis Bramston*. Later on, he wrote a very successful play for the two of us, *Double Act*, which has been performed in 27 countries and nearly as many languages.

"I loved working with GK. He was very generous if you said something funny. He used to kiss me at the end of the show and we would make more of it every week. Of course we were only faking as we were both terrified of breathing on one another. One night the production team dropped a lot of ping-pong balls down onto the set. GK came to me for my answer and as I turned my card, I said 'I can't get it in for the balls!' He fell to the floor."

Barry Creyton Remembers...

Barry Creyton explained, "My history with it was—this is a digression—when I went away to live in England, it was the end of the sixties and I had a decade of great exposure on Australian television. So I went away and had a nervous breakdown," he laughs, "before I pursued a very sane theatrical career in London. And in the course of getting well, I found gyms in a big way, and I added pounds to my size. And by the time I got back I was unrecognizable from the skinny guy that went away in the late sixties. So Graham nicknamed me 'Muscles' throughout the whole program. And at the end of every other show—I would *cringe* with embarrassment!—he would ask me to take my shirt off for the masses. Terrible! I mean, you know, you'd put your head down, rip off your shirt, and take a bow.

"Noeline he always kissed goodbye at the end of it. Dave Gray he always went to, and Dave would tell a very corny gag of some kind. Then they'd do quick goodbyes for all the—on the center one, down at the bottom, was an old friend of mine, Stuart Wagstaff, who's been on Australian television as long as I have, I guess; since the early sixties, as I was when I started. And he was always sort of solid, good old British sort of gentleman material, but with a wicked sense of humor.

"Carol Raye was a movie star in the forties [in Great Britain] and a stage star, came to Australia and was on the *Bramston* show with me in the sixties."

"It's funny, I just have the fondest memories of doing that show," he continued, "because you had none of the responsibility and all of the fun. It was not like hosting your own show, which I've done several times, and you have all of the responsibility then. If there's something wrong with the show, they don't blame the writers or anybody, they blame *you* if your name is in front of the television show. Always. And that's the case anywhere in the world. But we had none of the responsibility. That was the joy of just going in and playing off the laughs. There were some times literally I was helpless with laughter and simply couldn't speak. So Graham would just take it and we'd go on to the next one while I was just doubled over with laughter, you know, on the floor.

"He was so much in control of what he was doing and knew so much about timing, laughs, and playing comedy, which he was expert at, and picked his panel because we were as well. I mean, the three of us at the top had played comedy all our lives. Stuart had always played comedy as well. So he knew that he was going to get well timed statement, response, statement, response. He would never get in the way, if you had a gag. He would never get in the way of it, just as you would not get in the way of his.

"But if you got a little bit too explanatory or verbose, getting to your gag at someone, he'd simply put his microphone down to his side and say, 'Hurry up,' so no one could hear it. Then he'd pick it up again and you knew instantly you had to cut to the chase as quickly as possible. Well, sometimes it was not even as decent; 'Oh, get on with it, for [BLANK]'s sake!' He would say *something* the audience never heard, and then he would lift it up as though nothing had happened, you see. You were the one with egg on your face, you know."

What About The Boobs and Howard Cosell?

I asked Barry Creyton if the panelists ever had a drink during the lunch break between shows (After all, I *had* to ask!). "Never," he replied. "We did them always in the evening. We did them—I think we started taping at about seven at night. We did them all on a Monday and a Tuesday night, every week."

"We weren't drinking the whole time," agreed Ugly Dave Gray, who laughed, "No, no, I don't drink much. I spill most of it, actually!"

Ugly Dave Gray Remembers...

With his ever-present cigar, Manchester, England-born Graham David Gray started in nightclubs before moving into the game show world when in 1972 he hosted an Australian version of *Beat the Clock* (Later, beginning in 1979 he would host *Celebrity Tattle Tales* for a season, before hosting *Play Your Cards Right* from 1984 to 1985).

Of his famous name, he admitted, "That all started as a gag, actually. My wife and I were out with some people having dinner, many moons ago before I came to Australia, forthy-three years ago, and I cracked a couple of gags with the friends we were with, and everybody laughed except my wife. And they said, 'Don't you think he's funny?' and she said, 'Nah.' I said, 'Don't worry, I only married her because she's so dumb, she makes me look intelligent.' Quick as a flash she said, 'Look who's talking! He's so ugly, I only married him because he made me look attractive.' So people around the table said, 'When you go to Australia, why don't you call yourself Dave Ugly Gray. Put the 'ugly' in the middle.' And somebody else said, 'No, it doesn't roll off the tongue.' And somebody else said, 'Yeah, that's good, because every word is four letters, Ugly, Dave, Gray. Why don't you—?'

"So, when I came to Australia I didn't know anybody, and I went to see an agent to see if I could get in a club, and he said, 'What name do you go under?' So I said, 'Ugly Dave Gray.' And he said, 'Ugly Dave—? I can't put that in the foyer of the club!' I said, 'Oh, I've *always* used that, it's always been my name.' And, funny enough, the 'Ugly' caught on."

In 1976 he was cast in the straight dramatic role of Bunny Howard in early episodes of *The Young Doctors**, until his initial thirteen-week contract expired.

"When I first signed for the show we did, we didn't know if it was going to be a success because I was currently doing *The Young Doctors**, and I wasn't enjoying it because I was a real depressing part and everything, and Graham rang me and said, 'We're doing this shopw called *Blankety Blanks*, and I really want you to do it with me, and I said, 'But will it be a regular or just a one-off?' and he said, 'No, it will be a regular.' So I said, 'But I'm an actor now!' and he said, 'I know, I've seen you.' He said, 'I think you'd be better off doing this with me.' So we did it and when I signed the contract I said, 'How much is it?' And they said, 'Forty-five dollars a show.' And I signed for forty-five [Australian] dollars."

*=*The Young Doctors* was a popular Australian evening soap opera running from 1976 to 1983. A huge success on Australian television, it was later broadcast in the United Kingdom and the United States where it developed a cult following. .

Stuart Wagstaff remembers...

"I used to watch *Match Game* when I was living in L.A. from 1972 to 1975 and was delighted when the game came here and I was asked to be involved on a permanent basis," said regular panelist Stuart Wagstaff. He admitted, "I don't know why I was approached to do *Blankety Blanks*. I was a friend of and had worked with Kennedy for a long time, maybe he suggested it, I don't know. Also Tony Connoly had been a producer at Grundy TV for a while and I had done *Celebrity Squares* (an Australian version of *Hollywood Squares*) with him, so maybe that was the catalyst. Even so I am sure Graham K had right of approval for panelists; he is not one to suffer fools gladly.

"*Match Game* in the U.S. did not depend so much on the host as on the panelist. Graham Kennedy was a huge TV star, known as 'The King' and he made it a vehicle for himself and we were pawns. I think the U.S. version featured the panelists more than the host.

"The other panelists apart from Barry, Noeline and Dave Gray and Carol Raye were amongst others: actor/singers Trevor White and Jon English; very popular TV star/comic/musician Bobby Limb (now dead); his wife, comedienne Dawn Lake; Vaudeville performer Gloria Dawn (now dead); comedian Joe Martin (now dead); Mark Holden, pop singer; actress Ingrid Mason played the dizzy blonde but was in fact sharp as a tack; and lots of other performers, TV personalities, station identities, TV journalists and the odd visiting performer from U.S. or U.K. (who wondered what the hell they had walked into).

"The best panelists were Barry and Noeline and Noel Ferrier (now dead), all very funny. Ugly Dave Gray was a British comic who achieved fame with this show...a very good teller of old jokes! I think Noeline would have to be my favorite, but I'm biased. I've always been very fond of her. Carol Raye was fine, a friend of long standing...Ingrid Mason was perhaps the most intelligent player, actress Carmen Duncan was good."

And then Stuart mentioned another actress who was "beautiful and intelligent," who was "particularly inept at the game," which I found funny. Some things definitely *do* cross borders.

I asked if there were any panelists, guests or otherwise, who were pains to deal with. "Oh yes, there were a few who were pains in the neck, or three feet lower," he replied, and mentioned a couple of names, adding, "but Graham K had a wonderful way of putting down people who were smart-arses.

"Doing *Blankety Blanks* was like going to a party every time we recorded, it was immense fun amongst friends. The only bad part of it, was that it became so hugely popular, particularly with young people, that although I had a certain amount of recognition value after so many years in the business, it became a bit of a pain having all the kids latch on to one, although it did create a teen-age audience which happily I dragged into the theatre later!"

For The Record

For those of you hunting for *Blankety Blanks* souvenirs, if you poke around online auction sites, you may just find such anachronisms as *Graham Kennedy's Blankety Blanks*, a vinyl LP record featuring "hilarious snippets" from the show (Why didn't Gene Rayburn have one of these!?). Long before the advent of releasing popular TV programs on DVD and Blu-ray, fans could enjoy their favorite moments on the record player.

"On the disc is one of my favorite moments, I think," said Barry Creyton. "I couldn't speak, I was laughing so hard. I don't know if you know that a common Australian vernacular for genitalia is 'lunch,' and Graham asked this very dumb contestant—I think the question was, 'All the ladies at the picnic were shocked when they saw Barry Creyton's BLANK'—and the answer was obviously muscles, you know, that's what we all wrote down. She said 'lunch.' And none of us could speak; Noeline had tears running down her face, she was laughing so much, and it's on that disc."

The End of the Show

After three years hosting *Blankety Blanks*, Graham made the decision to end the show. "He was the one who made the decision," said Barry. "And I think he probably didn't want to do it after that. A very wise decision. He certainly didn't need the money, I don't think! So he could say when he wanted to start a show, and when he wanted to stop one. And I think it was probably a very good decision on his part, because people would get tired of it then. That's why.

"I think back to the *Bramston* show which I did which was satirical stuff, possibly the most groundbreaking and most successful television show Australian television's ever had, and I did that for a total of two years and then, way against what the network wanted, left. There was no point in going on because we didn't work to seasons in those days; so you did like forty shows straight in a year, one after the other, then I went on and did another forty shows right after that. And you start to not only burn out, but the public gets a little sick of the way you look."

Graham's Retirement

After his retirement, Kennedy went into physical decline. His biographer Graeme Blundell told a reporter, "I was fascinated with how Graham got old so quickly. Noeline [Brown] said he embraced old age early on." It didn't help that he suffered "two bad falls in six months, diabetes, no daily exercise other than hugging his Clydesdales, shooing Henry the Golden Retriever, lifting several glasses of red wine and four packs of cigarettes a day."

"He was a wonderful guy," said Barry Creyton, "but very reclusive in his later years....because he was such a recognized entity for so long. He just wanted to hide once he got a little older and got over all of that. I saw him on one trip back to Australia—naturally before his accident—and it was a great treat to see him. I was only back there for a short time and I traveled down to Noeline's house which was way in the country, and he lived nearby and he came up and we had lunch. The next year, I think, I was back again and I had someone with me, and Noeline said, 'Come up and try to have lunch', and Graham said, 'Is Barry alone?' and she said, 'No, he's got a friend.' And he said, 'No, I won't,' and I never saw him again after that. He just wouldn't do it; he wouldn't get together with anybody he didn't know well. However, on television that's not the impression you had from him; A very funny man."

In fact, as with Gene Rayburn, Graham gained a whole new generation of fans. "I was here [in L.A.] for seven years before I ever went back," said Barry. "They're repeating them all, of course, on cable. No residuals, I'm sad to say. But they were just as popular the second time around. Extraordinary! This is twenty years after the event."

Graham Kennedy passed away on May 25, 2005. His memorial service, which amounted to a state funeral, was covered live by three networks. "His last few months were comparatively peaceful," reported Stuart

Wagstaff. "Noeline Brown and her husband were wonderfully supportive."

And The Winner Is...

The suits may not have fully appreciated Graham Kennedy's talents, but his audiences sure did. "He got several popularity awards," reported Barry Creyton. "There's a well-known award in Australia called the Logie Award, from John Logie Baird, and he won it several times."

John Logie Baird (1888-1946) was the Scottish-born inventor of Television. Though others were developing their own systems at the time, Baird was the first to successfully publicly demonstrate television on January 26, 1926 from a laboratory in London (Bet you thought it was Edison!). Later, he also was the first to demonstrate color and stereoscopic television, big screen television, and ultra-short wave transmission. The award itself is comparable to the Emmy Awards in American TV. Graham Kennedy has won an unprecedented seven Gold Logie awards and in 1998 was inducted into the Logie Hall of Fame.

"The first time he won it—do you know the Grundy Organization, who produced the show? *Everyone* makes those speeches, you know, thanking God and their parents and their children and their wives and their husbands, and they cry and all that. Graham accepted his award and simply said, 'I'd like to thank *me* for having faith in the Grundy Organization.' And that's how powerful he was. Without him there wouldn't have been a show, and Grundy wouldn't have had the run they had with it. But it's my all-time favorite acceptance speech."

Remakes

The series was revived in 1985 and lasted a year, with Daryl Somers as the host and Noeline back on the panel, but as with the later *Match Games*, critics said it lacked either the chemistry or the wickedness of the original.

"Darryl Summers was quite different from GK as the host of the second incarnation of *Blankety Blanks*," observed Noeline Brown. "He used to get into costume at the drop of a hat. I enjoyed working with him, but it was quite a different show. By then I think it was a long way away from *Match Game*. I did see the later version, too, but only a couple of episodes. It didn't work. They did some silly stuff that took them out of the studio."

Oh yes, there was a later version. The show was again revived in 1996 and lasted until 1997 with emcee Shane Bourne (both revivals aired on the Nine Network). Panelists on this series included Rhonda Burchmore, Marty Fields, and Annie Rigby. One new segment was the 'Dob in a Mate' bit which featured Steven Jacobs taking to the streets to surprise somebody with the chance to win $1,000. The show sported an odd assortment of guest panelists during its run—even Gary Coleman made an appearance (Yes, *that* Gary Coleman)!

Of the later versions of the show, we can only say that there was only one Graham Kennedy. "Would I do it again?" said Stuart Wagstaff. "With GK yes, but this will never be possible. He is very unwell and not likely to improve. I would have to have terrific faith in whoever was chosen as host, nobody immediately leaps to mind. There in the old phrase, 'You can't re-heat cold porridge' and I think that's probably the best answer."

Blankety Blank

If Australia's *Blankety Blanks* was essentially a comedy show built around a game show format, then the British version, *Blankety Blank*, was more like a parody of a game show. The show debuted on BBC1 in 1979 with Irish DJ Terry Wogan as the first host and became—like its American and Australian predecessors—a bona-fide hit. Popular British comedian Les Dawson picked up the mantle in 1983 and hosted the show until 1991. The show *then* returned yet again and was hosted by comedian Paul O'Grady in his drag alter-ego 'Lily Savage'—first airing on BBC1, before being dropped in 2000 and being immediately picked up by ITV.

Terry Wogan
August 3, 1938-January 31, 2016

Wogan's saga is well known to audiences in the U.K. Before becoming the voice of the BBC, he worked as a bank clerk before noticing an advertisement in the *Irish Independent* for announcers for Radio Eireann. Thus began his long career in broadcasting, and by the early sixties he was a household name in Ireland. The BBC came a-calling and during the seventies and early eighties he was the voice of BBC Radio 2, with a wry, commentary style.

Host Terry Wogan and the Blankety Blank panel. Like Gene Rayburn, Wogan sported a long, skinny microphone.

At one point he hosted *Jackpot*, which was then Ireland's most popular game show. "It was a none-too-taxing game for cheap and cheerful prizes," he remembered, adding, "in many ways it prepared me for the depths and degradation of *Blankety Blank*—and it involved a wheel of fortune, from which the unfortunate contestants could select their chosen subject." But as relaxed as he was on radio, he confessed, "It was not really until the success of *Blankety Blank* on BBC 1, a good fifteen years later, that I felt able to relax and be myself in front of a television camera. It was horrific."

Such is many a performers' debut, but luckily, Wogan got better as the years wore on.

Wogan attributed his hosting *Blank* to the BBC TV's Head of Light Entertainment, who commissioned producer Alan Boyd to look for a 'vehicle' for Terry's talents. "Boyd," remembered Wogan, was "a mischievous Scot, with a genius for turning dross into what looked like gold, until you scraped off the surface, came up with *The Match Game*, a popular daytime show in the States, which featured minor celebrities and a host no one cared twopence about, who was remarkable only for his thin tubular microphone, which he waved about like a wand.

"Boyd thought it was just right for me...A hitch here, a tuck there...Why not call it after the Australian TV version—*Blankety Blank*? We did a couple of pilot shows, which proved nothing—because, as cannot be said too often, nobody knows anything in this business until the red light comes on. So we gave it a go, Boydie, the BBC, and me."

The Rules and Prizes

Blankety Blank's format deviated slightly from the American standard. There were no returning champions; two sets of players each played two rounds, with the winner advancing to The Super Match—at this point only the 'Audience Match' was played. The top three answers could earn 150, 100, or 50 points (called "blanks") which could be redeemed for what one website called "rather small prizes of descending crappiness (The Beeb never gave away big prizes on their game shows, until *Weakest Link* offered £10,000 in 2000)." Whichever winner scored higher in the Super

Match then played a Head-to-Head Match for a prize "roughly twice as nice as the one they'd won before."

Memories of The Show

"It was great," remembered British pop star-turned-announcer Ross King, who watched it as a kid and later grew up to be a celebrity panelist himself, "because it was such a huge mixture of guests that were on it. Pop stars to TV hosts to comedians to—especially as a kid, I remember it because you never knew who was going to be on it.

"I was on it when it was Les Dawson," said King, "and it was right at the end of Les's. I was hosting a few different shows in Britain at the time, and appearing in a few musicals and things. I was asked to be a guest on it, which was really freaky for me because it was a bit like the first time I went on *Celebrity Squares*, which of course is *Hollywood Squares* here, because it was that thing—it was a show you'd grown up watching as a kid. Terry Wogan, who'd hosted the first series, was a hero of mine—well, still is.

"It was so perfect for him," says King of the show during Terry Wogan's reign. "The British version was played *so* tongue-in-cheek. The whole thing was so ridiculous. They would groan at the question, the 'Blankety-Blank.' Also, the huge prize was a *Blankety-Blank* checkbook and pen! It was in the days in Britain, when they didn't give away any kind of prizes, or big prizes would be like a thousand Pounds." Contestants obviously were playing for the fun of it, rather than for big money. "And that was the way in which Terry did it. And it's quite interesting that the style of the hosts they have had are all very similar, in that the style is either self-mocking or put-down. And it's quite interesting that that's the common theme that ran through it. Wogan especially always put himself down, and then the game as well. And Les Dawson was very much, you know—his quotes would be, 'If this game gets any thinner, we'll have to bring a juggler on.' That kind of stuff."

The show featured a few semi-regular panelists over the years. "Kenny Everett was a regular," says Ross King. "And there was a lady called

Lorraine Chase, who was a model and then very famous for a commercial that ran in Britain, which was for Campari. And she became very famous for it because all she said was—because it was a very posh gentleman who [says to her], 'You know, you must have been wafted here, truly in the arms of paradise of angels,' and she went, 'Nah, Luton Airport.' She looked so beautiful and refined, but she talks like a real Cockney. So that was her, kind of a schtick. She's actually doing a soap in Britain at the moment called *Emmerdale*. She was a regular [panelist] as well. And I remember Les Dawson being on it as well, as a guest, when Terry Wogan did it. But Kenny was definitely a regular."

That Long Skinny Mike

It's worth noting that Gene Rayburn wasn't the only host to sport a long, skinny microphone: "One thing that I remember from the very first year," remembered Ross King, "is that Terry Wogan had a very unusual microphone, which was a bit like a car antennae. And it extended, and I think Kenny Everett, who sadly passed away—he was another great DJ—actually broke it during one show." So did the BBC have to get Terry another one? "I'm sorry, I don't know that he got another one! But I always remember that, that funny thing of him having this very strange [microphone], like a car aerial."

Wogan Remembers *Blankety Blank*

"From the start, I loved it," admitted Wogan. "At last, I was not trapped in a tuxedo, or behind a desk. The ridiculous microphone gave me something to do, with at least one hand. I could walk and talk where I liked, without looking for marks on the floor... *Blankety Blank* was the first time I felt as easy in front of a TV camera as I always had before a radio mike.

"It did not exactly set the woods on fire for the first series. Some of the early critiques might have shattered a more sensitive psyche...."

"But I loved the insignificant prizes. They made the whole thing work on a level . For me, it was the tackiness of the prizes that gave the show its distinctive flavor, that turned it into a tongue-in-cheek send-up of a game-show. A mug-tree, for goodness sake! A plastic bicycle, a star prize of a weekend in Reykjavik—and for all the contestants, winners and losers, a remarkably cheap combination of plastic and wood, that was the *Blankety Blank* Checquebook and pen...I have mine before me as I write, and dash away a manly tear at happy memories.

"*Blankety Blank* was a watershed for me, the start of a decade of extraordinary success and acclaim....After initial timidity, the stars began to rally around *Blanks*. David Jason, Henry Cooper, Shirley Ann Field, Paul Daniels, Lorraine Chase, the very young Michael Barrymore, Lennie Bennett, Jack Douglas, Mike Yarwood. As the show became more and more successful, we were beating off the great and the good. But we always found a special place for three special people: Beryl Reid, Kenny Everett and Larry Grayson.

"I don't know why Beryl took a smack to me; she could be difficult, temperamental, with others. With me, and on *Blankety Blank,* she was perfect. Beryl played it absent-minded, scatty, Larry with camp disdain, and Kenny? Well, Kennny bent my mike whenever I was foolish enough to get close to him.

"The younger viewers particularly loved Everett's madcap ways, and he was very popular at that time, with his own eccentric, anarchic TV show. I guested on it, a couple of times. I hope he liked me as much as I liked him: he died far too young. His Requiem Mass at Farm Street Church was too sad for words. I miss him yet, and Larry, and Beryl...

"The star attraction of BBC TV's Christmas 1979 was *Blankety Blank*, and it did not let them down; it topped the season's ratings for that year. I can't remember how many seasons I did of the show, but it never lost its appeal for the viewers. I gave it up because other things were in the pipeline, and although Jimmy Moir, head of Light Entertainment, did not agree at the time, it was the right decision. It was not a bad decision for Les

Dawson, either, for he picked up the silly microphone and ran with it successfully for several subsequent seasons."

Les Dawson
(February 3, 1931-June 10, 1993)

Manchester-born comedian Les Dawson took over hosting duties from Terry Wogan and to his surprise, the show continued its successful run.

Dawson reminisced about his *Blankety Blank* experiences in his autobiography, *A Clown Too Many* and wrote, "The BBC wanted me to take over from Terry Wogan on the show he had made his very own: *Blankety Blank*." Dawson noted that in Great Britain, "Terry Wogan is a legend in broadcasting, and I don't think there has been a more popular figure in this country for years. He possesses everything I haven't got: good looks and charm. How could I, a dumpy, craggy-faced comic, hope to take over from such a man? It was also a dangerous thing to do, taking over from an established host of a popular show."

In the end and to his credit, Les Dawson faced the challenge. "I had no choice. I still had a contract to fulfill with the BBC and I would only be away from home one day a week if I took *Blankety Blank*. It would be punishing but possible: a car would pick me up early Saturday morning, take me to London where I would tape two programmes* [*I just *love* the way the Brits spell words!—The author], then the car would bring me home on the same night, albeit the early hours of Sunday morning. That way, I could look after the children and my wife. There was another reason for having to take the quiz show job: money. The income tax had yet again denuded me of the filthy, and I have never been much of a saver.

"My friends now howled that I was out of my mind; my wife shook her head in disbelief and my confidence began to dissolve. It was decided that I would do a pilot run of the show to see what I was like on it...I was awful. I couldn't remember the rules, and I floundered but one thing did emerge: it was funny. So, in early 1984, I hosted twelve *Blankety Blanks* and my fears were shortlived: the viewing figures went from five million to ten million; after a hesitant start, the show came naturally to me and the

Comedian Les Dawson was *Blankety Blank's* second host

public obviously liked it. The first person to congratulate me on the success was Terry Wogan himself."

Dawson found great success with the show. But he was suffering from exhaustion. Not only was it a rough commute and taping schedule, but his wife Meg was quite ill with cancer of the spine. "Meg was only able to get about with great difficulty and it broke my heart to see the pain in her eyes. Frequently now, I found myself sliding into fits of depression and a feeling of 'What the hell is life all about' soured my outlook.

"After taping a show, instead of driving back home soon after the programme, I would get the driver to take me into the West End to the clubs, and there in those dimly lit places I would drink to excess...I was at a very low ebb."

He continued, "Early 1985 saw me working on another batch of *Blankety Blanks* which I was not destined to complete," he recalled, and with good reason—he was suffering from kidney failure and was rushed to the hospital in great pain. "I was in the intensive care ward, my kidneys had ceased to function, my blood pressure was almost nil and I was fighting for my life.

"For three long days and nights, those wonderful surgeons fought to save me. Meg had been told that I had a fifty-fifty chance of pulling through. One specialist told her bluntly that my resistance was so low, I could not combat any infection.

"Little did I know that the radio and the television were daily reporting my progress, little did I know that the national press had to be kept forcibly out of the hospital...I knew none of this until the morning I opened my eyes, grinned at a pretty nurse and asked her for a date...Thanks to God I had come through it all.

"The answer to the question 'Have all the things I've done been worth the effort?' came in the shape of sacks and sacks of mail from the public. Good will cards, get well cards, fruit, flowers filled the hospital to overflowing. There was a letter from an old age pensioner begging me to get well soon, and in the letter she'd pinned a pound note saying 'Get yourself a tonic with this money.' Thousands of children wrote to me expressing their concern and love...Yes, love there was in that sick room and the letters bore mute testimony to that fact. Show business opened its heart and the affection brought tears to my eyes. A young nurse came into my room and helped me to red through the heaps of mail. At one point she looked up and said in a trembling voice, 'It must be wonderful to know that so many people love you.'

"Yes, everything I had done had been worth it. I never knew how many lives had touched mine throughout the years."

Les Dawson ended his run with the show in 1990, and passed away three years later. In his memoir, Terry Wogan wrote, "Les Dawson is another who has passed away too soon, another with whom I felt a special rapport. When the BBC asked me to take over *Blankety Blank* again, after Les's passing, I would not consider it."

Paul O'Grady (AKA "Lily Savage")

Blankety Blank was brought back in 1998 hosted by Lily Savage (played by a cross-dressing Paul O'Grady—long before the premiere of *Rupaul's Drag Race* in the States). As was the case with Graham Kennedy (not to mention Groucho Marx's *You Bet Your Life*), the game itself was deemphasized to focus on Savage's antics, which included poking fun at the game show format; however, a rather decent vacation was now offered as the grand prize. BBC1 dropped the new version in 2000, but ITV quickly snapped it up. In fact, O'Grady's antics proved so popular the show was renamed *Lily Savage's Blankety Blank*.

"A drag queen is a cartoon," explained O'Grady. "I never felt like I was putting on women's clothes, but costumes. They were so outlandish. I was emulating a cartoon character that I'd invented. I never had the desire to click down the street of an afternoon. It belonged on stage and that was it."

His youthful nightclubbing in London inspired his Lily Savage persona. "I saw really stylised, classy acts, like the Disappointer Sisters. It was the burlesque element, the panto element that I liked. And they were sending up lots of old Hollywood stuff, which appealed to me.

Lily Savage displaying the coveted prize: a *Blankety Blank* "checquebook" and pen set.

"There was an edge to it that you didn't get in the theatre—theatre was safe. This was music hall, where you had to interact with the audience to survive."

But finally, Paul O'Grady had had enough, and "Lily Savage" retired as a game show hostess. O'Grady was matter-of-fact when asked why. "I never had an identity crisis, I got fed up wearing the makeup!" As he explained, "You'd glue four sets of false eyelashes together ahead of time. You'd block eyebrows out with mortician's wax, then paint them with spirit gum, wait for them to dry, put the clown white over and then blend your foundation, two shades. Add a bit of blusher, do all the eyes. Stick the lashes on, get used to them for a minute, then slap on the mouth and the beauty spot and that was it.

"You wear two pairs of dancer's tights so you don't ever need to shave legs. I'd never shave anything, just my armpits, because as a friend said, 'You don't want the Hanging Gardens of Babylon. I didn't have a hairy chest, and I'd wear lots of bangles and gloves to hide my arms. No way I was going down the shaving route, because you have got to lead a bleeding normal life, as well. There were always very clear lines for me."

Review Questions

1. The United States imports wines from France, oil from the Middle East, and cars from Japan, and in return exports BLANK to the outside world.

a. Burgers and fries and loads of ketchup
b. Moonshine from the stills in the hills
c. Our finest television programming

2. The best way to explain Graham Kennedy's status to an American is simply to state that in Australia, he was BLANK, BLANK and BLANK all rolled into one.

a. Patty, LaVerne and Maxine Andrews
b. Uncle Miltie, Johnny Carson, and Benny Hill
c. One part gin, a dash of vermouth, and a great big olive

3. Hosts of the UK's *Blankety Blank* included BLANK, BLANK and BLANK.

a. A radio host, a comedian and a drag queen
b. A nun, a priest and a rabbi
c. Larry, Moe and Curly

Answers: 1. c., 2. b., 3. a.

20

Let The Games Begin!

It was common practice for Milton Bradley and other game manufacturers to produce board games based on popular TV game shows (and popular sitcoms: witness the *I Dream of Jeannie* and *Laverne & Shirley* board games!). *Hollywood Squares*, *The $10,000 Pyramid* and *Beat the Clock* were all made into board games. And so was the ever-popular *Match Game*, courtesy Milton-Bradley, the largest board game manufacturer in the world.

Once upon a time (1860, to be exact) Mr. Milton Bradley (Yes, Virginia, there really *was* a Milton Bradley) started a lithography business in Springfield, Massachusetts, and in order to keep his business afloat, began producing a board game he called *The Checkered Game of Life*. The game was a huge success, and by 1880, Bradley expanded his business to include jigsaw puzzles. After his death in 1911, Bradley's company continued to grow and prosper, producing and marketing such classic games and activities as *Big Ben Puzzles* (1941), *Chutes and Ladders* (1943), *Candyland* (1949), *Yahtzee* (1956), *The Game of Life* (1960), and *Twister* (1966).

It makes sense then that a board game manufacturer and the producers of television game shows would cross paths.

The box cover for the second edition of the seventies version of the board game. While skeptical that either "Norma" or "Carl" could match Brett and Charles for star wattage (or in the bickering-and-bantering department), one hopes they had a lot of fun pretending they were seated on the celebrity panel.

"I remember clearly with *Password* playing that at home, before it was made, sitting on the sun porch with Daddy standing there," says Lisa Todman, Bill Todman's daughter. "He said, 'This is a new game. This is how it works.' It was just on paper—Milton Bradley hadn't made the home game yet! And I remember going to the office and doing run-throughs. There was a lot of gaming."

A 1963 article in *Sports Illustrated* noted that more than 125 million Americans watched and played GT games each week. each week.

"Daddy kept a white board at home, with the TV schedule on it," Lisa Todman continued. "They had so many shows. I think, when it was the most, we had fifty-three half-hour increments every week."

The Match Game Board Game

"As far as I know," said Ira Skutch, "Dick De Bartolo's questions were used in the board games. The physical part was designed by Milton-Bradley. And no," he added, "I never played it for fun."

According to Dick DeBartolo, the production company kept a file of all the questions used on the show, and gave this to the good folks at Milton-Bradley, who then designed the game (and no, Dick never played the board game either).

The original *Match Game* board game was introduced in 1963 and contained approximately one hundred perforated cards with six questions on each card, a plastic scoreboard tray with colored pegs and chips, six "scribble boards" (cardboard inserts with vinyl sleeves), six crayons, and a "generous supply" of wipe-off papers. Players simply tried to match their partner's answers to the questions—simple premise with the scoring done similarly to the TV show (points are given for matching two, with more points given for matching all three) though the point values are different to allow for longer game play, and there was no bonus round.

The game eventually went through six editions, plus a few high-end deluxe editions. The Fine Edition cost a whopping seven bucks and had the questions on slick-looking playing cards, instead of the perforated cardboard cards. The magic slates were covered by gold folders, and a dial was used to keep score, instead of the pegboard. This edition used the same scoring system as the 60s version of the show. The Collector's Edition of the game was identical to the Fine Edition, except that it was contained in an attractive leatherette case which buttoned shut. The very rare "Briefcase Edition" was contained in a hard plastic case with a handle for transport, perfect for carrying for a long trip by car or plane.

When *Match Game* was revived in 1973, so was the board game, and it was updated the same way the show itself was changed from the 1960s version of the show.

"I vaguely remember playing it in the office before it actually went on the market," says Kay Henley. "I had one for years but lost it in the earthquake."

Examples of the questions included the ubiquitous "Name a kind of muffin" (answers given were blueberry, bran, corn, toasted, and English), "Name a kind of store" (department, shoe, drugstore, grocery, variety), and "John likes to read BLANK" (sports, mysteries, comics, fast). But the questions did get slightly more sophisticated. My personal favorite was "Name a female comedy star." While the question itself is dull as dishwater, the answers they offered were Lucille Ball, Carol Burnett and Brett Somers. Frankly, I'm all for anything that celebrates the glory that is Brett.

Milton Bradley issued three editions of the 1970s version of the board game. The second edition came out in 1975 and featured better questions (though it still asked "name a kind of muffin").

By most accounts, the 1960s versions of the board game are far superior to the later 1970s versions, and by *all* accounts, the TV show is better than *any* version of the board games. Even so, the different board games are something of a collector's item among *Match Game* fans, and like most so-called 'collector's items,' can be found at garage sales for a quarter or in souvenir shops for fifty dollars. And if you're *really* lucky, you just may stumble across foreign versions of the game. That's right, Milton Bradley also created and sold board game versions of *Graham Kennedy's Blankety Blanks* in Australia and *Blankety Blank* in the U.K., based on those foreign versions of the show.

Additionally, in 1989 HarperCollins published *The Blankety Blank 'Supermatch' Book of Crosswords*, a paperback by Will Adams, who has written travel books and other puzzle books. The book was supposedly based on the Supermatch round of Britain's *Blankety Blank,* in which contestants were faced with a word and a blank

The internet age ushered in a new alternative to the board games: online versions of popular game shows. A computer version of *Match Game* was announced by Sierra Entertainment in 2001, but a finished game was never released. That's okay, because several of the *Match Game* fan sites on the internet featured online variations on the game, and that's just the start. While GSN (the Game Show Network) was airing reruns of Match Game episodes, they also featured an interactive online game designed to be played while simultaneously watching the reruns.

Review Questions

1. In order to keep his lithography business afloat, Milton Bradley marketed a board game called <u>BLANK.</u>

a. Checkers
b. The Checkered Game of Life
c. Pin the Tail on President Rutherford B. Hayes

2. When the seventies version of the *Match Game* board game asked players to name a famous female comedy star, their suggestions included <u>BLANK.</u>

a. Brett Somers, Carol Burnett, and Lucille Ball.
b. Brett Somers, Betty White, and Joyce Bulifant.
c. Kukla, Fran and Ollie.

3. By all accounts, the sixties versions of the *Match Game* board games are <u>BLANK</u>.

a. Superior to the *Laverne & Shirley* board game
b. Inferior to the *Happy Days* board game.
c.. Inferior to any TV version of *Match Game* itself.

Answers: 1.b., 2. a., 3. c.

21

The Match Game/Hollywood Squares Hour

The Match Game-Hollywood Squares Hour was a television first: a combination of two half-hour classic game shows into a single, one-hour package. Gene Rayburn hosted *Match Game*, while Jon Bauman hosted *Squares*; the two also served as panelists on each others' respective shows.

Mark Goodson Productions managed to negotiate successfully with the film studio Orion (which had the rights to *Hollywood Squares* at the time) to create this show, but a few decisions worked against them. For starters, Gene had been hosting a talk-variety show called *Saturday Morning Live* on WNEW in New York and wasn't thrilled with commuting again to Los Angeles again. But, hoping to have another big hit on his hands, he committed to it.

More than one person pointed out that, since Gene Rayburn had been brought back to host the *Match Game* half of the program, that it was odd that John Bauman was brought in to host the *Hollywood Squares* half instead of Peter Marshall. In his memoir, *Backstage With the Original Hollywood Square*, Peter wrote, "When it was announced there would be an hour block called *Match Game/ Hollywood Squares Hour*, I was sure they'd offer it to me, especially since Gene Rayburn was hosting *Match*

The not-so-dynamic duo: Jon Bauman and Gene Rayburn, co-hosts of *The Match Game-Hollywood Squares Hour*.

Game. Of course, that didn't happen, and Jon Bauman hosted the show. I kind of hate to admit that I was happy when it didn't even last one season."

The back-story was a little more convoluted.

"I had gotten the rights to *Squares,*" Peter told me, "and then Orion screwed me out of the thing—I won't even go into it. I didn't even mention it in the book but it was going to be Gene and I. I told them, 'Why don't you put *Jeopardy* back on?'—before Alex [Trebeck] went on—I said, 'It should be *Jeopardy/ Squares.*' That was a tremendous hit when it was on. And they decided to put *The Match Game* on and it was terrible the way they did it."

Unfortunately, Peter wasn't the only one who felt that way. When I mentioned the idea of *Jeopardy/Squares* to Ira Skutch, he laughed and said, "I don't think that's right either. I don't think those two shows would go together at all. *Hollywood Squares* was a comedy show, as was *Match Game.* That's why they put them together. They were both more or less guessing games, as opposed to knowledge games. I don't think *Hollywood Squares* and *Jeopardy* would have gone together at all. That's funny."

The History of *Hollywood Squares*

The original *Hollywood Squares* ran on NBC from 1966 to 1981 with Peter Marshall as host and nine celebrities seated in three rows of three. As with the *Match Game* panel, a lot of stars sat in those squares over the years, and the regulars and semi-regulars included Rose Marie, Clifford Arquette (as his folksy Charley Weaver character), George Gobel, and of course, the center square wasd famously occupied by Paul Lynde.

The rules were simple: Two contestants (one playing X and one playing O) would play a kind of tic-tac-toe game in which the players took turns picking a celebrity to answer a question. In the original show, the celebrities usually answered with a "zinger" joke answer before responding with a real answer, whether true or false. The contestant would either agree or disagree with the celeb's answer. Correctly agreeing or disagreeing with the celebrity's answer would capture the square. The first contestant to connect three squares in a row, horizontally, vertically or diagonally, would win the game.

Besides the *Match Game/Hollywood Squares Hour*, *Hollywood Squares* has been brought back a number of times over the years. Foreign versions have been done in the U.K. (known there as *Celebrity Squares*) and Australia (known variously as *Celebrity Squares*, *Personality Squares*, and *All-Star Squares*), as well as in Brazil, Singapore and even China!

The Rules

So instead of being paired up with *Jeopardy*, *The Hollywood Squares* was married off to *Match Game*. The premise itself was a busy mix: The first half of the show, hosted by Gene with Jon Bauman as a panelist, was played like the classic seventies version of *Match Game*—question asked, contestant giving their answer, celebs matching or not matching, with the tiebreaker played straight ("<u>BLANK</u> New Jersey" with contestants choosing possible answers by the numbers, such as "Atlantic City" or "Newark," with the first to match winning the round; another classic example was "Flash <u>BLANK,</u>" and this being the early eighties and all, the contestant and celeb matched with "Flash*dance*"). At the half-hour mark, the winner moved on to the *Hollywood Squares* portion of the game.

At this point, a large portion of the set—the third tier where the three other celebs would sit—would swing into place, completing the nine-seat configuration for the *Squares* half of the game. The three additional celebrities would then walk out onstage to be introduced, their names flashing on the enormous lighted screen behind them. Jon Bauman then hosted *Squares* as Gene took his place among the stars in the panel. As with classic *Squares*, the object of the game was for celebrities to answer questions with the contestant agreeing or disagreeing with the answer in order to win a tic-tac-toe formation in 'Xs' and 'Os'. The first Squares game was worth $100, the second $200, and each succeeding game worth an additional $100 until the time ran out. The contestants would also get

$25 per matching square, and if a contestant missed a question, the square went to the opposing contestant—apparently in an effort to save time. The contestant with the most money won, then went on to play the big money Super Match round (a la *Match Game*) which Gene would host with Jon back on the panel.

According to Robert Sherman, "There was one more really bad problem with the show. Even though *Match Game* and *Hollywood Squares* were paired up by NBC because of their similarities, they were two very different shows, so we had panelists who played one of the games very well but then were just awful at the other. And we had the same problem with contestants. The contestants could play *Match Game* or they could play *Hollywood Squares*, but most of the time, they couldn't play both. We had so many episodes where only half of the game was any good and then the other half was just dismal."

The Set

The production was moved from CBS Television City to the NBC studios in beautiful, downtown Burbank. Gone were the shag carpeting and running-lights; this set was sleek and modern, bordered by a nearly two-story lighted panel, signaling a major departure from the beloved game of the Brett-and-Charles era. Gone also were Brett and Charles—or rather, gone were *regular panelists*, save for Gene and Jon. (For that matter, Rose Marie, Karen Valentine, George Gobel, and of course the by-then late Paul Lynde were all also conspicuously absent from *Squares*.) Both Charles and Fannie made guest appearances, but there seemed to be a conscious effort to get away from the homey, cozy, cocktail-party atmosphere of the old *Match Game*—in other words, to boldly move from the seventies and land firmly in the eighties.

I mentioned that light board to Diane Janaver, who worked as contestant coordinator on the new version of the show. "Yes, I remember it well!" she laughed. "That was usually the aim, to bring it up to date and get it really current." Her summary of the finished product was, "It wasn't *terrible*, it just didn't have a good feeling."

Gene and Jon

Gene Rayburn himself later admitted that "Mark Goodson made a mistake in hiring Jon Bauman," Gene Wood said. "He took him out and bought him a whole wardrobe for the show, then ended up spending an hour after each show telling him what he did right and [usually, according to Gene] what he did wrong."

Gene Woods laughed when David Hammett asked about MGHS in an interview and said, "Rayburn was dragged kicking and screaming into that hour. Bauman was likeable, but his character was so foreign to TV. Jon's fate was of not keeping the show moving, plus his occasional pose as 'Bowzer' seemed out of place. Instead of being looked up to, he was doing schtick...and it didn't fit."

"The idea of *The Match Game-Hollywood Squares Hour* wasn't such a bad idea," observed Lynne Rayburn. "It was an intriguing thought to take these two popular shows and mash them together. But Bauman had been 'Bowzer' to the public for years. He performed at Woodstock and he was always in that character any time he was in public, so that's over a decade of Bowzer but no real familiarity with Jon Bauman. So even though Bauman had been a performer for years, he had no identity outside of that character. For the viewers, it was like a total stranger was hosting *Hollywood Squares*."

When I asked Judy Landers about appearing on the *Match Game-Hollywood Squares Hour*, she replied, "I loved him, Bowzer, I think that's what his name was. He was wonderful and fun and a great performer. Yeah, I never understood why they would put two hosts on one show...I mean, my sister and I have co-hosted things together, but we did it as a team, you know? We were 'the Landers sisters,' you know? So it was different than two totally different personalities. Maybe that's why it didn't work, because they were both so outstanding on their own, but together, I don't know."

"Well, actually, they didn't really work *together*," Diane Janaver pointed out. "I mean, you know, they would change places. That was about it. It wasn't like they were on a team, as Rayburn had been on the radio show as a team. They were just two guys that were both there. They didn't seem to have any particular rapport or any particular emotion. Jon was a nice guy, you know, he was funny and different from the other emcees. But I don't think they had any special anything between them."

Elliot Feldman, who wrote for *Match Game* beginning about 1975, was brought in to write for the new version. "Yeah, I worked for *Match Game-Hollywood Squares* with Gene Rayburn and Jon Bauman," he remembered. "That was kind of a failed idea. And the worst thing about that was Rayburn and Jon Bauman did not get along. And they were the co-hosts. You may want to get a hold of Jon Bauman. He's got a good sense of humor; he might be able to put that into perspective."

"So Gene and Jon actively did not get along?" I asked.

"Well," Elliot began with hesitation, "you've got to get verification on this: One show I think Gene whacked him on the head with his microphone. You've got to get verification on that."

The Lack of zingers

While writers had provided most of the stars with clever 'zingers' on the original *Hollywood Squares* (Peter Marshall: "Paul, why do motorcyclists wear leather jackets?" Paul Lynde: "Because chiffon wrinkles."), Mark Goodson was adamant—perhaps remembering the quiz show scandals of the 1950's when answers were secretly leaked to players—that panelists come up with their own material.

"Mark Goodson hated the original *Hollywood Squares*, and I mean it when I say that word," Robert Sherman told Adam Nedeff. "He hated it. He wrote an essay for some newspaper about how terrible it was that the show briefed the celebrities about the questions for each show, and how the show tried to justify it by putting a disclaimer in the end credits explaining what they had done. But Goodson argued that the disclaimer ran far too long and they only flashed it on the screen for a few seconds and the audience didn't have chance to take it in or understand what it meant. So if he was going to do *Hollywood Squares*, he was going to do it

Mark Goodson's way, even though the Heatter-Quigley way worked. So we had to re-invent the wheel."

Adam Nedeff himself observed, "Merrill Heatter had already figured out that *Hollywood Squares* didn't work with banter, just quick jokes. Questions were terse and straightforward, giving extra weight to the funny lines that the stars fired off. And the show had its policy in place that twenty-two questions had to be asked for each show."

"We were applying the *Match Game* science of question-writing to Hollywood Squares-style questions," continued Robert Sherman. "And one of the things we tried to do was anticipate reactions, the way we used to for the regular panelists on *Match Game*. Okay, so Goodson doesn't want us briefing the celebrities on questions and he doesn't want us preparing jokes for them. He insisted that we not do that or come anywhere near that. So we began slipping cues and key words into the questions. We would think of a really funny joke that somebody might give in response to the question, and then we'd re-write the question ever so slightly to include a word or a phrase that would steer the panelist

> Jon Bauman: "Which generally lasts longer, Alison: a good facelift or a good bulldozer?"
>
> Alison Arngrim: "I find a facelift *performed* with a bulldozer is usually quite effective."

into thinking of the same joke that we had thought of. Once in a while, you'd get a really good panelist who picked up on all of the hints we were dropping and fire off all of the jokes, but the vast majority completly missed what we were doing.

"What was unfortunate for us was that Goodson slowly realized the problems we were having, and as time went by, I think Goodson really began to regret ever saying a bad word about *Hollywood Squares*. I think deep down, he wished we would switch to writing the jokes and briefing the panelists, but doing that would have essentially required him to admit a mistake and risk losing face, because down the road, a reporter interviewing him might say, 'You said this about *Hollywood Squares* and now you're doing it yourself,' and Goodson would have to address that. And that was just the worst part of the whole experience. Everybody in the company from Mark Goodson on down knew how we could repair this, but we couldn't do it."

The Writers

Aside from *Match Game* veterans Dick DeBartolo and Elliot Feldman, other writers werer brought in to write questions (sans *Hollywood Squares*-styled zingers) for the show, among them, Marsha Keets Morris, Abbe Schorow, and Maxine Nunes.

Maxine Nunes remembered, "I was working as a researcher on another show and the guy who sat at the desk behind me was about to go off of lunch, and I said, 'Oh, where are you going?' and he said, 'Oh, there's an audition for writers for the *Match Game/Hollywood Squares*,' and I'm like, 'Oh, can I come?' He's probably still mad at me about that, because I got the job and he didn't.

"So I went and there was like—I'm sure you've heard about that—there was like, I don't know, a hundred people in this room at Goodson-Todman, sort of giving instructions how to write audition material for the show. And Bobby [Sherman] and Joe [Neustein] were there, and Bobby goes, 'So I guess everybody here has seen *Match Game*. Is there anybody here who hasn't?' And I'm the only one who raised my hand. So he explained basically, you know, you write a joke so that several answers come to mind. And the summer before that I had done a book with a friend of mine which were jokes where the rhythm matched the *Match Game* jokes, only they were much raunchier. The book was called *The Bloom is off the Rose*, and the joke was, 'You know the bloom is off the rose when...'"

In other words, it was a book full of <u>BLANK</u> questions.

"There were a lot of things in the book that you could turn into *Match Game* material. I understood the principles. ...And I handed mine in, and I called Bobby back the next day and said, 'Can I redo this?' because I thought, 'Oh my gosh, I can do them better,' and I really, really wanted the job. He said, 'Oh, you don't have to,' and he called to say I had the job. And then he called me and said, 'Well, you have the job. How much money do you need?' and I was like dumb, young, so I told him how much money I needed. But it turned out that the salary I got was several hundred dollars a week more than what I told him I needed, which was really a nice surprise. He didn't hold me to my low bid. So that's how I got on this show."

Today, Maxine is working on a mystery novel, in addition to the books she has already authored (*The Lace Ghetto* and *Backtrack*) and co-authored (*What's Really Wrong With You: A Revolutionary Look At How Muscles Affect Your Health*).

Celebrity Panelists

Yes, *The Match Game/Hollywood Squares Hour* had its share of stars on the show...though none of them was named Brett or Richard.

"People were used to Brett, Charles, Richard, and whomever else we had on the seventies show," observed Diane Janaver. "[In *Match Game-Hollywood Squares Hour*] there were so many people all the time, then so many more faces on *Hollywood Squares*, on getting switchover. I thought it was confusing and too long, and I understand why it only ran for a year. Not even! It ran less than a year. I think it was too big for its own good."

The celebrities were a hodge-podge mix of comedians, soap stars, and the occasional sitcom personality. Among the smart ones was Alison Arngrim, who spent most of the seventies playing the nasty Nellie Oleson on *Little House on the Prairie*. "So in the eighties I became queen of the game shows!" she laughed. "I mean, basically I'd just come off the show and I was trying to get on everything. 'Hello, hello, here I am!' So I was on every damn thing going.

Alison Arngrim, fresh off her stint as bad-girl Nellie Oleson on *Little House On the Prairie*, appeared on the *MG-HS* panel. At the top of the show her name was emblazoned on the screen as she entered the stage and curtsied to the studio audience. Opposite, dressed in "appropriate 1980's glamour queen clothes." (Both courtesy NBC)

"And I wore appropriate 1980's glamour queen clothes, and I remember the audition. I actually had to *audition* for *Match Game*, so they could see what kind of stuff you'd say. And the line that got me the job was, it was something about meat...some question about a butcher, and the big answer that everybody was putting in the blank was 'rump roast.' It was one of *those* kinds of questions. And you were supposed to say something cute and fun, and then your answer. So I did my rump roast answer like everybody else in the test game, but I said 'Well, I don't know if I can answer this question. I'm a vegetarian. I don't eat meat unless it has a

ALISON

pulse.' And they called me back the next day and said 'You are *so* doing this show!'

"It was during one of the *Hollywood Squares* segments with Bowzer, and he did the strangest things to his hair. He had really curly hair and he'd come in really early to hairdressing and he would straighten his hair. Strange.

"And they had a question about 'Which weighs more, a woman's breast or a Big Mac?' And I said, 'Well, I don't know if my breast weighs more than a Big Mac, but there have been over three billion served.' And people were like falling off the platforms. I remember Vic Dunlop stood up and turned around and shook my hand. And so I just said all these things. Actually, the average woman's breast weighs more than a Big Mac, in case you're wondering. So I said a lot of silly things, so they liked me. I also tended to win. This was in the old days—they didn't tell us any answers.

The set. (Courtesy NBC)

And they didn't write us jokes. They write everybody jokes now, they don't trust anybody to have a brain and be funny."

One theme week proved especially memorable when cast members from the classic show *Leave it To Beaver* were reunited (Ken Osmond as Eddie Haskell: "My, that's a lovely jacket you're wearing, Mr. Rayburn.") on the show. Jerry Mathers, Tony Dow and Barbara Billingsley, along with *Match Game* veteran Richard Deacon (who played 'Lumpy' Rutherford's father on the series) seemed to have a fine time as they traveled down memory lane with the viewing audience.

Nonetheless, The *Match Game-Hollywood Squares Hour* never found its stride and never really found its audience. Ratings were poor since it was pitted against *General Hospital*, still riding high on the crest of the Luke-and-Laura hoopla. And the lack of regular panelists and the lack of spontaneity added up to a lack of chemistry. It lasted barely a year—cancelled after thirty-seven weeks.

Ira Skutch was fairly discreet on the subject, saying only, "The *Match Game-Hollywood Squares* game didn't work at all in my judgment."

Review Questions

1. The *Match Game-Hollywood Squares Hour* was a blending of two <u>BLANK</u>.

a. Classic game shows.
b. Clashing personalities.
c. Network executives who should have known better, but had too many highballs (one of them ordered a Sazerac, but decided he doesn't really like brandy after all) at lunch and said "Okay" at the pitch meeting.

2. The *Match Game-Hollywood Squares Hour* faced stiff competition from <u>BLANK</u>.

a. Luke and Laura.
b. Laurel and Hardy.
c. The cast of *Leave it to Beaver*

3. According to Alison Arngrim, a woman's breast weighs more than <u>BLANK</u>.

a. Vic Dunlop.
b. A Big Mac.
c. Vic Dunlop eating a Big Mac.

Answers: 1. a., 2. a., 3. b.

22

Match Game 1990-1991

According to Adam Nedeff, "In early 1987, trade ads first appeared for a new version of Match Game, a joint venture of Mark Goodson Productions and Coca-Cola (which dabbled in film and television production during the 1980's). Curiously, some ads included a photo of Gene splashed across them, while some ads made no mention of a host whatsoever. The initial press release from The Television Program Source (the syndication firm that would distribute the show) even stated that 'a host for the new show is to be named.'"

"We absolutely wanted Gene involved, as I recall," confirmed Robert Sherman. "And we were very ambitious about the new version and thought for sure we would make it to air. We were confident enough that Mark Goodson commissioned several set designers to come up with some renderings of new sets. I remember the sets were drastic departures from what we had been using in the 1970's versions, and I recall thinking that all the designs they came up with were beautiful, but Mark Goodson didn't like any of them."

After Gene Rayburn was rejected as host of the new version of *Match Game* and Bert Convy had to be replaced due to illness, Ross Shafer was brought in as host of the 1990-1991 incarnation of the show.

The concept went through a series of changes taking a few years to hammer out. But at last in 1990 *Match Game* returned to daytime television, this time on ABC. The network was excited about the revival, but when someone suggested calling Gene Rayburn in to reprise his role as host, the reply was that by this point Gene, now aged seventy-two, was too old (According to Adam Nedeff, "Mark Goodson was somewhat on the fence about having Gene host the show again and offered the job to Jamie Farr at one point"), and instead Bert Convy was hired to host the new version. Convy shot the original pilot but sudden illness forced him to the sidelines, and he was replaced by comedian-host Ross Shafer. The following year, Bert Convy died of a brain tumor.

Regarding Bert Convy, Gene Rayburn admitted, "It's hard for me to be objective about him. But his style was not my style. I remember once, I hosted his show—*Tattletales*—with him as a player. And I found out later that after I had guest-hosted *Tattletales*, the producer was saying to him, 'Why don't you try doing this differently? This is the way Rayburn would so it...' And it had to do with the way he moved his body around when he was hosting. And Bert told the producer, 'I can't do that. I would never turn my back on camera.' He wasn't loose. He was a tight guy. He did fourteen shows on Broadway, though, so he had talent, I have to give him that."

The Celebrity Panel

Charles Nelson Reilly was back on the celebrity panel as the sole regular, though ventriloquist and comedian Ronn Lucas (with "friends" like Scorch the Dragon and Buffalo Billy) was later added. Initially, another ventriloquist had been hired for the show, but he wasn't ambidextrous, and while he could maneuver the puppet with his dominant hand, he couldn't write with the other. Lucas was called in as a last minute replacement and won the gig because he could control his puppets with one hand as well as write his answers on the cards with the other.

Charles' return to the show signaled a more conscious effort for the producers to try to recreate the feel of the 1970's show. Brett Somers was even brought in as a guest panelist a few weeks after the show debuted.

Of course, there were the occasional antics. One one episode, soap star Walt Willey of *All My Children* demonstrated his runway modeling moves, including giving his look to the camera while "modeling" his wristwatch. (Reminded of the incident, Ross exclaimed, "*Yes!* I forgot about the wristwatch modeling routine we did. Walt is a natural comedian and the women loved him.") The Halloween, 1990 episode featured Ross dressed as Count Dracula with the contestants and panel also costumed: Walt Willey (a wizard) and Jill Larsen (The Statue of Liberty). Brett donned a blonde wig and bow as Little Bo Peep while Charles wore a padded Superman suit. Vicki Lawrence was dressed as Little Red Riding Hood. Ronn Lucas dressed as Little Boy Blue while his dragon puppet Scorch was...a dragon. Suddenly Scorch rolled back under the desk, and when "he" sprang back up, "he" was wearing a "costume": Lucas had crafted and put on a Ross Shafer puppet. "I'm the most terrifying thing I could think of," said Scorch. "I'm a game show host. Not you, Ross," Scorch assured him. "Chuck Woolery!"

Gene Wood told Curt Alliaume, "Ross Shafer was nice, came out of the comedy circuit. But he was put into the middle of some heavyweights, like Charles Nelson Reilly. When Rayburn did it, he was in charge. I told Ross, 'You're one of the stars...you've got to get them to accede to your wishes.' But it was hard for him. The game may have come back a year or two too soon."

"Frankly our ratings were very good," insisted Ross. "History proves we were winning our time slots in most major markets—but the continuing interruptions with the first Gulf War coverage lost millions for ABC, so they wanted to cut corners anywhere they could. When this happened, Woody Frasier, a very smart man, offered ABC an extra half hour of *The Home Show* for free. It solved the network problem and we were bounced."

The Rules

"Two contestants, one a returning champion, competed in two rounds of classic *Match Game* with a twist: all six celebrities played each question, and $50 was awarded for every match. In addition, after each round of classic *Match Game*, a round of Match-Up! was played.

In Match-Up! a blank phrase was read, *a la* the classic Head-to-Head Match, and the contestant saw two choices on a hidden screen. The player secretly made his or her selection and the choices were then offered to the celebrity. The first Match-Up! lasted thirty seconds and paid $50 per match, while the second lasted forty-five seconds and paid $100 per match. Whomever had the most money after the second Match-Up went on to the Super Match—played in the same way as the 1978-1982 version, with the Audience Match values increased to $500, $300, and $200, and the Head-to-Head Match worth ten times that, or twenty with a good Star Wheel spin. If a player lost in the Audience Match, he or she played for $500 (or $1,000 if doubled) in the Head-to-Head Match.

The Set

Though he designed the now-iconic seventies *Match Game* set, Art Director James J. Agazzi actually preferred the more sleek Art Deco-inspired layout he designed for the 1990-1991 installment of the show.

"The 'Deco' style of the 1990-91 production came about because I was requested to come up with a different look," he reported. "Deco is one of my favorite design trends and is used a lot—or was—by many game show designers. The overall design was inspired by the design of a well known Deco camera shop in Los Angeles. The color scheme just happened. There were some minor problems with the turntable reveal of the host. By this time I do believe that—despite a new look—the concept for the show had taken on a 'tired' quality—a 'been there and done that' lack of energy that prevented this edition from being a success."

When I asked, just out of curiosity, which camera store inspired the set design, he replied, "The store front is probably now under protection to

The facade of The Darkroom camera shop at 5364 Wilshire Boulevard in Los Angeles inspired the set design for the 1990-1991 version of *Match Game*.

be preserved by some part of City Hall that does that sort of thing...It is on Wilshire Boulevard, west of La Brea on the south side of the street. It has been partially incorporated into the entrance of The Conga Room nightclub. It is all black plate glass and aluminum—resembling a giant camera. Hope you are not disappointed when and if you look it up."

Bert Convy hosting the original pilot for the all-new *Match Game*.

Even in these screen grabs taken from the pilot one can easily spot the architectural elements of the set inspired by The Darkroom camera shop seen on page 437.

Ross Shafer

"I had a good rapport with ABC because I had just done a late night show with Matt Lauer and Spencer Christian called *Days End,* and they were interested in doing something with me. But actually, Bert Convy was hired to host that version of *Match Game*; and when he fell ill and died, there was another round of host tryouts. I think about 100 people auditioned. Luckily, I got the call."

He continued, "There was *no* pilot. I was performing in Atlantic City at Harrah's and I got the call that I got the job—and would it be okay if a photographer from ABC came to the hotel for promo pictures. In those days I permed my hair and this was one day after a very tight perm. I looked like an idiot.

"After the first five tapings, one day's worth, Mark Goodson came to me and said, 'Who was hosting the show today? I thought we hired Ross Shafer but I didn't see him today.' What he meant was that I was supposed to add what he called 'Ross Humor' to the show. I did that and got the show cancelled in record time."

For the most part, Ross had nothing but praise for his *Match Game* experience.

"Regardless of what anyone says, Charles Nelson Reilly is the most reliable, funny comedian-actor I have ever worked with," he reported. "He is quick, fast, and the reason Johnny Carson called on him hundreds of times to guest his show. Betty White is the female version of Charles—so smart and sharp; *never* at a loss for something funny to say. On TV she makes you watch her because she is so unpredictable. Off stage she was a doll—never a prima donna even though her hit *Golden Girls* was big.

"I liked Jonathan Goodson a lot—a real regular guy, for a billionaire's son. Jonathan was a lawyer and had worked outside the family business for years, so his perspective was very genuine. I loved Mark Goodson. I was going through a divorce at the time, and he provided me with endless support and encouragement. He called me on the road when I was doing my comedy act to give advice. Great man.

"I also loved our producer Chester Feldman; he was like my own dad in many ways. Sharp. Funny. Lovable. And Chester was really bright about the game business. He was also outspoken about other hosts, which I liked. He once told me, 'Ray Combs isn't getting any better on *Feud*....After two years he should be taking that show up to the next level and he isn't." I knew I should heed those words. Gene Wood was a total pro. He did the warm-up as well as the announcing and couldn't have been kinder to a newcomer like me. The director Marc Breslow was friendly but intimidating; I really wanted to impress him because he had seen everyone and everything. Richard Simmons was a great guest, and my comedian friends Bill Kirchenbauer, Ronn Lucas, Fred Travelena, and Brad Garrett were always hilarious."

"There were *no* bad things about this show. It was fun to hang out with the stars because they were always fun *...The hours and money were great. I loved doing it and was very sad when it went off the air. We would come to work at noon every other Saturday-Sunday, have a nice lunch with the stars and crew, then tape all five shows in about three and a half hours and go home. The perfect job; I had lots of time to go out and promote the TV show and do my comedy act and corporate speaking engagements in between."

Today Ross continues as an Executive public speaking coach, working with top company executives one-on-one in (what else?) coaching them in public speaking. Additionally he is a comedy and game show consultant for TNN, Comedy Central, Bravo, Broadway Video, and the USA Network. On top of all this, he created a game show for the USA network!

Vicki Lawrence

Feuds, real or contrived, can always make for entertaining television (witness Brett Somers and Betty White trading barbs in classic *Match*

---

*=During our conversation, Ross annotated this statement when he privately named one particular guest whom he said "hated me and I think secretly wanted to host the show."

Game reruns). But sometimes plans to generate excitement through animosity can backfire. One episode in particular featured Ross Shafer apparently making digs at celebrity guest panelist Vicki Lawrence. Ross later admitted, "This was a feud 'gimmick' invented by one of the producers to boost ratings. I regret that I ever went along with it; especially considering that I later learned that Vicki was *not* in on the gag. It must have seemed cruel to her and I felt awful that I was dumb enough to participate."

Dolly Read Martin

"Well, actually, when I played that game, I just enjoyed the game so much," admitted Dolly Read Martin, who graced the panel of the seventies version quite a few times. "I think I didn't like where they had me sitting. They had me up where Brett sat and I didn't think I fit in very well there because it's hard to sit there. I mean, that's *Brett's* seat. I just enjoyed the show. I *totally* enjoyed the show. I missed Gene, of course, but it really didn't matter. I could play *Match Game* right here and enjoy it to death. I'm a very simple person, I guess."

Brett Somers

Brett Somers remembered being a guest panelist in 1990, but she missed working with Gene Rayburn hosting. "Whomever the network head was said, 'Well, you're too old.' He wasn't too old! He was fine, he looked great, you know, and they foolishly got somebody else, and it was stupid. It was terrible. I did it. Once. I was in California. So I went out and did the show, and it was terrible. Without Gene it failed. He was great. He was just a great straight-man."

Ross remembered when Brett Somers made a few guest appearances on the panel. "Yes, Brett was on the show but the wit and magic was gone. She was tired or felt like a fish out of water. Charles tried to regenerate the chemistry but Brett was slow and out of it. I felt sorry for her because there was a lot of pressure on her to recreate the old show." But he adds, "I watched the show in the 73-82 run. I loved Brett in the early days!"

Marcia Wallace

"I did the one with Ross Shafer," remembered Marcia Wallace. "And I enjoyed that, but it wasn't the same. Look, it was okay, and Ross Shafer was delightful, I loved Ross Shafer. He was delightful and I enjoyed doing it.

"I did quite a bit of it; I was married then, and Mikey was just born. That's when I told the story about—and they bleeped my answer! Now I *knew* I was going to get bleeped this time. But I told the story about, I was changing his diapers once, and Bingo the dog came sniffing around when he was on the floor and I was changing his diapers. I thought he was going to go from Pampers to Depends. But I said, 'Bingo! Get way, get away!' And he said, 'Oh, Mommy, no! I love it when Bingo looks at my penis!' He was three. And I of course thought, 'Somehow I'm going to work that in.'

"Now, this was almost ten years later; this would have been around 1990. But it still caused a lot of furor, and I was bleeped again, I'm pretty sure. But a lot of people, Charles, started talking about Bingo, and 'How do we get Bingo on the air?' 'I'd like to have Bingo on the floor here.' 'There's a place for Bingo up here on the upper tier.' So it got a lot of [mileage]."

Betty White

When asked about the differences between working on the previous versions of *Match Game* and the 1990 edition, Betty White replied, "Well, the sense of fun—they were trying to do a game show without the same— it was Gene's personality I think, and Richard Dawson's, that made the original *Match Game* work, and the sense of fun. And of course, Charles Nelson Reilly was incorrigible! And when they tried to do it as a more or less straight game show I think it lost some of its charm".

She had the grace to add, "I could be dead wrong," but I suspect she was on to something.

Elliot Feldman

Elliot Feldman, who wrote for the classic seventies version of the show, later wrote for the Ross Shafer version as well. "Yeah, I did that one and I did the [Michael] Burger one with Jay Wolpert," said Elliot. "They made a mistake not bringing in—oh, I shouldn't say that. Not bringing Robert Sherman in. He was sorely missed."

Like Betty White, Elliot felt that Ross Shafer focused too much on the game part of the show. "He'd leave out the jokes, and that to me was a mistake. To me, he should have zapped in the jokes more toward the time period. You want a harder edge, more straight on. I guess the Ross Shafer version was the eighties. They should have really brought it up to date instead of peeling it back to make it more conservative. The people tuned into the show not for the game, they tuned it in for the interaction."

Review Questions

1. When designing the set for the updated *Match Game*, James J. Agazzi was inspired by a <u>BLANK</u>.

a. Dive bar the producers frequented.
b. The hood of a Rolls-Royce
c. A camera shop on Wilshie Boulevard.

2. The pilot for *Match Game* was hosted by <u>BLANK</u>.

a. Bert Convy.
b. Vicki Lawrence
c. Old Man Periwinkle.

3. Producers for the show instigated a feud between <u>BLANK</u>.

a. The Hatfields and The McCoys.
b. Bette Davis and Joan Crawford
c. Ross Shafer and Vicki Lawrence

Answers: 1. c., 2. a., 3. c.

23

"The *Match* Is Back!"

Back like a boomerang it came!

After Mark Goodson passed away in 1992, his son Jonathan became president and CEO of Mark Goodson Productions. In the mid-1990s the company was bought out by All-American Television, which in turn would later be bought out by Pearson Television. In 2000 Pearson sold their TV division to Fremantlemedia, who currently owns the rights to *Match Game* (You practically need a scorecard to keep track of this stuff!).

Anyway, Goodson-All-American shot a pilot for a new version of *Match Game* in 1997 hosted by Charlene Tilton, the actress best known as Lucy on *Dallas*. "I have hosted a few things," Charlene told me. "It's a fun thing to do but—you know, if it's the right thing it's fun. You know, it can be a lot of fun."

Unfortunately, the resulting pilot was not much fun. The producers went back to the drawing board where the format was re-vamped and an all-new, syndicated, five-day-a-week version of *Match Game* debuted September 21, 1998. Michael Burger, whose previous credits included *Mike and Maty* and *Family Challenge*, was hired as host.

Michael Burger (*Mike & Maty*, *Home & Family*) was tapped to host the all-new version of *Match Game*, returning to national syndication in Fall 1998.

"*Match Game,* for me, has always been the crown jewel of game shows," admitted Michael. "So when it came about that they were going to bring the show around again, I put my name in the hat and the first go-around I got passed over for Charlene Tilton, who did a pilot for *Match Game*. It didn't go. You know, she shouldn't be hosting that any more than I should be the love interest on *Dallas*. It just didn't make any sense. So it came around a year later that Pearson, which is now Fremantle, said, 'Yeah, let's go do some run-throughs.' The run-throughs went great and they said, 'Let's go with it.'"

The set borrowed the sleek Art Deco design of the 1990-1991 *Match Game* set and gave it the color scheme of the British *Blankety Blank*. The new *Match Game* now featured a five-celebrity panel (down-sized from the usual six) and ditched the 'A' and 'B' choice of questions in favor of pun-laden categories. Two contestants competed in two rounds of classic *Match Game*. Matches were worth one point in Round One and two points in Round Two. The questions were less dependent on clever double-entendre and more often featured a more, shall we say 'obvious' sense of humor. The contestant with the highest score moved on to the Super Match, which featured a $5,000 prize.

Game show veteran Jay Wolpert (*Whew!, Hit Man*) joined on as executive producer partway into the project. Nell Carter, George Hamilton, Vicki Lawrence, and Judy Tenuta were the four regular celebrity panelists, with a single celebrity guest panelist rotating every week.

When two classic game shows returned to the airwaves that Fall of 1998, *TV Guide* stated the following: "CHEERS to the gaming spirit. It takes guts to resurrect such beloved game shows as *Match Game* and *Hollywood Squares* without the stars who won us over the first time around. But producers are betting that Whoopi Goldberg can take over where Charley Weaver left off, and if Vicki Lawrence, George Hamilton, and Nell Carter seem a rather odd match, well, Brett Somers and Fannie Flagg weren't exactly household names when CBS successfully revived *Match Game* in 1973. These classic contests deserve their bonus rounds. Somewhere Paul Lynde is smirking with delight."

The celebrity panel included (clockwise from upper left) Nell Carter, Vicki Lawrence, Judy Tenuta, and George Hamilton, along with a special guest panelist.

If Paul Lynde was smirking with delight over the success of the new *Hollywood Squares*, he may also have been smiling that his side was winning the old *Match Game* vs. *Hollywood Squares* rivalry. The critics seemed to feel that Nell and George were no Brett and Charles.

But occasionally Judy Tenuta proved a good match for Patti Deutsch. On one episode, Michael Burger read off the following: "They just found the world's oldest men's room. Wouldn't you know it, on the wall it says 'For a good time call BLANK.'"

After the contestant answered with, "Dick Clark," Vicki Lawrence quipped, "It's probably the oldest Dick she could think of!" When Michael Burger called upon Judy Tenuta to show her answer, she responded with, "Well, I was gonna go with 'Eve,' and then I thought 'Bea Arthur,' but I said 'Moms Mabley.'" (Comedy legend Moms Mabley was Judy's go-to answer, up there with Monty Hall as Patti Deutsch's.)

Guest panelist Rondell Sheridan brought down the house, though, when he exclaimed to the contestant, "Have you *seen* the game ever? Do you *wanna* win?" before showing off his card, which read "Eve." In the meantime Michael Burger wondered aloud, "And what's Dick Clark *doing* in the men's room?"

Michael Burger

Judy Tenuta, for one, loved woking alongsidee host Michael Burger. "Oh, he was great!" says Judy. "He was really—he would play off me 'cause I'd call him 'Daddy.' Like, he'd say, 'Alright kids, write your answers down.' I'd go, 'Daddy!' And then Nell started calling him 'Daddy,' so we were calling him 'Daddy' all the time. He was really good because he always kept it moving and always had a good comment. He was a good host."

Part of his appeal was his genuine appreciation of *Match Game*. "I can't impress upon you how much fun it was to step out onto that CBS lot, see that big eye there and then be in those hallowed halls and do the game that you grew up watching," he admitted. "There was no yelling, there was no screaming. I've been on shows where there was yelling and screaming, and

I don't like that. So that was my demand, if I had such a thing. That's 'Let's go have fun, let's not do this any other way.' And because it's a comedy show, it does help nicely with the outcome.

"I had so much fun doing that show. I was lucky enough to bring my best friend in to do the announcing, Paul Boland. He's a stand-up comic and impressionist. So what this audience got was an incredible day of entertainment. We did seven shows in one day; that was four, take a lunch break, and do three. So my buddy Paul who did the announcing and warm-up would come out and do part of his act, which he does all over the world and gets standing ovations. And then I came out, and the show was so loose and so fun with the stars that we had, they'd jump right on that 'fun afternoon' kind of feel.

"George Hamilton would tell stories that would crack the audience up. Nell Carter, bless her soul, would get up and sing. Vicki Lawrence was a riot, Judy Tenuta was always funny—those were our regulars. And then we [booked] some soap opera stars and whomever else we could get that wanted to play."

Nell Carter

(September 13, 1948 – January 23, 2003)

While best known to TV audiences for her two-time Emmy-nominated starring role on the hit sitcom *Gimme A Break*, Nell Carter is remembered by many for her dynamic breakout role in the rollicking, Fats Waller vaudeville-styled revue *Ain't Misbehavin'*, which ran for over 1,600 performances on Broadway. She won a Tony as Best Featured Actress in that musical, then three years later won an Emmy for reprising the role in a television production of the same musical.

Her obituary in *The New York Times* accurately noted, "She belonged to a select circle of theatrical pop-soul belters whose members reveled in high-powered vocal flamboyance. A typical performance by Ms. Carter reached into the fabric of a song and tore out its seams with feral flourishes.

"As a singer and stage personality, Ms. Carter was also a natural comedian. Her vocal style was descended from the humorous gutbucket blues of Bessie Smith by way of Dinah Washington, whose singing also conveyed a seam of earthy amusement."

George Hamilton

"I was never more surprised than I was by George Hamilton," admitted Michael Burger, "by how self-deprecating and how quick he was...I mean, just as funny and as witty as any stand-up worked at it. I'd get to know him. We'd go to dinner after the show and hung out, which is not a story for this book, but the life that George Hamilton leads makes you envious and in shock and awe. You go, 'Wow! Wow!' At the same time though, not at all egocentric about it, and more insecure about it than you'd think. Or maybe not insecure is the word, but certainly not gloating or boasting about it. He knows who George Hamilton is and he keeps that image alive in many, many ways.

"George Hamilton in fact started talking to this contestant who got to the end game, and he was a month or two away from getting married and hoping to make some money to help pay for that. George said, 'Well, if you do, I will pay for your wedding, or chip in on it', and he did that. I don't know the official upshot of that but George said, 'if it happens, I'm there'—whatever it was, he promised something, and I don't remember if he'd just show up for the wedding or wrote them a check or what. But the guy had a little inspiration to get it right."

Judy Tenuta

"Tenuta was funny," remembered Michael Burger. "She would get up on the desk and you could count on her for a laugh."

Judy herself explained how she came to join the *Match Game* panel. "What happened was, just like any production team, they're so creative they want to do a replay of something that was a success," she laughed. "But thankfully for me, they actually had me in mind. My agent called me—this is something I didn't even have to hunt for--my agent called, which is, you know, we love that because that's so rare—my agent called me and I thought he was joking because he goes, 'Well, you know they're going to do a new version of the *Match Game*, and the producers are really interested in you,' and I go, 'Yeah, yeah, yeah, okay.' You know, 'Pinch me when it really happens.'

"So a few months went by, and he would keep telling me periodically, 'Oh no, they're really interested, they really want to meet with you, blah blah blah blah blah'. Well, in the meantime I was busy filming something. I had a pet-project, with Greg [Glienna] actually, *Desperation Blvd.,* so I wasn't really paying a ton of attention. But then when we finished in April, I believe, or in May, my agent called me again and said, 'Listen, the producer wants to meet you', and I go, 'Great'. So we met and he kind of gave me a rundown of how the show was going to work, and then they wanted to use me.

"And then they had Vickie Lawrence, Nell Carter, and George Hamilton. We were the four mainstays, and then they were going to use rotating guests.

"And anyway, then after we had that meeting, he said, 'Listen, we're gonna all meet. I want you to meet Nell, and we're going to come to the production office.' So about a month later we did that and then we started shooting in, it was either June or July of '98.

"We had a lot of fun, I have to say," continued Judy, "although the producer was constantly breathing down my back because I would be the

> **Michael Burger:** "For one week only, The Apple Valley Preschool production of Hamlet—of course, this time the three-year-old Hamlet declares, 'To BLANK or not to BLANK.'"
>
> **Contestant:** "To *pee* or not to *pee!*"

little wild one and I'd jump on top of the desk, and I'd always show my outfit. You've gotta do it—well, you know, you want to make it fun for people, not just like, 'Okay, we matched.' "

The Questions

Elliot Feldman noted that the earlier Ross Shafer version of *Match Game* focused too much on the game itself and not enough on the jokes. "And the last version [in 1998-1999] was almost completely the opposite," he said. "There were too many jokes but it didn't move the game along, it kind of bogged it down. It's too bad. I guess that's my opinion, anyways."

"The angle we went with was to make the show very funny," said Michael Burger. "When *Match Game* came about, it was everything I could do to get myself in front of those people. What you find out however, watching the old shows and even the shows from the seventies is that what made those shows funny is what you *couldn't* say. "

"I remember one of the particular questions," says Judy Tenuta, "and I can't remember how it was worded, but it was something about 'flatulence.' And so the contestant put on some word meaning that, just a regular word, and Vicki said some word and it matched. And then I put 'butt song,' and they go, 'I guess we'll have to take *that*.' I was always trying to think of different synonyms, more fun ones."

Michael Burger continued, "You want to be so true to the show because it was such a great show, and then put a modern day spin on it without sacrificing why the show worked to begin with. And in the same way *Newlywed Game* and a lot of those shows just won't work now just because you can tune into any one of those stations and hear the things you're not supposed to hear and see the things you're trying to allude to. That being said, I still think it's one of the best structured games in the history of game shows.

"It's a perfect dynamic, and I would jump at the opportunity to do it again."

Vicki Lawrence

"Vickie Lawrence was great too," said Michael Burger. "In fact, we're neighbors; see each other in the market all the time, and then the show happens to get on the air, and we're still neighbors. We did everything but carpool. We'd talk about the show. We literally live a couple of miles from each other. And she was great, she was a go-to gal; she would give you the answer, she's a good game-player."

"Usually, Vickie and I were on the top row," remembered Judy Tenuta, "so it was Vickie, then a guest, then me. So they'd sandwich some poor innocent guy in between Vickie and I—we would have a field day. They'd usually be some soap star who had *no clue*, you know? And it was really fun because we could have our fun with him.

"Vicki was a riot. Sometimes I think they wanted to separate us because we were laughing. We were bad. We would take whosever in the middle and make mincemeat out of them. Yeah, we had a lot of fun."

> **Michael Burger (after reading Judy's answer, at a loss for words):** "Well, I'm not—come on—are you *kidding?*"
>
> **Judy Tenuta:** "Can I say that?"
>
> **Michael:** "Well, yeah, if we're doing late night cable in *Denmark!*"

Marcia Wallace

"I was never asked to do the one with [Michael Burger] because they changed it to five seats and Vicki did my part," admitted veteran panelist Marcia Wallace. "She was a regular. And they were wrong. I mean, I was really good on that show. But hey, it was on the air a very short time. I don't believe anybody ever watched it. And by the time of the nineties, they weren't interested in good game players, they were interested in plugging shows. That's why the seventies were such a glorious time for celebrity game shows, because they picked good game players."

The Guest Panelists and The Contestants

"It's a great show for stars to do, because you're not going to look dumb and these are not *Jeopardy!* questions, they're fun questions to think about, just fill in that blank," observed Michael Burger. "I think the show could've brought in some great unique celebs had it gone on, because I think celebs would have loved to have played it.

"And the contestants—there were auditions to get these contestants in there. They had a piece of paper they had to fill out with 'BLANK apple' and all that. If the contestant didn't get the idea of what the show was, they didn't make the cut, and there were a couple of instances where we narrowed down what we thought was the best of the best. So you may watch the show and say, 'Really? That was the best?' It *was*. You know, you want somebody that can play the game and have some fun.

"And you really do want these contestants to win. At the heart of any game show, you want to root for these guys. You do want to see them win and there was a lot to that, and I remember the hours I would spend going over these questions. Will they get this? Is it fair? You want to challenge them but at the same time you do want winners.

"I remember we were in the Bonus Round, and I forget the exact question, if it was 'BLANK Washington,' and you're trying to get them to guess, and as an expert host, I actually gave the answer away. Okay so...whatever I said, I actually gave the answer that I hoped they might give. So then we had to stop tape, and the host can't give both parts. And you really started to feel for these contestants where, between you and me and the audience it seems so simple, and then for the life of them they couldn't come up with what seemed like an obvious [answer].

"And I'll tell you, these stars *really* wanted to match for the five grand. There's nothing more than seeing them happy."

The Show Ends

"See, the problem was, in the big markets like New York it was on at a bad time, " reasoned Judy Tenuta. "In L.A. it was on at a good time, and then they moved it around. They would play it late at night, so that wouldn't help us. But I must say, in certain markets it stayed on really long. Like, for some reason in Florida—I don't know what was up with that! They kept showing it and showing it, and even to this day; I was just in Florida and I get recognized *constantly* there. I mean, I'll get off the plane and the baggage handlers—'Hey, Judy!' —You know, and old people—a huge demographic. I can't figure it out... They were coming out of the woodwork."

Haphazard scheduling was a big problem for the show finding its audience. Another problem was that, despite having four regulars on the panel, there was a constant search by the producers for the fifth wheel.

"You know," admitted Michael Burger, "they believe younger stars are going to attract a younger audience, which we went back and forth on. I think a show—if it's funny, it's funny, you know? But a new game show...Ashley Judd's probably going to take a pass on it, you know what I mean? I think we were lucky to get the people that we did, because in each one of their professions they are at the top of their game."

Yet another wrench thrown into the works was the length of the show. Judy Tenuta said, "I felt that the early ones, if you noticed, were a lot more casually paced." The classic 1973-82 *Match Game* episodes lasted a minute or two longer than the new version, making room for additional commercials and the revenue that advertising brings with it. Those few minutes may not seem like a lot on paper, in the world of television it can make a huge difference in how the game plays to the viewing audience. "It is what it is, so you make the show work," Michel Burger told me. "With a little less time, the game is structured just a shade differently."

So, once again, *Match Game* found its head on the cancellation chopping block.

"I was heartbroken that it went off the air, " admitted Michael Burger. "I was the first in and one of the last to leave Stage 33, which has a full history. You know, I hope we tried to make Gene Rayburn proud. I wanted that show to work more than anything."

Review Questions

1. Host Michael Burger felt *Match Game* was <u>BLANK</u>.

a. The crown jewel of game shows
b. Not nearly as good as catching a rerun of *Mama's Family*
c. The perfect place for Judy Tenuta to show off her accordian skills

2. Judy Tenuta's and Nell Carter's nickname for Michael Burger was BLANK.

a. Daddy
b. Susan
c. Moms Mabley

3. Mandel Ilagen graduated from *Match Game*-winning contestant to BLANK.

a. President of the Vicki Lawrence Fan Club
b. Fremantle executive, working on *The Price Is Right*
c. Michael Burger's chauffeur

1. a., 2. a., 3. b.

24

Match Game in the 21st Century

Game show fans got all aflutter when *Daily Variety* reported the following in its May 10, 2004 issue: "Imagine Gene Rayburn and a ridiculously long, skinny microphone, and you've got the idea behind *What the Blank?*, a new incarnation of the classic *Match Game* format in the works at Fox, with Fred Willard attached to host.

"Fremantlemedia, which owns the rights to *Match Game* and a slew of other classic quizzer formats, is onboard to produce the 21st century take on the 1970s hit. Pilot was taped Saturday in Los Angeles, allowing the show to be considered for a summer or fall bow.

"In the original *Match Game*, which aired both in primetime and daytime, a panel of six celebs—think Richard Dawson, Charles Nelson Reilly, Brett Somers—would offer a mix of silly and straightforward answers to host Gene Rayburn's fill-in-the-blank jokes. Contestants would do their best to figure out what the celebs were thinking; winning players got a shot at the bonus round, where they could win big money by guessing how audience members had filled in a blank.

"The *Match Game* bonus game, by the way, led Mark Goodson Prods. to create an even bigger hit: *Family Feud*. Both skeins remain in regular rotation on GSN (the net formerly known as Game Show Network."

But while the seventies version of *Match Game* put GSN on the map, the network passed on this new version of the show. In an interview for TVgameshows.net, Ian Valentine, the chief programmer for GSN, said, "Do you realize how difficult it would be to write a good *Match Game* question today? I don't think it can be done with consistency."

Gameshow Marathon

Nonetheless, in the summer of 2006 the show made a brief return. *Game Show Marathon* was hosted by Ricki Lake and announced by Rich Fields and featured six celebrity contestants competing in a six-week elimination tournament. Each week the celebrities would play a different classic game show—from *Let's Make a Deal* to *Press Your Luck*—with the celebrity contestants playing for their favorite charities.

The *Match Game* episode aired on June 22, 2006. The set reproduced the familiar early seventies cream, blue and orange set (shag carpeting and all!) and the celebrity panel boasted George Foreman, Kathy Griffin, and Bruce Villanch in the upper row, Adrianne Curry seated next to Adam Carolla in the lower row, with Betty White occupying her familiar place in the last seat (Betty was the only panelist from the classic seventies run to appear for this segment of *Gameshow Marathon*). Celebrity contestants Kathy Najimy and Lance Bass played for charity.

Ricki Lake used the same signature "long skinny" Sony ECM-51 telescoping microphone Rayburn used during the CBS version. The format was that of *Match Game PM*, except that in the Super-Match the Head-To-Head Match was played for fifty times the amount won in the two Audience Matches. Kathy Najimy won the game, scoring five matches to Lance Bass' three. Interestingly, Najimy had a backgound in game shows, havong appeaed as a civilian contestant on *Family Feud* in 1981 and on *The $25,000 Pyamid* in 1985.

What The Blank!

A few years after the *What the Blank!* pilot was shot, TBS commissioned a new pilot for a revived version as part of an overhaul of its late night television programming. On June 21, 2008, Andrew Daly hosted a pilot episode featuring Sarah Silverman, Scott Thompson and Norm MacDonald as the regular panelists, filmed on the same set used for the taping of the *Gameshow Marathon* episode.

"We shot the pilot in June," remembered Andrew Daly. "Our pilot was shot on an exact replica of the old set on the same stage at CBS and Scott Thompson was using Charles Nelson Reilly's old mic with the smiley face CNR drew on it with his Magic Marker all those years ago. It was surreal."

TBS eventually passed on the project in favor of *Lopez Tonight*, starring George Lopez.

Match Game On DVD

A special DVD boxed set titled *The Best of Match Game* was released on November 21, 2006 containing thirty uncut episodes of the show, with bonus features including a tribute to Gene, an interview with Brett, and the pilot of the original sixties *Match Game*.

"As indicated by its current number one status on GSN, *Match Game* continues to be a perennial favorite almost 25 years after its final original episode," said Jeff Hayne, Director of Acquisitions for BCI. "From host Gene Rayburn to regulars Brett Somers, Charles Nelson Reilly and Richard Dawson, celebrities became instantaneously recognizable because of their appearances on the show. We're excited to be bringing the series to DVD not only for its loyal original fans, but for their children to appreciate as well."

Among the favorite episodes included in the set was the infamous "School Riot" debacle, during which "Dumb Dora was so dumb, she sent her cultured pearls to BLANK." After the contestant answered with "School," Ira Skutch ruled Ed Asner's and Brett's answers, "College," to be a match. When Charles held up his card, he got the buzzer with what was written on it: "Scuba diving school," with the word "school" outlined in a box. After mild booing from the audience, and Charles arguing that while "scuba diving" was meant to be funny because the question concerned pearls, the box he drew emphasized the word "school," and after a minor kerfuffle, his answer got a pass.

Things immediatelty went south when Debralee Scott and Richard answered with "Finishing school," and got the buzzer. Both immediately protested that if college and scuba diving school weren't too specific to match, then finishing school should be an acceptable match. While Gene tried to keep things calm, the audience roared their disapproval, goaded on by the incensed Debralee and Richard.

In the end, Ira never backed down, and after the commercial break the camera focused on Charles, lying catatonic on the carpeted stairs. "Now, Charles," exclaimed Gene, "What is this going on?" and Brett ran over, reading the following explanation off her blue answer cards, "First victim of school riot. Man with shirt inside out found on school steps." (Charles was wearing a French-styled sailor's shirt with the seams visible on the outside, causing Gene and Brett to joke he was wearing his shirt reversed.) This episode possibly marked a turning point, as Richard's disenchantment with the show escalated after this incident.

Behind The Blank

A few days after the DVD release date, GSN aired *The Real Match Game Story: Behind the Blank*, an hour-long special about the history of the show, produced by Frank Sinton and featuring interviews with Goodson-Todman staffers and celebrity panelists.

As Virginia Heffernan wrote in her review of the special for The New York Times,

Audrey Davis, who worked on both the sixties and seventies versions of the show and recounted on camera her story about Jayne Mansfield borrowing then stretching out her t-shirt during a taping of the show, admitted, "I don't remember much about *Behind the Blank* except when I filmed my part. Rae Pichon and Dick De Bartolo were in the studio with me to tape their parts. It was nice to catch up and see some of the old gang on camera when the show aired. I wish I could find my DVD. I probably learned a few things that I never knew then, but can't remember a thing now! The only thing I can remember that was edited from tape to air in my interview was that they never showed the portion of my answer about working with Mariska Hargitay. Guess they were only interested in the Jayne Mansfield story!"

In her review of the program for *The New York Times*, Virginia Heffernan wrote, "On Sunday, GSN, which has found increasingly successful ways to exploit its small window on cultural history, chronicles the rise and fall of this blockbuster program. In *The Real Match Game Story: Behind the Blank*, we learn everything we'd ever need to know about the wacky leerfest that modeled the promiscuous, drunken, risqué, gender-bending behavior of '70's celebrities for an unlikely daytime audience—under the guise of being a quiz show."

Giving a nutshell synopsis of the show's history, she continued, "Mark Goodson's original idea was for a kind of guess-what-I'm-thinking show that would take advantage of that era's love of thought experiments; that soon became boring, and matches were not frequent enough. Someone suggested turning to bluer material, or at least hinting at blueness, and the rest is history."

"...The GSN back story plays Mr. Dawson as the evil foil to the sweet and fun-loving Mr. Rayburn, and indeed he comes across as sour and ego-driven. But he was clearly the best player at the silly '*Match Game*'; contestants were always choosing him as their foxhole teammate—when it came right down to it, the jokes were over and it was time to win some money.

"Mr. Dawson was tan, burned, and not bad-looking. He played—I had forgotten this—a kind of Simon Cowell role in the *Match Game* seat. But he had his eyes on what he thought of then as bigger things, by which he meant *Family Feud*, the game show he went on to preside over which went on to overtake the *Match Game* as the most popular daytime show.

"*Family Feud* is nothing if not a populist show. rather than guess at the habits of the Hollywood demimonde, with their life of blankety-blanks, contestants guess at only what others like them might say: it's about being average.

"But, in the usual American way, those family values have yeilded back. *Match Game* is, apparently, the No. 1 show on GSN these days—in 30-year-old reruns. Never say there's nothing to learn from game shows!"

Match Game Live!

Fans who couldn't get enough of *Match Game*, even with the DVD set and reruns of the show airing several times a day on cable, could search out the numerous live-action versions (and knock-offs) being played across the country. Bars and clubs in New York and Chicago have been hosting special game show nights with their own parodies of classic game shows like *Family Feud*, *Hollywood Squares*, *Pyramid*, and of course, *Match Game*.

One of the most popular proved to be *The MisMatch Game*, which grew out of a benefit performance put on by the L.A. Gay and Lesbian Center's Renberg Theatre on September 25, 2004. Named one of the Ten Best Performances of the Year by *The Advocate*, producer Dennis Hensley played host to a 'celebrity' panel that included Michael Airington as Paul Lynde, Patrick Bristow as Nancy Kulp, Jennifer Elise Cox as Elaine Joyce, Jack Plotnick as Evie Harris, Tony Tripoli as Charles Nelson Reilly, and special guest star Marcia Wallace as...well...Marcia Wallace!

"The audiences love it," Marcia told me. "It's *Match Game* without euphemism. But you can't just keep saying '[BLANK],' '[BLANK]' and '[BLANK].' You still hopefully try to be clever and find an answer that matches but is funny. This game is not as easy as it looks."

I asked Dennis Hensley what gave him the idea to stage (and host) the benefit. "The original idea began when I recreated the *Match Game* for my birthday," said Dennis. "It was such a hit that we wanted to do it again, so we pitched it to the Center as a benefit fundraiser.

"I loved the *Match Game* more than other shows because it just seemed like a big cocktail party. The game seemed secondary to the jokes and just the celebrities being silly and making dirty jokes with their celebrity pals. Also, the structure of the questions on *Match Game* is much better suited to comedy. As a kid, I thought *Match Game* made being an adult seem like so much fun. And the people with good senses of humor had the majority, which is how I wish the real world worked. If you were pretentious or took yourself too seriously, you were outnumbered on *Match Game*.

"The audiences have been great. When it's really cooking, I think the show is funny in a way that's uniquely its own. The best answers aren't dirty—though a lot of them are—but they're also smart and work on several levels. Some answers have been so brilliant that the audience gave them standing ovations."

Since Dennis Hensley hosted the initial benefit performance in 2004, *The MisMatch Game* has been revived as an occasional fundraising effort benefitting the Los Angeles LGBT Center. For fifteen years now their stage gameplay has raised over $150,000 benefitting homeless LGBT youth, senior citizens, and those needing medical assistance. A fine group of talented Los Angeles-based (and occasionally those visiting from the other coast) comedians and actors (including among many, many others Jackie Beat, Willam Belli, Julie Brown, Danny Casillas, Drew Droege. Nadya Ginsburg, and Sam Pancake) have donated their time and talents to this very worthy cause. Good for them!

Review Questions

1. Among those assuming Gene Raybun's mantle as host of revived versions of *Match Game* were <u>BLANK</u>.

a. Fred Willard, Andrew Daly, and Ricki Lake
b. Kukla, Fran and Ollie
c. Tony Orlando and Dawn

2. While shooting a new *Match Game* pilot in 2008, celebity panelists discovered <u>BLANK</u>.

a. A new planet in the Milky Way
b. The smiley face Charles Nelson Reilly drew with a Magic Marker
c. Dick Clark's original birth certificate carved in a stone tablet

3. Fans who can't get enough Match Game can <u>BLANK</u>.

a. Go jump in a lake
b. Content themselves with the DVD boxed set of episodes, reruns airing on cable, and live-action parodies taking place in bars across the country
c. Settle for poorly-written sitcoms on prime-time network television

Answers: 1. a.; 2. b., 3. b.

25

The All-New *Match Game* With Alec Baldwin

After a summer installment of *Celebrity Family Feud* found success, ABC decided to revive other nostalgic game show property. "We basically said, *Match Game* is the one, if we can attach the right talent," said Jennifer Mullin, co-CEO of FremantleMedia North America and an executive producer on the new *Match Game.*

So Fremantle reached out to Alec Baldwin. "He's got a dry sense of humor," said Mullin. "He's got the right sensibility." As it turned out, he was something of a fan of the original show. "There was a period when I was a kid," he admitted, "...where I would fake sick and stay home from school as much as possible. I always say that's where I refined whatever acting abilities I have, pretending I was ill so my mother wouldn't make me go to school. Once I hit that couch, there's nothing I wouldn't watch. I was pretty much raised by these kinds of daytime shows. This game show was one of them."

And so the project moved forward—which is to say, it looked backward. At the end of April, 2016 the official announcement was made: the network was placing their bets on game shows, promoting what it called a "Sunday Fun & Games Block," including the Steve Harvey-hosted

Celebrity Family Feud, the Michael Strahan-fronted *$100,000 Pyramid*, and an all-new version of *Match Game*, executive produced and hosted by Alec Baldwin.

"I would joke a couple years ago, when I started having more children, that I was going to end up hosting a game show to pay my bills," Baldwin laughed to *The Hollywood Reporter*. "Then this offer came in. The fact of the matter is ... they gave me a very generous amount of money for my charity. They gave me $1 million for my foundation to work just a few days. But the show is fun. Beth McCarthy, who I'd done *30 Rock* and *Saturday Night Live* with, is one of the best live TV directors in the business. And it's at 10 o'clock. We can do it a little looser, a little saltier. That surprised me. Some of the things people said in rehearsal were wickedly funny, and I wondered if we'd be able to say any of it on TV. But they're letting us. Hosting a game show is certainly not the only thing I want to do in life. But doing this and having fun with people, many of them my old friends—how can I say no to that?"

So Baldwin agreed to host the show and was surprised by the warm reception he received. "You'd think that doing these things would hurt you somehow. But it was announced I was doing this show, and in the ensuing two weeks, I got offered more jobs—this movie or that movie. I said to my agent, 'Don't they know I'm hosting *Match Game*?' We're all doing this to have fun and raise money for some causes."

The First Episode

There was a lot of speculation about this latest incarnation, most of which could be summed up with the following headline from a *Vanity Fair* article: "Can a New *Match Game* Bring Back the Ineffable [BLANK] of the Original?" The subtitle to the article illustrated the skepticism and snarkiness the new show faced when it asked, "And just how drunk will this version's celebrity panelists be?"

The first episode of the updated show opened with the announcer exclaiming, "Get ready to make a match!" instead of the traditional, "Get ready to match the stars!" Cynics wondered if contestants were no longer trying to match the stars, or perhaps (without the likes of Brett, Charles and Richard on the panel) there were no more "stars" left to match.

Of course, die-hard fans have to give any new production permission to find its own way of presenting the game. Any subsequent version doesn't negatively affect the classic versions of a game show. In fact, maybe the new versions only make the original seem better! Besides, anyone missing Brett, Charles and Richard can always turn to the reruns airing on cable or captured on the DVD boxed set.

"We're very much keeping it in the vibe of the seventies," Jennifer Mullin told *Vanity Fair*. "It will look and feel and sound like *Match Game*." So the show's producers made a conscious effort not to fix what wasn't broken in the first place. The same *Vanity Fair* article went on to introduce cosmetic examples including "the original funky bass riff that's playing in the show's current promos. Panelists will still sit before a light-bulb-trellis; they'll still be introduced as floating heads inside a sparkling, lo-fi spinning marquee."

The game play remained faithful to the classic version. "Formats aren't born overnight. They take time to get right," Mullin said. "The Goodson-Todman guys were masters at it. If it's not broken, don't fix it."

"No whammies so far for these nostalgic games," declared *The Hollywood Reporter*, while their reviewer Daniel Feinberg offered up his verdict following the show's premiere episode.

"I assume there's a comfort level that Baldwin will eventually ease into and that will include his panel interactions and his ability to hit the punchlines in the clues. For now, just as a jovial actor inhabiting an unexpected part, Baldwin is fun to watch and it's good to see him carrying over Rayburn's love for in-character clue readings, in this case a dismal-but-terrific Mick Jagger impression.

"The evolving rapport of the panel will be the aspect of *Match Game* that bears the most watching. Michael Ian Black has been seated in the Charles Nelson Reilly position in the upper right of the panel, and he's a solid pick to offer Reilly's erudite, spiky commentary. But there was little of that in the premiere, which concentrated more on O'Donnell's everywoman connection with the contestants and JB Smoove's dapper flirtations.

"... At least in the first episode, the panelists were carving out their own places, rather than finding points of interplay, and I wonder if chemistry can really be developed in a short summer run. To be sure, you can't produce Reilly/Brett Somers' interaction overnight, and it's surely better that they didn't try to force it. I laughed a few times and that's a start."

The Celebrity Panel

Some of the celeb panelists appearing during the ten-week run were clearly mor familiar with the game than others. Christie Brinkley (who admitted being more of a fan of *Hollywood Squares* and *Password*) admitted to not being familiar with the rules of the game, while Chris Colfer of *Glee*-fame explained, "When I was home sick, I'd watch all the reruns on GSN."

Along with sharing game-playing skills, recurring panelists Rosie O'Donnell and Tituss Burgess revisited the sparring between Brett and Charles without the banter feeling like it was forced. But as much as she might have been nominated a latter-day Brett Somers, Rosie also seemed to have channeled Richard Dawson in proving herself the most reliable player and the go-to partner for the Super Match bonus round (Alec Baldwin dubbed her "the Shakespeare of game shows" after yet another Super Match win). Ana Gasteyer's "literate and idiosyncratic" manner conjured up memories of Patti Deutsch's offbeat answers. One question referenced Baldwin and Gasteyer's infamous "Schweddy Balls" sketch from *Saturday Night Live*, which had in fact been written by Gasteyer. Baldwin read off the card, assuring the contestants, panelists and studio audience that the new "Schweddy Log" is the "best thing you'll ever put in your BLANK." After her fellow panelists responded with the obvious "mouth," Gasteyer displayed her answer: "Wood-burning stove."

And that's how you play the last seat on *Match Game*.

Boobs, Booze and Donald Trump

But as important as the celebrity panel is to the success of the show, so is the quality of the contestants. "It can be a little raunchy at times with their answers—we never know which way—so we just want people who can kind of roll with the punches and most importantly, get in that mindset of what the celebrities are thinking because you're trying to match their answers," said *Match Game* casting director Rebecca Greenberg.

And as John Teti wrote, " You cannot recapture the '70s, it's true, but unpretentious fun doesn't belong to one era. With that in mind, the creators of this revival achieved what long seemed impossible—a great new *Match Game*—by restoring the concept's original simplicity and letting smart players fill in the blanks."

But transferring any property from one era to another poses its own challenges. In order to work, fill-in-the-blank questions must be universal; writers rely on shared cultural (and pop-cultural) knowledge. But today's audiences are more diverse in background and experience than audiences in the seventies were.

"So they're reviving *The Match Game* with Alec Baldwin," former *Match Game* writer Elliot Feldman reported on his Facebook page. "He'll be able to handle the host gig much better than prior post-Rayburn hosts. The key, however, is the writing. It's very tricky and jokes can easily fall flat." And Elliot joked, "They should hire me, Joe Neustein, and Bobby. But that's one more pipe dream."

"We're trying to stay in the pop-culture zeitgeist, such as who's in the news, or a product, or an event, like the Olympics," said Jennifer Mullin. "We had a fun Baldwin brothers question, which Alec enjoyed reading. We had a Donald Trump question."

Match Game, she admitted, was built upon innuendo. "So we encourage a party spirit," she added. "It's playing at 10 o'clock at night; you can be a little bawdier." How does the show achieve this goal? According to legend, the answer was simple: vodka. Mullin herself downplayed any network-sanctioned lubrication, but conceded it was important for the celebrities to get in the right mood before taping. "We have the panel sitting around, talking, watching old episodes, and getting to know each other to build a sense of camaraderie," she stated, but she did add, "If they wish to have a cocktail, we can make that available to them."

"*Match Game* is all about showing people having a good time together," Wendie Malick observed, "so they got us all in a room together for an hour, hanging out and having cocktails, at about 2:30 in the afternoon! You tend to bond heavily, and quickly."

According to journalist Chancellor Agard, who attended the taping of one episode, "Each time the show paused for a commercial break, a man dressed in all black would walk on stage carrying a tray of drinks for the celebrity panelists (none for the contestants, because they have to win money, obviously)."

The cocktails were authentic, according to the cast. "Oh, they're real. They're definitely real," Chris Colfer attested. "I wasn't expecting to have a full bar when I walked in!" In fact, "It's a *gorgeous* bar," Ana Gasteyer declared, "and a good-looking bartender, which I think everybody appreciates. It's like Andy Cohen's [*Watch What Happens Live*] clubhouse; he's always got a hot bartender."

At the bar in the green room, "They have pretty much anything you want," continued Wendie Malick. "And they encourage you to drink, heavily. That's the secret to this show's success

"I've been here since 8:30 in the morning and I have been drinking since then," Cheryl Hines, who grew up watching the original show, told *Entertainment Weekly* at the end of the taping. "It's like college days."

With or without the help of the bartending staff, there was fun to be had. Let's face it, there's never going to be anyone like Brett and Charles. But that doesn't mean today's celeb panelists can't shake loose with some funny onscreen moments.

Chancellor Agard witnessed a taping featuring Leslie Jones and Leah Remini bonding together on the panel and reported in *Entertainment Weekly*, "Everyone at this panel seemed to be enjoying themselves, but Jones was definitely having the most fun. She was *all* over the place. She became invested in helping the contestants win money. At one point, she literally (and jokingly) walked off because the contestant did not go with the obvious answer... Her enthusiasm made you, the audience, care about the contestants winning. When they didn't get any points, you were disappointed. When they did get points, you were ecstatic."

The Former Governor

But Leslie Jones and Leah Remini aside, by far the most noteworthy celebrity to do a guest shot on the panel was former Alaska governor, Vice-Presidential candidate and conservative pundit, Sarah Palin. She appeared in the midst of one of the most volatile presidential campaigns in recent U.S. history and while she herself was not running, her status as a GOP representative made her a firebrand during the 2016 campaign.

On her Facebook page, Palin later wrote, "Nothing is more fun than the infiltration of traditionally liberal Hollywood; gives us a chance to interact with those who may assume they can't have much in common with a common-sense conservative. I always have a blast doing these pop culture venues!"

Though Alec Baldwin and Sarah Palin had previously clashed with their opposing political views (Palin famously showed up on *Saturday Night Live* in 2008 when Tina Fey did her famous impression of Palin, while the former governor declared "Stephen" was her favorite Baldwin brother) they greeted each other warmly on-camera.

"Sarah Palin is here because Tina Fey won't return my phone calls," Baldwin joked at one point, although he started the episode by addressing Palin, "I'm simply going to start by asking you what everyone is dying to know: what the hell are you doing here?"

Everyone, including Palin, laughed. She replied, "I've always enjoyed working with you, Alec. And really, I just thought, at this time, I want a challenge. I want to do the antithesis of what I should be doing."

Palin's compariots on the celebrity panel were Jack McBrayer, Leah Remini, Randall Park, JB Smoove, and Kristin Chenoweth. While a number of panelists started drinking wine and beer, Palin stuck with water. "I'm such a bore," she said.

No matter who sits on the panel, this is *Match Game*, after all, so the peremptory "Boobs" question had to be asked. Alec read off the following: "Did you hear Pinocchio has a sister? Every time she tells a lie, her BLANK gets bigger." The contestant's response? "Nipple!" he said, looking proud. Jack McBrayer, Leah Remini and JB Smoove went with variations on the classic *Match Game* answer, "Boobs," and the producers must have decided that was close enough, because Billy got all the points. When it was Palin's turn? "The most politically correct answer," she announced, holding her card which said "da bosom."

There was a question referencing Palin and her home state of Alaska: "Sarah Palin takes her pets to the groomer in Alaska. Once a week they manicure her moose, her caribou, and her BLANK." The audience reacted loudly.

At first Palin joked that she would refuse to answer, announcing to one and all, "I'm gonna filibuster," but she eventually played along. While the contestant answered with "Bison" and most of the celebrities answered "Bear," no one responded with what should have been the definitive answer, ahem, "Pussycat."

Palin turned out to be a good sport when it was her turn and held up her answer, "Her Alaskan golden nuggets!" The audience started booing loudly. "You can't boo her. She's a governor!" Baldwin admonished the crowd.

And this being the 2016 election season, the writers offered up a Hillary Clinton question as well. Baldwin read off the question: "Hillary Clinton just opened up a new magic show on the Las Vegas strip. For her final trick, she makes everyone's BLANK disappear." The contestant David chose "election ballots." No one matched. Randall Park and Leah Remini guessed "Donald Trump," and Sarah Palin guessed "brains."

The Verdict

The series received largely positive reviews from both critics and fans. Following the ten-week run, the network announced the series would be picked up, and *Match Game* was now officially back in busines!

Review Questions

1. According to one reporter, Leslie Jones' enthusiasm as a panelist made the audience <u>BLANK</u>.

a. Want to give her an Emmy, a Tony, an Oscar, and a cocktail.
b. Care about the contestants winning.
c. Become her new best friend and go shopping for handbags at Prada.

2. Ana Gasteyer's "literate and idiosyncratic" manner conjured up memories of <u>BLANK</u>.

a. Judy Tenuta's accordian-playing and wild dance moves.
b. Patti Deutsch's offbeat answers.
c. The song stylings of Martha Stewart's karoke version of *Love Shack*.

3. Alec Baldwin announced Sarah Palin was on the celebrity panel because <u>BLANK</u> wouldn't return his phone calls.

a. Brett Somers.
b. Tina Fey.
c. Hillary Clinton.

Answers: 1. b., 2. b., 3. b.

26

"I Wish I Had Cable..."

"*The Match Game* was never merely a TV game show. No matter the time of its broadcast, the show was a five-o'clock-somewhere cocktail party to which we were all invited, a raucous shindig populated by some of the wittiest personalities the small screen has ever seen. Sure, some of the stars couldn't spell their way out of a <u>BLANK</u>. But we were all too schnockered on laughs to mind. All game shows—not to mention, at-home game nights—will forever strive to be as inebriated and inebriating."

—Frank DeCaro, author of *Drag: Combing Through the Big Wigs of Show Business*, and former I've *Got a Secret* panelist.

When the number of cable TV channels exploded in the 1980's, people joked that one day there would be channels devoted to every little thing— a network devoted to soap operas, a network featuring nothing but cartoons, a network that showed nothing but (laugh, laugh) *game shows*...and then in time the joke became a reality.

GSN (formerly known as The Game Show Network) began airing on December 1, 1994, and over the rest of that decade, was added to more and more cable systems, satisfying those cable fans dissatisfied that fewer and fewer quality game shows had been produced. The seeming crown jewel of the network—which has shown everything from classic episodes of *The Newlywed Game*, the various *Pyramids*, and *Family Feud*—was *Match Game*. In recent years, GSN has produced a number of original game shows, including *Russian Roulette*, *Cram*, *Lingo*, and an updated version of *Press Your Luck*, and yet it was reruns of *Match Game* that drew in the fans. Today, three million viewers watch *Match Game* reruns each week. Think of it—reruns of reruns outpace the competition!

"Nobody ever really *admits* to watching game shows," grumbled Patti Deutsch. "They always preface it with 'When I was a kid and I was home *sick*, I used to watch.' Or waiters—they'll admit to watching it because that's what time they used to get off. But other than that it was always 'I was home sick.' So we would play to shut-ins. Little did we know."

Well, that may have been the way it *used* to be, but nowadays they play to more than just waiters and shut-ins. College students and hipsters have discovered the retro-chic classic game shows and turned them into cult classics. And some of *Match Game's* biggest fans are former panelists!

"I watch it more now than I have ever," Dick Martin admitted to me shortly before he passed away. "It's on every night...and it's such fun to see all the old gang. I love it! Because—I don't know, it's just such fun, and I see all these people that I know so well. And I play right along with it."

"Dick and I love to watch the reruns," confirmed Dolly Read Martin. "I love Tivo. Do you get Tivo?" When I said I currently did not, she gasped, "Oh, you've *got* to get Tivo!"

"I'm so bad with mechanical things," I lamented.

"Dick can't even plug in a light bulb," she laughed, "so I know what you mean. But even he knows how to do the Tivo. It's so easy. We Tivo all the time...Oh, it's fabulous, honestly. We bless Tivo every day, because you don't have to go find a tape and put it in. It just tapes somewhere in the atmosphere, God knows where. Details, details, details."

Even Scoey Mitchlll catches the reruns from time to time. "I miss a lot of them," he admitted, "but like I said, I'm not a game show watcher, but every now and then I'll be surfing through there and I'll come up, and I'll go, '*Ooh*, I'm on *television*!' My mother lives with me now. My mother is 104 and she really can't see it, but she hears my voice. So I catch it every now and then."

"My husband is a great game show watcher," admitted Joyce Bulifant, "and he always has it on, and he'll yell, 'You're on today!' And I might run through and look at it a second and say, 'Oh my gosh! What was I doing wearing something like *that*?'

And of course, the cast gets residuals from reruns of *Match Game*. "We get paid fifty cents a show," Patti Deutsch informed me. "Did you know that? Yeah. So you know, you sock that away, you've got fifty cents a show! It's bizarre, I think. And then when they rerun *Tattletales*, which my husband and I were on, we get a dollar, because we *each* get fifty cents. We're just rocking and rolling in our house, I tell you. Keeps the basset hounds in kibble."

When I mentioned that reruns of *Match Game* are shown about three times a day, Joyce Bulifant replied, "Isn't it amazing? And what do we get? Fifty bucks?" She laughed about the residuals and continued, "But that's not it. I mean, when the man told me the other day about his wife who was dying of cancer and that [watching *Match Game* reruns] was the bright spot of her day, Lord, that's enough. You don't need fifty dollars, whatever it is they give you."

More than fifty years after *Match Game* premiered on NBC, the show remains as popular as ever. At any given moment on eBay, the online auction service, fans are buying and selling *Match Game* board games, from the first 1963 edition to the 1970's editions. Type in the words *Match Game*, and you'll find dealers hawking signed photos of Brett Somers, and original tickets to see a taping at CBS for *Match Game '78*, still in mint condition. A signed 3x5 glossy photo of the late Gene Rayburn sold for

$94. A last-minute bidding war drove the price of a 1998 *Match Game* press kit, featuring 8x10 glossy photos of Michael Burger, Judy Tenuta, etc, along with press release and bios, to an astonishing $165. Maybe this doesn't compare to fans spending $30 million at the Sotheby's auction of the estate of Jackie Kennedy Onassis, but in the world of game show memorabilia, it's pretty impressive to witness.

Online there are tribute websites devoted to the show. Ryan Dziadosz proudly showed off the blurb that appeared in *Entertainment Weekly* listing some of the sites (including his own) and what they offered: everything from drinking games ("Charles asks for his nurse—2 drinks; Charles demands a nurse for an out of control Brett Somers—2 drinks...") to mini-biographies of celeb panelists to episode guides and still photos.

And then there are the reunions. While Brett and Charles never appeared in that bus-and-truck production of *Who's Afraid of Virginia Woolf?* (I'd have paid to see that—wouldn't you?) they were reunited not only on the Ross Shafer version of *Match Game*, but on December 2, 2002 they returned to Stage 33 of CBS Television City to shoot a special week of episodes on the new *Hollywood Squares*, hosted by Tom Bergeron. Sharing a square, they bickered and bantered like old times, proving they had lost none of their magic. Prior to that, Brett, Charles, and Betty White appeared together on the *CBS Early Show* on March 15, 2002 for a *Match Game Reunion*, where the three reminisced about Gene Rayburn and the show, and Brett dispelled the apparently very strong rumor that she was battling cancer at the time (Were people confusing her with Marcia Wallace?). Asked by the host about on-set drinking, Brett replied, "Absolutely, Absolutely. And all those people who said they weren't drinking...just lied!" When Betty White said, "I never saw the bar. Where'd you hide the bar?" Brett reprimanded her with, "Oh Betty, I'm ashamed of you!"

Hilarious stuff as far as I am concerned.

Today, GSN offers a handful of newly produced game shows (*Lingo, Win Tuition, Cram*, and others) in addition to its reruns of classic game shows; yet *Match Game* remains the network's highest rated show. This means that reruns of reruns are outpacing new programming! Few of the new shows seem to possess the cult power of *Match Game*, or even the original *Hollywood Squares*. Peter Marshall observed, "I used to like Fannie Flagg, I loved her on the show. They had style, I love people with style. Charles had style. Paul Lynde had style. I saw Marcia Wallace on my show the other day—she had style. Pleshette, Poston, they have style. And that's the problem with most of the game show hosts [today]. They don't have style. They do it, they do their job, but there's nothing personable about it. There's no personality there. They don't have style, it's that simple." It is worth noting that Peter said this completely without malice or arrogance; he was merely voicing what the fans seem to know instinctively.

Thus far, a *Match Game Movie* script hasn't yet been shopped around Hollywood, but in time, who knows? If they can transfer *The Brady Bunch*, *Scooby-Doo*, and *Charlie's Angels* from the small screen to the big screen and make money at it (they did it with *The Gong Show*! Twice!*) maybe the next ten years will have Drew Barrymore playing Brett Somers to Adam Sandler's Charles Nelson Reilly (Don't laugh! It could happen! After all, if Glenn Close could play a *singing* Norma Desmond...).

Enough schmaltz and enough eulogizing. Love it or not (if you bought this book, I'm assuming you at least *liked* it), in any of its incarnations it was indeed what Brianne Leary called a "cultural phenomenon," and more importantly, it was a fun game to play and a fun show to watch. There's nothing much left to say...except perhaps for the most fitting epitaph I ever heard, offered by Kay Henley: "I wish I had cable if for no other reason than to watch the old *Match Game* reruns."

---

*=*The Gong Show Movie* in 1980, and *Confessions of a Dangerous Mind* in 2002. Granted, *The Gong Show Movie* was a colossal flop, but why cloud the issue with facts?

27

"And Now a Word From Our Sponsors..."

There are a great many people to whom, for their help, I owe a debt of gratitude; chief among them are Kim Roach, who has proven to be a guardian angel on *multiple* levels, Mark Masaracchia, a longtime supporter of this book project, and most especially John F. Schultz, who introduced me to Kay Henley early on. But I must also acknowledge the following individuals and institutions who helped ease the process of information-gathering in some small or large way:

Harry Abrams, Abrams Artists Agency, The Academy of Television Arts & Sciences, The American Federation of Television and Radio Artists (AFTRA), James J. Agazzi, Kirstie Alley, Curt Alliaume, Gary Anderson of Score Productions, Darryl Armbruster, Adrienne Armstrong, Alison Arngrim, Ryan Arrington, Garrett Auriema, John Barnes, Bob Batche, Orson Bean, Ken Bichel, Seth Bier, Paul Boland, Mark Bowerman, Bradley University Library, Bart Braverman, Pam Braverman, Marc Breslow, *Broadcast, Programming & Production* magazine, Dr. Joyce Brothers, Noeline Brown, Michael Burger, Joyce Bulifant, Susan Burns, Annette Caggiano, Jack Carter, Brian Chenoweth, Dame Joan Collins, Jon Collins, Brian Connoy, Lee Costello, Barry Creyton, Patricia Cullen,

Jessica Curry, Dick DeBartolo, David Del Valle, Seamus Dever, The Directors Guild of America (DGA), Roger Dobkowitz, Todd Doughty, Patty Duke, Philippe Dunbar, Scott Dunbar, Alonso Duralde, Bobby Ellerbee, Elliot Feldman, Fannie Flagg, FremantleMedia, Edmund Hollander, Teresa Ganzel, Diego Garcia, Greg Glienna, Leonard Grainger, Francoise Gralewski, Dave Grzelak, David Hammett, Pat Harrington, Weston Harris, Chris Hart, Kitty Carlisle Hart, Jonni Hartman, Kay Henley, Dennis Hensley, Tom Hietter, Marsha Morris Hochfield, Karen Holland, Sandra Hollin, Mandel Ilagan, Jennifer Infante, Bob Israel and everyone at Score Productions, Diane Janaver, Larry Kase, Drew King, Ross King, Ken Kleiber and *That's Kentertainment!*, Gary Kleinman, Jack Klugman, Jean Kopelman, Bob LaBate, Chris Lambert, Audrey Landers, Judy Landers, Ruth Landers, Jeffrey Lane, Trish Lay, Stephen Lo, Sterling Long-Colbo, Ronn Lucas, Reverend Pam MacGregor, Jim MacKrell, Jeannette Mann, Peter Marshall, Dick Martin, Dolly Read Martin, David McGillivary, Edie McClurg, Mark Measures, Lee Meriwether, Scoey Mitchlll, R. Patrick Neary, Steven Neibert, Maxine Nunes, Jennifer Obakhume, T.J. O'Brien, Greg Palmer, Sharon Paz, Clive Pearse, Todd Pellegrino, Jennifer Peterlin, Rae Pichon, Robert Pine, Mark Quinn, Anthony Rapp, Charles Nelson Reilly, Cindy Ronzoni, Lindsay Rowan, Tom Rowan, The Screen Actors Guild (SAG), Debralee Scott, Ross Shafer, Robert Sherman, Lainie Sigesmund-Etzioni, Ira Skutch, Brett Somers, Reverend Jill Soyars, Angie Stark, Gerda Stark, Rick Stern, Dan Studney, Dennis Sullivan, Eric Szulczewski, Karen Tarleton-Holland, Jake Tauber, Rip Taylor, Maura Teitelbaum, Leslie Uggams, Pamela Usdan, Stuart Wagstaff, Marcia Wallace, Patrick Welborn, Marc Wheeler, John Whitaker, Alan White, Betty White (and her assistant Donna), Dave White, Shad Wilhelm, The Writer's Guild of America (WGA), Zoe Yeoman.

...And a *very* special thanks to my creditors for keeping at bay!

Bibliography

Books:

Bean, Orson—*Too Much Is Not Enough*, Lyle Stuart Inc., Secaucus, NJ (1988).

Cohen, Mark—*Overweight Sensation: The Life and Comedy of Allan Sherman*, Brandeis University Press, Waltham, MA (2013).

Dawson, Les—*A Clown Too Many*, Elm Tree Books, London (1985).

DeBartolo, Dick—*Good Days and MAD: A Hysterical Tour Behind the Scenes at MAD Magazine*, Thunder's Mouth Press (1994).

Fabe, Maxene—*TV Game Shows! A Behind the Screen Look at the Stars! The Prizes! The Hosts! and The Scandals!* (1979).

Ferguson, Ali—*Graham Kennedy's Blankety Blanks*, Horwitz Publications, Australia, (1977).

Holms, John P. and Wood, Ernest—*The TV Game Show Almanac: 50 Years of Facts and* Fun, Chilton Book Company, New York-Pennsylvania (1995).

Jones, Jenny with Patsi Bale Cox—*Jenny Jones: My Story*, Andrews McMeel Publishing, Kansas City, MO (1997).

Marshall, Peter, and Armstrong, Adrienne—*Backstage With The Original Hollywood Square*, Rutledge Hill Press, Nashville, TN (2002).

Middles, Mick—*When You're Smiling: The Illustrated Biography of Les Dawson*, Chameleon Books, London (1999).

Norbom, Mary Ann—*Richard Dawson and Family Feud*, Signet Classics (1981).

Skutch, Ira—*I Remember Television*, the Directors Guild of America and Scarecrow Press (1989).

Wallace, Marcia—*Don't Look Back, We're Not Going That Way: How I overcame a Rocky Childhood, a Nervous Breakdown, Breast Cancer, Widowhood, Fat, Fire, and Menopausal Motherhood and Still Managed to Count My lucky Chickens*, Off The Wall Press, Los Angeles (2004).

White, Betty—*Here We Go Again: My Life in Television* (1995) .
Wogan, Terry—*Is It Me?*, BBC Worldwide Limited, (2000).

Newspaper/Magazine/Online Articles:
Adams, Lee and Charles Strouse—*Bye Bye Birdie* (Theatre Program), 1960, New York.
Bolstad, Helen, *'Winners Circle'*, *TV Radio Mirror* May 1960, pages 38-9, 69-70.
Borden, Jane—*Can a New Match Game Bring Back the Ineffable [BLANK] of the Original?*, Vanityfair.com, June 24, 2016
Dahlbeck, Emily, *'A Stitch in Time'*, *Afternoon TV*, October 1974, Vol. 6, Num. 9, pages 20-1, 66, 68.
Bubbeo, Daniel—*Match Game Premiere Features Host Alec Baldwin, Rosie O'Donnell*, Newsday.com, June 24, 2016.
Duralde, Alonso, 'Charles in Charge,' *Advocate* Magazine, October 9, 2001.
Feinberg, Daniel—*'Match Game' and '$100,000 Pyramid: TV Reviews,* HollywoodReporter.com, June 27, 2016.
Heffernan, Virginia—*Filling in the Blanks on a Staple of Daytime*, *The New York Times*, November 25, 2006.
Klineman, Gary— *"Match Game '75: A Look at Daytime T.V.'s Number 1 Game Show,"* *Broadcast Programming & Production* magazine, September/October 1975, Volume 1 Number 3.
Kissell, Rick—*Alec Baldwin-Hosted 'Match Game' to Cap ABC's Sunday Summer Lineup*, Variety.com, April 28, 2016.
Lasher, Irene—*Patty Duke 'Fun Or Folly—She's Willing To Try.'* Calendar page 79. *Los Angeles Times* 16 June 2002.
Mitovich, Matt Webb—*Match Game Secrets Spilled: Pre-Game Drinking, Forbidden Doodles, and More*, TVLine.com, April 30, 2017.
Mitovich, Matt Webb—*Match Game vs. $100,000 Pyramid: Which ABC Reboot is Most Faithful?*, TVLine.com, June 27, 2016.
O'Connell, Michael—*How ABC Convinced Alec Baldwin to Host 'Match Game'*, HollywoodReporter.com, June 23, 2016.

Ryan, Joal—*Game-Show Great Dead,* E! Online News, December 22, 1999.

Starr, Michael—*The Starr Report: 'Match Game: Politically Incorrect Flashback,' New York Post,* 31 July 2001.

'Unmatched Host Adds Humor To TV Quiz Show,' *Sunday News TV Week,* May 9-15, 1965.

Teti, John—*Holy ___, the New Match Game is Really Good,* Tv.avclub.com, July 6, 2016.

Whitney, Dwight—'*The return of Oliver J. Dragon III: Along With Some Observations On The State Of Television From His Old Friend Burr Tillstrom,' TV Guide,* February 1970.

Websites:

Properly citing online reference material is a tricky business. Websites and links to articles come and go in the cyber world, and some articles and websites I checked early in my research no longer exist, at least in their present form. Of particular help were Curt Alliaume's *Match Game '75/Match Game P.M.,* Brian Connoy's website *Matchgame.org, The Match Game Home Game Home Page,* Greg Palmer's blogsite *Slow Boat to the Land of Parting Gifts,* and David Hammet's *A Conversation with...the Man* posted on Chris_Lambert.com. Other sites include Hasbro's company website, Classicsquares.com, Eyesofageneration.com, Spaceagepop.com, The Internet Movie Database (IMDb.com), and Realitynewsonline.com, which was the source for Eric Szulczewski's marvelous quote used at the beginning of Part II of this book.

Television Programs:

A&E Biography: Mark Goodson
E! True Hollywood Story: Family Feud
The Real Match Game Story: Behind the Blank

...and of course, reruns of *Match Game, Blankety Blanks,* and *Blankety Blank* in its various incarnations. My gratitude to the respective casts and crew members is enormous.

The Cast and Crew of *Match Game* 1962-1969

Original airdates: December 31, 1962-September 29, 1969 on NBC

Cast
Gene Rayburn—Host
Johnny Olsen—Announcer
Wayne Howell—Sub-Announcer

Directed by
James Elson
Mike Gargiulo
Ira Skutch
Rodger Wolf

Produced by
Robert Noah—Executive Producer
Jean R. Kopelman—Producer
Diane (Hoffacker) Janaver—Associate Producer

Unit Manager
Jules North
Glenn Botkin

Program Staff
Roselle Barnard
Ken Abernathy
Lenore Goldstein
Brian Hennessey
Rae Pichon
Audrey Davis

Editorial Staff
Dick DeBartolo—Writer ("*Questions prepared by*")

Theme Music
Bert Kaempfert—Composer (*A Swingin' Safari*)

Art Department
Otis Riggs Jr.—Set Designer
Ted Cooper

Celebrity Panelists

Don Adams, Edie Adams, Anna Maria Alberghetti, Alan Alda, Robert Alda, Marty Allen, Steve Allen, Fran Allison, June Allyson, Don Ameche, Morey Amsterdam, Paul Anka, Lauren Bacall, Jim Backus, John Barnes, Sandy Baron, Orson Bean, Joan Bennett, Candice Bergen, Edger Bergen, Shelley Berman, Carl Betz, Joey Bishop, Claire Bloom, Ray Bolger, Victor Borge, Lloyd Bridges, Dr. Joyce Brothers, Chelsea Brown, James Brown, Deborah Bryant, Abe Burrows, Edd Byrnes, David Canary, Kitty Carlisle, Judy Carne, Pat Carroll, Peggy Cass, Jack Cassidy, Joan Caulfield, Bennett Cerf, Sydney Chaplin, Dick Clark, Dorothy Collins, Shirl Conway, Barbara Cook, Bill Cosby, Wally Cox, Les Crane, Richard Crenna, Robert Culp, Bill Cullen, Bobby Darin, Don DeFore, Dom DeLuise, Selma Diamond, Phyllis Diller, Hugh Downs, Kier Dullea, Faye Emerson, Douglas Fairbanks, Jinx Falkenberg, James Farentino, Barbara Feldon, Fannie Flagg, Joan Fontaine, Paul Ford, Whitey Ford, John Forsythe, Arlene Francis, David Frost, Betty Furness, Joe Garagiola, Anita Gillette, Jack Ging, Mark Goodson, Leslie Gore, Gale Gordon, Robert Goulet, Joel Grey, Rosey Grier, Leonid Hambro, George Hamilton, Noel Harrison, Patricia Harty, Jill Haworth, Peter Lind Hayes, Mary Healy, Florence Henderson, Skitch Henderson, Darryl Hickman, Connie Hines, Dustin Hoffman, Hal Holbrook, Sally Ann Howes, Marty Ingels, Art James, Jane Anne Jayroe, Arte Johnson, Van Johnson, Milt Kamen, Howard Keel, Dorothy Kilgallen, Alan King, Durward Kirby, Sandy Koufax, Abbe Lane, Peter Lawford, Carol Lawrence, Michele Lee, Jack E. Leonard, Sam Levenson, Bill Leyden, Robert Q. Lewis, Shari Lewis, June Lockhart, Dorothy Loudon, Anita Louise, Diana Lynn, Sue Lyon, Giselle MacKenzie, Gordon MacRae, Meredith MacRae, Sheila MacRae, Jayne Mansfield, Mickey Mantle, Peter Marshall, Raymond Massey, Denny McCain, Roddy McDowell, Darren McGavin, Ali McGraw, Ed McMahon, Barbara McNair, Julia Meade, Vaughn Meader, Audrey Meadows, Jayne Meadows, Don Meredith, Ethel Merman, Dina Merrill, Robert Merrill, Mitch Miller, Liza Minelli, Sal Mineo, Gary Moore, Rita Moreno, Henry Morgan, Chester Morris, Robert Morse, Don Murray, Jan Murray, Bess Myerson, Barry Nelson, Phyllis Newman, Hugh O'Brian, Pat O'Brien, Helen O'Connell, Patrick O'Neal, John Payne, Bert Parks, E.J. Peaker, Joe Pepitone, Tom Poston, Paula Prentiss, Carmel Quinn, Tony Randall, Elliot Reed, Lee Remick, Burt Reynolds, Sharon Kay Ritchie, Joan Rivers, Pernell Roberts, Cliff Robertson, Dale Robertson, Steve Rossi, Nipsey Russell, Mort Sahl, Soupy Sales, Diana Sands, Vidal Sassoon, George Segal, Rod Serling, William Shatner,

Ann Sheridan, Allan Sherman, Nancy Sinatra, Roger Smith, Ann Sothern, Bart Starr, Connie Stevens, Rise Stevens, Jacqueline Susann, David Susskind, Pat Suzuki, Gloria Swanson, Y.A. Tittle, Mel Torme, Leslie Uggams, Brenda Vaccaro, Vivian Vance, Marilyn Van Derbur, Bobby Vinton, Eli Wallach, Dionne Warwick, Betty White, Maury Wills, Flip Wilson, Jane Withers, Jo Anne Worley, Jane Wyatt, Gretchen Wyler, Jane Wyman, Carl Yastrzemski, Alan Young, Henny Youngman

The Cast and Crew of *Match Game* & *Match Game P.M.* 1973-1982

Directed by
Marc Breslow—Director

Produced by
Mark Goodson—Executive Producer
Joel Hecht—Associate Producer
Mark Sherman—Associate Producer
Robert Sherman—Associate Producer
Ira Skutch—Producer
Jake Tauber—Associate Producer
Bill Todman—Executive Producer

Original music by
Score Productions
Art Direction By
James J. Agazzi
Arlene Alen (as Arlene Allen)
Peter Clemens
Production Management
Rita Burton—Production Supervisor
Bruce Chamberlain—Production Supervisor
Roxie Wenk Evans—Production Supervisor
Carl Ginex—Production Manager
Mike McDaniel—Production Supervisor
Tom Richmond—Production Supervisor

James W. Ripple—Production Supervisor
Andrew J. Selig—Production Manager
Nancy Bradley Ward—Production Supervisor
Sound Department
Janice Bendiksen—Sound
Larry Eaton—Sound
Don Helvey—Sound
Bob Marencovich—Sound
Jerry Martz—Sound
Joseph McNeil—Sound
Other Crew
Ray Angona—Technical Director
Tom Barnes, Jr.—Lighting director
Patricia Berlly—Stage Manager
Buddy Borgen—Stage Manager
Lee Brougham—Video
Theodore Cooper—Creative Consultant: Goodson-Todman
Steve Cunningham—Technical Director
Willie Dahl—Stage Manager
Audrey Davis—Stage Manager
Roger Dubkowitz—Production Assistant
Roger Dubkowitz—Program Staff
Andrew Felsher—Production Assistant
Elin Frankel—Program Staff
Allyn B. Fried—Prize Coordinator
Sandi Gough—Production Assistant
Robert Gray—Associate Director
Sid Grosfield—Stage Manager
Dick Harwood—Stage Manager
Kay Henley—Celebrity Coordinator
Ed S. Hill—Lighting Director
Rick Hiner—Lighting Director
Diane Janaver—Contestant Coordinator
Mary Lieberman—Assistant to Producer
Mary Lieberman—Production Assistant
Michael J. Malone—Music Supervisor
Bob Marencovich—Technical Director
Bruce Nielson—Lighting Director

Giovanna Nigro—Stage Manager
Patricia A. Fass Palmer—Assistant to Producers
V. Dale Palmer—Lighting Director
Teresa A. Pfiffner-Krebsbach—Production Assistant
Doug Quick—Stage Manager
Phil Ramuno—Stage Manager
Jim Rice—Technical Director
Harry Rogue—Stage Manager
Karen Russak—Production Assistant
Jim Smith—Stage Manager
Nancy Stevenso—-Video
Pat Stine—Lighting Director
Harry Tatarian—Technical Director
George Thompson—Technical Director
Stephanie Voltz—Production Assistant
Stephanie Zilgitt—Production Assistant

Editorial Staff
Dick DeBartolo—Writer
Elliot Feldman—Writer
Joel Hecht—Writer
R. Patrick Neary—Writer
Joe Neustein—Writer
Jake Tauber—Writer
Marcia Morris—Writer

Celebrity Panelists

Don Adams, Jack Albertson, Elizabeth Allan, Jonelle Allen, Morey Amsterdam, Steve Allen, Bill Anderson, Loni Anderson, Adam Arkin, Lucie Arnaz, Ed Asner, Jim Bacus, Kay Ballard, Adrienne Barbeau, Bob Barker, Rona Barrett, Jon 'Bowzer' Bauman, Orson Bean, Meg Bennett, Valerie Bertinelli, Joey Bishop, Amanda Blake, Larry Blyden, Tom Bosley, Bill Braverman, Charlie Brill, Foster Brooks, Dr. Joyce Brothers, Chelsea Brown, Johnny Brown, Joyce Bulefant, Gary Burghoff, Raymond Burr, Abe Burrows, Judy Carne, Didi Carr, Jack Carter, Peggy Cass, Jack Cassidy, Brian Patrick Clark, Marty Cohen, Gary Collins, Joan Collins, Didi Conn, Hans Conreid, Bert Convy, Gary Crosby, Pat Crowley, Bill Cullen, Robert Culp, Jamie Lee Curtis, Bill Daily, Abby Dalton, James Darren, Richard Dawson, Clifton Davis, Phyllis Davis, Richard Deacon, Lynn Deerfield, Gloria DeHaven, Pat Delany, Patty Deutsch, Phyllis

Diller, Jody Donovan, David Doyle, Tom Dreesen, Denise DuBarry, Patty Duke, Nanacy Dussault, Leslie Easterbrook, Stephanie Edwards, Ann Elder, 'Mama' Cass Elliot, Wesley Eure, Michael Evans, Nannette Fabray, Sharon Farrell, Melinda O. Fee, Pat Finley, Gail Fisher, Fannie Flagg, Joe Flynn, Anitra Ford, Rosemary Forsyth, John Forsythe, Arlene Francis, Eva Gabor, Don Galloway, Joe Garagiola, Beverly Garland, Dick Gautier, Lynda Day George, Bennye Getteys, Anita Gillette, Stu Gilliam, George Gobel, Sydney Goldsmith, Ronny Graham, Fred Grandy, Shecky Greene, Rosey Grier, Holly Halstrom, Tom Hallick, Marvin Hamlisch, Pat Harrington, Jo Ann Harris, Julie Harris, Jennilee Harrison, Gina Hecht, Robert Hegyes, Marilu Henner, Linda Kaye Henning, Dwayne Hickman, Polly Holiday, Earl Holliman, Erica Hope, Larry Hovis, Susan Howard, Tab Hunter, Gunilla Hutton, Peter Isacksen, Kate Jackson, Conrad Janis, Dawn Jeffory, Arte Johnson, Carol Jones, Carolyn Jones, Jack Jones, Jackie Joseph, Elaine Joyce, Steve Kanaly, Betty Kennedy, George Kennedy, Sarah Kennedy, Tom Kennedy, Richard Kiel, Freeman King, Mabel King, George Kirby, Jack Klugman, Guich Koock, Bernie Kopell, Kukla & Ollie (Burr Tillstrom), Nancy Kulp, Audrey Landers, Judy Landers, Michael Landon, David Landsberg, Nancy Lane, Hope Lange, Ted Lange, Carol Lawrence, Miss Michael Learned, Brianne Leary, Michelle Lee, Ruta Lee, Helaine Lembeck, Sheldon Leonard, Robert Q. Lewis, June Lockhart, Julie London, Richard Long, Allen Ludden, Meredith MacRae, Bill Macy, Lorrie Mahaffey, Robert Mandan, Irlene Mandrell, Penny Marshall, Peter Marshall, Dick Martin, Dolly Martin, Ron Masak, Mitzie McCall, Edie McClurg, Barbara McNair, Anne Meara, Lee Meredith, Lee Meriwether, Ethel Merman, Donna Mills, Juliet Mills, Scoey Mitchlll, Mary Ann Mobley, Rita Moreno, Henry Morgan, Jaye P. Morgan, Pat Morita, Louisa Moritz, Greg Morris, Kate Morrow, Jack Narz, Leslie Neilsen, Phyllis Newman, Randi Oakes, Ken Olfson, Alan Oppenheimer, Buck Owens, Ron Palillo, Lorna Patterson, Richard Paul, Minnie Pearl, Janice Pennington, Donna Pescow, Joann Pflug, Robert Pine, Tom Poston, Juliet Prowse, Sarah Purcell, Lynn Redgrave, Della Reese, Charles Nelson Reilly, Alejandro Rey, Barbara Rhoads, Madilyn Rhue, Susan Richardson, Marcia Rodd, Esther Rolle, Donald H. Ross, Nipsey Russell, Soupy Sales, Isabel Sanford, Joe Santos, Debralee Scott, Avery Schreiber, William Shatner, Charles Siebert, Joe Silver, Dick Smothers, Brett Somers, Suzanne Somers, Joanie Sommers, Louise Sorel, Diane Soviero, Jim Staal, Skip Stephenson, Lilibet Stern, Connie Stevens, Kaye Stevens, McLean Stevenson, Trish Stewart, Barbara Stuart, Susan Sullivan,Don Sutton, Loretta Swit, Rip Taylor, Melody Thomas, Richard Thomas, Mel Tillis, Charlene Tilton, Fred Travalena, Willie Tyler & Lester, Bobby Van, Abigail Van Buren, Conny Van Dyke, Monique Van Vooren, Robert Vaughn, Robert Walden, Marcia Wallace, Marjorie Wallace, Jimmie Walker,

Laurie Walters, Betty White, Mary Wickes, Tudi Wiggins, Anson Williams, Paul Williams, Shelley Winters, Alfie Wise, Gene Wood, Jo Anne Worley

The Cast and Crew of *The Match Game-Hollywood Squares Hour* 1983-1984

Hosts
Gene Rayburn—Host (*The Match Game*)
Jon 'Bowzer' Bauman—Host (*The Hollywood Squares*)

Announcer
Gene Wood—Announcer

Sub-Announcers
Rich Jeffries
Johnny Olsen

Directed By
Marc Breslow—Directer

Written By
Dick DeBartolo—Writer
Elliot Feldman—Writer
Marsha Morris—Writer
Maxine Nunes—Writer
Abbe Schorrow—Writer

Original Music By
Edd Kalehoff (Theme)

Art Direction
Dennis Roof

Produced by
Joseph Neustein—Producer

Robert Sherman—Producer

Celebrity Panelists

Steve Allen, Bill Anderson, Alison Arngrim, Rod Arronto, Lew Ayers, Frank Bank, Jon 'Bowzer' Bauman, Bruce Brown, Ed Begley Jr., Barbi Benton, Barbara Billingsley, Sorrell Booke, Bart Braverman, Jimmy Brogan, Thom Bray, Lois Bromfield, Ellen Bry, Jm J. Bullock, Gary Burghoff, Blake Clark, Marty Cohen, Nathan Cook, Teri Copley, Lydia Cornell, Richard Correll, Bill Cullen, Bill Daily, Abby Dalton, Sybil Danning, Linda Dano, Richard Deacon, Phyllis Diller, Robert Donner, Vic Dunlop, Nancy Dussault, Rene Enriquez, Bob Eubanks, Fern Fitzgerald, Fannie Flagg, Stan Freberg, Arlene Francis, Leonard Frey, Gallagher, Teresa Ganzel, George Gobel, Fred Grandy, Arsenio Hall, Victoria Holleman, Jennilee Harrison, Rebecca Holden, Elaine Joyce, Salli Julian, Gordon Jump, Mary Page Keller, Jayne Kennedy, Ken Kerchival, Richard Kline, Elyse Knight, Ted Knight, Audrey Landers, Judy Landers, Michael Lembeck, Jaylene, Twyla Littleton, Larry Linville, Gloria Loring, Dorothy Lyman, Debra Sue Moffet, Larry Manetti, Dick Martin, Jerry Mathers, Constance McCashin, Edie McClurg, Pat McCormick, Matt McCoy, Eddie Mekka, Jayne Meadows, Brian Mitchell, Kim Miyon, Richard Moll, David Oliver, Ken Osmond, Richard J. Porter, Markie Post, Tom Poston, Phil Proctor, Bill Rafferty, Gene Rayburn, Helen Reddy, Tim Reid, Charles Nelson Reilly, Roxie Roker, David Ruprecht, Mark Russell, Nipsey Russell, Pat Sajak, Soupy Sales, Joe Santos, Stephen Schmetzer, Charles Siebert, Martha Smith, McLean Stevenson, Nancy Stafford, Jim Stahl, Skip Stephenson, Shawn Stevens, Alan Thicke, Fred Travelena, Shannon Tweed, Willie Tyler and Lester, Bonnie Urseth, Deborah Van Valkenburgh, Tom Villard, Nedra Volz, Lyle Waggoner, Chuck Wagner, Marcia Wallace, Jimmie Walker, Jeri Weil, Jesse Welles, Jamie Widdoes, Tom Wiggin, Anson Williams, Michael Winslow, Alfie Wise, Karen Witter

The Cast and Crew of *Match Game* 1990-1991

Cast
Ross Shafer—Host
Gene Wood—Announcer
Bob Hilton—Sub-Announcer

Directed By
Marc Breslow—Director

Produced By
Chester Feldman—Producer
Jonathan M. Goodson—Producer
Mark Goodson—Executive Producer

Written By
Dick DeBartolo—Writer
Randal Wetzel—Writer

Celebrity Panelists

Joe Alaskey, Rebeca Arthur, Michael Barymore, Rhonda Bates, Bruce Baum, Roger Behr, Jm J. Bullock, John Byner, Lorenzo Caccialanza, Lisa Canning, Nell Carter, Vince Champ, Stuart Damon, Phyllis Diller, Jane Eliot, Dana Fleming, Diane Ford, Beverly Garland, Brad Garrett, Marjorie Goodson-Cutt, Ilene Graff, Khrystyne Haje, Deborah Harmon, Lynn Herring, Christopher Hewitt, Fiona Hutchinson, Anne-Marie Johnson, Arte Johnson, Diana Jordan, Sheila Kay, Bill Kirchenbauer, Richard Kline, Audrey Landers, Judy Landers, Jill Larson, Vicki Lawrence, Chris Lemmon, Gloria Loring, Ronn Lucas and Friends, Gloria Loring, Meredith MacRae, Dick Martin, Dolly Martin, Brad Maule, Daphne Maxwell-Reid, Paula McClure, Edie McClurg, Andi Metheny, Roger E. Mosley, Pat Musick, Susan Norfleet, Erin O'Connor, Tom Parks, Jonathan Prince, Charles Nelson Reilly, Soupy Sales, Bob Sarlotte, Avery Schreiber, Richard Simmons, Brett Somers, Nancy Stafford, Perry Stephen, Pam Stone, Robin Strasser, Sally Struthers, Jason Stuart, Carol Susskind, Lauren-Marie Taylor, Rip Taylor, Shelley Taylor-Morgan, Deborah Tranelli, Fred Travalena, Shannon Tweed, Tom Villard, Jimmie Walker, Marcia Wallace, Betty White, Mary Wickes, Walt Willey, Karen Witter, Jo Anne Worley, Jacklyn Zeman

The Cast and Crew of *Match Game* 1998-1999

Cast
Michael Burger—Host
Paul Boland—Announcer

Produced By
Jay Wolpert—Executive Producer
Kevin Belinkoff—Producer

Match Game 101

Susan B. Flanagan—Producer

Directed By
Randall Neese—Director

Written By
Howard Kuperberg—Writer
Hennen Chambers—Writer
Arnie Meissner—Writer
Steve Sussman—Writer
Jay Wolpert—Writer

Michael Burger's Wardrobe by
Zanetti

David S. Heifetz—Costumer

Celebrity Panelists
James Avery, Lauralee Bell, Downtown Julie Brown, JM J. Bullock, Nell Carter, David Chokachi, Eddie Cibrian, Coolio, Kevin Eubanks, Gil Gerard, Jason George, George Hamilton, Windsor Harmon, Pamela Hill, Richard Jeni, Kathleen Kinmot, Lorenzo Lamas, Vicki Lawrence, Robin Leach, Mario Lopez, Brad Maule, Shemar Moore, Phil Morris, Joshua Morrow, Nolan North, J. Eddie Peck, John Salley, Rondell Sheridan, Kin Shriner, Ben Stein, Kristoff St. John, Judy Tenuta, George Wallace, Fred Willard

The Cast and Crew of *Match Game* 2016-Present

Cast
Alec Baldwin—Host
Steve French—Announcer

Directed By
Beth McCarthy-Miller—Director
Ron de Moraes—Director

Celebrity Panelists

Jason Alexander, Pamela Anderson, Tichina Arnold, David Arquette, Skylar Astin, Morena Baccarin, Ike Barinholtz, Tyson Beckford, Jillian Bell, Sandra Bernhard, Valerie Bertinelli, Jason Biggs, Michael Ian Black, Wayne Brady, Christie Brinkley, Tituss Burgess, Anna Camp, Tisha Campbell-Martin, Mario Cantone, Adam Carolla, Lynda Carter, Josh Charles, Michael Che, Kristin Chenoweth, Erika Christensen, Chris Colfer, Laverne Cox, Sheryl Crow, Whitney Cummings, Chris D'Elia, Jason DeStefano, Taye Diggs, Michael Ealy, John Early, Abby Elliott, Edie Falco, Donald Falson, Jenna Fischer, Sutton Foster, Rick Fox, Viveca A. Fox, Judah Friedlander, Ron Funches, Kenny G, Ana Gasteyer, Nikki Glaser, Adam Goldberg, Max Greenfield, Judy Greer, David Alan Grier, Darrell Hammond, Colton Haynes, Cheryl Hines, Tyler Hoechlin, Oliver Hudson, Rob Huebel, D. L. Hughley, Ice-T, Gabriel Iglesias, LaToya Jackson, Gillian Jacobs, Caitlyn Jenner, Anjelah Johnson-Reyes, Leslie Jones, Orlando Jones, Ellie Kemper, Julie Klausner, Jane Krakowski, NeNe Leakes, Sugar Ray Leonard, Joe Lo Truglio, Justin Long, Natasha Lyonne, Wendie Malick, Joshua Malina, Eva Marcille, Debi Mazar, Jack McBrayer, Tim Meadows, Debra Messing, Isaac Mizrahi, LaMorne Morris, Matthew Morrison, Bobby Moynihan, Niecy Nash, Jerry O'Connell, Rosie O'Donnell, Sarah Palin, Randall Park, Chris Parnell, Kal Penn, Jay Pharoah, Mekhi Phifer, Busy Philipps, Maggie Q, Colin Quinn, Leah Remini, Caroline Rhea, Sam Richardson, Andy Richter, Jason Ritter, Adam Rodriguez, Rupaul, Horatio Sanz, Amy Sedaris, Sherri Shepherd, Kevin Smith, Raven-Symoné, J.B. Smoove, Martha Stewart, Ice-T, Kenan Thompson, Joe Lo Truglio, Neil deGrasse Tyson, Sheryl Underwood, Bubba Watson, Johnny Weir, Alexandra Wentworth, Pete Wentz, Casey Wilson, Scott Wolf, Bellamy Young, Sasheer Zamata, Constance Zimmer
...And counting!

About the Author

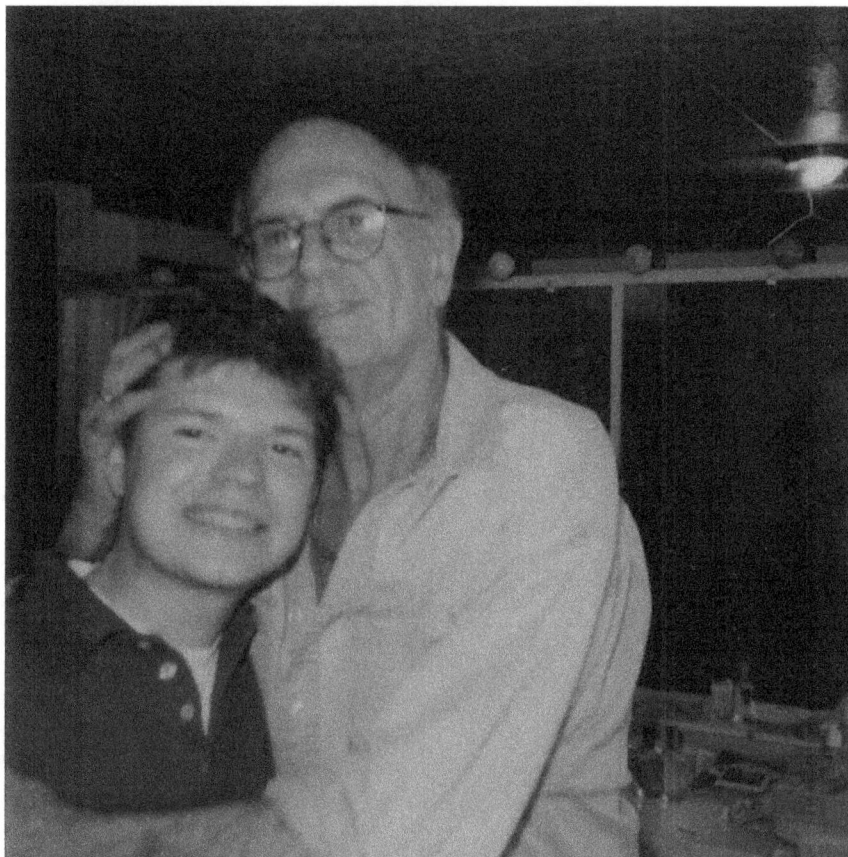

Author A. Ashley Hoff with Charles Nelson Reilly, following a performance of his one-man-show at The Canon Theatre in Beverly Hills in May, 2002.

Having previously worked in talent agencies in Chicago and Los Angeles, A. Ashley Hoff encountered many of the surviving hosts, writers, directors, producers, and celebrity panelists connected with *Match Game* in its various incarnations. He lives in Los Angeles. This is his first book.